UNDERSTANDING
DEVELOPMENT
& LEARNING
Implications for Teaching

Michael C Nagel
and
Laura Scholes

UNDERSTANDING
DEVELOPMENT
& LEARNING
Implications *for* Teaching

OXFORD
UNIVERSITY PRESS
AUSTRALIA & NEW ZEALAND

OXFORD
UNIVERSITY PRESS

Oxford University Press is a department of the University of Oxford.

It furthers the University's objective of excellence in research, scholarship, and education by publishing worldwide. Oxford is a registered trademark of Oxford University Press in the UK and in certain other countries.

Published in Australia by
Oxford University Press
253 Normanby Road, South Melbourne, Victoria 3205, Australia

National Library of Australia Cataloguing-in-Publication entry

Creator: Nagel, Michael C., author.
Title: Understanding development and learning : implications for
  teaching / Dr Michael C Nagel, Dr Laura
  Scholes.
ISBN: 9780195519655 (paperback)
Notes: Includes bibliographical references and index.
Subjects: Learning.
  Human growth.
  Learning, Psychology of.
  Nervous system–Growth.
  Inclusive education.
Other Creators/Contributors:
  Scholes, Laura, author.
Dewey Number: 370.1523

Edited by Susan Keogh
Cover design by MC Drawn
Text design by Watershed Design
Typeset by diacriTech, Chennai, India
Proofread by Anne Mulvaney
Indexed by Glenda Browne
Printed in China by Leo Paper Products Ltd

CONTENTS

1 WHAT IS LEARNING?   1

2 THE LINKS BETWEEN HUMAN DEVELOPMENT AND LEARNING   29

3 UNDERSTANDING BRAIN DEVELOPMENT   64

LIST OF FIGURES

LIST OF TABLES

PREFACE

> The transformation of learning theory over a century and of its attempted application to schooling is remarkable. Scientific research on learning has produced changed concepts of knowledge itself, new criteria for what counts as competent performance and as intelligence, new principles for instruction, and even new theories of how educational organizations work.
>
> (Resnick, 2010, p. 186)

Understanding Development and Learning! The title of this book could not be more appropriate for anyone interested in learning and particularly for those who are teaching or have aspirations to teach. The title itself is closely linked to the disciplinary field of educational psychology and the authors of this book have a deep passion for understanding learning and, more importantly, using this understanding to enhance the learning of others. Not all that long ago we were trained to be teachers; at that time, our collective understanding of learning was limited in scope and depth, and was often secondary to an emphasis on teaching. While our initial journey into the education profession commenced before the information age of the twenty-first century, research into learning has grown exponentially since that time—so much so that education or 'schooling' has shifted from a focus on teaching and learning to an agenda premised on learning and teaching. This is a welcome change for educational psychology, which some years ago also recognised that the pre-eminent link between education and psychology is learning and not instruction (Renninger, 1998).

In some sense, the volume of work you are about to engage with maintains many elements that you might encounter in educational psychology texts. Educational psychology is a branch of psychology and a vast landscape that specialises in understanding learning and teaching in educational contexts (Santrock, 2011). Given that this volume of work's primary aim is to assist future teachers in developing their understanding of learning and enhance their craft as educators, the tenets of educational psychology provide an appropriate framework for helping to achieve that goal. But, while educational psychology offers a framework, *Understanding Development and Learning* also draws on contemporary research and ideas drawn from a nascent discipline know as 'neuro-education' (neuroscience education).

The linking of neuroscience to education has a relatively short history. In itself neuroscience is a relatively new discipline encompassing neurology, psychology and biology (Goswami, 2004). Since the late 1990s, an exponential growth in neuroscientific research has taken place due to advances in brain-imaging technologies that allow researchers to look at the brain in action. Today those technologies have continued to improve, allowing even further insights into the inner workings of the brain and helping to establish the beginning of the twenty-first century as the age of brain–mind science (Goldberg, 2001).

The proliferation of neuroscientific research noted above has also facilitated a growing consensus that brain research is relevant to educational and child-rearing contexts, given that it is now possible to look inside a human brain as it processes stimuli from the environment and 'thinks' (Byrnes,

2007; Carew & Magsamen, 2010; Nagel, 2012a; Posner & Rothbart, 2007; Shonkoff & Levitt, 2010). This sentiment is likely to have contributed to the emergence of neuro-education from the disciplines of neuroscience, education and psychology in an effort to take brain research into the classroom and also to provide a forum for further research in this interdisciplinary field (Campbell, 2012; Carew & Magsamen, 2010; Tokuhama-Espinosa, 2011). In 2009 a major milestone linking neuroscience and education occurred at Johns Hopkins University in Baltimore, Maryland. The inaugural Neuroscience Research in Education Summit brought together more than four hundred leading researchers to further develop neuro-education by blending the collective fields of neuroscience, psychology, education and cognitive science to create more effective teaching methods and curricula, and, ultimately, to inform and transform educational policy (Carew & Magsamen, 2010). While the exact origin of the term 'neuro-education' is unclear, it has now become part of the nomenclature of a number of education and research programs across prominent universities and research institutes around the globe (Nagel, 2012a).

The inherent links between pedagogy and curriculum within neuro-education should be self-evident for all who are interested in contemporary educational psychology and schooling. Education is about enhancing learning; neuroscience is about understanding the mental processes involved in learning. Concomitantly, while neuro-education can investigate some of the basic processes involved in learning such things as literacy and numeracy, it also explores cognitive control and flexibility, motivation, social and emotional experience and, most importantly, learning to learn (Royal Society, 2011). Perhaps the seminal and visionary work of Leslie A. Hart (1983) entitled *Human Brain and Human Learning* more simply sums up the importance of neuro-education by noting that teaching without an awareness of how the brain learns is like designing a glove with no sense of what a hand looks like.

If classrooms are to be places of learning then the brain—the organ of learning—must be understood and accommodated. *Understanding Development and Learning* focuses on human development and learning through developing a deeper understanding of how these important areas are connected to the developing brain and mind. Neuro-education is at the heart of this endeavour and frames much of the discussion throughout the following chapters. Importantly, information derived from neuroscience is presented in a way that is accessible to educators and accompanied with practical suggestions and examples for linking science to the art of teaching.

ABOUT THE AUTHORS

Dr Michael C Nagel (BEd, MEd, PhD) is an Associate Professor in the School of Education at the University of the Sunshine Coast, where he teaches and researches in the areas of cognition, human development, behaviour and learning. He is the author of a number of journal articles and books on child development and learning, with a particular focus on the pediatric brain. Dr Nagel is a feature writer for 'Jigsaw' and the 'Child' series of magazines, which offers parenting advice to more than one million Australian readers and has delivered over 300 workshops and seminars for teachers and parents nationally and internationally.

Dr Laura Scholes (BEd, MA, PhD) is a Research Project Manager in the School of Early Childhood, Faculty of Education, Queensland University of Technology. Her teaching experience spans undergraduate and postgraduate programs in the fields of Literacy, Early Childhood, Human Development and the Sociology of Education. Her work in the School of Early Childhood includes professional development with the Jiangsu International Foundation for Education Excellence (JIFEE) in China. Dr Scholes' research is in the fields of children's moral development, gender and education, and literacy development. She has published in a range of scholarly education journals, contributed to book chapters and has recently co-authored a book entitled *Teaching for Active Citizenship in Early Education Classrooms: Research Insights from the Fields of Moral Values and Personal Epistemology.*

ACKNOWLEDGMENTS

We wish to acknowledge the myriad of individuals who assisted us in various ways in the construction of this text. First, our children, who sometimes found us so engrossed in our work that we forgot we also had to 'parent': their unquestionable support means the world to us.

We also would like to acknowledge the reviewers whose comments and ideas helped shape this volume of work. Concurrently we wish to acknowledge the editors who refined our writing and taught us a great deal. And we particularly would like to thank all of the staff at Oxford University Press who persevered with us, provided much guidance and helped us shape, what we think, is a text rich with theory and practical ideas for all educators and those striving to become educators.

Finally, we wish to acknowledge all of the wonderful teachers who work so hard to provide exemplary learning opportunities for their students. Teaching is indeed a noble profession and we hope the following pages provide a valuable tool for those who take on the important role of positively influencing their students' development and learning.

The authors and the publisher wish to thank the following copyright holders for reproduction of their material.

Cover: Stocksy/Studio Firma

Elsevier for figure 3 from Jing Yang et al 'Neural changes underlying successful second language word learning: An fMRI study', Journal of Neurolinguistics, 2015, volume 33, pages 29–49, figure 8.1; **Oxford Univeristy Press** for Maude Beauchemin et al, 'Mother and Stranger: An Electrophysiological Study of Voice Processing in Newborns', Cerebral Cortex, 2011, figure 5.3; **PNAS** for figure 2 from M. Ingalhalikar et al. 'Sex differences in the structural connectome of the human brain', 2013, volume 111 no.2, figure 5.4; **Shutterstock**, p.3, p.31, p.92, p.123, p.155, p.185, p.217, p.247, p.285.

Every effort has been made to trace the original source of copyright material contained in this book. The publisher will be pleased to hear from copyright holders to rectify any errors or omissions.

GUIDED TOUR

Each chapter opens with clearly defined **learning outcomes** to direct your learning and help you focus on the key points of the chapter.

LEARNING OUTCOMES

As you read through this chapter and undertake the exercises at the end, you will gain the ability to complete these tasks successfully:

→ describe the differences between learning as a 'product' and learning as a 'process'

→ describe traditional models of teaching and 'schooling' in Western countries and articulate how such models are often denoted as a factory-line method of education

→ describe and discuss the term 'learning' in conjunction with theoretical perspectives of learning, while identifying key aspects of prominent theoretical orientations to learning.

Key terms listed at the beginning of each chapter highlight important concepts that will be addressed. Definitions are provided in **margin notes** to aid your understanding as you read through the text.

KEY TERMS

- behaviourism
- positive reinforcement
- negative reinforcement
- humanism
- social learning theory
- constructivism

Behaviourist orientations to learning

Behaviourism
A field of psychology concerned with individual behaviour.

The term behaviourism stems from the early works of John Watson (1913, 1914, 1925), who believed that the key to understanding learning could be found through the analysis of behaviour. Watson was an American psychologist whose initial research work focused on

See Chapter ❾ for more detail on the sociocultural influences on boys' and girls' development.

differences between boys' and girls' language and literacy development but now there are opportunities for these differences to be observed. In this chapter, we talk about biological 'sex' differences and the biological and physiological make-up of males and females; 'gender' usually refers to the socially constructed attributes, including social roles and behaviours. In Chapter 9, we talk about the socially constructed attributes and behaviours associated with gender.

Linkage margin notes direct you to further material on key topics in other parts of the text.

Setting the scene case examples open each chapter with an illustrative, classroom-based example or dilemma to set the context, and the questions that follow invite you to examine your own opinions, reactions and responses to the scenario before reading on.

SETTING THE SCENE

It's Friday and, like on all Fridays, the students of Mr Kahan's Year 5 class are getting ready for their weekly spelling and number facts quiz. Chloe takes out her notebook, writes the date and the numbers one to twenty. Chloe likes the first part of the quiz where she has to spell ten words randomly selected from the weekly word list each student receives on Monday. Chloe likes spelling and rarely makes a mistake but, when the next ten questions are random number facts recited by Mr Kahan, she does not usually do as well. Chloe is a good student and works hard but for some reason she seems to struggle with multiplication facts and routinely makes a number of errors during the maths part of the quiz. She studies hard during the week but it seems that multiplication is something she cannot master, not in school anyway.

1 Can you recall a time in your life as a student when you may have experienced something similar to Chloe's experience above? Were there times when what you were 'learning' in school did not seem to sink in, or when you found it difficult to demonstrate what you had learnt?

2 In your opinion, why is it that some students may struggle with learning particular things in an educational context? What is learning and how do we measure it? As a future teacher how will you determine what students have learnt?

3 The word 'learning' is often taken for granted and not always easily defined. Before working through this chapter write a definition of learning and be prepared to review that definition when the information in the chapter has been covered.

Something to think about sections offer interesting case studies, research and practice examples to broaden your thinking on important topics.

SOMETHING TO THINK ABOUT 1.2

GENIE: A CASE STUDY IN THE DEPRIVATION OF STIMULATION

In terms of learning, experiences or the lack thereof matter. Chapter 2 presents neuroscientific evidence of how experiences shape the neural architecture of the mind but, long before researchers could look at the inner workings of the brain, examples of what happens when children are deprived of certain experiences provided a great deal of support for the work of Maslow and others. One tragic story is particularly compelling.

On 4 November 1970, a social worker discovered a thirteen-year-old girl who, by all accounts, had been forced to flounder helplessly within an environment Maslow might have noted as the bottom of his hierarchy. This young girl, who was later named 'Genie' by social

Ask yourself...

Fortunately, it is unlikely any teacher will ever deal with children who experienced a life anything like Genie's. But we do know that children who grow up in impoverished regions or neighbourhoods or whose basic needs are not being met outside school do end up in classrooms. What does Maslow's hierarchy suggest would be the most important considerations to attend to when encountering disadvantaged children?

Ask yourself questions appear regularly throughout the text, prompting you to reflect on what you are learning and think critically about the complex issues addressed.

Full colour diagrams and illustrations throughout the text help to clarify and bring ideas to life.

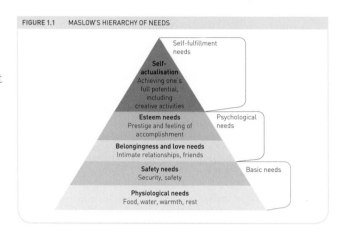

FIGURE 1.1   MASLOW'S HIERARCHY OF NEEDS

Self-fulfillment needs

Self-actualisation
Achieving one's full potential, including creative activities

Esteem needs
Prestige and feeling of accomplishment

Psychological needs

Belongingness and love needs
Intimate relationships, friends

Safety needs
Security, safety

Basic needs

Physiological needs
Food, water, warmth, rest

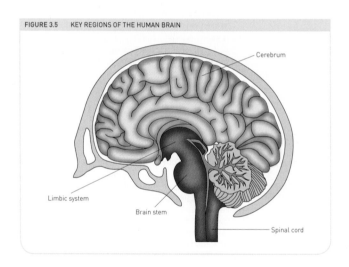

FIGURE 3.5   KEY REGIONS OF THE HUMAN BRAIN

Cerebrum

Limbic system

Brain stem

Spinal cord

CHAPTER SUMMARY

This chapter explored the broad topic of human development and learning. The beginning of the chapter unpacked three basic issues that surround aspects of human development, including: nature versus nurture, discontinuous development versus continuous development and universality versus diversity. These three issues have framed discussions of human development for years and still play a role in shaping research and ideas around how children grow and mature.

Chapter summaries bring together the key points and link chapter content back to the learning outcomes identified at the start of the chapter.

Implications for teaching

As noted early in the chapter, many generations of students experienced a factory-line approach to being educated. For many years students were viewed as *tabula rasa*, a Latin term meaning 'blank slate', and the role of a teacher was to fill that empty void with the knowledge that was deemed important at the time. From the 1970s onward, researchers began to articulate aspects of learning as a process as much as a product. Concurrently, the advent of technology which has given rise to an age of seemingly endless information calls into question the need or actual possibility of pouring a continuing exponential growth of information and/ or knowledge into the heads of students. For some researchers and theorists there is still a worrying trend, at a systemic level, to perpetuate a factory model through the continued use of standardised testing and many other artefacts of twentieth-century schooling. The issues with standardised tests are covered in Chapter 10 but foreshadowed here as an example of something you may have personally experienced and might now question as a valid mechanism

Implications for teaching sections demonstrate how research can influence teaching practice in a variety of ways.

Comprehension-based **Study questions** at the end of each chapter assist in revision and **Practical activities** are designed to allow you to further your thinking and provide opportunities to put theory into practice.

PRACTICAL ACTIVITIES

1 *While on practicum*, document the methods used to determine when or how learning has occurred. List all of these in one of two columns in a table under the headings 'Product' and 'Process'. Is one column larger than the other and, if so, what does that indicate to you? Could you design different ways to determine what, if any, learning has occurred?

2 *While on practicum*, jot down any examples of particular theoretical approaches to learning that you observe during the course of your practicum. Are some theories more apparent than others? Do some approaches resonate better with your own beliefs about learning and, if so, how might you engage with such approaches as a teacher?

STUDY QUESTIONS

1 What are the five broad theoretical orientations presented in the chapter? Note the main focus of each.

2 What is the difference between positive and negative reinforcement? List some examples of each in a classroom context.

3 What are the five levels of the Maslow's hierarchy of needs? List some ways in which you might be able to help students meet basic and psychological needs at school.

4 Social learning theory is important in terms of behaviour and learning. What does this theory mean for you as a future teacher and potential role model for your students?

5 What are the primary differences between cognitive constructivism and social constructivism? Provide examples of each in relation to educational and pedagogical contexts.

FURTHER READINGS

Armstrong, S. (2008). *Teaching Smarter with the Brain in Focus: Practical Ways to Apply the Latest Brain Research to Deepen Comprehension, Improve Memory, and Motivate Students to Achieve*. New York, NY: Scholastic.

Baron-Cohen, S., Tager-Flusberg, H. & Lombardo, M. (Eds.) (2013). *Understanding Other Minds: Perspectives from Social Cognitive Neuroscience* (3rd ed.). Oxford, UK: Oxford University Press.

Carpenter, L. (2010). Understanding autism spectrum disorder. In M. Hyde, L. Carpenter & R. Conway, *Diversity and Inclusion in Australian Schools* (pp. 267–279). Melbourne, Australia: Oxford University Press.

Diamond, M. & Hopson, J. (1999). *Magic Trees of the Mind: How to Nurture Your Child's Intelligence, Creativity, and Healthy Emotions from Birth through Adolescence*. New York, NY: Penguin Putnam.

Fiske, E. (Ed.). (1999). *Champions of Change: The Impact of the Arts on Learning*. Retrieved from Arts Edge: The Kennedy Center: http://www.artsedge.kennedy-center.org/champions/

Hyde, M., Carpenter, L. & Conway, R. (Eds.) (2014). *Diversity, Inclusion and Engagement* (2nd ed.). Melbourne, Australia: Oxford University Press.

Jensen, E. (2000). *Different Brains, Different Learners: How to Reach the Hard to Reach*. Thousand Oaks, CA: Corwin Press.

Unesco (1994, June). *The Salamanca Statement and Framework for Action on Special Needs Education*. World Conference on Special Education Needs for Education: Access and Quality, Salamanca, Spain.

VIDEO LINKS

Roger Slee Education and Inclusive Communities—Article 2
https://www.youtube.com/watch?v=Hjc4430D8As

A speech given in New Zealand by Professor Roger Slee, who is the director of the Victoria Institute for Education, Diversity and Lifelong Learning; simultaneously signed.

Principals Australia Institute: *How Inclusive Is Your School*
https://www.youtube.com/watch?v=F2-FjRBjGx0

Overview of inclusion and diversity.

WEBLINKS

Australian Advisory Board on Autism Spectrum Disorders
http://www.autismadvisoryboard.org.au/

Information on autism spectrum disorders from the websites of the Advisory Board's member organisations.

Children and Young People with Disability Australia (CYDA)
http://www.cda.org.au/

CYDA is the national peak body that represents children and young people (from birth to 25 years) with disability.

Gifted and Talented Education
http://www.curriculumsupport.education.nsw.gov.au/policies/gats/index.htm

Support for teaching gifted and talented students from the New South Wales Department of Education.

Further reading lists and annotated **video** and **weblinks** direct you to key additional resources related to each chapter.

GLOSSARY

Affective
Of or having to do with emotions or the feeling of emotion.

Anxiety
A negative emotional state that can impair performance and engage the body's stress-response system.

Culture
Knowledge, beliefs, values, morals, laws, customs, traditions and artefacts common to members of society.

Developmental tasks
The meeting of developmental challenges arising from maturation, context and sense of self.

A consolidated **Glossary** at the end of the book provides a quick reference to help you with unfamiliar terms and concepts.

WHAT IS LEARNING?

> There are more than 50 different theories of learning in the field of educational research. The presence of so many theories of learning may be interpreted as a kind of diversity that we may, or perhaps should, celebrate. But this fact can also be interpreted in a very different manner: as both demonstrating and hiding the complexities of learning. These are the complexities of a reality that are mostly taken for granted, leaving them unavailable for reflection.
>
> (Jorg, Davis & Nickmans, 2007, p. 147)

LEARNING OUTCOMES

As you read through this chapter and undertake the exercises at the end, you will gain the ability to complete these tasks successfully:

→ describe the differences between learning as a 'product' and learning as a 'process'

→ describe traditional models of teaching and 'schooling' in Western countries and articulate how such models are often denoted as a factory-line method of education

→ describe and discuss the term 'learning' in conjunction with theoretical perspectives of learning, while identifying key aspects of prominent theoretical orientations to learning.

KEY TERMS

- behaviourism
- positive reinforcement
- negative reinforcement
- humanism
- social learning theory
- constructivism

It's Friday and, like on all Fridays, the students of Mr Kahan's Year 5 class are getting ready for their weekly spelling and number facts quiz. Chloe takes out her notebook, writes the date and the numbers one to twenty. Chloe likes the first part of the quiz where she has to spell ten words randomly selected from the weekly word list each student receives on Monday. Chloe likes spelling and rarely makes a mistake but, when the next ten questions are random number facts recited by Mr Kahan, she does not usually do as well. Chloe is a good student and works hard but for some reason she seems to struggle with multiplication facts and routinely makes a number of errors during the maths part of the quiz. She studies hard during the week but it seems that multiplication is something she cannot master, not in school anyway.

After school, Chloe heads home and helps Mum and Dad in the convenience store they own, as her parents' first language is not English and sometimes Chloe needs to become a translator. Chloe really enjoys working in the store and often is behind the counter where she unknowingly uses some of the very same maths skills she struggles with in school. Often her friends will come in and their love of lollies is evident in the volume of sweets they choose and through the money spent when Chloe calculates the cost of many of the items in her head before using the very old cash register they currently have in the store. It is clear in her interactions with her friends and others who shop in her family store that Chloe's math skills are superior to those she demonstrates most Fridays.

1 Can you recall a time in your life as a student when you may have experienced something similar to Chloe's experience above? Were there times when what you were 'learning' in school did not seem to sink in, or when you found it difficult to demonstrate what you had learnt?

2 In your opinion, why is it that some students may struggle with learning particular things in an educational context? What is learning and how do we measure it? As a future teacher how will you determine what students have learnt?

3 The word 'learning' is often taken for granted and not always easily defined. Before working through this chapter write a definition of learning and be prepared to review that definition when the information in the chapter has been covered.

INTRODUCTION

This chapter aims to develop your understanding of the broad, and often taken-for-granted, concept of *learning*. Defining learning is not always easy and at times seems ambiguous with a myriad of intricacies and idiosyncrasies, making one single definition very difficult to attain. Indeed, the word 'learning' itself has a number of meanings depending on the context in which it is used, but it is the core business of educational institutions and, as such, warrants some detailed exploration. Those embarking on a career as an educator or those already in charge of learning and teaching in any educational environment would do well to draw together their own learning about learning in order to ensure that the art and science of their craft are up to date and serving the interests of their students. And while we agree that the complexities of learning are often taken for granted—as noted in the opening quote—we do not share the overall sentiment of the authors. Theories surrounding human development and learning are available for reflection and should be the core of any educator's philosophical meanderings and practical applications in an education environment. This chapter is the beginning of such reflection and understandings.

Before exploring learning in greater detail, we need to note a few important provisos. First, learning is not confined to schools and indeed starts long before a child enters a classroom. Some might argue that learning begins about seventeen days after conception and this will be discussed later. Second, learning is an integral component of being human. Human beings do two things very well: survive and learn. Our capacity for learning has offered the human race a degree of flexibility and adaptability far surpassing any other species on the planet (Ormrod, 2008). Every day we learn and continue to learn, although we may not be fully conscious of when learning is occurring. We are designed to learn and, under the right conditions, we do so very well through complex interactions with others via various environmental stimuli and activities, and through serendipitous moments when we take in a great deal of information through all of our senses.

Finally, it is important to remember that learning is not always easily measured or something attributable to a select group of individuals. In many educational contexts, and arguably too often, learning is associated with test or achievement scores, some demonstrable outcome or some measure of cognitive ability or scholastic aptitude. This, in turn, suggests that the role of a teacher is to deliver curriculum and then design mechanisms to see how much 'learning' has occurred, where any errors are, and make adjustments to ensure that students acquire the requisite content or skill set to be measured. But not all learning is necessarily measurable or quantifiable and, while we are all capable of learning, there are also many things that can affect our learning. Significantly, many generations of teachers were provided guides or texts related to the psychology of learning that paid little, if any, attention to the role of emotions, feelings, personalities, relationships or environments on learning (Claxton, 1999). We now know that learning is not simply something that occurs via the transmission of knowledge from one person to another. Learning is often a complex enterprise involving more than just the cognitive attributes of the mind or isolated as test scores or grades. We learn very well and contemporary research also tells us that we can learn to learn more effectively and that teachers can be an integral part of the learning process. Therefore, this chapter has been set out as the beginning of the journey of understanding development and learning and as the starting point for expanding your own learning on the road to enhancing, and positively engaging with, the learning of your own students or what is more commonly referred to as *teaching*.

DEFINING TEACHING

Understanding Development and Learning's focus is on learning, and in particular, learning that takes place in schools. It is therefore important to also unpack notions of teaching given the dynamic nature between learning and teaching in educational settings. In a similar way to unpacking definitions of learning, attempting to define teaching is equally as arduous. We have all experienced teaching and not all of the teaching we received occurred in schools. Parents and family members, friends, coaches, celebrities, religious leaders and many others including the family pet can teach us a thing or two. In terms of educational settings, the modern profession of teaching was created at about the same time as the first school systems and before this time anyone who had something to offer in the way of learning could open a school or apply to the local community to teach in its school (Vick, 2013). Such individuals were not required to have formal teaching qualifications but this changed markedly with the introduction of schooling for the masses. The evolution of modern 'schooling' is discussed later in this chapter but it is noteworthy here to reiterate that defining teaching, or indeed a theory of teaching, is not only difficult to do but highly contestable.

Perhaps one of the reasons surrounding the difficulty in defining teaching is evident in the reality that most people in Western societies have been to school and have experienced some form of teaching or another. Having grown up in schools, many adults believe they know how to teach because they watched teachers for many years (Darling-Hammond et al., 2005). Many individuals will eagerly form opinions on what constitutes 'good' or 'bad' teaching and, by association, good or bad 'schooling'. These opinions, in turn, shape and are shaped by the prescribed social purposes of education as constituted by political, social and cultural agendas. In Western societies this has seen theories of teaching taking on particular practices—or *pedagogies*—and much of that practice emerged from the industrial era. Generations of students have been the recipients of this particular form of teaching whereby a substantive amount of pedagogy has focused on the transmission of information or knowledge, understanding or wisdom to students in an oral or written framework; teaching is set out to inform, instruct, explain or enlighten (Ackoff & Greenberg, 2008).

The traditional knowledge transmission model of teaching born out of the industrial era is still evident in many contemporary educational settings. The implications of such an approach are wide-ranging and noted throughout this chapter where appropriate. In terms of teaching, such a model reinforces a rather simplistic and intuitive notion of teaching; someone knows something and then teaches it to others (Darling-Hammond, 2006). The measure of the success of that model is usually some form of assessment and, while it has succeeded for some students, it has also left many more behind. Indeed, mountains of research have demonstrated that the notion of transmission teaching doesn't actually work most of the time (Darling-Hammond, 2006). This model of teaching is still very prominent in many contemporary schools and is symptomatic of debates surrounding what constitutes good teaching and, by association, good learning. Worryingly, such debates have been around for many decades as eloquently encapsulated in the work of American curriculum theorist, B. O. Smith who, in 1963, stated: 'We are a long way from a comprehensive theory of teaching, grounded in a clear cut system of concepts and backed up by empirical evidence. To develop a general theory ... will require bold explorations which take into account of what has been done, but which are in no means bound by past failures and successes' (p. 10).

TEACHING IN THE TWENTY-FIRST CENTURY

While it may be that we are still 'a long way from a comprehensive theory of teaching', there does seem to be an increasing consensus that a knowledge transmission model of teaching is ill suited for learning and learners in the twenty-first century. Teaching that focuses on transferring knowledge rarely takes into account the experiences and needs of students. Instead such a mindset tends to place curriculum, predetermined content and assessment as the standard approach of educational endeavour and as such is likely to be unsuccessful for a majority of learners given the diverse nature of student populations in Western schools (Darling-Hammond, 2006). Indeed, research evidence indicates that overall student achievement improves through a more contemporary theory of teaching whereby teaching has these aims:

→ draws out and works with the pre-existing understandings that students bring with them
→ explores subject matter in depth in an effort to provide a firm foundation of factual knowledge
→ integrates the teaching of metacognitive skills (Donovan, Bransford & Pellegrino, 2000).

In addition to the significant considerations of teaching made by all the theorists above, a final important aspect of any contemporary theory of teaching must recognise that learning and teaching are intimately linked. Teaching is a complex activity that exists in a reciprocal relationship with learning and as such theories and knowledge of teaching must begin with deep understandings of human development and learning (Darling-Hammond, 2006). For developmental psychologists such a claim goes without saying, while new theories and approaches to teaching in educational contexts not only recognise the important links between human development and learning, but also the importance of understanding neurological development as it pertains to learning (see, for example, Donovan et al., 2000; Kalantzis & Cope, 2008; Ormrod, 2008; Tokuhama-Espinosa, 2011). The next section and the remaining chapters of *Understanding Development and Learning* adopt this framework in that it is our belief that, while defining teaching is important, understanding learning and learners is central to any successful contemporary educational endeavour.

DEFINING LEARNING

As the previous section demonstrated, defining the word 'learning' is not an easy proposition. Is learning the product of some type of endeavour, is it a process or is it both? How do we know if something has been learnt? Must all learning be set in a context of performance or assessment or is it possible to learn something without even realising it? These questions are central to this chapter and a long history of research and debate. Perhaps one of the reasons that learning is often difficult to define, or narrowly understood, can be situated in many people's experiences of schooling. After all, in Western countries the vast majority of people have been to school and they have a view of learning that is well established and linked to teaching. Indeed, it is likely that when most people hear the word 'learning' they often think of schools, yet this is problematic for a number of reasons.

First, and as noted in the previous section, not all learning occurs in schools. Most children arrive for their first day of formal education with a great deal of knowledge along with a vast array of skills and attributes they learnt long before walking into a classroom. Some would argue that most learning is done at home, at work or outdoors and as such schools are but one domain where learning can occur (Ackoff & Greenberg, 2008).

Second, the type of learning that has occurred in most Western schools, including those in Australia, Canada, the United Kingdom and the United States, has been premised on a factory-line model of production (Ackoff & Greenberg, 2008; Darling-Hammond, 2006; Robinson, 2011). Within this model students were typically viewed as empty vessels and a teacher's role was to progressively fill up students' minds with the information necessary for a successful future and productive citizenship (Nagel, 2013a). Today, this form of educating has its own inherent difficulties and issues, not least of which is that it was designed during the industrial era and is still the standard approach for many educational institutions trying to engage learners who are arguably remarkably different from any other generation of students. This is discussed in some detail later in this chapter.

Finally, at a time when information continues to grow exponentially and where students can access a seemingly infinite array of sources of information, our understanding of learning has also changed. Not long ago, schools were the primary source of information and knowledge for students. Today, young people can access information 24/7 within the palm of their hands and this strengthens the point made earlier: not all learning occurs in schools. Because learning is not isolated to schools, and in an effort to gain greater insights into broad notions of learning, it is important for us to look at learning through various lenses. This is achieved in the following sections by looking at how learning has been approached in educational contexts, contemporary understandings of learning and various theoretical perspectives of learning, past and present.

SOMETHING TO THINK ABOUT 1.1

LEARNING STYLES

Are you a visual, auditory or kinaesthetic learner? You are probably none of the above and all of the above but none of that matters in terms of educational contexts and learning in general. There is no credible evidence that learning styles exist and yet many teachers and schools spend time, energy and resources trying to determine their students' learning styles and adjust their pedagogy and curriculum accordingly. A number of current educational psychology textbooks also still embrace 'learning styles' concepts and advocate the practice of determining preferred learning styles to enhance educational outcomes (Pashler, McDaniel, Rohrer & Bjork, 2008).

The concept of 'learning styles' or 'learning modalities' is not a new educational phenomenon and likely arose from psychological taxonomies related to theorising about individual personalities. From such taxonomies a number of theories related to learning styles have emerged over the past decades. In Australia the most popular models are those derived from Neil Fleming's VARK theory, which is now typically promoted through inventories used ▶

▶ to determine if a student is a visual, auditory or kinaesthetic learner (Scott, 2010). But, as noted earlier, any attempts to modify one's teaching to cater to such notions of learning modalities is time wasted, given the lack of any evidence to support such activities. Two key questions are why such misguided notions continue to permeate many school corridors and professional development sessions and what might be a better alternative to such endeavours.

The answer to the first question is multifarious but it could be that, in an attempt to provide an egalitarian educational context for all, it is commonly proposed that teachers need to know how their students learn. The truth is that most students learn in very similar ways and we should not confuse 'styles' with abilities, interests and background knowledge: three factors important for learning and supported by an abundance of research. Focusing on individual abilities, interests and background therefore provides insights into the answer to the second question and a foundation for improving learning and educational outcomes. Rather than trying to discover the illusionary learning style of each student, teachers would do much better to consider content modalities and craft their pedagogy, as much as possible, around their students' levels of prior knowledge, abilities and interests (Willingham, 2009).

Ask yourself...

1   Have you ever participated in some inventory to uncover your learning style? If so, what actions did you take to support your style of learning? What were the outcomes of such endeavours?

2   Given that student abilities, interests and background knowledge appear repeatedly in educational and psychological research as important factors for improving educational outcomes, what does this mean for you as a future teacher? Consider the age of the students you wish to teach and provide a list of strategies for engaging with such important considerations.

A BRIEF HISTORY OF 'LEARNING' AND 'TEACHING' IN WESTERN SCHOOLS

In order to garner some insights into the history of learning and teaching in schools it is also important to briefly look at the history of schools themselves for the two are intimately linked. In the context of human undertakings, the concept of universal education has a relatively short history. Born out of the seventeenth century, and influenced by various religious movements, basic schooling for all children only became a national aspiration in most Western countries in the nineteenth century (Resnick, 2010). Before the nineteenth century, schools were very different from what they are today and accommodated in multipurpose buildings with only a handful of children, no set curriculum and where learning could be characterised as being achieved through rote memory work (Vick, 2013).

THE RISE OF THE FACTORY MODEL

The introduction of mass schooling to the general public was influenced by a number of contextual factors and delivered in very specific formats. In its earliest incarnations, teaching within schools reinforced rote learning and was generally catechismal in nature; individuals were asked a series of questions culled from religious texts and expected to provide standardised answers (Resnick, 2010). The advent of the industrial era also played a role in shaping education and with the growth of industry support for public education grew, transforming schooling from limited provision to widespread and hierarchical education systems (Carl, 2009). Interestingly, while the content of school curricula changed during this time to include basic arithmetic, geography, history, some science and a broader range of texts for reading and writing, the methods of teaching and learning in the classroom remained remarkably unchanged (Resnick, 2010). Some might argue that the function of schools during this time was to mirror the productivity of factories and, as such, schools were to teach social and citizenship skills; students arrived as blank slates, requiring the teacher to fill them in with knowledge in a system set up to ensure efficient and standardised functioning of all parts of the system (Ackoff & Greenberg, 2008).

The precise relationships between industrialisation and the rise of public education are difficult to pin down but there does appear to be a correlation between the spread of industry and the rise of mass public schooling (Carl, 2009). What is clear is that the factory model of education has strongly influenced notions of learning and teaching and is still evident in many schools today (Robinson, 2011). Within this model, learning and teaching are similar to production lines in a factory: start with a raw product (student), add information via the expert (teacher) and learning and knowledge is the end product. There is also an assumption in this model that for every bit of teaching there should be an equal amount of learning and that this can be accurately measured (Nagel, 2013a).

There are a number of issues associated with such a view of learning and teaching, not least of which is that such a model does not take into account the diverse needs and attributes of individuals, nor does it recognise the myriad factors that influence all aspects of learning. These will be covered throughout *Understanding Learning and Development* but it is also significant to note here that the current climate of raising educational 'standards' is predominantly underpinned by a factory model whereby all children can learn if the standards are correct and delivered through 'quality' teaching. Standardised tests, rankings of students and/or schools and rhetoric surrounding a 'back to basics' foundation of education elicit romanticised notions of 'traditional' schooling and a tacit endorsement of industrial-line education but rarely take into account theories of learning or the nature of human learning. In the twenty-first century, where students are active consumers of information and creators of knowledge, contemporary understandings of learning deserve to be centre stage of any educational endeavour and curriculum aspirations. This begins with looking at various theories of learning, past and present.

THEORIES OF 'LEARNING', PAST AND PRESENT

There's nothing so practical as a good theory.

(Lewin, 1951, p.169)

Kurt Lewin, considered by many as the father of modern social psychology, was concerned throughout his work to integrate theory and practice (Kolb, 1984). But the linking of theory to practice is not always easily achieved. Anecdotally speaking, our collective experience in the field of education has often witnessed many debates linking theory to practice. It is not uncommon to hear teacher mentors tell their prac students to forget what they are doing at university because now they are in the real world! It is also not uncommon for students to question the purpose of studying theory when the everyday realities of the classroom often seem far removed from the philosophical or scientific meanderings of a textbook. These may seem to be broad generalisations but experience suggests otherwise. Therefore, it is important to note the significance of examining theories before engaging in such activity.

One of the major goals of educational psychology is to understand learning and teaching; research becomes an important tool in achieving this objective. Research, on the other hand, allows for the collection of data and from such data various theories can be derived and further research conducted to validate a theory or create a new theory. Of itself, a theory is a framework that can be used to identify and explain relations among natural, observable phenomena (Fiske, 2004). Research and theory development are part of a cyclical process and new theories are used to fill gaps in any existing explanations of a particular phenomenon. Educational psychologists and educators have a long history of developing theories around child development and the phenomenon of education. We have a number of theories related to cognitive development, for example, that have affected many aspects of educational endeavour. Importantly, good theories can posit causal relations, attempt to find coherence, form good narratives, aim for simplicity in explanation, are testable, solve problems and inform practice (Fiske, 2004).

WHAT IS LEARNING?

Given the importance of linking theory to practice, it should be apparent that, in an educational context, many theories related to learning have been developed over time. Some of these theories continue to influence education today, while others are new and exciting to the field. To explore some of these important theories we begin by asking a very significant question: what is learning? In many educational psychology textbooks, learning is often defined as a relatively permanent change in behaviour, knowledge and thinking skills as a result of experience (see, for example, Krause, Bochner, Duchesne & McMaugh, 2010; Santrock, 2011). This definition appears very straightforward and concise but, as noted earlier, learning is far more complicated than what can be found in singular definitions. In educational contexts, learning is generally considered as an outcome or an objective suggesting some change in a student and as such embodies the types of definition presented above. It is noteworthy that an approach that benchmarks learning in terms of some measure of *change* or an *outcome* will, by necessity, emphasise learning as a 'product'. Too often this product is quantified by a grade or mark that, in turn, presumes that the higher the mark, the greater the learning that has taken place. This can be problematic, especially if we consider whether a person needs to perform or produce something in order for learning to have happened (Merriam, Caffarella & Baumgartner, 2007). Fortunately, in the last couple of decades we have witnessed some significant changes in how learning is conceptualised and subsequently seen expanded notions of learning emerge that go beyond simply being the product of some form of scholastic endeavour.

The work of Saljo

Changing conceptions of learning beyond that of it being a product is most evident in the work of Professor Roger Saljo, who is considered by many as a pioneer in contemporary research into learning. Professor Saljo is professor of education and educational psychology at the University of Gothenburg, Sweden, and in the late 1970s he published a seminal piece of work that has influenced learning theorists since. In this study, Saljo (1979) found that students conceptualised learning within five categories:

1 *Learning as a quantitative increase in knowledge*: Learning is the acquisition of information and 'knowing a lot'.
2 *Learning as memorising*: Learning is storing information that can be reproduced.
3 *Learning as acquiring*: Learning is acquiring facts, skills and methods that can be retained and used as necessary.
4 *Learning as making sense or abstracting meaning*: Learning involves relating parts of the subject matter to each other and to the real world.
5 *Learning as interpreting and understanding reality in a different way*: Learning involves comprehending the world by reinterpreting knowledge.

The significance of Saljo's (1979) work lies in the fact that the conceptions of learning demarcate learning as both a product and a *process*. As a process, learning includes changes in the way people understand, experience or conceptualise the world around them.

Consequently, learning can be experienced as something external (something that happens as a result of an experience) and something internal (something a person does in order to understand the world) (Nagel, 2013a). Saljo's (1979) work has since been reinforced through a plethora of studies involving people of varying ages in a number of different learning contexts (Purdie & Hattie, 2002).

The earlier work of Marton and Saljo (1976) also found that if students viewed learning as simply reproductive (i.e. rote memorising and replication of information) rather than as a process of making meaning and reflection then they were less likely to construct well-organised concepts regarding their learning. In other words, an individual's conceptions of learning will actually affect their own learning. Guy Claxton, a renowned author and Professor of the Learning Sciences at the University of Bristol Graduate School of Education, has noted that 'how well people learn is shown to be a function not only of the learning tools they possess, but the implicit beliefs they have picked up' (1999, p. 33).

IMPLICATIONS FOR TEACHING

A further important aspect of Saljo's work is that it is not meant to imply that there now exists a universality of meaning with reference to learning, demarcated as categories and described by Saljo (1979) and others. In educational contexts, learning is often defined according to different socially and culturally established conventions and, as such, teachers and students may exhibit a variety of approaches to learning in different situations depending on content, context and the demands of a particular task (Richardson, 2005). Concurrently, an individual's personal and cultural beliefs are often used to support various assumptions about learning and we all make assumptions about learning whether we realise it or not (Nagel, 2013a). Assumptions are made about what is important for students to learn; who can learn and why; and what strategies can be used to enhance learning (Bransford, Derry, Berliner, Hammerness & Beckett, 2005). To that end there are also a number of assumptions about learning and theories of learning that are worthy of scrutiny and elaboration.

First, and in an educational context, it is significant to remember that what is taught is not always the same as what is learnt. Students are not empty vessels waiting to be filled but rather are individuals who arrive in school with a diverse set of experiences and skills that are always part of any learning experience (Nagel, 2013a). Second, because learning is both a product and a process, traditional views of teaching along with Western societal assumptions about learning are often too narrowly defined and focus too heavily on tangible outcomes such as assignments and exams (Claxton, 1999; Robinson, 2011). Finally, and as noted throughout this chapter, learning is often taken for granted but it is too ambiguous a concept to articulate in a single sentence. As the quote from Jorg et al. (2007) at the start of this chapter shows, there are more than fifty theories of learning, which are ultimately unable to be covered in a single volume of work such as this textbook. Instead, a number of prominent perspectives of learning important to our understanding of formal education are presented and, as a learner, it is up to you to take what you know, pull it apart, add to it and ultimately form new ideas, understanding and conceptions of learning. This will be a significant component of your own understanding about development and learning and to help facilitate this process you will need to undertake several tasks:

→ examine some key theories of learning
→ think about your own beliefs of learning and question your own experiences of learning as you explore new theories of learning
→ reflect on ideas underpinning your understanding of learning
→ develop your understanding of learners and their developmental needs.

These points are intended to guide your learning and it is likely that you have already begun to engage in some of these ideas as this chapter has progressed. At this point, it is timely to look at some perspectives and theories of learning that have shaped educational practice and are still influential today.

THEORETICAL ORIENTATIONS TO LEARNING

As we have seen, learning is best understood as both a process and a product. But looking at learning as a process (rather than an end product) requires us to focus on what happens when learning takes place and such explanations help to frame various theoretical orientations of learning (Merriam et al., 2007). Five of the most commonly referred to orientations to learning that can be found in psychology and educational psychology include these:

→ behaviourist orientations to learning
→ cognitive orientations to learning
→ humanistic orientations to learning
→ social cognitive orientations to learning
→ constructivist orientations to learning.

Each of these orientations to learning, along with the key individuals who have helped shape or influence them, is explored below. It is important to note that there often is a degree of overlap between and among the orientations. As you read and develop your own understanding of learning, you will see commonalities and points of convergence emerging out of the details of each specific orientation. Another important consideration related to the theoretical orientations you are about to explore is that learning and human development are intimately intertwined and each orientation should be considered as an overview.

Other chapters in this text will give greater attention to aspects of human development and in particular neurodevelopment and the importance of human development to learning and education.

Behaviourist orientations to learning

Behaviourism
A field of psychology concerned with individual behaviour.

The term **behaviourism** stems from the early works of John Watson (1913, 1914, 1925), who believed that the key to understanding learning could be found through the analysis of behaviour. Watson was an American psychologist whose initial research work focused on animal studies but then controversially was applied in a human study involving an infant who would become famously known in psychology circles as 'Little Albert'. Watson and a graduate student by the name of Rosalie Rayner set out to prove that they could condition a fear response in a child or, in other words, have a child *learn* to be afraid (Watson & Rayner, 1920). In order to achieve this task they started exposing nine-month-old Little Albert to a series of stimuli, including a white rat, and found that the young boy showed no fear towards any of the items presented to him. The next part of the experiment saw the rat presented to Albert again but this time it was accompanied by the hitting of a metal pipe with a hammer behind, and out of view, of the child. Understandably, Little Albert was so startled by the loud bang he began to cry. Watson and Rayner repeated this over and over again to the point where Albert began to cry as soon as he saw the rat, even when the banging had been stopped. In essence Little Albert learnt to be afraid of the rat. The ethics of such an experiment are very problematic, not least of which because it is believed that Albert's fear was never deconditioned.

Behaviourists believe that observable stimuli produce observable behaviours, as in the study done by Watson and Rayner (1920), and as such *learning* can be conditioned through changes to the stimuli. One of the foremost behavioural theorists to expand on the work of John Watson was Burrhus Frederic (B. F.) Skinner. Skinner too was a prominent American psychologist and was the Edgar Pierce Professor of Psychology at Harvard University from 1958 until his retirement in 1974. Skinner (1953, 1963) described learning as an enduring change of behaviour resulting from external events, be they conscious or unconscious. For Skinner, learning occurred when some event or condition (stimulus) triggered an action (response) and those actions, which were rewarded in some manner, were likely to be repeated (learnt) (Nagel, 2013a). Both Skinner and Watson have contributed a great deal to our collective understanding of learning and two of the standout behaviourist terms associated with their work and often observable in schools are *classical* and *operant conditioning*.

CLASSICAL CONDITIONING

Classical conditioning focuses on the learning of involuntary emotional or physiological responses such as fear, sweating or increased muscle tension vis-à-vis some form of stimuli

(Santrock, 2011). The example of Little Albert could be considered classical conditioning, albeit with rather negative consequences. In an educational context, classical conditioning can be involved in both negative and positive experiences in a classroom or school. For example, a child may associate pleasurable feelings with a particular classroom due to its visual appeal, while another classroom may elicit fear or anxiety because the teacher in the room is overly critical. In this sense teachers can play both an implicit and explicit role in classical conditioning and must always reflect on their practice to ensure that any conditioning that is occurring is positive.

OPERANT (INSTRUMENTAL) CONDITIONING

For behaviourists, *operant conditioning*, which is also sometimes called *instrumental conditioning*, is a form of learning in which the consequences of a behaviour produce changes that will increase or decrease the probability that the behaviour will reoccur (Santrock, 2011). The consequences of the behaviour usually take the form of reinforcement or punishment whereby reinforcement increases the probability that a behaviour will reoccur, while punishment decreases the probability of repeated behaviours. The word 'reinforcement' actually means to strengthen the behaviour and reinforcement can be both positive and negative (Domjan, 2014). **Positive reinforcement** is easily explained and readily observable in schools and homes alike. In school, common positive reinforcers include praise, special privileges, high marks, scholarships, tokens, prizes, trophies, awards, certificates and public recognition. Even something as simple as a smile from a teacher can act as a positive, and powerful, reinforcement. **Negative reinforcement**, on the other hand, refers to the removal of unpleasant events or experiences after a desired behaviour is performed. A teacher may create a sense of surveillance by staring at a student until the student performs the desired behaviour, thereby eliminating the uncomfortable sense of someone watching over them.

> **Positive reinforcement** The addition of a pleasurable or desirable stimulus after a desired behaviour is exhibited.

> **Negative reinforcement** The removal of an undesirable stimulus or object after a desired behaviour is exhibited.

Positive and negative reinforcement are commonplace strategies in schools, where the standard mindset is changing behaviour. Perhaps one way to remember the difference between the two is that in positive reinforcement something is added, while in negative reinforcement something is subtracted or removed. Both strategies are regularly used in educational contexts and behaviourists believe that, for learning to occur, the role of the teacher is to create an environment of optimal conditioning: to provide the appropriate stimulus via the curriculum and follow this with some measure of positive or negative reinforcement (reward or punishment) (Nagel, 2013a).

The use of rewards and punishment is still quite prevalent in schools, particularly in terms of behaviour management strategies. There are a number of issues associated with such approaches to learning and behaviour, especially in terms of motivation and ethical considerations related to punishment. This is covered in greater detail later (in Chapter 7), but it is important to note here that an over-reliance on operant conditioning can actually hinder learning by focusing on extrinsic, rather than intrinsic, forms of reinforcement. Equally significant is that both rewards and punishment operate on an 'if you do this, you get that' strategy and are dictated by someone other than the learner (Kohn, 1999). Behaviourism also tends to neglect the contribution of cognition and cognitive skills to any learning process, especially in terms of more complex forms of behaviour such as problem solving. The important links between cognition and learning are very significant considerations for any teacher and educational context and as such are noted in the next section.

See Chapter ❼ for a detailed examination of motivation.

Cognitive orientations to learning

Cognition is a term that essentially means 'thought' and refers to the mental processes involved in comprehension and acquiring knowledge through experiences and the senses (Santrock, 2011). Such mental processes are often described as higher order functions of the brain encompassing language, imagination, perception, planning, thinking, remembering, judging and problem solving. Cognition is an important area of study across a number of disciplines but its meaning can vary slightly from one field to another. For example, in psychology and cognitive science, cognition is often depicted as an information-processing model within the mind, while a branch of social psychology known as *social cognition* focuses on attitudes, attribution and group dynamics (Blomberg, 2011; Sternberg, 2012). The dynamic nature of educational environments encompasses aspects of all disciplinary fields associated with 'cognition' but in terms of learning there are a number of significant aspects surrounding a cognitive orientation to this process.

One of the most important aspects of cognitive orientations to learning is that of human development. For cognitive theorists, learning is intimately linked with developmental changes and a gradual increase in the sophistication of mental processes. For example, researchers know that the mind of a two-year-old child is vastly different from that of an adolescent. This will obviously affect all aspects of learning and cognitivists focus on internal mental processes such as insight, executive control, attention, memory and perception as they apply to development and learning. Cognitive orientations to learning also focus on how learners manipulate information and make meaning out of information and experience. Deriving from this orientation is an underlying framework where learning is often delineated as the acquisition of new knowledge.

THE INFORMATION-PROCESSING MODEL

One of the foremost models of knowledge acquisition in a cognitive orientation to learning is the *information-processing model*. In this model, a great deal of emphasis is placed on how children process information through attention, memory, thinking and many other complex cognitive processes. The information-processing model emphasises that children manipulate information, monitor it and strategise about it while actively making sense of their experiences and modifying their own thinking in response to environmental demands (Nagel, 2013a; Santrock, 2011). The model itself often portrays cognitive endeavour as being similar to how computers process information, while cognitive psychologists often use analogies to computers to help explain the relation between cognition and the brain (Martinez, 2010). This view of cognition is often criticised for being overly simplistic in that human thinking, cognitive activity and learning cannot be easily described in the same manner as binary equations and the rigid algorithmic framework associated with computers (Ormrod, 2008). But, in an educational context, there are a number of important strengths in this model, particularly with its focus on understanding how memory operates and in developing pedagogy to assist in advanced problem-solving skills. This model is also an appropriate framework for much of the information and discussion in *Understanding Development and Learning*, given our emphasis on understanding processes and functions of the brain and mind in connection with child development. Indeed, many of the features of this model are evident throughout this book and in particular in exploring contemporary understandings of attention and memory as they pertain to human development and learning.

Human development is an important aspect of cognitive orientations to learning. The field of psychology has seen a number of theorists working in the area of human development and learning and many of these individuals and their work are examined in later chapters. But the important nexus between development and cognition is being heavily influenced by newer understandings of the human brain that are also presented throughout *Understanding Learning and Development* and form the underpinning framework of this entire volume of work.

Humanist orientations to learning

Humanist orientations to learning tend to pay less attention to aspects of cognition and give greater attention to student needs, emotions, values and self-perceptions. Born out of *humanist psychology* in the 1950s, this orientation to understanding psychology and learning emerged as an alternative to behaviourism's overly 'scientific' methods and psychiatry's focus on mental illness and disturbance (Nagel, 2013a). It is noteworthy that, before the 1950s, the early twentieth century had a number of individuals who could be noted as pioneers in humanist education. Inspired by the work of Jean-Jacques Rousseau, Friedrich Froebel and others, Maria Montessori, John Dewey and Rudolf Steiner embodied humanist philosophies in their writing and educational endeavours (Snowman et al., 2009). Today, Montessori and Steiner schools can be found in many Western countries, while the work of Dewey has been instrumental in shaping education and social reform since his earliest writings in the late 1800s.

Humanism is a system of thought that is predominantly concerned with the human experience, recognising the uniqueness of human beings and the qualities of life that

Humanism
A philosophical and/or ethical position that emphasises and values the agency of human beings.

contribute to our humanity (Nagel, 2013a). A central tenet in humanism is the value of human worth and dignity. In an educational context, this is translated into the practice of shaping the whole child with a view to improving his or her character. Academic performance, motivation and behaviour are linked specifically to the learning environment, whereby supportive classroom cultures promote enhanced self-esteem, intrinsic motivation and overall well-being and success (Snowman et al., 2009). And while humanist educators such as Dewey and Montessori continue to influence educational endeavour, the work of two key twentieth-century psychologists has also added a great deal to humanist orientations to learning.

Maslow's hierarchy of needs

Abraham Maslow was an American psychologist who is best known for creating a 'hierarchy of needs', which is a theory of psychological health predicated on fulfilling innate human needs. For Maslow, people have an innate drive to satisfy various needs that he organised into a hierarchy of five levels presented as a pyramid (see Figure 1.1).

As evident in Figure 1.1, Maslow believed that basic needs must be met before any higher levels can be achieved. If a learner's physiological, safety and belongingness needs are not met, then factors like self-esteem—which are integral to academic success—cannot be attained. This alone says much about the probable impact of poverty and socio-economic disadvantage on learning (Martinez, 2010). Contemporary neuroscientific studies support

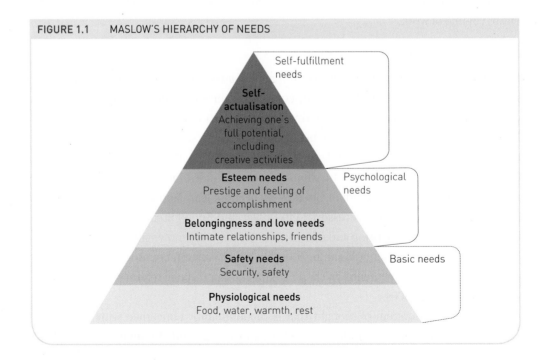

FIGURE 1.1   MASLOW'S HIERARCHY OF NEEDS

Maslow's work in that children raised in environments where basic needs are not met and where positive relationships are unavailable are subjected to high levels of stress which in turn negatively affect most aspects of their development and learning (McEwen, 2002; Nagel 2012a; National Scientific Council on the Developing Child, 2004, 2005, 2007; Shonkoff, 2010; Shonkoff & Levitt, 2010; Shore, 1997).

Notwithstanding the importance of meeting basic needs as depicted in Maslow's hierarchy, self-actualisation is the centrepiece of Maslow's theory and something he himself was deeply interested in. Maslow's research interests focused on studying psychologically healthy people in order to understand them and apply his findings so that others could more fully realise their potential for psychological health, growth and overall fulfilment (Martinez, 2010). In terms of learning in an educational context, Maslow's work asks educators to put student needs at the forefront of any learning situation, rather than those of the teacher or curriculum (Nagel, 2013a). Another humanist psychologist who complements Maslow in terms of meeting the needs of students and influencing education is Carl Rogers.

Rogers: nurturing students

Carl Rogers was a psychotherapist who pioneered a new approach to helping people cope more effectively with their problems and is widely regarded as one of the most influential psychologists in American history (Snowman et al., 2009). Rogers initially worked with delinquent children, becoming increasingly interested in child guidance and therapy. He formed the view that the key aspect for positive therapies could be found in setting up supportive environments and relationships rather than psychoanalytic techniques. Rogers's work transcended clinical practice and he became interested in education, where he argued that a teacher's goal should be to nurture students rather than direct their learning (Krause et al., 2010). For Rogers, learning was about personal change and growth and he believed that human beings had an inner drive towards self-fulfilment and a natural potentiality for learning. He believed that, within a nurturing environment, learners should be free to learn, explore and reach their full potential and that the best learning came from 'doing' (Nagel, 2013a). In one of his works, which embodies his philosophy in its title, *Freedom to Learn*, Rogers sets out a number of principles for learning and most notably acknowledges that a teacher's role is not just to deliver a curriculum but to give equal measure and attention to the intellect and emotions of each and every individual learner (Rogers, 1969).

The influence of the work of Carl Rogers and Abraham Maslow on learning and education cannot be understated. This is evident in contemporary educational rhetoric, which positions teachers as 'facilitators' and stresses the importance of meeting the 'needs' of each individual learner. Their work embodies humanist orientations to learning and emphasises that, for learning to occur, the heart of any educational endeavour must focus on personal and emotional development within a caring and supportive environment where student needs, desires, personal values, self-perceptions and motivations are considered. The importance of the learning environment also plays a central role in social cognitive orientations to learning.

SOMETHING TO THINK ABOUT 1.2

GENIE: A CASE STUDY IN THE DEPRIVATION OF STIMULATION

In terms of learning, experiences or the lack thereof matter. Chapter 2 presents neuroscientific evidence of how experiences shape the neural architecture of the mind but, long before researchers could look at the inner workings of the brain, examples of what happens when children are deprived of certain experiences provided a great deal of support for the work of Maslow and others. One tragic story is particularly compelling.

On 4 November 1970, a social worker discovered a thirteen-year-old girl who, by all accounts, had been forced to flounder helplessly within an environment Maslow might have noted as the bottom of his hierarchy. This young girl, who was later named 'Genie' by social workers, lived most of her childhood from the age of eighteen months in an environment of extreme deprivation. It appears that sometime before her second birthday, Genie's father confined her to a small room, often tied to a 'potty' chair. It was also discovered that some nights Genie was bound in a sleeping bag and forced to sleep in an enclosed crib with a cover of metal screening all around it. Genie was not allowed to speak to anyone; her mother and brother, who rarely left the family home, were forbidden from speaking to her. By the age of thirteen when she was discovered, Genie was almost entirely mute. It should come as no surprise that she had severe emotional difficulties but it may surprise some to know that she was physically underdeveloped and her stature was more typical of an eight-year-old than a teenager. Genie was promptly removed from her environment and her parents charged with child abuse but many of the secrets of the abuse remain untold as her father committed suicide before standing trial. Genie herself received extensive treatment but much of the damage was irreversible (Curtiss, 1977; Newton, 2004). Today, the case of 'Genie' is used by researchers to highlight what happens when humans are deprived of the very circumstances Maslow argues are necessary for learning and how lack of stimulation can lead to lifelong developmental problems.

Ask yourself...

Fortunately, it is unlikely any teacher will ever deal with children who experienced a life anything like Genie's. But we do know that children who grow up in impoverished regions or neighbourhoods or whose basic needs are not being met outside school do end up in classrooms. What does Maslow's hierarchy suggest would be the most important considerations to attend to when encountering disadvantaged children?

Social cognitive orientations to learning

As is tacitly suggested in the title, *social cognitive orientations* to learning imply a link between relationships, cognition and learning. In itself a social cognitive orientation to learning incorporates elements of both behaviourist (operant conditioning) and cognitive (information-processing) theories. Social cognitive orientations to learning emphasise how behavioural and personal factors interact with the social and physical environment; the roots of this orientation are derived from a framework known as social learning theory (Bandura, 1976).

SOCIAL LEARNING THEORY

The principal architect behind social learning theory is Stanford University Emeritus Professor of Psychology Albert Bandura. In the 1960s, Bandura conducted a series of famous experiments that have become collectively known as the 'Bobo doll study'. In different variations of these experiments, children were able to observe a woman beating up a Bobo doll and using aggressive language. (A Bobo doll is a large inflated doll with a sand base that rocks easily to and fro and when struck always returns to an upright position unless unexpectedly deflated.) When provided opportunities to engage with the Bobo doll, those children who witnessed violent and aggressive behaviour modelled the same behaviour, with or without any encouragement, rewards or punishment. Bandura's work is significant because it departs from behaviourism's insistence that all aspects of behaviour and learning are directed by some form of reinforcement or reward. Unlike the behaviourist Skinner, Bandura believes that human beings think about the relationship between their behaviour and consequences; social learning theory is arguably a transition between behaviourist and cognitive orientations to learning.

Over time Bandura's explanations for learning gave more attention to cognitive factors such as attention, memory, rehearsal and motivation and he relabelled his earlier work on social learning theory to social cognitive theory (Woolfolk & Margetts, 2013; see also Bandura, 1986, 1997, 2001). But the key principles underpinning both social learning theory and social cognitive orientations to learning suggest that people can learn by observing the behaviours of others and the outcomes of those behaviours (Nagel, 2013a).

TRIADIC RECIPROCALITY AND LEARNING VERSUS BEHAVIOUR

Another significant difference between behaviourism and social cognitive orientations to learning is that, unlike the central tenets of behaviourism, a social cognitive orientation recognises that learning can occur without a demonstrable change in behaviour. In other words, people can learn through observation alone and their learning may not necessarily be shown in their behaviour; observation and learning do not necessarily require imitation or mimicry (Nagel, 2013a). Social cognitive orientations to learning also recognise the role of the physical and social environments on behaviour and learning. For example,

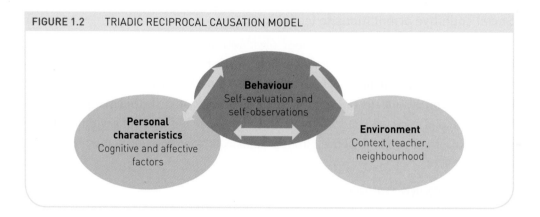

FIGURE 1.2   TRIADIC RECIPROCAL CAUSATION MODEL

Behaviour
Self-evaluation and self-observations

Personal characteristics
Cognitive and affective factors

Environment
Context, teacher, neighbourhood

school resources, the consequences of actions, the nature of a task, the use of reinforcement or punishment or both, other people, group dynamics and the actual physical size of a classroom can all affect learning according to social cognitive theorists (Nagel, 2013a; Snowman et al., 2010; Woolfolk & Margetts, 2013). Consequently, the environment, behaviour and individual characteristics such as cognitive and emotional factors influence and are influenced by one another and form a model that Bandura (1986) refers to as triadic reciprocality or what others call the triadic reciprocal causation model (Snowman et al., 2010; Woolfolk & Margetts, 2013).

The work of Bandura and other social cognitive theorists has had, and continues to have, an impact on our understanding of behaviour and learning in an educational context. One of the most important considerations derived from this work and highlighted by Bandura is an assumption that people, and not environmental forces, are the predominant cause of their own behaviour (Snowman et al., 2010). According to Bandura (2006), 'people are self-organising, proactive, self-regulating and self-reflecting. They are not simply onlookers in their behaviour. They are contributors to their life circumstances, not just products of them' (p. 164). This places a great deal of emphasis on many aspects of development and highlights the importance of the learner in any educational context. The final orientation to be explored in this chapter complements this view.

SOMETHING TO THINK ABOUT 1.3

THE NEEDS OF TEACHERS

The social environment of a classroom and school is not only important in terms of student development and learning but also is an important consideration in terms of teacher performance and well-being. Schools are places where human interaction is central to teaching and learning and the work of Bandura (2006) and others is not only important for considering pedagogy, student outcomes and student welfare but also significant when considering teacher welfare. For example, teachers are among the highest white-collar ▶

▶ professionals in self-reported work-related stress; such stress is often a major contributing factor to teacher burn-out (Johnson et al., 2005). There has been a great deal of research into stressors present in the teaching environment, highlighting a number of contributing factors, including class size, high-stakes testing, challenging student behaviours and school management structures to name a few (see, for example, Ballet & Kelchtermans 2009; Montgomery & Rupp, 2005). Aside from the potential health issues associated with burn-out, it is also evident that as teachers burn out, their tolerance, relationships with others and concern and care for their students decline along with associated lowering of outcomes in terms of student achievement (Black, 2001; Cozolino, 2013). Interestingly, just about every correlate of teacher burn-out links directly or indirectly to the negative effects of social and emotional disconnection, suggesting that future teachers would benefit greatly from training that includes a strong emphasis on the social and emotional skills required to succeed personally and as a teacher (Cozolino, 2013). It is important for future and current teachers to constantly ensure they take care of their own well-being and hierarchy of needs within the social milieu that exists when working with young minds in an educational context.

Ask yourself...

1   In your experiences as a student, have you encountered any teachers who may have appeared to be burnt out? Conversely, did you engage with teachers who seemed to have an endless supply of energy and enthusiasm? What do you think might have been contributing factors to each and within particular contexts?

2   A number of studies have shown that teachers who experience more positive emotions related to their work are more resilient, intrinsically motivated and better able to cope with the demands of their job. What strategies, if any, do you have to deal with stress and foster your own resilience? What might you be able to do with students to build positive emotions in your classroom?

Constructivist orientations to learning

Not too dissimilar to some of the other orientations presented above, constructivist orientations to learning (constructivism) share a number of related perspectives and theorists. Dewey, Montessori, Steiner, Piaget and Vygotsky are historical influences within aspects of this orientation to learning (Martinez, 2010; Merriam et al., 2007; Snowman et al., 2009). One leading theorist has gone so far as to describe constructivism as 'a vast and woolly area in contemporary psychology, epistemology and education' (von Glaserfeld 1997, p. 203). Perhaps the woolliness in this area stems from a variety of perspectives that have been labelled constructivist and, while there does not appear to be one easily defined constructivist theory, the simple underlying premise for constructivists is that learning is a process of constructing meaning; it is how people make sense of their experience (Merriam et al., 2007). Beyond that premise there are significant differences among constructivist

> **Constructivism**
> A theory of learning whereby individuals construct knowledge and meaning from their experiences.

theorists as to the role of experience, the nature of reality, what knowledge is of interest and whether the process of making meaning is primarily an individual or social one (Steffe & Gale, 1995). The distinction between whether a person constructs their learning and understanding through a social process or as an individual is an important one. This dichotomy has seen the emergence of the two most prominent versions of this orientation: *cognitive constructivism* and *social constructivism.*

COGNITIVE CONSTRUCTIVISM

Cognitive constructivism focuses on the individual and the role of cognition in accommodating new information in existing conceptual frameworks or schemes. The overlap with a cognitive orientation to learning is fairly self-evident and may be considered an extension of Jean Piaget's work. Indeed, some view Piaget as a constructivist and perhaps the most important originator of cognitive constructivism (Martinez, 2010). Within this branch of constructivism, making meaning relies on an individual's cognitive capacities and abilities, whereby meaning is constructed via the individual's previous and current knowledge structure; learning is the product of an internal cognitive activity; and learners actively construct knowledge and understanding (Merriam et al., 2007; Nagel, 2013a). In an educational context, this orientation suggests that learning is accommodated through providing experiences that 'induce cognitive conflict and hence encourage learners to develop new knowledge schemes that are better adapted to experience. Practical activities supported by group discussions form the core of such pedagogical practices' (Driver, Asoko, Leach, Mortimer & Scott, 1994, p. 6). It is significant to note that, while cognitive constructivism focuses on the individual, classrooms that embody such practices are recognised as places where individuals are actively engaged with others as they attempt to understand and interpret phenomena for themselves and where the 'teacher's role is to provide the physical experiences and to encourage reflection' (Driver et al., p. 7). This stands in contrast to the theoretical foundations of social constructivists.

SOCIAL CONSTRUCTIVISM

Social constructivism also focuses on the construction of meaning but emphasises the use of *cultural tools* (for example, language, mathematics, diagrams, approaches to problem solving) as a fundamental influence on making meaning. Social constructivists often refer to the learning process as a form of negotiating meaning, given the links between one's cultural tools and the necessity of engaging socially in talk and activities about shared problems or tasks (Merriam et al., 2007; Snowman et al., 2009). For social constructivists, making meaning is a dialogic process and, while a learner's cognitive capacities are important, it is the cultural tools at learners' disposal that shape learning through authentic, real-life activities to create common or shared understanding of some phenomenon (Nagel, 2013a; Snowman et al., 2009). The works of the Lev Vygotsky and Jerome Bruner are often associated with this orientation. Briefly, Vygotsky viewed learning as an activity socially mediated through the symbols and language of a culture, while Bruner advocated a discovery approach to learning via the use of problem solving (Krause et al., 2010).

Although cognitive and social constructivists emphasise different aspects of learning, they are not completely incompatible. In his description of constructivist epistemology, Windschitl notes that 'learning is an act of both individual interpretation and negotiation with other individuals' (2002, p. 142). Each approach does not deny the value of the other and all forms of constructivism understand learning to be an active, rather than a passive, endeavour (Merriam et al., 2007). In an educational context, learners are viewed as self-regulated and active participants in their learning and active 'constructors' of meaning through individual and group endeavour. For constructivists a fundamental consideration is the student, and so too is the fostering of positive student–teacher relationships.

See Chapter ❾ for a detailed look at the work of Vygotsky and Bruner.

CONCLUSION

It should be apparent that the orientations to learning noted in this chapter maintain important considerations in terms of all aspects of educational endeavour. It should also be apparent that the divergence of ideas found within each orientation posits a degree of legitimacy in views of learning as being complex and multifarious (Claxton, 1999). Generations of teachers have drawn their insights from the theories and theorists noted throughout this chapter and many continue to do so. Importantly, we should never assume learning to be a simple, taken-for-granted notion of the daily interactions between teachers and students in schools. Nor should teachers or those training to be teachers assume that they have learnt all they need to learn about learning once they take charge of a classroom. As noted in the Introduction of *Understanding Learning and Development*, neuroscience has made great strides into the discipline of education and our understanding of human development while also providing teachers with new understandings of learning. Chapter 2 continues this journey into understanding learning by exploring the important links between human development and learning.

CHAPTER SUMMARY

This chapter opened with the question 'what is learning?' This approach provided you with an opportunity to look at learning as both a product and process and draw an understanding of the differences between each. This led to an exploration of the subtle differences between teaching and learning and a brief history of each in Western school settings, underpinned by the claim that some current practices of 'education' do not align well with a number of theories of learning, particularly as they relate to contemporary students. In order to support such a claim a number of prominent orientations, or theoretical perspectives, of learning were presented. It is important to reiterate that there is a vast number of theories of learning; those that have been explored represent a select group that, to date, have and continue to have prominence in educational practice. Various aspects of behaviourist, cognitive, humanistic, social cognitive and constructivist orientations to learning are likely to play a part in your career as a teacher and a broad overview of each was offered to assist in your development as a teacher.

Implications for Teaching

As noted early in the chapter, many generations of students experienced a factory-line approach to being educated. For many years students were viewed as *tabula rasa*, a Latin term meaning 'blank slate', and the role of a teacher was to fill that empty void with the knowledge that was deemed important at the time. From the 1970s onward, researchers began to articulate aspects of learning as a process as much as a product. Concurrently, the advent of technology which has given rise to an age of seemingly endless information calls into question the need or actual possibility of pouring a continuing exponential growth of information and/or knowledge into the heads of students. For some researchers and theorists there is still a worrying trend, at a systemic level, to perpetuate a factory model through the continued use of standardised testing and many other artefacts of twentieth-century schooling. The issues with standardised tests are covered in Chapter 10 but foreshadowed here as an example of something you may have personally experienced and might now question as a valid mechanism for determining any degree of learning. Indeed, one important question for you to continually reflect on in your personal practice is 'am I teaching the way I was taught?'

This question is an important one; like standardised tests, it is explored in more detail in Chapter 10 under the term 'apprenticeship of observation' (Lortie, 1975). At this stage, after working through this chapter, it is important to keep this phrase in mind as you explore the following questions.

Ask yourself...

1   After working through the chapter, has the definition of learning that you were asked to write at the beginning of the chapter changed? If so, how?

2   Given your experiences as a student, have there been times when you felt your learning was enhanced or optimised? If so, under what conditions did this occur?

PRACTICAL ACTIVITIES

1 *While on practicum*, document the methods used to determine when or how learning has occurred. List all of these in one of two columns in a table under the headings 'Product' and 'Process'. Is one column larger than the other and, if so, what does that indicate to you? Could you design different ways to determine what, if any, learning has occurred?

2 *While on practicum*, jot down any examples of particular theoretical approaches to learning that you observe during the course of your practicum. Are some theories more apparent than others? Do some approaches resonate better with your own beliefs about learning and, if so, how might you engage with such approaches as a teacher?

STUDY QUESTIONS

1 What are the five broad theoretical orientations presented in the chapter? Note the main focus of each.

2 What is the difference between positive and negative reinforcement? List some examples of each in a classroom context.

3 What are the five levels of the Maslow's hierarchy of needs? List some ways in which you might be able to help students meet basic and psychological needs at school.

4 Social learning theory is important in terms of behaviour and learning. What does this theory mean for you as a future teacher and potential role model for your students?

5 What are the primary differences between cognitive constructivism and social constructivism? Provide examples of each in relation to educational and pedagogical contexts.

FURTHER READING

Blakemore, S. J. & Frith, U. (2005). *The Learning Brain: Lessons for Education*. Oxford, UK: Blackwell Publishing.

Claxton, G. (1999). *Wise Up: The Challenge of Lifelong Learning*. New York, NY: Bloomsbury Publishing.

Darling-Hammond, L. & Bransford, J. (Eds.) (2005). *Preparing Teachers for a Changing World: What Teachers Should Learn and Be Able to Do*. San Francisco, CA: John Wiley & Sons.

Donovan, M. S., Bransford, J. D. & Pellegrino, J. W. (Eds.) (2000). *How People Learn: Brain, Mind, Experience and School*. Washington, DC: National Academy Press.

Jorg, T., Davis, B. & Nickmans, G. (2007). Towards a new, complexity science of learning and education. *Educational Researcher Review, 2*(2), 145–156.

Lee, H. S. & Anderson, J. R. (2013). Student learning: What has instruction got to do with it? *Annual Review of Psychology, 64*, 445–469.

Martinez, M. E. (2010). *Learning and Cognition: The Design of the Mind*. Boston, MA: Allyn & Bacon.

Robinson, K. (2011). *Out of Our Minds: Learning to Be Creative* (2nd ed.). West Sussex, UK: Capstone Publishing.

Tokuhama-Espinosa, T. (2011). *Mind, Brain, and Education Science: A Comprehensive Guide to the New Brain-Based Learning*. New York: W.W. Norton.

VIDEO LINKS

Crash Course: *The Bobo Beatdown—Crash Course Psychology #12*
https://www.youtube.com/watch?v=128Ts5r9NRE

A succinct clip highlighting the impact of Albert Bandura's work on our understanding of behaviour and learning with a look at interesting learning concepts associated with his work.

Study.com: *Constructivism: Overview and Practical Teaching Examples*
http://study.com/academy/lesson/constructivism-overview-practical-teaching-examples.html

A concise look at constructivism and its application within classrooms.

WEBLINKS

Center for Innovation in Teaching and Learning http://cte.illinois.edu/resources/topics.html

A useful website with a number of links to theoretical and practical resources and ideas for the classroom.

Framework for 21st Century Learning http://www.p21.org/our-work/p21-framework

Although it is based in the United States with a view to enhancing educational structures and practices there, this site offers resources and ideas for engaging learners through contemporary understandings of learning, society and culture.

THE LINKS BETWEEN HUMAN DEVELOPMENT AND LEARNING

2

 Walk upstairs, open the door gently, and look into the crib. What do you see? Most of us see a picture of innocence and helplessness, a clean slate. But, in fact, what we see in the crib is the greatest mind that has ever existed, the most powerful learning machine in the universe.

(Gopnik, Meltzoff & Kuhl, 1999, p. 1)

LEARNING OUTCOMES

As you read through this chapter and undertake the exercises at the end, you will gain the ability to complete these tasks successfully:

→ understand and describe the important links between human development and learning

→ describe basic issues found in theories of human development

→ understand key aspects of physical, socio-emotional and cognitive development and how they relate to learning

→ describe and discuss Piaget's theory of cognitive development.

KEY TERMS

- emotional regulation
- temperament
- attachment
- schemata
- developmental tasks

Ms Hicks was quite excited by the realisation that in this, her first year of teaching, she would be teaching Year 1 students. She could hardly wait for them to arrive and start the school year with her. But she was unaware of the drama to unfold when Oliver arrived that morning. Oliver seemed a bit shy and somewhat anxious when he entered the classroom with his mother. He seemed to cling to her quite closely. Ms Hicks suggested that Oliver join some of the other children who were playing with blocks and puzzles on the carpet. With a little encouragement from his mum, Oliver moved to the carpet and started to do one of the many puzzles that had been set out. Ms Hicks learnt that Oliver was an only child and he had been home schooled until this year. That did not matter much to Ms Hicks who felt that Oliver would be quite comfortable in the class. It was only when Oliver's mother made her way to the door that Ms Hicks realised that things may not be as easy as she had first thought.

As Oliver noticed his mum leaving, he leapt up and quickly ran to her side, grabbing her leg. He appeared very anxious and distraught and, although his mother repeatedly told him she would be back later, his grip on her leg tightened. When Ms Hicks approached the pair Oliver let out a horrendous scream that startled the other children, some of whom were beginning to show a bit of distress at the events taking place around them. One little girl, Sophie, began to cry while others looked on in a mixture of surprise, curiosity and anxiety. Ms Hicks need to do something to calm the situation and she suggested that Oliver's mum stay for a few more minutes until he settled down and felt more relaxed. Oliver's mum agreed and escorted Oliver back to his puzzle on the carpet. Oliver reluctantly sat down but watched carefully as his mother returned to a chair next to Ms Hicks's desk. After a few minutes, and while Oliver was distracted, his mother quickly left the classroom at the advice of Ms Hicks. When Oliver realised that she had gone, he ran for the door and bolted into the playground, screaming for his mother. Ms Hicks gave chase and caught up with Oliver as he stood sobbing uncontrollably. She walked with him back to the classroom where he then found a place in the corner of the room and sat on his own. Oliver refused to move from that spot until the first break of the day when he joined the other children in their designated eating area and, while he ate the snack provided by his mother, it was clear he was still in a state of distress. Oliver's anxiety only disappeared when his mother arrived at the end of the day to collect him and take him home. Ms Hicks explained how the day had gone and noted that she felt that each day would improve ... it would just take some time.

1   The scene presented above is not an entirely unusual one for many teachers. Some children arrive at school for the first time with varying 'attachment' issues and find it difficult to settle in. What might you do if faced with similar circumstances? How might you help your students, regardless of age, feel safe and relaxed?

2   The links between human development and learning are important considerations for teachers. As you progress through this chapter, consider how aspects of human development may affect your pedagogical practice. Depending on the age of students you wish to work with, keep notes of those aspects of human development you think will need careful consideration in your planning.

INTRODUCTION

The important links between *human development* and learning will be discussed in this chapter. It should be evident to most people that learning is intimately linked with human development. Human development is not isolated to physical development but rather encompasses a number of other important domains; studying human development allows us to understand how humans change from conception to adulthood and on into old age and death (McDevitt & Ormrod, 2013). *Understanding Development and Learning* focuses on human development as it pertains to the early stages of life and through the school years, given that an understanding of human development and learning is an important framework of knowledge for future teachers. As a child matures and develops, so too do a number of important skills and attributes. With maturation and growth come improvements in physical coordination, emotional regulation, attention, memory and many other important factors associated with learning and overall development. Interestingly, some aspects of development seem to change overnight while others require much longer periods of time. But changes do occur and often surprise us.

Emotional regulation
The capacity to understand, accept and manage one's emotions.

In the eyes of some it is problematic when individuals who work in the areas of education and child development or psychology use personal anecdotes or refer to their own family members as sources of information or evidence to support research studies. But many times personal anecdotes offer varying opportunities for one's own work or light-bulb moments that provide insights into an individual's beliefs or ideas about the work they do. Such a moment occurred for us when listening to a story conveyed by one of our colleagues some years ago when his son had returned from one of his first days of school as a Year 1 student. On this day, the young boy excitedly told his dad that he had to draw a picture of his family for school the next day. Given his background in learning and teaching, the father's initial thoughts focused on concerns about homework at such an early age, but his son's overwhelming desire to do what he was asked overrode any concerns and he proceeded to help his son by finding a space on the kitchen table for him to engage in his early artistic best. He recalled how his son sat there staring at the paper, looking deep in thought and seemingly perplexed about where to begin. Our colleague, as a parent, felt that this would be a fairly straightforward exercise but, a few minutes later, the young lad conveyed his sense of puzzlement to his father that, in turn, left Dad in his own state of bewilderment. The son asked, 'Dad, how do you think I should draw our family?' His father mentioned that there were coloured pencils or markers and he could start by drawing his mum if he liked. 'No, no ... should I do it *portrait* or *landscape*?'

This anecdote is offered to impart a view around the central premise that adults should never underestimate what children know and learn and that a child's capacities for learning occur long before we might think. This is an important consideration given that, as late as the 1970s, many psychologists believed that newborn infants were only capable of automatic responses and could not think (Gopnik, Meltzoff & Kuhl, 1999). We now know that this is simply not the case and that, even during foetal development, a child is learning a great deal about the world. At birth this learning explodes and is closely aligned with many aspects of human development. As we said at the start of this chapter, an understanding of human development and its links to learning are of paramount importance for all educators: that is why *Understanding Development and Learning* adopts such a perspective.

A FRAMEWORK BUILT ON THEORY AND DOMAINS OF DEVELOPMENT

Looking at aspects of human development and learning has a fairly long history across numerous research and academic disciplines. There are many texts available that focus specifically on child and adolescent development at the nexus with learning and education. Research questions in the field of human development and learning are diverse and expansive. For example, while some researchers focus their efforts on understanding why and how most children acquire language in the first few years of life, others might be more interested in examining whether biological and environmental influences on development and learning are fixed or variable. Such is the range of research in this important area that it is beyond this text to cover all the research that is available. Instead, the following pages begin by looking at some important theoretical perspectives related to human development and learning, followed by a general overview of particular domains of development. Later chapters focus on specific aspects of neurological development that underpin all other domains of development. The overall intent of such an approach is founded on a number of important factors.

First, this approach provides a framework for developing an understanding of the human growth process as it relates to the diverse learning styles and needs of students, whether they are starting school for the first time or preparing for life after high school. Examining various aspects of human development also provides future teachers with a deeper understanding of the many different pathways children can take as they grow and develop and the impact of rapidly changing environments on such development.

Second, exploring aspects of human development also provides opportunities for understanding a child's life, learning from a child's perspective and understanding the important links between various domains of development. For example, many parents and educators may not be aware of numerous studies noting the significant links between cognitive and social development in infants after the onset of independent movement—crawling and walking—(Eliot, 2000). In other words, many aspects of human development are intertwined and an educator's knowledge and understanding of this has implications for how they interact with students and for all aspects of their didactic and pedagogical endeavour. It is important for educators to understand that their students are not only developing cognitively or intellectually but also socially, emotionally and physically. Any understanding of learning must take into account that what happens in a classroom is not only about content and lessons but also about processes, contexts and relationships.

Finally, a foundational understanding of the links between human development and learning also provides educators with the opportunity to better understand their own life and learning experiences on the way to becoming self-reflective practitioners. Individual experiences and beliefs about many aspects of human development are anchored in particular social, historical and cultural contexts. To that end, examining various theories of human development and their links to learning not only builds an educator's understanding of this important topic but also fosters opportunities for enhanced self-understanding and personal growth. In turn, this growth and opportunity for self-reflection can help educators to become more creative, innovative and effective.

This journey begins by looking at some historical perspectives on human development and issues arising out of such perspectives. Such an approach is best initiated by looking at basic issues associated with human development.

BASIC ISSUES IN HUMAN DEVELOPMENT

Look across any child development text and you will find references made to three basic issues associated with any explanation of the developmental changes that take place during childhood. We take a similar approach due to the fact that these issues, to date, still appear unresolved. The first issue focuses on how genetic or innate factors and the environment combine to influence development: *nature versus nurture*. The second issue looks at whether development is something that occurs in succinct and identifiable stages or whether it is something that is more gradual and not easily labelled according to age or any other benchmark: *discontinuous versus continuous*. And the third issue centres on which aspects of development are universal and which may vary among individuals or cultures or both: *universality versus diversity*.

NATURE VERSUS NURTURE

In the study of human development, 'nature' refers to the inherited characteristics and tendencies that influence development while 'nurture' focuses on the environmental conditions that influence development (McDevitt & Ormrod, 2013). Questions of whether development is primarily the product of genetics and other internal causes or whether it is produced by the effects of the environment external to the individual continue to position some researchers on one side of the debate or the other. It is likely that human development results from the complex interplay of both nature and nurture whereby they work as 'partners' in most aspects of a child's growth (McDevitt & Ormrod, 2013). Recent studies across various fields of neuroscience and developmental psychology further suggest that the nature versus nurture argument is actually a moot point and that child development cannot be encapsulated solely by one position or the other (Nagel, 2012a). For example, it has long been assumed that children who grow up in disadvantaged neighbourhoods face higher hurdles to success than children in neighbourhoods that are better off. But one study found that, within disadvantaged environments, the effects of growing up were also influenced by a child's innate temperament: anxious and fearful children were more likely to face long-term mental health issues while calmer children were better able to manage the stress associated with disadvantage and not suffer any deleterious and ongoing developmental problems (Bush, Lengua & Colder, 2010). To that end, *Understanding Development and Learning* adopts the position that in terms of human development, and by association learning, nature and nurture work in tandem with each having a degree of influence on the other and on any developmental trajectory.

Temperament
A person's way of responding to novel events or experiences while regulating emotional impulses.

DISCONTINUOUS VERSUS CONTINUOUS

Whenever parents, teachers or researchers alike speak of child development they often refer to stages. The 'terrible twos' is reserved for two-year-olds; adolescence has been described as a stage of heightened hormonal stress (Hall, 1904). Describing childhood in stages usually refers to certain periods of time when children display certain behaviours. Stage theorists generally believe that each stage of development, be it cognitive or otherwise, is qualitatively different from that in earlier or later stages and that changes from one stage to another are discrete, reflecting discontinuity of development (Bjorklund, 2005; Bjorklund & Blasi, 2012). For example, Jean Piaget's theory of cognitive development (see Chapter 1) is one of the most recognised and widely used frameworks for describing how a child's mind matures over four distinct stages. While Piaget's work is still widely considered by many as a seminal force in describing cognitive development, not all theorists believe that age-related changes necessarily reflect distinct and discrete stages of development.

A contrasting view of development posits that changes are mainly quantitative in nature, and so changes of quantitative abilities are said to exhibit continuity of development, with development occurring gradually (Bjorklund & Blasi, 2012; Salkind, 2004). For example, neuroscientific and developmental psychological research tells us that as children age they are able to hold more things in memory, know the meaning of more words and process information faster (Bjorklund, 2005; Eliot, 2000; Nagel, 2012a). These are quantitative or measurable changes that gradually occur over time and are not bound by succinct stages.

Not too dissimilar to the nature versus nurture debate, aspects of development are likely to be both discontinuous and continuous depending on what one is looking to describe, and the issue itself represents an artificial choice between alternatives (Salkind, 2004).

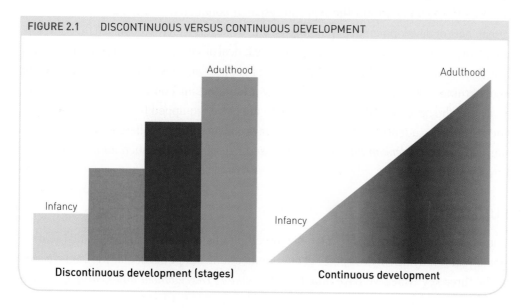

FIGURE 2.1   DISCONTINUOUS VERSUS CONTINUOUS DEVELOPMENT

Adulthood

Infancy

Discontinuous development (stages)

Adulthood

Infancy

Continuous development

Some theorists suggest that it is best to look at discontinuity and continuity as a continuum whereby the actual shape of change over time reveals that such changes are of both types (Kagan, 1971; Salkind, 2004). While Figure 2.1 offers a pictorial representation of the issue, *Understanding Development and Learning* adopts the view that child development does indeed maintain both discontinuous and continuous notions of development, depending upon what aspect of development is being observed, measured or described.

UNIVERSALITY VERSUS DIVERSITY

When we look at young children, unless significant disabilities are present, all children learn to sit, walk and run almost invariably in that order (McDevitt & Ormrod, 2013). Such developmental changes are said to reflect a certain degree of universality; the changes are evident or common across all individuals in all contexts. In contrast, other developmental changes are highly individual. Distinct differences are apparent and may be noted as reflecting a degree of diversity in development. For example, while temperament is an important aspect of emotional and social development evident in all children, there is evidence noting individual differences in the development of children's temperament style and that individual aspects of neurodevelopment play a role in shaping a child's overall temperament (Rothbart, 2004, 2007; Santrock, 2011). Some researchers have even labelled such differences as ranging from an 'easy' child to a 'slow-to-warm-up' child to a 'difficult' child (Chess & Thomas, 1977; Thomas & Chess, 1991).

It is probably safe to assume that most people would be able to identify aspects of universality or diversity or both in terms of child development. Most parents have witnessed aspects of each within and among their own children. Perhaps the greatest distinction between the two lies within the types of research conducted or the focus of interest of researchers or developmental psychologists. But, while it is widely recognised that development is a process of change demonstrating a great deal of similarities among children at any age, there is also substantial variability among people at all ages. In terms of development and learning, both universality and diversity are important considerations for teachers. Teachers who have an understanding of both are better equipped to plan learning experiences for their students as a group while always considering the differences among those same students. *Understanding Development and Learning* adopts such an understanding throughout its pages.

SUMMARY

The study of human development is a highly complex field. Many researchers and theorists spend years studying single aspects of development and adopt particular positions related to the three key issues we have noted. *Understanding Development and Learning* emphasises that a strict dichotomy between nature and nurture, for example, is overly simplistic; all aspects of human development will maintain components of nature and nurture, discontinuity and continuity, and universality and diversity. As you progress through each chapter you will see aspects of each issue presented both explicitly and implicitly, depending on their importance. Looking at physical, cognitive and social and emotional development as key domains of development further helps to set a framework for understanding the complexities of human development and the links between it and learning.

SOMETHING TO
THINK ABOUT
2.1

MONEY CAN BUY ORAL LANGUAGE SKILLS

One of the most important components of school success is a child's language and literacy ability. Researchers have known this for many years and literacy is one of the most important benchmarks used by educators and politicians alike when it comes to notions of minimum standards and teacher or school efficacy. Significantly, the future literate capacities of a child are influenced long before the child arrives at school. This is evident in many studies telling us that comprehensive language development, a precursor to literate success, is something that is nurtured early in life in the home environment.

In a landmark study, Hart and Risley (1995) found what many researchers had suspected for years: that children differ greatly in when they begin to learn language. But what Hart and Risley uncovered was that, above all else, the single greatest determinant in the nurturing of language is relative economic advantage. In their study, Hart and Risley identified that children living in poverty, children born into middle-class homes and children with professional parents were having similar language experiences but children in more economically privileged families heard some things much more often; as a result, their vocabulary and language capacities surpassed those of children in lower economic or middle-class conditions. In two-and-a-half years of observing forty-two families for an hour each month to determine what typically went on in the homes of children learning to talk, Hart and Risley found that, in terms of words heard, the average child in the lower socio-economic context was having half as much vocabulary experience (616 words per hour) as the average middle class child (1,251 words per hour) and less than one-third that of the average child in a professional family (2,153 words per hour). There are a number of contributing factors to this phenomenon but of importance here is that frequency matters, and that children born into homes with fewer economic resources have fewer language experiences thereby potentially creating future learning and 'schooling' disadvantages.

Interestingly, a recent study by researchers at Stanford University further demonstrates the impact of socio-economic standing on vocabulary development. Published in 2013 and led by Dr Anne Fernald, researchers found that, by eighteen months of age, children in different socio-economic groups displayed dramatic differences in their vocabularies. By age two the disparity in vocabulary development grew significantly (Fernald, Marchman & Weisleder, 2013). In this study children sat in a parent or caregiver's lap as images of two objects were shown on a screen. The parent wore sunglasses to eliminate any undue influence on the child as they listened to a voice recording identify one of the objects by name and use it in a sentence (for example, 'Look at the truck'). The researchers filmed the child's eye movements, tracking which image the child looked at and how long the child looked at the object in milliseconds. Children from lower socio-economic backgrounds were slower at identifying the correct object and ▶

▶ spent less time looking at it; by two years of age, they were performing at the same level in terms of speed and accuracy as eighteen-month-olds from higher socio-economic backgrounds. In other words, children of higher socio-economic backgrounds had larger vocabularies, sooner and at all ages. The importance of this study cannot be underestimated, given that many related studies have shown that differences in trajectories of language development established by three years of age tend to persist and are predicative of later school failure or success (Fernald et al., 2013). And now, the evidence suggests that components of school success can occur long before a child's third birthday or before they engage in any formal learning and teaching environments.

Ask yourself...

1 What do you think might contribute to the differences in vocabulary development across socio-economic boundaries as noted in the studies above? How would such differences in vocabulary affect curriculum and pedagogy in schools?

2 While it is apparent that pedagogy and curriculum may need to be adjusted to accommodate the types of disparities noted above, what school or systemic structures or policies might also be affected?

DOMAINS OF HUMAN DEVELOPMENT

Historically, texts designed to prepare future teachers with a greater understanding of the links between human development and learning begin such a journey by looking at physical development, cognitive development and socio-emotional development. *Understanding Development and Learning* follows a similar pattern but the fundamental framework underpinning this text is derived from contemporary neuroscientific research. Chapter 3 looks at neural development in great detail but it is important to bear in mind, while reading this chapter, that all aspects of development are intimately linked to that of the brain. As a child's brain matures and develops, so too do all aspects of physical, cognitive, emotional and social development. The intent of this chapter is to give a broad overview of the important aspects of each of these domains, followed in the next chapter and throughout the text with a more detailed focus on brain development and its links to all other aspects of development and learning.

See Chapter ❸ for a detailed look at brain and neural development.

PHYSICAL DEVELOPMENT

Physical development is sometimes taken for granted: it seems to happen without our noticing and is often viewed as being of lesser importance to cognitive, emotional or social development (Bjorklund & Blasi, 2012; Krause, Bochner, Duchesne & McMaugh, 2010). This may be due to the fact that, as a child's body grows and changes, such changes are easily visible compared to the other domains. It may also be that when people think of physical growth, they think primarily of changes to the body and forget that an important aspect of physical development is the development of the brain and nervous system. Therefore, it is significant to note that physical development involves more than just predictable changes in a child's shape, size and motor control, and actually reflects the biological changes that underlie psychological development (Bjorklund & Blasi, 2012). For example, cognitive development is influenced by physical development because the brain and associated development of motor skills affect the development of thought patterns.

Notwithstanding the important links between physical development and other domains of development, this section of the chapter focuses predominantly on changes related to growth and the body. For the purpose of organisation and in an effort to provide a suitable framework for looking at all aspects of development, it is common practice in human development research and literature to describe development in terms of particular periods. These periods include *infancy* (birth to 18–24 months of age), *early childhood* (2 to 5 or 6 years of age), *middle childhood* (6 to 11 or 12 years of age) and *adolescence* (10 or 12 years of age to late teens or early twenties). Within adolescence it is also not uncommon for some to break that period into *early adolescence* (10–14 years) and *late adolescence* (14–18 years). For simplicity, we will use infancy, early childhood, middle childhood and adolescence. You may note that these age periods mirror particular educational frameworks—early childhood, to primary age to high school—but it is equally important to note the fluidity of ages within each group. Simply stated, it is not really possible to put finite ages on these periods of development, given the maturational and developmental variability between children; for example, some children enter pubescence and adolescence earlier than others. But these periods do offer a framework for exploring development, starting with physical development.

Infancy

Compared to most other mammals, motor maturation and physical development are rather slow in humans due to the complexity of the brain regions responsible for such development (Nagel, 2012a). Worth noting here is that not all parts of the body grow at the same rate and that growth not only reflects changes in size but also in proportion. In utero and post-natally, the body spreads from head to foot—*cephalocaudal development*—and from its centre to periphery—*proximodistal development* (see Figure 2.2).

At birth a child is rather immobile with the exception of being able to turn its head and move its limbs, often in a seemingly uncontrollable fashion. Over the course of the next twelve months, many changes occur and, by one year of age, a child will have moved from simply

FIGURE 2.2   CEPHALOCAUDAL AND PROXIMODISTAL DEVELOPMENT

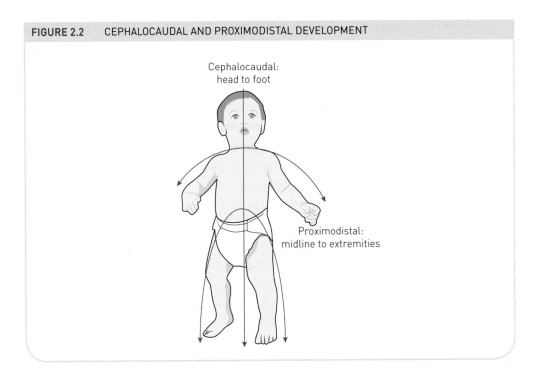

rolling over, to crawling, standing and eventually walking. The transition to walking is an important one; research has shown that crawling appears to strengthen neural pathways associated with vision, understanding of space and planning of movement (Bell & Fox, 1997). Crawling is also an important milestone in terms of developing emotional understanding in that a child's innate curiosity coupled with increasing mobility will be tempered by parental concerns over where to go; parents and care-givers will start to say 'no' and children start to learn that their actions affect the emotions of others (Campos, Kermoian & Zumbahlen, 1992; Krause et al., 2010). The links between crawling and various other aspects of development help to remind us that as the body grows and develops, so does the mind and that the environment plays a part in this development.

As the infant's muscles continue to grow, improved neural communication in the brain allows signals from the motor cortices to travel more rapidly and efficiently to various muscle groups throughout the body (Herschkowitz & Herschkowitz, 2004; Nagel, 2012a). Associated changes in both *gross* and *fine motor skills* are also evident over time. Gross motor skills involve large muscle groups of the trunk and limbs and whole body movements, such as rolling, clapping, throwing and running, while fine motor skills require small muscles of the mouth, arms and hands to work together to perform precise and refined movements (Nagel, 2012a). In terms of developmental goals and learning, gross motor skills play an important role in a child's exploratory behaviours and later schoolyard activities, while fine motor systems are associated with learning to read, write and interpret information (Berninger & Richards, 2002).

Between one and two years of age, the child's body continues to grow and coordination improves. A child will soon be walking independently and become much more mobile. Fine motor skills continue to improve and children of this age will soon be able to hold two or three objects in a hand, take toys apart and put them back together and begin to drink from a cup and feed themselves. Running and jumping soon become part of a child's gross motor repertoire, while throwing and catching abilities also develop quickly.

Early childhood

Physical development during early childhood continues to change rapidly in terms of both gross and fine motor skills. The acquisition and development of motor skills is so significant that most preschool and early childhood programs in Australia and New Zealand attach great importance to it (Krause et al., 2010). Visit any such environment and you will notice the promotion of gross motor skills through apparatus set up to allow children to climb, hop, roll, run, jump, skip and throw balls or other appropriate objects. Children will develop their fine motor skills through painting, using crayons, manipulating dough and clay or any measure of activities that require manipulation of the fingers and hands.

During the early childhood years, the development of motor skills also occurs through children's spontaneous activities and those organised by parents. Young children often seem to be in perpetual motion with boundless energy, and, as they actively engage in the world, they are simultaneously developing both gross and fine motor skills. This is a good example of how nature and nurture intermingle; physical development has a predetermined maturational path but experiences in the environment play a role in moving a child along that path. This continues into middle childhood; as children enter primary school, motor skills continue to improve.

Middle childhood

During middle childhood, the pace of physical change lessens from that of early childhood. Playground games along with participation in a variety of extracurricular activities contribute to physical development and lend themselves to the refinement and recombination of existing motor skills. It is noteworthy that, while changes in weight and height are gradual, speed, coordination and agility increase markedly (O'Donnell et al., 2012). Such changes have also been linked to various emotional, social and cognitive outcomes. As physical functions strengthen and become more refined, so too do a child's self-esteem and confidence (O'Donnell et al., 2012). Engaging with other children in physical activities also enhances a range of social skills, while concentration, memory and various aspects of learning also improve (Krause et al., 2010).

The importance of physical activity and play to physical development cannot be understated. A plethora of studies tells us that, as children move from infancy into early childhood and middle childhood, physical activity and movement are crucial for all aspects of physical development, along with all other aspects of development and school achievement and success. For example, physical activity and exercise have been linked to improved perceptual skills, verbal ability, mathematical ability, school readiness, attention, emotional self-control and aspects of memory (Nagel, 2012a). Perhaps this is why physical education is such an important part of the school curriculum with a requirement in Australia of at least two hours of physical activity for children in middle childhood (Krause et al., 2010).

Adolescence

Next to infancy and toddlerhood, adolescence is perhaps the next stage of physical development that is demonstrably noticeable. The onset of puberty brings with it a myriad of physical changes, ranging from visible changes in body shape to changes in sex hormones and brain structures. Changes to the brain are covered in greater detail in Chapter 3 but it is important to remember that, while the body begins to mirror adult shape and size through adolescence, the brain takes somewhat longer, resulting in many adults wrongly thinking that a teenager who is physically similar to an adult is also cognitively and emotionally mature.

During the earliest stages of adolescence, both boys and girls grow taller with a decreasing proportion of body fat to bone and muscle. Sex differences in growth spurts are evident: girls generally show the greatest physical changes between the ages of ten and fourteen, while changes in boys appear a couple of years delayed with the most significant between the ages of twelve and sixteen. As puberty begins to take hold, which is on average at eleven years of age for girls and fourteen years of age for boys, glandular changes and changes to the reproductive systems begin to emerge. The onset of menstruation in girls is followed by growth in the size of the breasts, extension of the uterus and growth in body hair, particularly underarm and pubic hair. For boys, lengthening and widening of the penis coincides with growth and thickening of pubic hair. Boys' voices will gradually deepen and the emergence of body and facial hair is evident. These major changes in both boys and girls present various challenges related to physical appearance and identity formation and come at a critical time in their schooling. The physical changes are also accompanied by social, cognitive and emotional changes. Sensitivity to such changes is an important skill for teachers as they help adolescents to navigate not only the curriculum but also the challenges associated with adolescence.

Final thoughts

There is broad variation in the physical development of one individual to the next. Within such variation are some general principles characterising physical development that are worth remembering when working with children in an educational setting. These principles have been succinctly stated in the work of McDevitt and Ormrod (2013, pp. 150–153):

→ different parts of the body mature at their own rates
→ children's bodies function as dynamic changing systems
→ each child follows a unique growth curve
→ as children grow, functioning becomes increasingly differentiated and integrated
→ physical development maintains both quantitative and qualitative changes
→ children's health is affected by their involvement in numerous environments.

These points, in conjunction with those offered earlier in the chapter, offer general guidelines related to age and physical maturation. But it is particularly important to emphasise that individual variations in physical development occur as a result of a number of other factors including gender, physical disabilities and the environment. For example, differences in growth rate and height have been observed among individuals in other countries and this may be related to diet, prevalence of various diseases and various health issues (Eveleth & Tanner, 1991; Krause et al., 2010). Therein lies yet another example of the merging of nature and nurture in that the 'ultimate size and shape that a child attains as an adult is the result of a continuous interaction between genetic and environmental influences' (Eveleth & Tanner, 1991, p. 176). Given the range of potential differences, it is incumbent upon teachers not only to maintain a broad understanding of physical development but also to reflect on their practice in relation to engaging with children in any learning environment. This is equally true when looking at other areas of development.

SOCIO-EMOTIONAL DEVELOPMENT

The linking of the concepts of social development and emotional development is deliberate and purposeful. While it is not uncommon to see child development and educational psychology texts deal with each individually, there is also a growing number of researchers and authors who prefer to merge these two aspects of development. *Understanding Development and Learning* adopts a similar approach for two important reasons. First, the interconnected nature of emotional development with that of being able to engage with others is self-evident; as children grow and mature emotionally, so does the scope and breadth of their relationships and social interactions. Social engagement, in turn, provides an avenue for continued emotional development; considerable volumes of work tell us that social interaction is critical for all aspects of development and long-term health (Nagel, 2012a; see also Gervais, 2009; Shonkoff, 2010; Wismer-Fries & Pollack, 2007). Second, taking this approach also assists in further emphasising the interconnected nature of all aspects of development while simultaneously constructing a framework for later chapters, which are underpinned by an understanding of the complexities and interconnected nature of the human brain. As the brain matures, so too do all aspects of development. Understanding key components of socio-emotional development and well-being is becoming increasingly recognised as a key factor in ensuring any measure of school success.

The importance of socio-emotional development cannot be understated. Socio-emotional development is a significant aspect of development; teachers need to have a degree of familiarity and understanding with it, given that socio-emotional development provides the foundation for how we feel about ourselves and how we experience others. A child's understanding of who they are, what they are feeling, what others might be feeling and what they can expect to receive from others are important concepts at the heart of their social and emotional wellness. Such understandings also influence all other areas of development. For example, cognitive, motor and language development can be greatly affected by how children feel about themselves and their ability to express ideas and feelings. Importantly, social and emotional milestones are often harder to pinpoint than signs of physical development. This should not be surprising, given that such milestones occur in the mind as a child's brain matures and develops. Importantly, human beings are, by nature, social beings and a child's social competencies are founded on emotional maturity and well-being. In order to develop a broad understanding of socio-emotional development and milestones of such development, it is prudent to look at what 'emotions' actually are, and various theories and perspectives related to emotions and emotional development.

Emotions, feelings and emotional development

For most people, emotions (sometimes referred to in neuroscientific literature as *affective states*) are something easily displayed but often not well understood. For example, many people might use the terms 'emotions' and 'feelings' interchangeably but in reality they are not the same thing. Emotions are best described as mental or physiological states, while feelings are the perceptions of those emotional states (Damasio, 2004). In other words, emotions result from the activation of particular perceptual circuits in the brain and specifically in concert with the limbic system, while feelings are the representations made as a result of such activity: emotions precede feelings (Damasio, 1999; Nagel, 2012a). For example, if you were walking down an unfamiliar street and passed someone's house where a large dog ran to the fence and barked loudly at you, a number of things would occur. An 'emotional' response would see your senses capture that stimulation, allowing various regions of the brain to work in concert with one another and convey a response suggesting you should pay attention to the stimulation and act. This emotional response would likely lead to you 'feeling' surprised, anxious or afraid; words you would use to describe this experience to others.

The subtle definitional nuances between the terms 'emotions' and 'feelings' are not necessarily problematic in *Understanding Development and Learning*. Both will be used, depending on the context provided, and the distinctions between the two should become increasingly apparent as the chapter progresses and as aspects of emotional development are explored. Before an overall exploration of socio-emotional development, a few important terms—*primary* and *secondary emotions*, *empathy*, *temperament* and *emotional regulation*—are worthy of some initial explanation. Later in the chapter, we refer to related terms, including *attachment*, *perspective taking* and *social referencing*.

Primary and secondary emotions

The displaying of emotions comes quite naturally to people. *Primary emotions*, sometimes referred to as 'basic' emotions, are evident in the earliest stages of life and are likely a product of a human being's innate survival mechanisms. While most experts agree on the existence of primary emotions from which all other emotions derive, there is yet to be a consensus reached on what these emotions might be. A commonly followed theory, based on the work of Paul Ekman (1970, 1999; see also Ekman & Friesen, 1971), posits that there are six basic emotions: happiness, sadness, fear, disgust, surprise and anger. From these emotions emerge *secondary emotions*, resulting from social and cultural interactions in the environment (Menon, 2000; Panksepp, 2004).

Secondary emotions are learnt emotions as children develop and engage with people and the environment around them. These emotions appear to develop between fifteen and eighteen months of age and also reflect an individual's emerging cognitive development, especially in relation to a child's ability for self-awareness (Lewis, 2008). In order to feel pride, for example, a child must be aware that he or she has successfully completed a task; such awareness is linked to maturation and cognitive development. Importantly, some secondary emotions not only depend on one's own awareness of self but also on an awareness of other minds. Such awareness can be linked to other people's expectations of, or reactions to, a child's behaviour and this awareness improves with age. A child will likely learn the emotions of guilt and shame, for example, when a parent displays signs of being upset or unhappy with particular behaviours. These learnt secondary emotions take time to develop, may be culturally specific and rely on improved cognitive abilities.

Empathy

A very important component of emotional and social development is *empathy*. Some would suggest that empathy is an important example of *perspective taking* and *social cognition* (Bjorklund & Blasi, 2012). Empathy relates to a person's capacity to experience the same feelings as another person, particularly when another person is sad, anxious or in any similar form of distress (Eisenberg, Eggum & Edwards, 2010). Infants appear to demonstrate primitive forms of empathy by shedding tears when they hear another infant cry, but this type of behaviour is involuntary, relies a great deal on mimicry and is not indicative of empathetic responses requiring self-conscious thought (Nagel, 2012a; see also Berk, 2006;

Decety & Michalska, 2010; Dondi, Simion & Caltran, 1999). Like all secondary emotions, the capacity to feel empathy for another person improves with age and is influenced by the actions of others. Parents who are warm and respond to their children's needs enhance empathetic behaviours in their own children; children who demonstrate greater degrees of empathy also display more socially appropriate behaviours and are more responsive to the social behaviours of others (Findlay, Girardi & Coplan, 2006; Zhou et al., 2002). Empathy is also closely linked to another significant component of emotional and social development: temperament.

Temperament

Temperament is a term often used by developmental psychologists to refer to 'personality' in infants and young children (Bjorklund & Blasi, 2012). Researchers often disagree on the details of what does and does not constitute temperament but it is generally recognised as a child's typical way of responding to novel stimulation, events or experiences along with a capacity to regulate impulses (Kagan & Fox, 2006; Rothbart & Bates, 2006; Rothbart, Sheese & Conradt, 2009). Most researchers agree that temperament is comprised of biological, genetic and environmental factors, and, as such, is another example of the interplay between nature and nurture. Arising from this interplay is the concept of *goodness of fit*.

Goodness of fit is an important consideration when looking at temperament and refers to a child's individual temperament and the particular environment in which he or she is raised (Chess & Thomas, 1977, 2000). Having a 'good fit' does not mean that an adult and child have the same temperament but rather that the adult accepts and accommodates a child's rhythms and dispositions (McDevitt & Ormrod, 2013). The longest-running study of temperament, following individuals from infancy to adulthood, found that most children fell into three types of temperament:

→ The 'easy' child—easily falls into routines, is happy and adapts well.
→ The 'difficult' child—experiences difficulty with routines, does not adapt well to new experiences and tends to react intensely and negatively to anything new.
→ The 'slow-to-warm-up' child—is inactive, has a negative mood, reacts mildly to environmental stimuli and is slow to adjust to new experiences (Chess & Thomas, 1977).

The study also found that many children did not strictly fit into any one of the patterns—but demonstrated many combinations of patterns—and that temperament was a major factor in a person's probability of experiencing psychological problems or coping well with stress (Chess & Thomas, 1977). Importantly, these researchers also found that parenting practices can modify temperament, which arguably parallels aspects surrounding the development of 'emotional regulation'.

Emotional regulation

One of the most important aspects of emotional development at the nexus of social interaction is that of emotional regulation. Generally speaking, emotional regulation refers to a person's capacity to understand and accept their emotions, and to manage such emotions when necessary to engage in appropriate social behaviour. Learning to regulate emotions is perhaps one of the most important tasks of early childhood (Cole, Martin & Dennis, 2004; Davis, Levine, Lench & Quas, 2010; Eisenberg & Spinrad, 2004; Fox & Calkins, 2003). Having 'good' emotional regulation skills allows individuals to control urges and limit impulsive behaviours during emotional distress. In an educational context, numerous studies have identified that children who demonstrate good emotional regulation appear to do better across all aspects of 'schooling' (see, for example, Blair, 2002; Blair & Razza, 2007; Eisenberg, Valiente & Eggum, 2010; Valiente, Lemery-Chalfant, Swanson & Reiser, 2008).

Emotional regulation often makes references to notions of delayed gratification (Mischel, Ebbesen & Zeiss, 1972) or impulse control, or can be referred to as 'self-regulation', 'emotional control', 'affect regulation' or 'emotion management' (Bell & Wolfe, 2004; Cole et al., 2004). It should be apparent that underlying each of these terms is the fundamental notion of controlling emotional responses; as such, emotional regulation provides another example of the important links between cognition and emotion. As children grow they become increasingly able to exercise voluntary control over behaviours and act according to social expectations. Concurrently, the development of emotional regulation and a capacity for controlling impulses depends on a number of individual characteristics along with the types of social actions encountered. Barring any form of developmental problems, the capacity to regulate one's emotions generally improves over time. Emotional regulation is integral to social development and, like most other areas of emotional development, it depends on aspects of both nature and nurture, as evident in the earliest stages of life.

SOMETHING TO THINK ABOUT 2.2

THE MARSHMALLOW TEST

The ability to regulate one's emotions in terms of delayed gratification is an important aspect of behaviour, motivation and learning. It also turns out that a child's capacity for delayed gratification, or what some might commonly refer to as self-control, can have long-lasting consequences.

In a remarkable series of studies that began in the 1960s at Stanford University, researchers explored delayed gratification in children with a simple but very effective test. Led by Professor Walter Mischel, a psychologist now at Columbia University, researchers presented individual pre-schoolers with plates of treats, such as marshmallows, in a controlled laboratory (Mischel & Ebbesen, 1970; Mischel et al., 1972). The child was then told that the researcher had to leave the room for a few minutes, but not before offering the child a choice. If the child waited until the researcher returned, the child could have a second marshmallow but if he or she couldn't wait, the child could ring a bell and the researcher would come back immediately but ▶

▶ the child could only have one marshmallow. In other words, the child could have one treat immediately or two later when the researcher returned after fifteen minutes had passed.

The immediate observations were interesting and saw that some children jumped up and ate the marshmallow as soon as the researcher left the room while others wriggled uncomfortably in their chairs as they tried to restrain themselves and a few managed to wait the entire time and receive their reward. More observations were to follow over the next forty years as the participants moved through school and life; the findings of many studies make for very interesting reading. It turns out that, as the years rolled on, those children who resisted temptation presented far fewer behavioural problems at school and actually ended up having higher scores on university entrance exams. They also had lower levels of substance abuse, lower likelihood of obesity, better responses to stress, better social skills as reported by their parents and friends and generally better scores in a range of other life measures (Mischel, 2014). Those who were less successful at resisting the marshmallow as children not only performed poorly on self-control tasks as adults but also showed different measures of brain activity. Those adults who displayed greater self-control as children had greater activity in the prefrontal cortex, the region of the brain that controls many executive functions—including decision making—while the ventral stratum, a region that processes desires and rewards, showed boosted activity in those with lower self-control (Casey et al., 2011).

In summary, the marshmallow test not only allowed researchers to observe the delayed gratification of children but follow them into adulthood. Time and time again, those who waited patiently for the second marshmallow succeeded in whatever capacity was measured, suggesting that emotional regulation and delayed gratification appear critical for success in school and life.

Ask yourself...

1   There is some evidence to suggest that, like many other aspects of human development, emotional regulation is part nature, part nurture. If that is the case, what might your role as a teacher be in helping develop emotional regulation with your students? How might you go about doing this for the particular age group you wish to work with?

2   How might the findings of the marshmallow test influence how you use rewards in your class?

Socio-emotional development—key features across childhood

At the risk of stating what might appear very obvious to most, during the earliest stages of life, empathy, temperament and emotional regulation are very immature. What may not be so obvious is that emotional development, and by association socio-emotional development, is as important as cognitive development. A human being's capacity to combine intelligence with empathy, for example, is what separates us from all other species (Hrdy, 1999). During infancy such capacities are very rudimentary. Infant children arrive with innate survival instincts intact but with only a few basic emotions and emotional competencies. Through time, children's repertoires of emotions expand as they develop physically, explore the world around them and engage with others. Such exploration entails social cognition and, as children move from infancy through toddlerhood, such understanding contributes to social competence, interpersonal sensitivity and an awareness of how the self relates to others in a complex social world (Thompson, 2006). This awareness is linked to the role models around a child; a child's socio-emotional development not only relies on individual traits such as temperament but also on the actions and interactions of others (Bandura, 1976).

The importance of engagement with others in terms of development begins early in life when infants demonstrate a capacity for *social referencing*. Social referencing is evident in children around twelve months of age and refers to the act of looking at someone else for clues about how to feel or respond to a particular object or event (Stenberg, 2009; Thompson, 2006). For example, a toddler who receives a new toy will likely approach and engage with it if his or her mother is smiling or avoid it if the mother shows disgust or fear. Social referencing also plays an important role in attachment and *perspective taking*.

Attachment
An emotional bond between an individual and attachment figure, usually the primary care-giver.

ATTACHMENT

Attachment is regarded as one of the most important aspects of socio-emotional development and is the primary source of a child's security, self-esteem, self-control and social skills (Eliot, 2000; Nagel, 2012a). Attachment forms in the early stages of life between infants and their mothers and has been described as a 'lasting psychological connectedness between human beings' (Bowlby, 1969, p. 194). This description highlights that, while mothers are important, the security of attachment also resides in many other relationships.

Like other aspects of emotional development, attachment changes over time. During infancy, children are understandably most closely attached to their primary care-givers and may appear distressed or anxious when separated. Often referred to as 'separation anxiety', this normal and important reaction peaks somewhere between ten and eighteen months of age and then gradually begins to fade as language and cognition improves (American Academy of Pediatrics, 2009; Nagel, 2012a). The nature of attachment changes over time as human beings mature and as relationships evolve. These changes are also intertwined with an individual's ability to engage in *perspective taking*.

PERSPECTIVE TAKING

Perspective taking refers to our ability to relate to others by being able to take their point of view and perceive their thoughts, feelings and motivations (Bjorklund & Blasi, 2012). This ability develops gradually as children mature and become less egocentric in their thinking. For example, pre-schoolers have a tendency to assume that other people believe and see the world as they do (Bjorklund & Blasi, 2012). Higher-level perspective-taking skills continue to improve through adolescence and into adulthood and, as children progress into higher levels of perspective taking, their abilities to relate to others, solve problems and communicate more effectively also improves (Burack et al., 2006). Some researchers consider perspective taking to be an important component of empathetic behaviour and, as noted above, empathy—and indeed all other aspects of emotional development—matures and improves over time (Lamm, Batson & Decety, 2007).

SUMMARY

In the early stages of life there is much developmental work to be done. To reiterate: all aspects of development are interrelated and rely on one another, and another important developmental capacity linked to socio-emotional development is that of language development. Chapter 5 looks at language development and its links to learning in greater detail but it is appropriate here to highlight the connections between socio-emotional development and language.

See Chapter ❺ for a detailed look at language development and learning.

In the earliest days of life, children are not able to talk but studies tell us that, even in utero, children are learning the sounds of language by eavesdropping on their mother's conversations (Nagel, 2012a). After birth, children begin paying close attention to language and, regardless of culture, learn their mother tongue effortlessly from babbling at six months of age to using full sentences by age three (Kuhl, 2004). It is through social interactions that much of this development occurs and, somewhere between the ages of two and three years, children begin to talk about emotions that they and others experience. At this age children also begin to realise that emotions can be connected to a person's desires. Parents and other family members play an important role in this development through modelling particular emotional responses. Recent research suggests that young children's social understanding is related to how often they experience adult communication related to the thoughts and emotions of others (Taumoepeau & Ruffman, 2008). By the time they have reached middle childhood, children will have typically learnt to talk comfortably about emotions, express their emotions during play, remain composed in the face of strong emotions and anticipate the kind of situations that are likely to be upsetting or enjoyable (Macklem, 2010; McDevitt & Ormrod, 2013).

As language improves and as children move through middle childhood and adolescence, their capacity for expressing emotions and emotional regulation also improves along with an understanding that emotional expressions do not always reflect people's true feelings (Saarni, Campos, Camras & Witherington, 2006). Children also begin to realise that when they are upset they can ask for support or help from peers or adults, try to change the way they are thinking about a troubling situation or substitute one activity for another to help alleviate stress or anxiety (Davis et al., 2010). These sets of skills reflect a degree of emotional and social intelligence (Goleman, 1995, 2006) that will continue to improve with age. But, during adolescence, and in spite of enhanced communication skills, socio-emotional development faces new challenges and presents many issues and considerations.

Adolescence is perhaps best characterised as a time of marked behavioural, hormonal and physical change (Blakemore, den Ouden, Choudhury & Frith, 2007). There is little denying that, during adolescence, socio-emotional development also changes and grows in complexity as children transition into adulthood. Peers become increasingly significant in the relationships and lives of adolescents as they look to shape their identities and gain greater independence. Sensation seeking and taking risks emerge as significant factors in socio-emotional development; much of this can be linked to substantive changes in the brain and cognitive abilities over time. Chapter 3 explores neural development and brain maturation in greater detail and sheds light on the foundational framework underpinning neurodevelopment with all other aspects of development. But a brief overview of cognitive development is warranted here.

SOMETHING TO THINK ABOUT 2.3

THE ADOLESCENT BRAIN AND THE ANTICIPATION OF SOMETHING GOOD

Earlier in this chapter, you looked at aspects of emotional regulation as it pertained to young children and was explored through the 'marshmallow test'. Reward systems in the brain play an important role in emotional regulation and behaviour, yet may work differently in children and adolescents. Indeed, reward-seeking behaviours during adolescence have been widely studied with some surprising and interesting results, particularly for teachers.

One of the important components of reward-seeking behaviour is the neurotransmitter that lingers in the limbic system—the region of the brain primarily responsible for processing emotions and memories—and is called dopamine. This important chemical in the brain gets greater attention in Chapter 5 but here it is timely to consider the following. The brain is a pleasure-seeking organ where dopamine works in concert with a structure known as the ventral striatum. When we have thoughts of gain (monetary, emotional or other rewards) dopamine is elevated in the ventral striatum and we feel good, but thoughts of loss decrease dopamine. In other words, when we are rewarded, or simply anticipate a reward, there is an increase in dopamine levels associated with the expectation of that reward and we feel good. In an educational context, this can mean that, when students experience an enjoyable activity, there is an associated surge in dopamine and a sense of pleasure but this surge can also occur in the anticipation of an enjoyable activity. So powerful is dopamine that it is often referred to as the pleasure chemical of the brain and levels of dopamine are affected by emotion, memories of past experiences and stress among other factors. Elevated dopamine levels are also associated with activities in the prefrontal lobe associated with attention, decision making, sequencing, motivation and other executive functions (Willis, 2009). Importantly, the reward systems of the brain work a bit differently during adolescence.

One of the most fascinating findings related to the adolescent brain is that adolescents show heightened activation of the ventral striatum in anticipation or receipt of rewards compared with adults, coupled with less activation in the prefrontal cortex relative to adults (Casey, Jones & Somerville, 2011). Moreover, the concentration of dopamine in the reward systems of the ▶

▶ brain is highest during adolescence (Casey et al., 2011). Finally, it also seems to be the case that, although adolescents appeared primed for rewards, small tangible rewards for simple tasks ignite a reward response in children and adults but get less response in adolescents (Casey & Caudle, 2013; Spear, 2010; Willis, 2009). Taken in its entirety, the reward system of the adolescent brain will likely affect motivation, behaviour and learning in different ways from the brains of younger children, given evidence showing that adolescents seek immediate and substantive rewards over long-term gain and are more inclined to seek experiences that create high-intensity feelings usually through sensation seeking, taking risks or novel activities (Nagel, 2014).

Ask yourself...

1 Given that the adolescent brain is maturing and its reward systems may operate somewhat differently from the brains of children or adults, what does this mean in terms of motivation and engagement for learning? How might you motivate adolescents differently from young children?

2 One of the most common considerations or challenges associated with the reward systems of the adolescent brain is a heightened proclivity for taking risks. The elevation of dopamine during adolescence at the nexus with sensation seeking often sees adolescents engage in undertaking high-risk activities. In what ways could you as a teacher within a school individually, or with the assistance of colleagues, provide pro-social risk-taking activities that are safe yet may meet the needs of adolescents?

COGNITIVE DEVELOPMENT

Cognitive development focuses on the development of our thought processes and how these processes influence how we understand and interact with other people and the world around us. *Cognition* refers to the acquisition and manipulation of knowledge through conscious effortful processes and unconscious automatic processes. Deciding what to include in this section of *Understanding Development and Learning* is a conscious cognitive activity; recognising a celebrity's face on the television in the background happens automatically or unconsciously.

The study of cognitive development involves the regular, age-related changes in children's cognition over time as well as individual differences in such cognition (Bjorklund, 2005). A number of prominent theorists have studied cognitive development and are noted throughout this text, depending on their framework for such study. Lev Vygotsky and Urie Bronfenbrenner, for example, premise much of their work on the sociocultural influences surrounding cognitive development and are explored in detail in Chapter 9. While there is no single general theory of cognitive development, perhaps the most historically influential theory as it relates to learning and education was developed by the Swiss psychologist Jean Piaget.

See Chapter ❾ for an extensive look at the work of Vygotsky and Bronfenbrenner.

Cognitive development according to Piaget

The work of Jean Piaget has extended across a number of decades and his theory of cognitive development has provided many central concepts in the field of developmental psychology. Piaget's work tended to focus on the growth of intelligence, which he understood to be the ability to more accurately conceptualise the world and perform logical operations. His ideas were initially developed by observing children. He found the reasoning of children intriguing, particularly when they gave wrong answers to logical questions. Piaget noticed that a child's reasoning ability seemed to improve with age. From his observations and his work with children, the foundations of his theory were formed and focused on the developing brain's acquisition of schemata (Piaget, 1954). Schemata or schema are units of mental organisation—or what some have described as the 'mental representation of an experience'—which help form knowledge and develop intellect (Kagan, 1970). Piaget believed that schemata are flexible in quality and quantity and that they develop and change as a child moves through various stages of cognitive development. Indeed, the idea that children progress through qualitatively distinct yet interrelated stages of cognitive development is central to Piaget's work but he also stressed a number of processes as being integral within and across each stage (Salkind, 2004). These processes help to shape and reshape schemata and include *organisation* and *adaptation*. Adaptation, in turn, is achieved through *assimilation* and *accommodation*.

*Schemata
The mental representation of an experience.*

For Piaget, organisation—or the tendency to combine physical or psychological processes or both into a coherent whole—not only represents an important component of cognitive development but is also critical for survival. For example, touching a hot object signals the nervous system to pull the hand away, an act which requires the cooperation of the nervous, muscular and skeletal systems (Salkind, 2004). The interrelated nature of such actions, according to Piaget, demonstrates how one structure does not exist independently of another but is coordinated with each, thereby providing the essence of organisation and demonstrating forms of intelligence (Bjorklund, 2005). Organisation, in turn, represents how schemata play a part in integrating structures into higher order systems through maturation and experience; a week-old infant has one scheme for sucking and another for hand and arm movements but before long these two schemes coordinate into a new scheme known as 'thumb sucking' (Bjorklund, 2005). With each new experience, a child's schemata change, particularly when they require some measure of adaptation.

See Chapter ❷ for a detailed discussion of Piaget's work.

ADAPTATION, ASSIMILATION AND ACCOMMODATION

Adaptation is perhaps the most important component of Piaget's theory, given his emphasis on the links between cognitive development, experiences and the environment. As the term suggests, adaptation refers to some form of adjustment to the environment and for Piaget this is accomplished through assimilation or accommodation or both.

Assimilation is the process through which all knowledge is acquired as individuals incorporate new experiences into already existing schemata (Salkind, 2004). For example, a child with a pre-existing schemata for a dog due to early experiences of the family's pet poodle encounters a dachshund for the first time and acknowledges it as a dog in spite of the differences to the pet. For the child, the dachshund is still a dog, given its primary characteristics, and this information is assimilated into the schemata for 'dogs'.

Accommodation, on the other hand, requires a different approach. Accommodation is the term Piaget used to describe what happens when we must change pre-existing ideas in order to fit in new information (Piaget, 1952). The dog example above proves useful once again. Let us say that the child encounters a Great Dane for the first time and upon seeing this large canine refers to it as a horse. At this point the child is assimilating information into existing schemata about horses and, given the animal's size and stature, believes it has encountered another version of a horse. But, after some intervention by the parents, proclaiming that the Great Dane is not a horse but another type of dog, the child now accommodates this new information to change his or her schemata for dogs once again. The balance that is attained through the processes of assimilation and accommodation as individuals adapt to new experiences was referred to by Piaget as the concept of *equilibration* and Piaget believed that it is the desire to always reach equilibration that provides the motivational force driving our assimilation and accommodation processes (Santrock, 2011).

EQUILIBRATION

Piaget's notion of equilibration is important to learning or, perhaps more succinctly, it is disequilibrium that motivates learning. A desire to reach equilibration, according to Piaget, is the key motivator in development and learning while learners themselves must be active in this process (Inhelder & Piaget, 1958). The active participation of the learner occurs through discrete stages of development, marked by qualitative differences, rather than a gradual increase in number and complexity of behaviours, concepts and ideas. To Piaget, cognitive development was a progressive reorganisation of mental processes as a result of maturation and environmental experience, and evident through various capacities for reasoning as noted within each stage (see Table 2.1).

TABLE 2.1 PIAGET'S STAGES OF COGNITIVE DEVELOPMENT

Stage	Approximate age range	Key characteristics	Characteristics of intelligence	Examples of behaviour and thinking
Sensorimotor	0–2 years	→ Develops an understanding of the world through sense and motor activities. → Goal-directed activity increasingly replaces reflex actions. → Development of object permanence occurs—the understanding that objects continue to exist even when they cannot be seen.	Intelligence is limited to the child's own actions on the environment.	→ Reaching for objects. → Imitation and memory processing becomes evident. → Looking for lost objects.
Preoperational	2–7 years	→ Development of language and other symbol systems. → Egocentricity (focus on self as more important than others). → Logic applied in one direction only.	Intelligence is symbolic, expressed via language imagery and other modes permitting children to mentally represent and compare objects out of immediate representation.	→ Intuition at problem solving. → Inability to empathise. → Uses gestures, signs, sounds and words to represent and convey meaning.
Concrete operational	7–12 years	→ Ability to apply logic in hands-on activities. → Thought is less egocentric. → Concrete experiences used to solve problems but unable to mentally manipulate conditions unless they have been experienced.	Intelligence is symbolic and logical (e.g., if A is greater than B and B is greater than C, then A must be greater than C).	→ Games are governed by rules. → Development of the idea of conservation—the ability to recognise that certain properties (e.g., volume) stay the same despite a change in shape or appearance. → Development of the idea of irreversibility—the mental ability of reversing physical or mental processes.

▶ TABLE 2.1   PIAGET'S STAGES OF COGNITIVE DEVELOPMENT

Stage	Approximate age range	Key characteristics	Characteristics of intelligence	Examples of behaviour and thinking
Formal operational	12+ years	→ Able to think abstractly, form hypotheses, solve problems in a systematic fashion and engage in mental manipulations.	Intelligence is notably more sophisticated, allowing for higher order processes to occur.	→ Development of scientific, rational thought. → Concern about identity and social issues becomes evident.

Adapted from the works of Bjorkland & Blasi, 2012; O'Donnell, Reeve & Smith, 2009; Snowman et al., 2009; Vialle, Lysaght & Verenikina, 2005.

PIAGET'S AGE-RELATED STAGES

As identified in Table 2.1, Piaget's theory consists of age-related stages and distinct ways of thinking. The *sensorimotor* stage represents the time of infancy to two years, where children move from reflexive to representational development. At the beginning of this stage, infants show little more than reflexive patterns but, by the end of this stage and in conjunction with the use of language, they display far more complex sensorimotor patterns and start to use words to represent objects.

The second Piagetian stage lasts from approximately age two to seven and is known as the *preoperational* stage. During this stage of cognitive development, children use more symbolic than sensorimotor thought but operational thought is not yet apparent. The emergence of pretend play and the use of language along with the representation of people, houses, cars, clouds and many other aspects of the world through scribbling offer examples of symbolic thought. Significant limitations of thought in this stage are evident through the concepts of *egocentrism* and *centration*. Egocentrism refers to a child's inability to distinguish between one's own perspective and that of another person, while centration involves the ability to focus attention on one characteristic to the exclusion of others (Santrock, 2011). For example, children in this stage are usually unable to take on the perspective of another or to understand important concepts such as conservation. To adults it is obvious that a litre of liquid is the same regardless of the shape and size of a container, while three-year-olds are unable to make such observations and rely on the size and shape of the container to determine volume. This changes as children move through the concrete operational stage.

The *concrete operational* stage, according to Piaget, extends from age seven to eleven and it is during this time that children start to use logical reasoning in place of intuitive reasoning, but this can only be applied to concrete objects and current events. In other words, while children think in an organised and logical fashion when dealing with concrete information they receive directly, their mental operations work poorly with abstract ideas (Berk, 2006). Abstract thought emerges in Piaget's last stage.

Around age eleven, children enter the formal operation stage in which they develop the capacity for abstract reasoning and scientific thinking. As children move into adolescence they also become capable of hypothetical and deductive reasoning along with proposi-tional thought—the ability to evaluate the logic of propositions without referring to real-world circumstances. Adolescents are also capable of reflecting on their own thoughts and, by association, they think more about themselves in both concrete and abstract terms. Interestingly, the capacity for abstract thinking as evident in this stage of development and through adolescence does not necessarily parallel rational and responsible decision mak-ing during the teenage years. This is likely due to very important maturational and struc-tural changes to the brain during the teenage years, which are explored in greater detail in Chapter 3. But it is worth noting here that while advances in technology, neuroscience and developmental psychological research suggest that Piaget may have been mistaken in some aspects of his theory, his theory continues to influence educational practice.

See Chapter ❸ for an extensive discussion of how the brain develops.

SUMMARY

The influence of Piaget's work on education cannot be understated. Piaget did not explicitly relate his theory to education but his ideas have been adopted by others and applied to educational policies and programs in Australia and numerous other countries. In terms of learning and education, Piaget's legacy is undeniable. Notions of individual learning, discov-ery learning, flexibility in the curriculum, the centrality of play in children's learning, and the use of the environment and experience are but a few examples of contemporary educational initiatives derived from Piaget's work. Piaget also helped to emphasise notions of 'readiness' and developmentally appropriate curriculum, while reminding educators to appreciate the intelligence and skills a child brings to a task. His ideas also acknowledge that errors should never be stigmatised as they are integral to learning and our understanding of how children solve problems (Krause et al., 2010). Finally, Piaget's work, like the framework of *Understand-ing Development and Learning*, asks educators to focus on the process rather than the end product of learning: perhaps his greatest contribution to educational practice.

SOME FINAL THOUGHTS ON HUMAN DEVELOPMENT AND LEARNING

It is important to reiterate that all aspects of development are interconnected and will, by association, affect learning. Developmental trajectories also play a part in behaviour and this will also affect learning. One useful way to conceptualise the overall links between human development and learning may be evident through a broad adaptive lens or frame-work known as a **developmental tasks** approach (Sroufe, 1979). Developmental tasks closely align with Piaget's notion of adaptation and are premised on the idea that, in order for a person to adapt, there are developmental challenges that must be met and that may arise from biological maturation, families and society or the developing self (Masten & Braswell, 1991). Table 2.2 shows the key developmental tasks over a child's lifespan that have the potential to influence learning. But it is important to note that, similar to information pre-sented throughout this chapter, an approach focusing on developmental tasks emphasises

Developmental tasks
The meeting of developmental challenges arising from maturation, context and sense of self.

See Chapter **❾** for a detailed discussion of the roles of context and the environment on development and learning.

normative development or the assumption that every child will go through these phases with varying degrees of ease (Gentile, 2014). While normative frameworks for development are helpful in setting benchmarks for what we might expect from children at certain ages, it is equally important to note that context and environment play a significant role in development and learning: this is discussed throughout *Understanding Development and Learning* but most notably in Chapter 9.

TABLE 2.2   KEY DEVELOPMENTAL TASKS OVER A CHILD'S LIFE

Approximate age range	Physical development	Socio-emotional development	Cognitive development	Developmental tasks
0–12 months	Most notable yet unobservable change is occurring in the brain with the development of neural networks.	Expression of emotions begins to develop with evidence of the early stages of emotional regulation.	Learning occurs and is exhibited through imitation, habituation, discrimination, classical and operant conditioning.	Developing a trusting relationship with a care-giver is the key task for healthy development.
1–2½ years	Children grow in strength, coordination and mobility and begin to develop measures of independence as they explore the world around them.	Social gestures begin to emerge and children begin to understand themselves as distinct from others. Independence of actions and feelings of competence become part of socialisation processes while children are beginning to learn to regulate and control their emotions and expressions of behaviour.	While language begins to become more sophisticated and communication skills improve, cognition is still constrained by limited memory abilities, the inability to think logically and/or abstractly and difficulties in distinguishing between fantasy and reality.	Acquisition of language and social norms help to form an understanding of how to act in new or ambiguous situations and internalise rules and values. Early attachment relations and the development of those relations remain key tasks.
2½–5 years	Physical development continues to improve in terms of gross and fine motor skills. Play behaviours affect development as children engage in greater varieties of games and activities with siblings, peers and adults.	Emotional regulation develops as children learn to be aware of standards of behaviour and using those standards to guide their actions and words. Empathetic behaviour begins to emerge in conjunction with the emergence of theory of mind. Being able to differentiate their own point of view from that of another is still difficult for children in this age group. Adult role-playing is an important aspect of development emerging at this time.	Children are beginning to learn to classify objects, organise things along particular dimensions (e.g., height) and deploy attention to specific tasks, but they tend to be able to focus on one piece of information at a time and ignore irrelevant stimuli.	The most important developmental task at this stage is learning self-control and self-regulatory behaviours, including reflecting on one's actions, tolerating frustration, delayed gratification and adjusting behaviour to suit particular situations.

▶

▶ TABLE 2.2   KEY DEVELOPMENTAL TASKS OVER A CHILD'S LIFE

Approximate age range	Physical development	Socio-emotional development	Cognitive development	Developmental tasks
5–12 years	Continued changes in weight and height occur gradually while speed, coordination and agility increase markedly. Such changes affect a child's self-esteem and confidence, while engaging with other children in physical activities can enhance a range of socio-emotional and cognitive skills.	The forming of friendships and working with others helps to foster the development of self-concept in the context that one's sense of self is defined in part through relationships with others. Emotional regulation continues to improve, which also plays a part in relationships and peer group formations.	The distinction between appearance and reality develops along with a growing capacity for looking at more than one perspective at the same time. Tendencies to initiate activities, explore and seek out learning experiences along with improved work ethics and goal-directed behaviours emerge and develop.	Perhaps the main developmental task during this stage focuses on relationships: forming friendships, learning how to be part of a peer group, and how to adhere to group norms.
12–18 years	Pubescence signals a change in reproductive systems with resultant changes in hormones and many physical attributes. Physical growth can occur rapidly and varies between the sexes, which in turn plays a role in emotional development as it pertains to body image.	Taking risks, novelty and sensation seeking are indicative of changes in socio-emotional development. While major cognitive changes are occurring, emotions often drive behaviour.	The ability to think in abstract terms emerges and improves over time. Attention and concentration skills also improve. Adolescence is also a time when the brain goes through a major stage of reconstruction and maturation that in turn influences behaviour.	Developing deep levels of trust and closeness with both same-sex and opposite-sex peers is fundamentally important. The formation of one's own identity also becomes an important developmental task as adolescents gain greater autonomy and responsibility at home and school.

Adapted from the works of Aber & Jones, 1997; Gentile, 2014; Krause et al., 2010; Masten & Braswell, 1991; Mischel et al., 1972; O'Donnell et al., 2012; Sroufe, 1979, 1995; Sroufe, Cooper & DeHart, 1996; Sroufe, Egeland & Carlson, 1999.

CONCLUSION

An understanding of human development and its links to learning is important in educational contexts. Importantly, human development is not focused purely on physical development but covers all aspects of the development of the body and mind. Equally important, educators must take care not to focus any understanding of learning exclusively to cognitive development. Learning, like human development, is a highly complex activity. As a child grows from infancy, through childhood and adolescence into adulthood, understanding the interplay between development and learning is critical when considering all aspects of pedagogy and didactic endeavour.

Another significant consideration in the context of human development and learning is the interconnected nature of all aspects of development. Cognitive, physical and socio-emotional development work in concert together and are a product of nature and nurture. The subtleties of this are explored throughout *Understanding Development and Learning* but it is important to emphasise again that learning is intertwined with all aspects of development; as such, the links between the two are undeniably important in all facets and stages of formal education.

CHAPTER SUMMARY

This chapter explored the broad topic of human development and learning. The beginning of the chapter unpacked three basic issues that surround aspects of human development, including: nature versus nurture, discontinuous development versus continuous development and universality versus diversity. These three issues have framed discussions of human development for years and still play a role in shaping research and ideas around how children grow and mature.

After looking at these basic issues, the chapter explored the three main domains of human development. Physical development was considered from infancy to adolescence along with insights into the development of gross and fine motor skills.

The examination of socio-emotional development began with looking at the differences between emotions and feelings along with the differences between primary and secondary emotions. With those differences in mind, the chapter explored aspects of development surrounding empathy, temperament and emotional regulation, all important developmental areas of interest for teachers given their interplay with behaviour and learning.

The final part of the chapter focused on cognitive development and, in particular, the work of Jean Piaget. While some aspects of Piaget's work are being questioned and influenced by recent advances in neuroscience, his ideas and theories continue to inform our overall understanding of cognitive development and remain an integral aspect of teacher training. Piaget's view of schemata is an important consideration for any future teacher.

The chapter closed by exploring a 'developmental task' approach to linking human development and learning with key developmental tasks provided for your consideration as a future teacher.

Implications for Teaching

One of the most important aspects for understanding the links between human development and learning is that each child is unique and each child's developmental timelines will vary. This is partly nature and partly nurture, given the dynamics between a child's innate capacities and the environment he or she grows up in. Importantly, and noted most significantly in Chapter 10, there isn't any evidence to suggest that you can somehow accelerate a child's cognitive abilities and, by association, learning. Piaget's findings clearly show the existence of stages of cognitive development that span a number of months and years. This is important for parents and teachers alike, given the last couple of decades has seen a proliferation of books and resources developed by educators purporting to somehow enhance children's intelligence and cognitive abilities. The evidence of the efficacy of such programs is scant, contentious and arguably worrisome. For example, one study found that young children who watched DVDs that were purported to enhance vocabulary development actually experienced deficits in their vocabulary compared to children who did not engage with that 'learning' tool (Zimmerman, Christakis & Meltzoff, 2007). This suggests that a degree of caution and scrutiny is warranted by teachers when presented with resources and tools that are marketed as enhancing cognitive development or any aspect of human development. Indeed, even Peter Huttenlocher, Professor Emeritus at the University of Chicago and widely considered one of the fathers of developmental cognitive neuroscience, was concerned with trying to accelerate learning when he noted:

> One has to consider the possibility that very ambitious early enrichment and teaching programs may lead to crowding effects and to an early decrease in the size and number of brain regions that are largely unspecified and that may be necessary for creativity in the adolescent and adult. The neurobiologic studies of crowding effects introduce the caveat that too much early learning may under some conditions become detrimental to the learning of later acquired skill. (2002, p. 214)

Ask yourself...

1   After working through the chapter, what do you think are the key aspects of human development that will affect your teaching practice and the learning of the students?

2   Given the age of the students you wish to work with, what important components of socio-emotional and cognitive development will you need to keep in the forefront of your planning?

PRACTICAL ACTIVITIES

1   *While on practicum*, observe children of various ages and see if you can identify what stage they may be at when placed within Piaget's theoretical framework. Can you identify how teachers use Piaget's work either explicitly or implicitly?

2   *While on practicum*, jot down any examples you see of children who demonstrate potential issues in terms of human development. For example, the scene at the beginning of the chapter noted how one student might have attachment issues. Can you identify any others in your practicum context?

STUDY QUESTIONS

1   What are the three basic issues in human development? Describe the characteristics of each.

2   Why are physical activity and play so important in terms of physical development?

3   What are the differences between emotions and feelings? Primary and secondary emotions?

4   What is emotional regulation and why is it so important in terms of behaviour and learning?

5   Outline each of Piaget's four stages of development and the main characteristics of each.

6   What are 'schema'? Why are they important in terms of learning?

FURTHER READING

American Academy of Pediatrics (2009). *Caring for Your Baby and Young Child: Birth to Age Five* (5th ed.). New York, NY: Bantam.

Bell, M. A. & Wolfe, C. D. (2004). Emotion and cognition: An intricately bound developmental process. *Child Development, 75*(2), 366–370.

Bjorklund, D. F. (2005). *Children's Thinking: Cognitive Development and Individual Differences* (4th ed.). Belmont, CA: Wadsworth/Thomson Learning.

Damasio, A. (2004). Emotions and feelings: A neurobiological perspective. In A. S. R. Manstead, N. Frijda & A. Fischer (Eds.), *Feelings and Emotions: The Amsterdam Symposium (Studies in Emotion and Social Interaction)* (pp. 49–57). Cambridge, UK: Cambridge University Press.

Eisenberg, N., Valiente, C. & Eggum, N. D. (2010). Self-regulation and school readiness. *Early Education and Development, 21*(5), 681–698.

Eliot, L. (2000). *What's Going On in There? How the Brain and Mind Develop in the First Five Years of Life.* New York, NY: Bantam Books.

Gervais, J. (2009). Environmental and genetic influences on early attachment. *Child and Adolescent Psychiatry and Mental Health, 3*(25), 1–12.

Goleman, D. (1995). *Emotional Intelligence: Why It Can Matter More than IQ.* New York, NY: Bantam Books.

Goleman, D. (2006). *Social Intelligence: The New Science of Human Relationships.* London, UK: Hutchinson–Random House.

Gopnik, A., Meltzoff, A. N. & Kuhl, P. K. (1999). *The Scientist in the Crib: What Early Learning Tells Us about the Mind.* New York, NY: Harper Collins Publishers.

Macklem, G. L. (2010). *Practitioner's Guide to Emotional Regulation in School-Aged Children.* New York, NY: Springer Science + Business Media.

Mischel, M, (2014). *The Marshmallow Test: Understanding Self-Control and How to Master It.* London, UK: Bantam Press.

Nagel, M. C. (2012). *In the Beginning: The Brain, Early Development and Learning.* Melbourne, Australia: ACER Press.

Nagel, M. C. (2014). *In the Middle: The Adolescent Brain, Behaviour and Learning.* Melbourne, Australia: ACER Press.

Salkind, N. J. (2004). *An Introduction to Theories of Human Development.* Thousand Oaks, CA: Sage Publications, Inc.

Shonkoff, J. P. (2010). Building a new biodevelopmental framework to guide the future of early childhood policy. *Child Development, 81*(1), 357–367.

VIDEO LINKS

Igniter Media: *The Marshmallow Test*
https://www.youtube.com/watch?v=QX_oy9614HQ

A short, and entertaining, clip of a contemporary rendition of Mischel's seminal work. Worthy of watching to get a sense of differences in children in terms of impulse control, emotional regulation and delayed gratification.

Davidson Films: *Piaget's Developmental Theory: An Overview*
https://www.youtube.com/watch?v=QX6JxLwMJeQ

This concise look at Piaget's work, as narrated by Professor David Elkind, provides some interesting examples of real-life differences in children based on their particular stage of development.

WEBLINKS

Centre on the Developing Child—Harvard University
http://developingchild.harvard.edu/

While this website tends to focus on the early years of development, it does provide key resources and links for developing an informed understanding of those things that both enhance and hinder human development and, by association, learning.

Learning and Cognitive Development
http://www.parentingcounts.org/research/cognitive-learning

This section of a parenting website offers an array of research and news articles along with videos covering numerous aspects of human development as it pertains to learning and behaviour.

3 UNDERSTANDING BRAIN DEVELOPMENT

> A father comforts a crying newborn. A mother plays peekaboos with her ten-month-old. A child care provider reads to a toddler. And in a matter of seconds, thousands of cells in these children's growing brains respond. Some brain cells are 'turned on', triggered by this particular experience. Many existing connections among brain cells are strengthened. At the same time, new connections are formed, adding a bit more definition and complexity to the intricate circuitry that will remain largely in place for the rest of the children's lives … We didn't always know it worked this way.
>
> (Shore, 1997, p. ix)

LEARNING OUTCOMES

As you read through this chapter and undertake the exercises at the end, you will gain the ability to complete these tasks successfully:

→ describe and discuss important components of the brain as they pertain to behaviour and learning

→ discuss the role of key aspects of brain development during the early years and adolescence

→ explain the links between environmental stimulation and brain development and highlight this in terms of learning windows and deprivation

→ discuss the key roles of the limbic system and frontal lobes in terms of learning.

KEY TERMS

- neuromyths
- neuroplasticity
- experience-expectant stimulation
- experience-dependent stimulation
- learning windows
- prefrontal cortex
- executive functions

Mr Ricci studied to become a primary teacher in the mid-1980s. During this time, he was taught to construct lesson plans using cognitive, affective and psychomotor objectives as a blueprint for developing worthwhile teaching and learning experiences. In his mind, and as suggested by his lecturers, thinking, feeling and doing underpinned his planning but each of these was distinct from the other. Recently he attended a conference that focused on the brain and learning and was astounded to find out just how intimately connected thinking, feeling and doing were in terms of how the brain actually processes information. He was equally amazed at how much information about the brain and mind had been discovered since he left university some thirty years ago. Indeed, some of the most recent information about how the brain learns had only been articulated in popular literature and textbooks during the last decade. Armed with this new-found knowledge and a renewed passion for his own learning, Mr Ricci decided to share what he had learnt about the brain with his colleagues at his next staff meeting. The reaction was very mixed. For some of his colleagues, any understanding of the brain was something they did not have time to worry about, given the amount of curriculum content they had to cover. Some felt that the information Mr Ricci offered was not really something they could engage with, as they felt that systemic structures would not allow them to do so in any real pragmatic fashion...the big picture was too big! But some were as excited as he was and wanted to know more, particularly in terms of how the brain matured and how this affected behaviour and learning. They were also very interested in how emotions can play such an important role in learning and in so many different ways. Armed with these new insights, some of the staff decided to create their own professional learning group and, along with Mr Ricci, extend their own learning of the brain and the potential links of these new understandings to their practice as classroom teachers.

1 How much do you know about the human brain? Can you list a series of dot points of information about the brain and how it develops over time?

2 During your pre-service teacher education, have you attended any courses or classes that focused on aspects of the brain, its development and the implications of this for you as a teacher? Do you think this is important? Why or why not?

3 What do you think might be important to know about the human brain as it pertains to learning and teaching? As you progress through this chapter, be sure to note any links between brain development, learning and teaching that you think are important for teachers to be aware of.

INTRODUCTION

Chapter 2 provided a general overview of aspects of human development and learning. This chapter looks to extend that by focusing on what is central to all aspects of human development and learning: the developing human brain. Since the early 1990s, advances in neuroscience and technology have provided a wealth of information on the human brain; this information is now being articulated across a number of disciplines, and informing policy and programs related to education and child care. For example, studies now tell us that Piaget may have underestimated the competencies of infants and pre-schoolers and overestimated the value of discovery learning (Berk, 2006). Brain research is providing insights into all aspects of development, while providing greater clarity and detail of the links between human development, learning, health and well-being and education. So prolific has been the incursion of neuroscience into education that the term 'neuro-education' has now surfaced in the literature and research, while courses in brain development are becoming part of tertiary education courses and ongoing professional development for teachers (Carew & Magsamen, 2010; Nagel, 2014). *Understanding Development and Learning* is also underpinned by research into the human brain and this chapter focuses on how the brain develops as a platform for examining the links between such development and learning. Before exploring the intricacies of the developing brain, it is useful to briefly mention some important points related to brain research and their potential links to learning and educating young minds.

See Chapter ❷ for a review of Piaget's theories.

At the start, it should be emphasised is that what scientists currently know about the development and function of the human brain is infinitesimal compared to what they do not know. We are only beginning to understand the 1.3 kilogram universe between our ears that has been described as the most unimaginable thing imaginable (Hooper & Teresi, 1986; LeDoux, 1998). Concurrently, linking neuroscience to education is also in its infancy and, while numerous researchers across a variety of disciplines continue in their attempts to bring the two together, there is still much work to be done. This has led to a number of misinterpretations of the available science and also a number of **neuromyths** associated with linking neuroscience to the pragmatic desires of educators. Many of these issues and errors will be dealt with throughout *Understanding Development and Learning* but we also recognise and acknowledge that, as time progresses and the science around the brain advances, we too must be open to critique and changing our claims in the future where need be. Too often there is a strong desire within educational contexts for immediate quick-fix solutions resulting in the misreading or misuse or both of the research (Howard-Jones, 2010). We have attempted, in *Understanding Development and Learning*, to present the science as best as possible with a view to having future and practising teachers reflect

Neuromyths
The misuse or misinterpretation or both of neuroscience to perpetuate educational myths.

and question their practice where appropriate and not present grandiose platitudes for changing the face of education. We ask you to keep this in mind while working through all chapters and when making decisions about your own practice.

A second important consideration is based on something self-evident for anyone working in an educational context—teachers are interested in how the brain works but do not have time to pore through the plethora of studies that may enhance what they do in the classroom and school environment. Paul Howard-Jones (2010, p. 34) sums this up most eloquently by noting that 'while scientists argue and theorize, educators are stuck with the task of implementing solutions today'. Chapter 4, and indeed the remainder of *Understanding Development and Learning*, has been set out with a view to providing future and present educators ideas for implementing solutions today by offering insights drawing educational and developmental psychology together with neuroscience. Importantly, these insights are drawn from the best available evidence today, presenting scientific insights into the developing brain juxtaposed with educational practice. To that end scientific details are minimised so that a broader picture of the links between neuroscience and education may be presented en route to a greater understanding of the connections between brain development, behaviour and learning. This journey begins with looking at how the brain takes shape not long after conception and how it develops through the early years of childhood.

THE DEVELOPING BRAIN—THE EARLY YEARS

For some years now, medical practitioners and researchers have been able to view aspects of child development in the womb using computerised images of body parts produced by sound waves: what is more commonly referred to as *ultrasound imaging* (Nagel, 2012a; Shore, 1997). And while ultrasound is rather limited in terms of understanding overall brain development in utero, recent research and advances in technology can now provide information about the most important structures of the developing brain (see, for example, Jakab et al., 2014; Schopf et al., 2014). Such advances in technology are providing a wealth of information related to overall brain development. For example, we know that the brain's most profound growth spurt occurs during gestation, followed by intense growth in the early years and major structural changes during adolescence (Willis, 2009). Technology is also providing us with a greater understanding of how the mind develops into the marvellous organ of learning that separates humans from all other species on this planet. Before looking at this developmental journey it is appropriate here to draw a measure of distinction between the terms 'brain' and 'mind'.

BRAIN AND MIND

It is common for people to use 'brain' and 'mind' synonymously but there are subtle differences between the two worth some elaboration. There is a long history of discourse and debate related to what constitutes a human mind and how it is different from the brain but such discussions are beyond the scope of this text. Instead, a neuroscientific perspective is most suitable in drawing some distinctions between the two. When discussing the brain, scientists are generally referring to all of the structures, processes and functions of the electrochemically driven mass of tissue held within our skulls and responsible for the mechanics and physiology of all that we are able to do (Nagel, 2014). The mind, on the other hand, is a product of the brain and plays a central role in intelligence, consciousness, language, thinking and metacognition (Nagel, 2012a, 2014). In essence, the mind is something the brain does; while they are intimately connected and influence one another, it is the activity of our minds that separates us from all other living things (Pinker, 2009). Daniel J. Siegel, author and clinical professor of psychiatry at the UCLA School of Medicine, offers an eloquent and detailed description of the mind:

> Mind relates to our inner subjective experience and the process of being conscious or aware. In addition, mind can also be defined as a process that regulates the flow of energy and information within as a process that regulates the flow of energy and information within our bodies and within our relationships, an emergent and self-organising process that gives rise to our mental activities such as emotion, thinking and memory. Subjective experience, awareness and an embodied and relational process that regulates the flow of energy and information are fundamental and interdependent facets of mind. (2012, p. 1)

While the differences in describing the brain and mind are subtle, they are more apparent in the early stages of life as the brain matures and develops (see the discussion on cognitive development in Chapter 2); Piaget used this understanding to shape his theory related to stages of development. As a child grows and matures, the mind becomes much more adept at performing highly complex processes. But, in the earliest stages of life, there is much to be done for this to happen and the starting point occurs at a stage referred to as *neurogenesis*.

NEUROGENESIS

As the word suggests, neurogenesis refers to the generation of neurons; this process begins about seventeen days after conception when the neural tube forms, which in turn leads to the formation of the brain and spinal cord. Neurons differ from other cells in the body, most notably in their structure and ability to transfer information to one another. There are

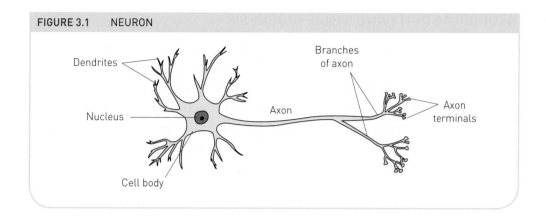

FIGURE 3.1   NEURON

Dendrites

Branches of axon

Axon

Nucleus

Axon terminals

Cell body

different types of neurons but they all share the same general structure (Figure 3.1): they all tend to have a bulb-like structure (*nucleus*) with sprouting branches (*dendrites*) and a tail-like structure referred to as an axon with terminals (*axon terminals*) at the end that pass and receive chemicals from other neurons (Nagel, 2012a).

The generation of neurons occurs at a frenetic pace. It has been estimated that approximately 250 000 neurons emerge every minute, while peak production might see several hundred thousand cells each minute, but this process begins to slow about four months into gestation (Brown, Keynes & Lumsden, 2001; Garrett, 2009; Herschkowitz & Herschkowitz, 2004; Nagel, 2012a; Ropper & Samuels, 2009). It is important to note that the generation of neurons occurs somewhat in parallel with the emigration of these neurons to different regions of the developing brain, later followed by a rapid process of cell death known as *apotosis*. While it may sound somewhat sinister, the brain actually produces more neurons than necessary and apotosis is an important developmental process of programmed cell death, ensuring the brain eventually operates with the greatest efficiency; too may neurons would prove costly in terms of energy expenditure and efficiency. Although 50 per cent of the neurons produced are eliminated between six months of gestation and one month after birth, an infant's brain still has far more neural connections than it actually needs as an adult (Lenroot & Giedd, 2007). During adolescence, a similar process to apotosis—known as *synaptic pruning*—occurs whereby the brain remodels itself by discarding unused synaptic connections (Nagel, 2014). (Synaptic pruning is an important stage of refinement for the brain and is covered in greater detail later in the chapter.) Significantly, while both apotosis and synaptic pruning are important in terms of structuring the neural architecture of the mind to become more efficient, it is during the early stages of life that the brain is busy setting up a system of interconnectivity unrivalled by anything within the known universe.

NEUROPLASTICITY AND SYNAPTOGENESIS

The generation of neurons is but the first step in the development of the brain. As neurons emigrate they begin to speak to each other through an electrochemical impulse known as a *synapse*. The communication between neurons is an important step in the hard-wiring of the brain and this process is, arguably, representative of the first and earliest stages of learning, given that such communication occurs as the brain receives stimulation from the environment and adapts accordingly: nature and nurture working in tandem. This process is also an example of neuroplasticity, an important concept for learning as it relates to the brain's capacity for changing in response to stimulation from the environment. At a more technical level, neuroplasticity allows neural networks to extend, reorganise, prune, correct or strengthen themselves through acquiring new information, obtaining feedback and reorganising associations between new and prior knowledge (Willis, 2010). Neuroplasticity is an important consideration in terms of learning and educational contexts and we will refer to it throughout *Understanding Development and Learning.*

The developing communication between neurons is referred to as *synaptogenesis* and peak production of connections does not occur until sometime in the first year of life (Nelson, de Haan & Thomas, 2006). Synaptic connections continue to grow throughout the first three years of life and, by the time a child reaches age four, it will have more connections and burn three times as much energy as its paediatrician (Shore, 1997). It is the synaptic transmission of information that is responsible for developing the long-term 'hard-wired' neural circuitry of the brain and this process would not be possible if not for the presence of *neurotransmitters*.

Neurotransmitters are a very important component for the communication between neurons to occur. They act as a chemical messenger between the dendrites of one neuron and the axon terminals of another at the synaptic level (see Figure 3.2). Neurotransmitters impact on the activity, longevity and overall maintenance of synaptic connections and neurons themselves and include some familiar names such as *dopamine* (mainly involved in emotion, reward systems and movement), *serotonin* (memory, mood, temperature regulation) and *melatonin* (sleep) (Gibb, 2012; Nagel, 2008). It should be self-evident that given what they influence, as briefly noted above, neurotransmitters play an important role in behaviour and learning. This is arguably most evident during adolescence when the brain goes through significant alterations and maturational change. This is explored later in the chapter but for now it is significant to reiterate that the presence or absence of particular neurotransmitters influences behaviour and all levels of brain activity from actions of impulsivity and restfulness, to feelings of anger and ecstasy to thinking and attention (Chugani, 1996; Shore, 1997; Nagel, 2008).

Neuroplastic
The ability of
brain to reorg
neural pathw
via sensory
stimulation a
new experien

FIGURE 3.2   SYNAPTIC TRANSMISSION OF INFORMATION

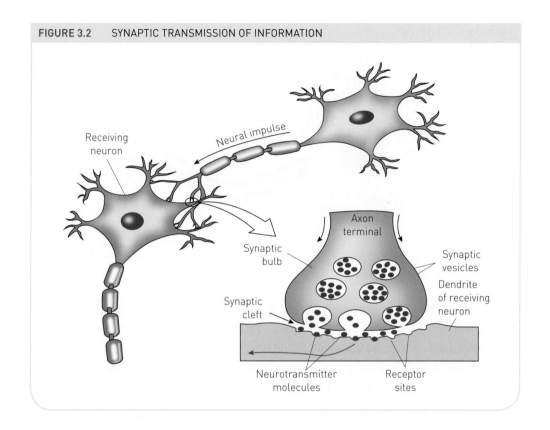

THE ROLE OF MYELIN

A final important component for understanding early brain development and, in particular, the developing neuro-circuitry of the mind is that of *myelin*. Myelin is a white fatty material, often referred to as the white matter of the brain, that grows and wraps itself around the axons of neurons (Figure 3.3). At birth a child has very few myelinated axons and it takes almost three decades for the brain to become completely myelinated. In terms of how the brain communicates, myelin acts as an insulator and conductor; the more myelin the brain has, the more expeditious and efficient the communication between neurons. The production of myelin, referred to as *myelination* or *myelinisation*, is a key process in brain development because it massively accelerates the speed of signals between neurons, which in turn promotes greater synaptic connectivity (Blakemore & Frith, 2005; Howard, 2006; Nagel, 2012a).

THE IMPORTANCE OF STIMULATION

As noted above, early development of the brain requires a number of processes to occur but perhaps the most studied aspect of development is the number of synapses and synaptic connections (Blakemore & Frith, 2005), which in turn is arguably the most important

FIGURE 3.3   MYELIN

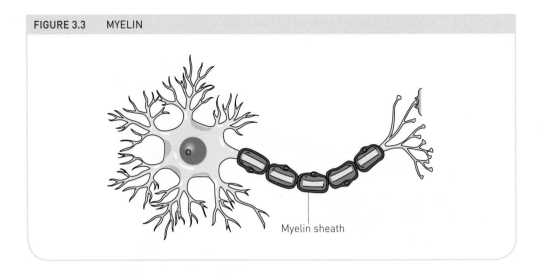

Myelin sheath

aspect of development in terms of learning. While brain connections are being produced in utero, it is after birth that these connections start to grow and change at a rapid rate; most brain cell connections are made in the first year of life. Which connections survive and grow and which fade away and die is a product of nature and nurture. The genes a baby inherits from its parents and its early experiences both play a role in shaping the neuro-architecture of the brain. Scientists also know that it is in the first three years of life that a child's brain is taking in a great deal of sensory data; experiences via stimulation from the environment continue to play a significant role in shaping a child's brain and mind.

The need for stimulation is an important component of building the neural superhighway of the brain but that does not mean that a child need necessarily be exposed to as many learning experiences as possible during the early years (Blakemore & Frith, 2005; Nagel 2012a, 2012b). In some contexts, the importance of stimulation has morphed into an agenda of urgency or misinformation suggesting that as much be done as possible with toddlers and young children to ensure they have the best chance at a successful academic career. Indeed, the notion that you can somehow enhance the brain through some measure of hyperstimulation or a plethora of early learning instruction has now become a pervasive neuromyth that may actually do more harm than good. Concerns over the use of neuroscience towards enhancing learning during the early years mirror similar concerns at the turn of the millennium around aspects of 'developmentally inappropriate practice' and are worthy of some mention here.

Since the 1980s researchers and scholars have warned that increased academic pressure on young children, often referred to as 'hothousing', may result in increases in various anxiety disorders associated with stress (Burts, Hart, Charlesworth & Kirk, 1990; Elkind, 1986; Gallagher & Coche, 1987; Isenberg, 1987). The reasons surrounding increases in academic pressure on younger and younger children over the last few decades are multifarious and expansive and as such beyond the scope of this text. What is clear is that advances in neuroscience and the merging of neuroscience and education have seen the emergence of a number of myths regarding early learning that closely resemble that of, and are often used to bolster, hothousing. In other words, brain science, in numerous circumstances, has been used to further the notion that the younger you 'educate' a mind, the better—resulting in a plethora of brain-enrichment toys, early learning devices and programs advocating increased education where more may actually end up being less (Nagel, 2012b). Unless a child lives in extreme poverty, violence, isolation or social and emotional deprivation, the natural everyday environments children find themselves in promote strong neural development and a healthy start to learning (Hirsh-Pasek & Golinkoff, 2004; Nagel, 2013a). There is scant, if any, scientific evidence to support notions that special stimulation or enrichment activities early in life lead to some measure of advanced brain development, improved intelligence or academic prowess (Nagel, 2012a; Shonkoff, 2010; Shonkoff & Phillips, 2000). A closer look at sensory stimulation and deprivation along with myelination helps shed light on why this might be.

SOMETHING TO THINK ABOUT 3.1

HOW SOON DO INFANTS THINK?

Over the last three decades researchers and scientists have learnt a great deal about the human brain and how the mind develops. Concurrently, various branches within cognitive neuroscience have uncovered a great deal about how children learn and behave, and have even called into question previous theories of cognition. Even the esteemed work of Jean Piaget on theories of cognitive development (as outlined in Chapter 2) have gained much scrutiny. If you recall from the previous chapter, Piaget suggested that, at the earliest stages of life, infants were incapable of higher order thinking; that belief permeated psychology texts for many years. But there have been a number of studies suggesting that perhaps Piaget and others did not give infants enough credit. For example, in a study conducted originally with fourteen-month-old children and then with nine- and eleven-month-old infants, researchers found that, as early as nine months of age, children were capable of what some might consider rather sophisticated thinking. In these studies the researchers would present replicas of real-world objects and model particular actions. A toy dog would be shown taking a drink of water and then the researcher might model the starting of a toy car with a key and giving a person a ride. Later, the child was not given the same toys but instead might be presented with a different animal, such as a fish, anteater or rabbit, and different vehicle; without prompting, the infant would typically act out similar scenarios: animals drank water, forklifts, aeroplanes, buses and other vehicles were driven. In other words, the children did not simply mimic a dog drinking and car driving but, given different objects, were able to generalise the correct actions or properties of the objects presented to them (Mandler & McDonough, 1996; McDonough & Mandler, 1998). What studies such as these tell us is that we are only beginning to understand how the brain and mind work; we can never underestimate the capacities of all children, regardless of age or stage of development.

Ask yourself...

1   Given that young children may be able to do more than we might anticipate, what are some of the possible implications of this when engaging with young minds in an educational context?

2   As a teacher, what can you do to ascertain potential capabilities of students in your classroom?

STIMULATION AND DEPRIVATION: TWO SIDES OF THE SENSORY COIN

Experiences matter to the brain! As noted earlier, synaptogenesis relies on the genes of an individual (nature) and the stimulation, via experiences, that individual has (nurture). In other words, stimulation plays a major factor in shaping our minds and is further broken down into two categories—experience-expectant stimulation and experience-dependent stimulation (Greenough, Black & Wallace, 1987; Markham, Black & Greenough, 2007). Experience-expectant stimulation relates to those ordinary day-to-day experiences the brain requires for particular hard-wiring to occur. Early research labelled these important developmental experiences as 'critical periods' but they are now more commonly referred to as 'sensitive periods' of development (Johnson, 2005; Thomas & Johnson, 2008). The term itself is a broad one that applies whenever the effects of experiences on the brain are unusually strong during a limited period of time (Knudsen, 2004). For example, at birth an infant's sight is very poor and each day the brain must receive visual information through the eyes to allow for the hard-wiring of sight to occur. Generally speaking, and barring any physical impairments, the simple opportunities to view the world provides the necessary stimulation for the brain to develop all the necessary mechanism for visual processing and sight. This is true of all the senses and a number of other important developmental capacities; it appears that children enter the world prepared for certain abilities that unfold as long as the brain receives the stimulation it expects (Bjorklund, 2005; Nagel, 2012a).

Experience-dependent stimulation differs in that this type of stimulation refers to adaptive processes arising out of the specific contexts or unique features of a particular environment (Nagel, 2012a). Experience-dependent processes are those things children learn as they engage with the environment, giving rise to individual differences across various developmental domains (Nelson, 2000). For example, while the brain *expects* to hear language in order to develop all aspects of oral language skills and auditory processing, what and how a child learns to communicate also *depends* largely on the language that is heard. This is explored in greater detail in Chapter 5 but at this stage it is important to note that perhaps the most significant difference between what the brain depends on

Experience-expectant stimulation
Those ordinary day-to-day experiences the brain requires for the particular hard-wiring of important connections.

Experience-dependent stimulation
The experiences that act as adaptive processes in shaping the brain's hard-wiring and may be most commonly referred to as learning experiences.

and what it expects lies in the fact that experience-expectant processes would apply to all children, while experience-dependent processes are likely to be far more individual in type, frequency, duration and what could rightly be thought of as 'learning' experiences (Nagel, 2012a; see also Bjorklund, 2005; Black, Jones, Nelson & Greenough, 1998; Diamond & Hopson, 1999; Greenough & Black, 1992; Greenough et al., 1987).

Learning windows

Experience-dependent stimulation is an important component of development and learning but it is neither necessary nor desirable to expose a young child to as many learning experiences as possible during the early years (Blakemore & Frith, 2005). Brain development and maturation extends over a number of years in human beings and an important aspect of this development is myelination, or the increasing of white matter as discussed above. Instead of trying to somehow hyperstimulate learning, it is better to bear in mind that there seem to be opportune times to engage in particular learning experiences and these periods of time have become known as **learning windows**, shown in Figure 3.4 (Nagel 2012a, 2013a; see also Chugani, 1994, 1996; Chugani, Phelps & Mazziotta, 1987, 1989; Diamond & Hopson, 1999; Eliot, 2000; Herschkowitz & Herschkowitz, 2004; Hirsh-Pasek & Golinkoff, 2004).

Learning windows Optimum times of neural maturation when the brain requires certain types of stimulation to create or stabilise long-lasting neural connections.

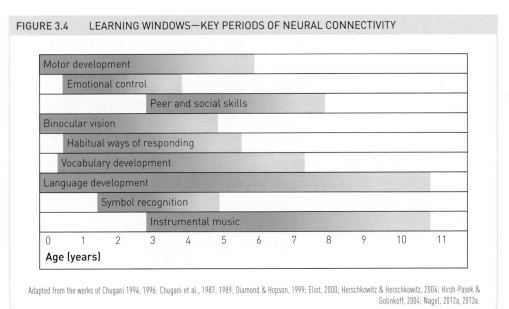

FIGURE 3.4   LEARNING WINDOWS—KEY PERIODS OF NEURAL CONNECTIVITY

Adapted from the works of Chugani 1994, 1996; Chugani et al., 1987, 1989; Diamond & Hopson, 1999; Eliot, 2000; Herschkowitz & Herschkowitz, 2004; Hirsh-Pasek & Golinkoff, 2004; Nagel, 2012a, 2013a.

The concept of particular windows for learning parallels research related to 'sensitive periods' but a significant difference is that learning windows never completely close. Instead, learning windows offer the optimum time for engaging in particular modes of stimulation but adults can certainly engage in some of those same activities later in life; it would likely just be a bit more laborious for the aged brain. Having the appropriate stimulation at the right time can also be linked to the production of myelin: the more white matter, the more efficient the brain becomes—and myelination takes a number of years to complete.

The production of myelin in the brain is a process more analogous to running a marathon than a sprint. We also know that myelination occurs in a relatively predictable manner, from inside to out and back to front (Aubert-Broche, Fonov, Leppert, Pike & Collins, 2008; Deoni et al., 2011). From an evolutionary standpoint, this is purposeful in that the controlling of a number of bodily functions via the brain stem along with emotional and fight or flight systems in the limbic system or mid-brain need to mature sooner than the higher analytical process found in the prefrontal lobes. Interestingly, recent studies have also suggested that, when a human is learning something, this may also promote the development of myelin (Hofstetter, Tavor, Moryosef & Assaf, 2013; Yeung et al., 2014). But it is important to note that the focus of such studies has been linked to disease prevention in ageing brains and, as yet, there isn't any evidence suggesting that extra tuition can make a young brain mature faster or better. In terms of learning, it appears that the brain has a predetermined plan of development and perhaps the most substantial factor related to stimulation is not doing more but rather ensuring that a child's brain is not deprived of important experiences.

SOMETHING TO
THINK ABOUT
3.2

ROMANIA'S ORPHANS: A CASE STUDY IN BRAIN STIMULATION

One of the most interesting findings related to experiences and the developing brain can be found in studies looking at what happens when you deprive the brain of important stimuli during its development. For many years, it was well known that long-term neglect and abuse during childhood could result in a range of developmental difficulties. And while there are those who mistakenly, and sometimes misleadingly, use neuroscience to promote programs and products with a view to enhancing a child's brain through some measure of hyperstimulation or 'enrichment' program, perhaps of greater concern are those children who live in environments devoid of adequate stimulation. Sadly, children who were raised in orphanages in Romania provide an example of what happens when the brain is deprived of the stimulation it expects to experience.

During the latter part of the twentieth century and under the reign of Nicolae Ceausescu, the Romanian government looked to enhance its future economic workforce through an increased birth rate. All forms of contraception and abortion were banned, the state guided family planning and women were encouraged, through state policy and taxation, to have a minimum of four or five children. Such policies led to an array of human rights abuses and by 1989 witnessed the institutionalisation of over 170 000 children in overcrowded and appallingly inhumane conditions (Zeanah et al., 2003). The result of Ceausescu's bold social experiment witnessed vast numbers of children with severe problems across all developmental domains. Neuroscientific studies even demonstrated impaired capacities in regions of the brain associated with the central nervous system and socio-emotional processing when compared to children raised outside such institutions (see, for example, Chugani et al., 2001; Marshall, Fox & BEIP Core Group, 2004). To that end, the evidence is quite incontrovertible: abuse and neglect result in developmental problems, in turn resulting in behavioural and learning problems among many other potential problems.

Ask yourself...

1 What might be some of the potential consequences for students who live in conditions of extreme poverty or disadvantage?

2 Given the potential for children entering a classroom from an environment of disadvantage, what are key considerations when working with such children in an educational context?

It should be self-evident that limiting or depriving a child of various sensory stimuli will have an impact on that child's developing brain. Moreover, studies into the deprivation of sensory stimulation have a substantive history in animals and, tragically, numerous examples of such deprivation in human beings have also provided evidence of the importance of providing healthy contexts for children to grow and mature. As discussed above, there are particular experiences that the brain expects in order for normal development to occur. For example, animal studies have shown that if you deprive healthy mammals with opportunities to see for a period of time after birth the result can be impaired vision or complete lack of sight (Hubel & Wiesel, 1970; Wiesel, 1982; Wiesel & Hubel, 1963). Importantly, the ground-breaking work of these studies noted that the deprivation of visual stimuli did not result in physical damage to the brain or optic nerve. Instead, it appears that such deprivation robbed the brain of the necessary stimulation to hard-wire for sight. This important research has also influenced medical practice in humans: the early treatment or removal of cataracts in children is now seen as critical for ensuring proper development of sight, while adults who develop cataracts are not at risk of going blind as they are already hard-wired for sight. The deprivation of stimulation is generally something that, fortunately, only occurs in extreme conditions. (An example of such extremes is presented in Chapter 5.)

SUMMARY

The formation of the brain begins in utero and changes rapidly at birth. The genesis of neurons and the communication that occurs through synapses is an important factor in hard-wiring the brain and this process is influenced by both nature and nurture. As the brain's information superhighway develops, it does so with the assistance of myelin. Myelin, or the white matter of the brain, takes over twenty years to fully develop. As white matter increases, the brain becomes more efficient and expeditious in processing information. Finally, the brain expects and depends on various types of stimulation to develop optimally and ensure all other aspects of development occur unabated. All of these processes are important to development and mediated through various regions and structures of the brain, the topic of the next section of the chapter.

STRUCTURES OF THE BRAIN

Understanding the various structures of the brain begins with recognising that, when examined independently or collectively, those structures are simple only in name. As noted earlier, what is known about the brain is dwarfed by what is not known. But what is known can offer important insights into understanding students and informing educational practice.

It is beyond the scope of *Understanding Development and Learning* to identify and elaborate on the full range of neural structures in the brain and how these may influence who we are and what we do. Indeed, the complexity of the neural structures in the brain are vast in scope and detail so it is perhaps more appropriate in this context to adopt a more general perspective. In adopting such a position we can identify three areas of prominence in the brain and the important structures within each that are pertinent to developing a greater understanding of overall human development and learning. These three areas include the *brain stem*, *limbic system* and *cerebrum* (see Figure 3.5).

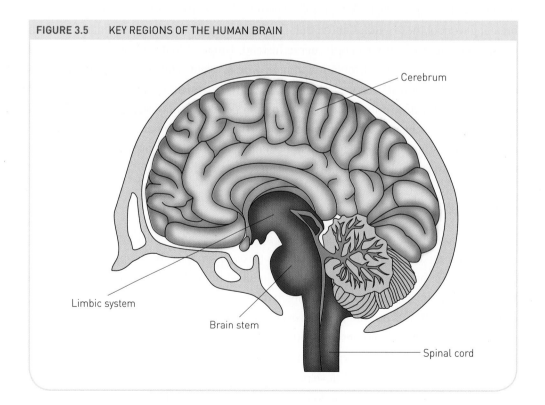

FIGURE 3.5   KEY REGIONS OF THE HUMAN BRAIN

Cerebrum

Limbic system

Brain stem

Spinal cord

THE BRAIN STEM, CEREBRUM AND LIMBIC SYSTEM

The brain stem is a collective term representing a number of smaller structures that connect the brain to the spinal cord. This region of the brain is responsible for functions not under conscious control and is where human survival responses such as fight-or-flight are initiated. For example, nuclei that are the centres for respiratory (breathing), cardiac (heartbeat) and vasomotor (blood pressure) activities are housed in the brain stem as are the mechanisms that control vomiting, sneezing, swallowing and coughing (Carter, 2009; Sweeney, 2009). It is also worth noting that an important structure known as the cerebellum sits just above the brain stem and some estimates suggest that it contains about 50 per cent of the brain's neurons (Andersen, Korbo & Pakkenberg, 1992; Sylwester, 2005). The cerebellum is a very complex structure and plays a role in sensorimotor integration, motor coordination and the coordination of cognitive functioning and various thought processes (Berninger & Richards, 2002; Diamond, 2012; Herschkowitz & Herschkowitz, 2004). The cerebellum is a good example of the interconnective nature of the brain in that this structure plays a role in moving our muscles and shaping our thoughts.

Sitting just above the brain stem and residing in the middle of the brain is the limbic system. The limbic system is often simplistically described as the emotional part of the brain and, while processing emotions is a key activity in the limbic system, other important activities also occur in this region. The limbic system plays a central role in processing environmental stimuli and processing memories, and it connects the lower regions of the brain responsible for motor and autonomic functions with the higher regions of the cerebrum responsible for cognitive thought. The limbic system also plays a role in sleep patterns, regulation of bodily functions, attention, hormones, motivation, the production of most of the chemicals in the brain and numerous other mechanisms that influence and shape our behaviour (Nagel, 2012a). Four important structures within the limbic include the *amygdala*, *thalamus*, *hypothalamus* and *hippocampus*, and their primary functions are noted in Figure 3.6.

The structures within the limbic system are not limited in the activity they do as suggested in Figure 3.6, but the activities noted are the most significant in terms of behaviour and learning. It is also important to remember that each structure influences the other and they do not work in isolation from other parts of the brain. The limbic system also plays an active role in many higher thought processes that occur in the most advanced part of the human brain, the cerebrum.

The cerebrum is the largest and topmost part of the brain. When asked to visualise a brain, it is this area that most people would likely think of and it is this area that separates humans from all other species. The outer layer of the cerebrum, known as the *cerebral cortex*, is mostly comprised of *glial cells*: the 'grey matter' of the brain. Glial cells provide

FIGURE 3.6   KEY STRUCTURES IN THE LIMBIC SYSTEM

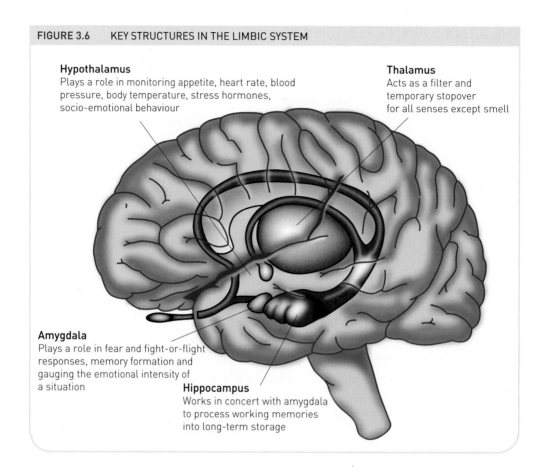

Hypothalamus
Plays a role in monitoring appetite, heart rate, blood pressure, body temperature, stress hormones, socio-emotional behaviour

Thalamus
Acts as a filter and temporary stopover for all senses except smell

Amygdala
Plays a role in fear and fight-or-flight responses, memory formation and gauging the emotional intensity of a situation

Hippocampus
Works in concert with amygdala to process working memories into long-term storage

protection and support for neurons, which comprise the white matter of the brain due to the presence of myelin.

The frontal lobe

The cerebrum also consists of the two hemispheres of the brain with each having a parietal, occipital, temporal and frontal lobe. Each lobe, in turn, is responsible for a number of functions but perhaps the most pertinent in terms of learning is the *frontal lobe*. In evolutionary terms, the frontal lobe is the youngest part of the brain. In educational terms, it is where higher order thinking and many other important functions occur; some aspects of language, problem solving, emotional regulation, attention, concentration, planning, decision making, responsible thinking and judgment are but a few of the activities mediated in the frontal lobes, and in particular the prefrontal cortex (Nagel, 2014; Nelson et al., 2006). These activities, as well as others, fall under the umbrella term executive functions, and are critical for development and learning. Many of these capacities emerge towards the end of

Prefrontal cortex
The region of the frontal lobes directly connected to every distinct function of the brain and responsible for coordinating and integrating most brain functions.

Executive functions
An umbrella term for the regulation and control of cognitive processes, including aspects of memory, reasoning and numerous higher order skills.

the first year of life but executive functioning continues to improve and develop through adolescence and into adulthood (Byrnes, 2007). It should be emphasised that executive functioning is part of the maturational timeline of the brain, which is one of the reasons cognition and emotional regulation vary markedly depending on age. Equally significant to note is that children who grow up in adverse environments resulting from neglect, abuse or exposure to violence may experience levels of impairment in the development of executive functioning skills (Evans & Wachs, 2010; Lengua, Honorado & Bush, 2007; Maughan & Cicchetti, 2002).

Notwithstanding any measure of impairment due to adverse circumstances, executive functioning takes some time to fully develop. The prefrontal cortex is the last thing to mature with full maturation occurring in the third decade of life (Giedd, 2004; Kuhn, 2006). Had Piaget had the technology available to him at the time he may have, therefore, reconsidered his view that abstract reasoning was assured around twelve or thirteen years of age. That is not to say that twelve-year-olds cannot think abstractly; it just means that humans get better at doing so with age. Indeed, many of the executive functions and higher order cognitive activities that adults take for granted seem to operate differently during the teenage years when the brain goes through profound developmental changes.

THE DEVELOPING BRAIN AND ADOLESCENCE

From the outset it may be best to define the term 'adolescence' in the context of development and learning. Depending on whom you may ask and where they live, finding a consensus on a definition of adolescence is not easy to achieve. This is due to the fact that the word adolescence, derived from the Latin term *adolescere* meaning to 'go into adulthood', is generally defined differently depending on social conventions and cultural contexts. Most people associate adolescence with the teenage years but from a neurodevelopmental standpoint, linking adolescence with pubescence is perhaps a better starting point. Pubescence is a medical term denoting a change in the reproductive system that mirrors the beginning of changes to the brain (Nagel, 2013a). For some young people, this begins before they turn thirteen and, like denoting timelines for puberty and bodily changes, delineating the exact time when the brain begins to change is highly individualistic. Developmental changes depend on age, experience and hormonal changes, but it is commonly accepted that major changes to the brain occur between the ages of twelve and nineteen with full development and maturation being completed sometime into adulthood (Giedd et al., 1999; Paus et al., 1999; Sowell, Thompson, Holmes, Jernigan & Toga, 1999).

SYNAPTIC PRUNING

One of the most appropriate ways of thinking about the changes to the brain during adolescence is that of a brain under reconstruction. This is a time of significant growth and development and one of the main changes occurs through the discarding of unused neural connections. Known as 'synaptic pruning', this process occurs during the teenage years and sees a significant reduction in the grey matter of some regions of the brain while overall brain volume increases (Giedd et al., 1999; Sowell, Thompson, Tessner & Toga, 2001). Increases in the brain's white matter are evident in most regions of the brain, while grey matter peaks in the frontal lobes around eleven years of age in girls and twelve years in boys (Giedd et al., 1999). There are also differences between boys and girls in other regions of the brain where temporal lobe grey matter peaks at 16.7 years in girls and 16.2 years in boys while parietal lobe grey matter peaks at 10.2 years in girls and 11.8 years in boys (Giedd, 2004). The thinning and thickening of grey matter during adolescence is thought to reflect changes in the size and complexity of neurons, not a change in actual number (Giedd, 2004). The end result of these changes is that the brain eventually becomes more efficient by getting rid of unused connections and enhancing and strengthening the connectivity of those that remain; the adage 'use it or lose it' is most appropriate in this context (Giedd, 2004; Nelson et al., 2006; Thompson et al., 2000). In terms of learning, this change suggests that the activities that an adolescent continually engages in support the ongoing growth and proliferation of neural connections. In an educational context, introducing a second language to a thirteen-year-old as an elective for only one year is likely a waste of time in terms of long-term retention and use; for new tasks and skills to be maintained they must be practised over time or they will be pruned (Willis, 2009).

HOT AND COLD COGNITION

A second consideration of adolescent brain development relates to the increase in white matter. As discussed earlier, white matter represents the fatty material known as myelin. Myelin will increase dramatically over adolescence, making the brain quicker and more efficient in terms of processing information. The timing of myelination appears to depend on age, environment and genetics but, while a significant growth in myelin occurs in the prefrontal lobes, this occurs later than in many other regions of the brain, including the limbic system (Casey, Getz & Galvan, 2008; Fuster, 2002). This may be one reason adolescents seem to run high on emotion and, at times, make decisions that may lack a measure of responsible thinking—their limbic system overrides the analytical part of the brain. The notion that various executive functions, including higher order thinking, can be influenced by emotional state or where cognition is coloured by emotion is referred to as *hot cognition* (Hongwanishkul, Happaney, Lee & Zelazo, 2005). *Cold cognition*, on the other hand, refers to executive functioning devoid of emotional influence (Roiser & Sahakian, 2013). Both hot and cold cognition are evident in people of all ages but, during adolescence, hot cognition often takes precedence, particularly in the company of peers and as a driving force towards sensation-seeking or risk-taking behaviours (Casey & Caudle, 2013; Dahl, 2001; Nagel, 2014; Reyna & Farley, 2006; Spear, 2010, 2013). It may be the case that the earlier maturation of the limbic system intersecting with significant developmental changes in the cerebrum is a major contributor to greater reactive behaviours during adolescence where emotions take centre stage. Concurrent changes in particular neurotransmitters during adolescence may also be complicit in these not-thought-through behaviours as well as other actions.

NEUROTRANSMITTERS

As described earlier in the discussion of the developing brain during the early years of life, neurotransmitters play an important role as chemical messengers during synaptic activity. It is worth noting here that, during adolescence, there appear to be significant fluctuations in melatonin, serotonin and dopamine (Spear, 2007). A closer look at each of these important chemicals offers further evidence of the substantial changes in the brain during adolescence and how these may affect learning.

Melatonin

Melatonin is a neurotransmitter that plays an important role in the regulation of the system that monitors the sleep–wake cycle associated with our circadian rhythms. This important chemical is produced in the centre of the brain by the *pineal gland*. When our environment is dark, the pineal gland at the centre of the brain ensures that melatonin levels are increased, inducing drowsiness. There is some evidence suggesting the secretion of melatonin declines during puberty, which in turn affects an adolescent's sleep cycle (Carskadon, 2002; Carskadon, Acebo & Jenni, 2004). Anecdotally, generations of parents and teachers alike can attest to the fact that, during the teenage years, sleep patterns do seem to vary. Significantly, sleep is very important in terms of memory consolidation.

Serotonin

While fluctuations in melatonin may influence adolescent sleep cycles, variations in serotonin will affect mood and behaviour. Serotonin is one of the most widely distributed chemicals in the brain. While it helps to keep people calm and relaxed, it also plays an important part in social behaviour (Siegel & Crockett, 2013). Given its distribution across various regions of the brain, it is not surprising that serotonin plays a role in a number of mood fluctuations, including those associated with anxiety, arousal and impulse control. Low levels of serotonin have been linked to depression, sleep disorders and a number of behavioural disorders (Howard, 2006; Nagel, 2014; Sylwester, 2005). Individuals suffering from chronic depression are often prescribed medication to enhance the uptake of serotonin in the brain. Of interest here is that there appears to be a temporary decline in the levels of serotonin during adolescence. Female adolescents appear especially susceptible to even lower levels of serotonin at certain times, given that serotonin levels are also influenced by oestrogen; elevated levels of oestrogen during a teenage girl's menstrual cycle result in elevated levels of serotonin, while low levels of oestrogen see corresponding declines in serotonin (Bethea, Lu, Gundlah & Streicher, 2002; Brizendine, 2006; Chugani et al., 1999; Dahl, 2003; Panksepp, 2004). Fluctuations in this important calming neurotransmitter suggest that serotonin may be complicit in increased impulsivity and greater health risks associated with depressive behaviours during adolescence (Nagel, 2014).

SOMETHING TO THINK ABOUT 3.3

WHY TEENAGERS WON'T WAKE UP FOR SCHOOL

One of the most intriguing patterns of behaviour that changes during adolescence is that of sleep. As children enter puberty and progress through their teenage years, their sleep patterns can change markedly, characterised by later times of falling asleep to difficulties in awakening in time to get to school. It has long been known that, as children age, their sleep time reduces but, during a time of profound brain maturations and alteration, adolescents need more than nine hours of sleep to operate optimally. Going to sleep at midnight only to get up early in the morning for school is highly problematic. In itself, sufficient sleep is very important during periods of brain maturation and essential for learning and memory development. One study (Hansen, Janssen, Schiff, Zee & Dubocovich, 2005) found that adolescents perform better in the afternoon than in the morning and similar studies suggest that school hours may actually be contributing to sleep deprivation in adolescents. To make matters worse, there is growing evidence that the light emitted from computers and handheld devices can also negatively affect sleep, and diminish the total number of hours of deep sleep necessary to perform at one's best (Cajochen et al., 2011). Given that we could now refer to today's adolescents as 'screenagers', it should be self-evident that a good number of students who arrive for class in the morning are sleep deprived and not performing to their best. This is supported by a large body of evidence noting a clear association between sleep disturbance and poor school performance (Pagel & Kwiatkowski, 2010).

Ask yourself...

1   When working with adolescents in an educational setting, what considerations related to morning classroom endeavour might need to be considered?

2   What could schools do to help alleviate or accommodate changes to sleep patterns associated with the onset of puberty and adolescent maturation?

3   Research examples of schools that have looked to accommodate the evidence on adolescent sleep patterns in a proactive fashion by changing policy and practice.

Dopamine

Finally, but certainly of no lesser importance, dopamine levels also appear to vary during adolescence. Dopamine is sometimes referred to as the 'pleasure' chemical in that elevated levels of dopamine elicit positive feelings and, under some circumstances, sheer euphoria: one of cocaine's chemical targets is dopamine. Regions of the brain associated with novelty seeking, rewards and risky behaviour are influenced by dopamine. Both animal and human studies identify elevated levels of dopamine during adolescence, particularly in males and particularly in response to certain experiences (Casey et al., 2008; Chambers, Taylor & Potenza, 2003; Galvan, 2010, 2012; Spear 2000a, 2000b). Dopamine has also been implicated in diverse developmental and cognitive operations including, but not limited to, learning, decision making, motor skills and neuroplasticity (Galvan, 2012). The implications surrounding changes in dopamine levels during adolescence in relation to learning are linked predominantly to rewards and motivation and an immature prefrontal cortex.

As noted earlier, the area of the brain that is the last to mature, and where executive functioning thrives, is the prefrontal cortex. Many of the structures within the limbic system develop and mature sooner and are influenced by various neurotransmitters in the brain. Such maturation has been shown to correlate with various measures of cognitive functioning and emotional regulation (Nagel, 2014). For example, adolescents tend to perceive risks differently from adults, seek immediate rewards rather than value long-term goal-directed behaviours and display exaggerated emotional responses for many things adults would consider mundane or uninteresting. Taken in its entirety, developmental changes to the brain during adolescence, and indeed through the lifespan, are worthwhile considerations for all aspects of human development and learning and, by association, education.

CONCLUSION

Current generations of teachers and future teachers now have an opportunity to have a far greater understanding of the human brain than any previous generation of educators. Advances in technology have provided important insights associated with brain development throughout the lifespan and teachers are well placed to take advantage of this information to inform and enhance their own practice. From understanding the earliest stages of development and the significant changes that happen to the brain in the early years of learning through to insights into the major structural and functional changes that occur during adolescence, teachers are better placed now more than ever to engage with such findings for the betterment of all students. Developmental psychologists and all who are interested in theories associated with learning are also reshaping previous understandings of the brain and mind, for the brain is the heart of learning.

Greater understanding of how the brain develops, the role of sensory stimulation from the environment, structures and functions of the brain and changes in the brain during key developmental time frames offer more informed understanding of all other aspects of development. Our knowledge of cognitive, socio-emotional, physical and language development in association with neuroscientific perspectives on memory, motivation, intelligence and behaviour continues to grow and reconfigure the seminal work of others. For example, while Jean Piaget provided a framework for understanding cognitive development that maintains a degree of currency today, we now know that his understanding of infant cognition and the development of abstract thought are somewhat erroneous. We also know regions of the brain associated with higher order cognitive processes, emotion and survival are intimately connected in ways not previously understood, which in turn reminds us that learning is far more complex than ever imagined. This becomes clearer as we progress through the rest of *Understanding Development and Learning* and continue to link neuroscience with learning. A focus on memory in the next chapter moves us along this path.

CHAPTER SUMMARY

This chapter focused on an important aspect of development as it pertains to learning and behaviour: the development of the human brain. Over the last three decades researchers have learnt a great deal about the brain and its development. These insights offer important questions and considerations of how best to engage with this information in an educational environment. Our exploration of the development of the brain began with a look at the differences between 'brain' and 'mind' and then moved into how the brain develops in the early years of life. Important concepts such as 'neuroplasticity' and 'learning windows' were examined within a framework of understanding how the brain forms its neuro-architecture within an electrochemical milieu of neurotransmitters and environmental stimuli.

The second part of the chapter explored various regions of the brain and their roles across a number of cognitive and socio-emotional parameters. This then led us to look at the amazing restructuring of the brain that occurs at the onset of puberty and through adolescence. Important processes were examined along with related behavioural manifestations associated with the adolescent brain. The role of the neurotransmitters melatonin (sleep), serotonin (mood) and dopamine (sensation seeking and risk taking) were described as they pertain to adolescent behaviour and some of the implications of this on learning, and by association pedagogy, were offered.

Implications for teaching

As noted at the beginning of the chapter, what is known about the brain is much less than what is unknown; linking neuroscience to education is not only a work in progress but also one in its infancy. It is significant that, as neuroscientific research continues to grow almost exponentially, much of the current evidence supports theories of learning discussed through-out *Understanding Development and Learning*. For teachers then, perhaps one of the concepts related to the developing brain that they could focus on is the role of emotions in learning and how simple acts of approval or sarcasm can influence student outcomes. Psychologists have known for quite some time that our moods play a role in how we learn and behave but neuroscience tells us that how we engage with students can instantly influence chemicals in the brain and our approach to tasks or challenges. Experiences of stress and pleasure provide good examples of such influence.

It is now widely accepted that stress can negatively affect learning, particularly if the stress is associated with internal beliefs of ability or perceived hindrances to learning (LePine, LePine & Jackson, 2005). Part of the reason for this is that, when sensory information elicits a stress response in the brain, most of the brain's resources are allocated to a fight-or-flight response. Pleasurable experiences, on the other hand, can elevate neurotransmitters such as dopamine, promoting not only pleasurable feelings but also enhanced motivation and aspects of memory (Blakemore & Frith, 2005; Willis, 2010). In an educational context, therefore, it could be argued that how a teacher responds to a student in any situation can have a direct effect on the neurophysiology of the brain and, by association, behaviour and learning.

Ask yourself...

1   As a future teacher, what are some things that you can do to help alleviate stress in a learning context?

2   What strategies can you employ to develop a positive learning environment?

3   It is a truism that classrooms are diverse in terms of student needs, interests and behaviour. As a teacher, what are some important considerations for you to ensure that you are able to maintain a positive outlook given this diversity and how can you take care to ensure you do not fall into fight-or-flight responses?

PRACTICAL ACTIVITIES

1   *While on practicum*, discuss with your mentor teacher(s) any opportunities they have had to learn about the human brain. Have they had any training during their own time at university or any professional development in this area? Take note of any opportunities they have had and what their own opinions of the topic are. Do their views resonate with Mr Ricci, as described in the opening of this chapter, or are they uninterested in the topic?

2   *While on practicum*, discuss with your mentor teacher(s) what strategies they use to develop a positive atmosphere and alleviate student stress where possible. Follow this conversation up with your peers at the school or university and see if you can develop a list of ideas to enhance your practice.

STUDY QUESTIONS

1   What are three main structures of the brain and what are their primary responsibilities?

2   What are three important neurotransmitters and what primary role does each play in terms of behaviour?

3   Briefly note the differences between experience-expectant stimulation and experience-dependent stimulation. Depending on the age of the students you wish to teach, jot down some examples of how you can provide experience-dependent stimulation.

4   What is the fundamental difference between sensitive periods of development and the concept of learning windows? Given the information about learning windows as presented in this chapter, what might be some proactive policy measures that could be implemented to take advantage of certain opportunities for learning?

5   Given the profound changes in the brain during adolescence, what might some of these changes mean in terms of engaging adolescents to enhance pedagogy and outcomes? By way of example, consider changes to the reward systems of the brain.

FURTHER READING

Blakemore, S. J. & Frith, U. (2005). *The Learning Brain: Lessons for Education.* Oxford, UK: Blackwell Publishing.

Byrnes, J. P. (2007). Some ways in which neuroscientific research can be relevant to education. In D. Coch, K.W. Fisher & G. Dawson (Eds.), *Human Behavior, Learning and the Developing Brain: Typical Development* (pp. 30–49). New York, NY: Guilford Press.

Campbell, S. R. (2012). Educational neuroscience: Motivations, methodology, and implications. *Educational Philosophy and Theory, 43*(1), 7–16.

Carew, T. J. & Magsamen, S. H. (2010). Neuroscience and education: An ideal partnership for producing evidence-based solutions to guide 21st century learning. *Neuron, 67*(5), 685–688.

Donovan, M. S., Bransford, J. D. & Pellegrino, J. W. (Eds.) (2000). *How People Learn: Brain, Mind, Experience and School.* Washington, DC: National Academy Press.

LeDoux, J. (1998). *The Emotional Brain: The Mysterious Underpinnings of Emotional Life.* New York, NY: Simon & Schuster.

Martinez, M. E. (2010). *Learning and Cognition: The Design of the Mind.* Boston, MA: Allyn & Bacon.

Nagel, M. C. (2012). *In the Beginning: The Brain, Early Development and Learning.* Melbourne, Australia: ACER Press.

Nagel, M. C. (2014). *In the Middle: The Adolescent Brain, Behaviour and Learning.* Melbourne, Australia: ACER Press.

Pinker, S. (2009). *How the Mind Works.* New York, NY: W.W. Norton.

Tokuhama-Espinosa, T. (2011). *Mind, Brain, and Education Science: A Comprehensive Guide to the New Brain-Based Learning.* New York, NY: W.W. Norton.

VIDEO LINKS

Maine Children's Growth Council: *Infant Brain Development—The Critical Intervention Point*
https://www.youtube.com/watch?v=_0EYXx9iI64

A short interview on infant brain development with Dr Jill Stamm from Arizona State University. Although sponsored by 'Libraries for the future', this short snippet succinctly encapsulates some of the most important experiences necessary in the early stages of brain development.

National Core for Neuroethics: *Matching Adolescent Education with Brain Development by Sarah Jayne Blakemore in Brain Matters! Vancouver*
https://www.youtube.com/watch?v=cId5BEiSXns

An interesting podcast with Dr Sarah Jayne Blakemore, looking at adolescent brain development and the potential implications of this development for education.

WEBLINKS

Neuroscience for Kids
http://faculty.washington.edu/chudler/neurok.html

A useful website about neuroscience and the brain designed by the University of Washington for teachers and students.

DANA Foundation
http://www.dana.org/

This site is the product of a private philanthropic organisation that supports brain research through grants, publications and educational programs and offers numerous resources for understanding the brain.

4 LEARNING, THINKING AND INTELLIGENCE

> The development of an intelligent, responsible human being is not an automatic internal process that takes place in spite of environmental factors, and it is not an external process of moulding a pliable child into a predetermined shape chosen by parents and teachers. It is a lively process of give and take in which children explore their boundaries and limits. Sometimes they accommodate to adult expectations and, sometimes, quite naturally, they resist.
>
> (Miller, 2007, p. 457)

LEARNING OUTCOMES

As you read through this chapter and undertake the exercises at the end, you will gain the ability to complete these tasks successfully:

→ describe and discuss the notion of intelligence and theories that have contributed to our understandings

→ discuss the areas of the brain associated with intelligence and thinking

→ explain the links between nature and nurture in terms of cognitive capacities

→ discuss the implications of Western notions of intelligence on classroom practice.

KEY TERMS

- cognitive ability
- intelligence quotient (IQ)
- general mental ability
- triarchic model
- multiple intelligences
- emotional intelligence

Kelly Springfield was very excited about the beginning of the school year. The allocation of classes had been made and Kelly could see she was going to have twins Jessica and James in her Year 4 class. Kelly had taught the twins' sister, Mia, a couple of years earlier. She had been an extremely bright girl who learnt quickly and received very high grades for her work. Mia had excelled at reading and writing and was also a model student, engaged in her work and excited about learning. Kelly assumed that Mia had a high intelligence.

The twins were active members of the class, but by the end of term one Kelly was getting very frustrated with Jessica and James and a little perplexed. Both Jessica and James needed constant redirection as they moved around the classroom at times when students were supposed to be seated and working quietly. They both seemed bored a lot of the time and were always looking for other activities to do, such as art. Kelly had also done a range of testing and both Jessica and James were well below the class average in reading. A little concerned, Kelly had put the twins on an intense reading program and spent extra time hearing them read. But they were hard to keep engaged in the reading activities and did not seem to be improving. Although Kelly wanted to talk with the twins' mother, she was a little reluctant as she thought the twins' underachievement might be viewed as a reflection of her teaching. She thought that, if there was a problem with the twins' cognitive capacities, their mother would have already approached her about it. Sometimes their older sister Mia came by after school and collected them from class. She seemed very responsible and conversations with her indicated she was doing very well at school now she was in Year 7. Kelly was at a bit of a loss.

1   Is it reasonable for Kelly to expect the twins to be the same type of student as their sister Mia? Why? Why not?

2   Do you think the difference in the twins and Mia's scholastic endeavours is related to intelligence? Why? Why not?

3   Discuss some factors that may be affecting the twins' outcomes in reading.

4   Discuss some strategies Kelly could try with the twins to improve their reading outcomes.

INTRODUCTION

Cognitive ability
Brain process of
acquiring knowledge
and understanding.

The notion of a general cognitive ability or 'intelligence' is an elusive concept that is difficult to define and measure. How do you define intelligence? Is there one general intelligence or do we possess multiple intelligences? We have difficulty conclusively defining the term 'intelligence' in a way that fully considers individual cognitive capacities and the development of culturally specific abilities. Add to the mix ongoing debates about the role of nature and nurture in intelligence, or intellectual capabilities, and you have a thought-provoking, controversial topic! You may already have been involved in debates about whether intelligence is fixed or changeable and the role of genetic inheritance and environmental factors. Although the concept of intelligence is often quantified and discussed, unlike a child's foot size or height, it cannot be precisely measured, only indirectly evaluated through individual performance. This abstract, broad concept can be considered from a psychological perspective as the ability to solve problems; from a multiple-intelligences approach as at least eight specific cognitive capacities; from a sociocultural perspective as the ability to use the tools of the culture; and within triarchic theory to also include practical know-how (Table 4.1 shows some of the different perspectives on intelligence as a concept).

A neuroscientific approach to understanding intelligence involves understanding the brain's role in intelligence and factors that enable or constrain the development of such capacities. Individual differences in general intelligence have been associated with differences in brain structure and function. One theory of the neural bases of intelligence—the Parietal-Frontal Integration Theory of Intelligence (P-FIT)—describes a network of frontal and parietal brain regions as the main neural basis of intelligence (Colom et al., 2009). In this way general intelligence involves multiple cortical areas throughout the brain (Colom et al., 2009). But recent research suggests that the brain basis of intelligence could be extended to consider other parts—the posterior cingulate cortex and subcortical structures—as relevant for intelligence (Basten, Hilger & Fiebach, 2015). A common finding in contemporary neuroscience research is the understanding that intelligence is likely to be distributed across brain regions rather than located in one particular region and relies on neural connectivity, efficiency and overall cognitive organisation (Gazzaniga, Heatherton & Halpern, 2010). As we have noted on many occasions, the current era of extensive research on the brain and the underpinnings of mind processing continues to lead to new developments and understandings.

TABLE 4.1 APPROACHES TO NOTIONS OF INTELLIGENCE

Traditional intelligence		Multiple-intelligences		Neuroscience
Charles Spearman	General mental ability 'g' Specific mental ability 's'	Robert Sternberg	Triarchic theory: analytic, creative, practical	Distributed neural connections in the frontal and parietal lobes are related to higher intelligence
Alfred Binet	Stanford-Binet IQ test	Howard Gardner	Eight frames of mind	
Raymond Cattell	'Crystallised' and 'fluid' intelligence	Daniel Goleman	Emotional intelligence	

The notion of intelligence is often associated with a person's cognitive abilities to learn and demonstrated in school performance, abstract thought, self-awareness, emotional knowledge, memory, planning, creativity and problem solving. Many parents make the mistake of comparing the academic achievements of their children by suggesting one may be more intelligent than another because he or she received better marks in a school report. There is more to the story than grades and an intelligence quotient (IQ). While individuals may be described as intelligent due to their scholastic endeavours, contemporary notions of intelligence and different models provide many ways of conceptualising intelligence. In this chapter we will consider some of the traditional and contemporary models of intelligence. We will also consider the contributions of neuroscience to our current understandings. Neuroscience techniques are accelerating our understanding of how the brain works, with imaging technologies that identify brain areas and the relationships among them that underlie psychological processes central to education, including learning, memory, attention and reasoning. Interest in the neural basis for individual differences in these processes and for their complex integration forms the basis for most conceptual understandings of human intelligence (Haier & Jung, 2008). In this chapter we will look at how our rational brain evolves and how the very things that we as adults take for granted, in relation to higher order thinking processes, are nowhere near complete in children.

Intelligence quotient A number representing a person's reasoning ability.

MEASURING INTELLIGENCE

How is intelligence defined or measured? Is intelligence solely determined by biology or can it be developed? What does it mean when we describe a student as 'intelligent' and how do we account for children's differences in cognitive ability? As a teacher will you refer to students as 'bright' or 'clever'—what will that mean to you? The nature of general cognitive ability indicates that intelligence is a valid construct but that does not equate to being fixed (Adey, Csapo, Demetriou, Hautamaki & Shayer, 2007). Findings from the Human Genome Project, an international project exploring how genes work, suggest that the variance in cognitive ability is not easily explained by genetic markers (Nisbett et al., 2012). While twin studies show that genetic influences continue to affect cognitive ability into old age (Pedersen, Plomin, Nesselroade & McClearn, 1992), intellectual development also depends on elements such as diet and adequate nourishment; exposure to illnesses; the physical and social environment including economic status; parental education and income (Duchesne, McMaugh, Bochner & Krause, 2013). It is precisely because this general cognitive ability is malleable that it offers such a powerful opportunity to educators (Adey et al., 2007).

Quantifying or measuring how individuals process information, think and learn is largely a Western notion that draws on the skills that are valued in a particular society. Non-Western societies do not always value the same skills or place priority on the same abilities as Western societies (Grigorenko et al., 2001). For example, while Western societies value speed in problem solving, indigenous conceptions of intelligence in communities such as sub-Saharan Africa also value social qualities such as respect, obedience, diligence and readiness to share (Grigorenko et al., 2001). In a similar way, conceptions of intelligence among the Baganda and the Batoro in Africa are described as socially oriented behaviour of benefit to the collective (Wober, 1974). Intelligence is equally hard to assess in traditional Western ways in particular cultures, as children in places such as rural sub-Saharan Africa are more familiar with clay as a medium of expression than they are with pencil and paper. We must then be cautious when considering the measurement of intelligence and the cultural bias that impede parity of participation by students.

While Western notions of cognitive abilities tend to consider intelligence as involving high levels of competence in literacy, numeracy and technological skills, there continues to be disagreement about the concept, structure and origin of intelligence. In some educational settings, intelligence tests are used in a variety of ways and are often linked with a general aptitude and capacity for understanding and learning. In most Western societies, intelligence is conceptualised as some form of mental ability and often valued in terms of 'more is better'. Such notions, coupled with advances in neuroscientific research, have seen a burgeoning and highly profitable industry targeting parents who wish to do all they can to ensure that their child is the next Einstein (Nagel, 2012a). Needless to say, the hype surrounding building super brains and the reality are two very different things. In this chapter we will shed some light on these discrepancies and offer a cautious look at intelligence in relation to individual brain development and implications for learning, thinking and your role as an educator. Cautious, because much of what we know about intelligence is speculative and much of what is offered to educators is very contentious and continues to be informed by neuroscience (Nagel, 2012a). But it is important to have a clearer understanding of what intelligence is, how it is linked to brain development and how teachers can enhance normal, healthy development of an intelligent mind.

SOMETHING TO
THINK ABOUT
4.1

WHAT IS INTELLIGENCE?

Are we too quick to judge what intelligence is? Consider these examples. Perhaps all but one of them would not be judged as intelligent by the conventional standards of achievement at school—but are those judgments necessarily correct?

Kayla had never liked school much and just scraped through Year 12. She tried a variety of different jobs before finding her niche working with an interior designer. After several years, she found she could mostly pick what style of design customers would like simply from the clothes they wore and the way they spoke.

Nate is tolerating school until he can leave and get an apprenticeship with a panel beater. He knows he is not one of the smart kids. He fills his notebooks with doodles of decorated hotrods but his art teacher is not that enthusiastic about them. He can't wait until he gets his own car and has the chance to paint it with elaborate designs.

Growing up in a small rural town, Bindi knows she's never going to be a rocket scientist. She loves her two horses and spends every spare moment with them. She can often predict how they will behave from the weather or what's happening around them. She wouldn't mind being a vet but she knows she'll never get the marks.

Ivan doesn't have any close friends at school. He often gets picked on for being a nerd and usually spends his lunchtimes in the library, working on apps. He plays a lot of chess and has beaten most of the competitors his age in local competitions. His hero is Bill Gates and he dreams of coming back to school as a globally successful internet entrepreneur. In the meantime, he's thinking of wagging PE: it's soccer and he's dreading it.

Some of the following processes are often associated with intelligence.

1   The ability to solve problems
2   The ability to adapt to everyday experiences
3   The ability to judge, comprehend and reason
4   The ability to be creative
5   The ability to communicate using interpersonal skills
6   The ability to understand objects and symbols
7   The ability to think rationally
8   The ability to interact with the environment

Ask yourself...

Read the list of processes above and for each, consider the following questions.

1   How much of our intelligence is influenced by genetics?
2   How much of our intelligence is influenced by experiences?
3   How do cognitive abilities interact with other aspects of functioning?
4   Are there sex differences in intelligence?
5   Is intelligence locally influenced or is intelligence a global capacity?
6   How can you measure intelligence?
7   Are there multiple intelligences?

CHARLES SPEARMAN AND THE 'G' FACTOR

At the beginning of the twentieth century, Charles Spearman (1904, 1925) assisted in developing the construct of intelligence as an innate ability. An English psychologist, he argued that a range of similar cognitive attributes could be measured and therefore interpreted as a measure of intelligence demonstrating a general mental ability or 'g'. He also noted differences in how individuals performed according to the items in the tests, with some people excelling in language-related activities and others outperforming on recall of lists of digits. He explained this as specific mental abilities or 's'. His work has been referred to as a 'two-factor theory of intelligence' (Spearman, 1904, 1925). He believed that some people were endowed with higher levels of 'g' and specific mental abilities associated with 's'. Spearman's work remains influential today in that his notions of general mental ability or 'g' are arguably what is measured using intelligence tests and these measurements—now referred to as IQ (intelligence quotient) scores—do appear to be fairly stable predictors of performance in school and academic settings as well as performance in certain careers. The impact of Spearman's work has helped shape numerous complementary theories of intelligence over the last hundred years.

General mental ability
Broad mental capacity that influences performance on cognitive ability.

ALFRED BINET AND INTELLIGENCE QUOTIENT (IQ)

At about the same time that Spearman was designing his theory of intelligence, the French psychologist Alfred Binet (1916) was asked to develop a test to help determine which children might not be able to learn in school and therefore should be sent to special schools. To this end, Binet created the first intelligence test. It has since been modified and refined, with the most common iteration being the Stanford–Binet test still used today to ascertain an IQ score. IQ scores are based on comparisons with other people and this is represented in a bell-curve graph, resembling a camel's hump (see Figure 4.1). Most people (around 68 per cent) will score within the hump, between a range of 84 and 116. This is also evident in children: roughly seven out of ten children will have similar 'normal' IQ scores with about 15 per cent below 83 points and 15 per cent above 117 (Hirsh-Pasek & Golinkoff, 2004). It is important to keep in mind that, while testing can assist in distinguishing intellectual disability from normal intelligence in babies and young children, it cannot distinguish moderate differences in intelligence within this age bracket. IQ test scores become stable through childhood, are fairly reliable around age eight and settle around adult scores at roughly age twelve (Carter, 2000). IQ tests have also been identified as culturally biased and often only serve as indicators of the kind of learning that takes place in schools; as such, their effectiveness as a determinant of overall human intelligence must always be scrutinised in terms of intent and context (Nagel, 2012a). It is also important to note that contemporary IQ tests mirror Spearman's recognition of the existence of considerable variability on how individuals perform on different types of items in intelligence tests.

FIGURE 4.1   THE DISTRIBUTION OF IQ SCORES IN A TYPICAL POPULATION

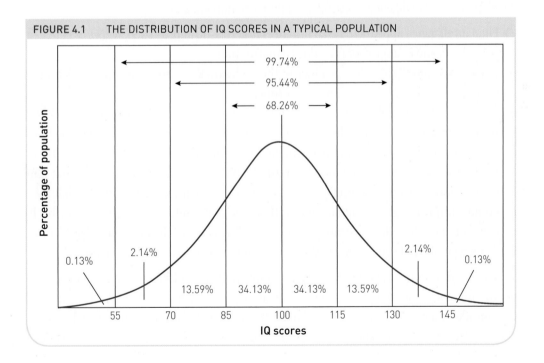

RAYMOND CATTELL: CRYSTALLISED AND FLUID INTELLIGENCE

Notions of *crystallised* and *fluid intelligence* proposed by Raymond B. Cattell (1987) provide a useful foundation for unpacking the nature and nurture of intelligence. An English and American psychologist who studied under Charles Spearman, Cattell expanded on Spearman's notion of general mental abilities. Cattell believed that general intelligence is multifarious with many factors at work to produce intelligences that he broadly separated into fluid and crystallised. Fluid intelligence or fluid reasoning depends on non-verbal abilities and an individual's ability to detect relationships among stimuli and process this information effectively, expeditiously and efficiently. In other words, the processing of stimuli drives a person's ability to think or act quickly. Reasoning and problem solving in this way is grounded in physiology, particularly neurophysiology. This form of intelligence includes inductive and deductive reasoning. Crystallised intelligence, on the other hand, is culturally based fact-oriented knowledge; it refers to those skills derived from accumulated knowledge and experience, good judgment and social skills. Such skills stem from learning and acculturation. This form of intelligence tends to improve with age, as experiences tend to expand one's knowledge (Cattell, 1987).

Cattell's work illustrates three important considerations related to intelligence and the development of intelligence or cognitive abilities in individuals.

→ Fluid intelligence appears to be an innate characteristic and, as such, will vary between individuals and change over time due to maturation.
→ Crystallised intelligence is a product of the contextual environment and the learning experiences facilitated for children over time.
→ Most importantly, while some types of testing may offer insights into general abilities, studies have shown that children who possess similar fluid intelligences, but come from different cultural backgrounds, perform differently on 'crystallised' tasks (Nagel, 2012a). In other words, some testing may be culturally biased and, as such, any tests that aim to articulate a measure of intelligence must be scrutinised carefully to ensure that they do not disadvantage individuals due to their social or cultural background—or both. Children will often demonstrate attributes, abilities and what might be referred to as some type of intelligence beyond the scores offered in pencil-and-paper IQ tests.

The fluid nature of intelligence is an important consideration in the context of neurophysiology and the overall nature of intelligence. This is particularly evident if we consider that fluid intelligence is linked to brain maturation or what psychologists and child development experts refer to as 'cognitive development' or 'general ability'.

Cognitive development and intelligence are inextricably linked and years of studies have demonstrated that a child's ability to understand abstract concepts and perform certain cognitive tasks improves with age (Siegal & Varley, 2002). Therefore, it is important to look at the links between brain maturation and the nature of intelligence (see Figure 4.2) before embarking on notions of how to nurture intelligence in a healthy and positive way within the classroom.

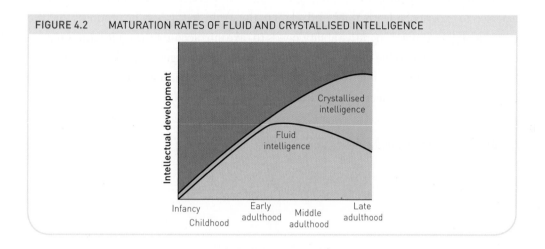

FIGURE 4.2   MATURATION RATES OF FLUID AND CRYSTALLISED INTELLIGENCE

NOTIONS OF MULTIPLE INTELLIGENCES

ROBERT STERNBERG'S TRIARCHIC THEORY

As teachers, we are interested in teaching for thinking; that is, how students *produce* knowledge rather than how they merely *reproduce* it. We are interested in stimulating students' effective thinking and intelligent behaviour. Some of the oldest, most familiar and most widely accepted descriptions of intelligence in Western societies are those linked to cognitive abilities or factors thought to be involved in intellectual performance. This is an area in which Robert Sternberg (1997, 2012), an American psychologist and Professor of Human Development at Cornell University, has achieved eminence, through his broad view of intelligence.

According to Sternberg (1997), traditional notions of intelligence represent a relatively narrow set of cognitive abilities or capabilities. He defines human intelligence as 'mental activity directed toward purposive adaptation to, selection and shaping of, real-world environments relevant to one's life' (Sternberg, 1985, p. 45). In other words, he describes it as the mental activity necessary for adaptation to, as well as shaping and selecting of, any environmental context. In this way, he proposes that intelligence is not just reactive to the environment but also active in forming it. That is, people have an opportunity to respond flexibly to changing situations. Intelligence, then, is a collection of abilities that allow a person to experience, learn, think and adapt to the world. In this way, he proposes that the concept of 'g', or general cognitive ability, needs to take into account the multifarious nature of cognitive ability and the influence of context, including changes that take place through the lifespan. His theory is referred to as the triarchic model of intelligence as he identified three key aspects of intellectual capacities, shown in Figure 4.3 (Sternberg, 1997).

Triarchic model
Characterises intelligence in terms of distinct components: analytical, creative, practical.

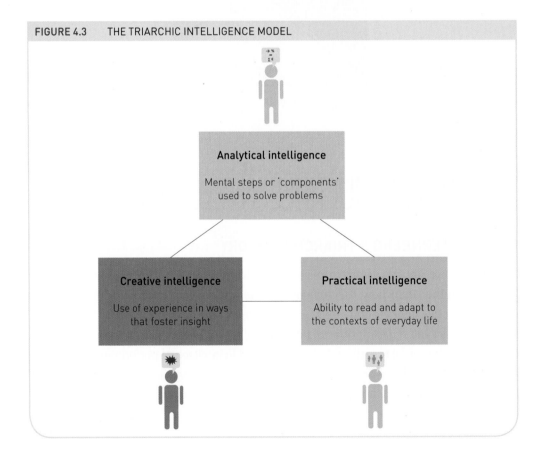

FIGURE 4.3   THE TRIARCHIC INTELLIGENCE MODEL

Analytical intelligence

Mental steps or 'components' used to solve problems

Creative intelligence

Use of experience in ways that foster insight

Practical intelligence

Ability to read and adapt to the contexts of everyday life

Sternberg's triarchic model of intelligence includes three elements: analytical or componential intelligence; creative or experiential intelligence; and practical or contextual intelligence. His view of intelligence revolves around the interchange of analytical, practical and creative aspects of the mind.

STERNBERG'S TRIARCHIC MODEL OF INTELLIGENCE

Robert Sternberg is an American psychologist born in New Jersey in 1949. Sternberg's life is testament to the fact that performing well in tests is not necessarily an indicator of one's true capabilities! His interest in psychology began early in life due to his personal suffering of test anxiety. After Sternberg repeatedly did poorly on exams due to anxiety, he began to believe that testing was not an accurate measure of his actual knowledge and abilities. Sternberg then developed his very first intelligence test, which he named the Sternberg Test of Mental Ability (STOMA). Sternberg then went on to develop the triarchic model of intelligence that is defined as consisting of analytical, creative and practical intelligence.

Analytical (componential intelligence)

Traditional notions of intelligence involve executive processes used in solving problems and making decisions. These executive processes are involved in regulating how the mind acts in terms of abstract thinking and logical reasoning, verbal and mathematical skills.

Creative (experiential intelligence)

Creative thinking and processes allow us to do tasks, including perceiving problems in our long-term memory, perceiving relations between objects, and applying relations to another set of terms. This component of intelligence also involves the ability to generate new ideas and deal with novel situations.

Practical (contextual intelligence)

Practical intelligence, the knowledge acquisition component, is used to obtain new information, choose relevant from irrelevant information, and to selectively combine the various pieces of information gathered. It is sometimes termed 'street smarts' or the ability to apply knowledge to the real world (Sternberg, 1985, 1997).

While Sternberg's background is in the science of measuring mental capacities, his stance on standardised testing and intelligence do not support traditional views. Sternberg notes that psychometric intelligence tests only measure analytical thinking and memory skills, and do not account for other essential components of intelligence. That is, most IQ tests measure only the componential/analytical component in intelligence. According to Sternberg, traditional educational systems value 'componential' intelligence most highly, and tests are designed largely to assess this type of intelligence—composed primarily of linguistic and logical-mathematical abilities. He argues that two other kinds of intelligence: contextual (the source of creative insight) and 'experiential' (the 'street smarts' of intelligence) are of enormous value to society, yet not reinforced nor given much opportunity to develop in many traditional classrooms.

Ask yourself...

1   What are the implications of the three components of intelligence for teachers? How will you facilitate experiences to account for these different facets of intelligence?

2   Pick a common classroom experience that requires students to engage in producing a tangible product. List and detail the processes involved in the experience and how students could engage analytical, creative and practical practices.

Sternberg's explorations of intelligence move beyond traditional notions as he considers intelligence as more than a static score, arguing that it is malleable and takes into consideration contextual influences such as culture, gender, age, parenting style, personality and schooling. According to Sternberg (2010), students with different triarchic patterns present differently in schools: that is, students with high analytic ability tend to have the skills valued by schools. Creatively intelligent students might not conform to teacher expectations, while practically intelligent students might not demonstrate the skills required to do well in the classroom. Of course, most school tasks are not purely analytical, creative or practical, with opportunities to learn through all three intellectual approaches.

GARDNER'S EIGHT FRAMES OF MIND—MULTIPLE INTELLIGENCES

Multiple intelligences
Theory that proposes several independent forms of human intelligence exist.

Howard Gardner (1983) first proposed a model of multiple intelligences in his book *Frames of Mind: The Theory of Multiple Intelligences*. He continues to build upon this work as Professor of Cognition and Education at the Harvard Graduate School of Education. As part of his theory, he argues that there is a range of cognitive abilities and that these abilities are distinct and therefore not necessarily related. In this way, a child in your classroom who finds mathematics easy and quickly picks up concepts such as addition, subtraction and multiplication may not be more intelligent than a child who takes longer in mastery. A child who takes longer to grasp these concepts may be approaching the mathematical concepts from a fundamentally different perspective on a more complex and deeper level or might excel in other learning domains.

Gardner proposes eight specific types of intelligence:

→ *linguistic*: the ability to use language. Sensitivity to the meaning of words, the order among words, and the sound, rhythms, inflections and meter of words (for example, poets).

→ *logical-mathematical*: the capacity to process mathematical operations and conceptualise the logical relations among actions or symbols (for example, mathematicians, scientists).

→ *spatial*: the ability to think three dimensionally and conceptualise and manipulate large-scale spatial arrays (for example, aeroplane pilot, sailor), or more local forms of space (for example, architect, chess player).

→ *bodily-kinaesthetic*: the ability to use one's whole body, or parts of the body (like the hands or the mouth), to solve problems or create products (for example, dancer).

→ *musical*: sensitivity to rhythm, pitch, meter, tone, melody and timbre. May entail the ability to sing, play musical instruments and/or compose music (for example, orchestral conductor, composer).

→ *interpersonal*: the ability to interact effectively with others. Sensitivity to other's moods, feelings, temperaments and motivations (for example, negotiator, successful teachers).

→ *intrapersonal*: sensitivity to one's own feelings, goals and anxieties, and the capacity to plan and act in light of one's own traits (for example, psychologist or counsellor).

→ *naturalistic*: the ability to make consequential distinctions in the world of nature as, for example, between one plant and another, or one cloud formation and another (for example, farmers, ecologists) (adapted from Gardner, 2015).

There has been some discussion about a ninth intelligence, *existential intelligence*, manifested when an individual is concerned with reasoning about the meaning of life, demonstrating they are spiritually smart or have metaphysical intelligence. The possibility of this intelligence has been alluded to by Gardner but has not been added. According to Gardner, IQ tests measure only linguistic and logical-mathematical abilities.

SOMETHING TO THINK ABOUT 4.3

MULTIPLE INTELLIGENCES IN PRACTICE

Gardner's model of multiple intelligences has been applied to education and has implications for classroom practices. According to Gardner (2011), education should develop intelligences and help people reach educational goals that are appropriate to their particular spectrum of intelligences. Gardner also believes that individuals possess the capacity to develop several intelligences and, at any one moment, a child will have a unique profile, due to genetics (heritability) and experiential factors. In this way, children have their own unique configuration of intelligences that teachers should take into account when teaching, mentoring or facilitating experiences. He argues that ideas, concepts, theories and skills should be taught in several different ways. That is, when you are teaching your students about the arts, sciences, history or maths you would present the ideas in multiple ways.

Ask yourself...

1 If you were developing students' capacities for understanding the concept of measurement, how could you present this in multiple ways? Pick a year level and list your strategies and expected outcomes.

2 If you were developing students' skills to paint, how you would present this to children in several ways? Pick a year level and list your strategies and expected outcomes.

3 Revisit the setting the scene scenario at the beginning of the chapter. Do you think Kelly would have benefited from understanding Gardner's model of multiple intelligences when she was trying to understand differences in the academic performances of the twins and their sister Mia? Why or why not?

Gardner cautions that the eight specific types of intelligences should not be confused with learning styles. In fact the idea of learning or thinking styles has been subject to criticism (Peterson, Rayner & Armstrong, 2009). While Gardner sets out distinct intelligences, he opposes the idea of labelling learners with a specific intelligence, as each child possesses a uniquely personal blend of all the intelligences.

As with all theories, there are of course critiques of Gardner's model. Psychologists, including Sternberg, have pointed to the lack of empirical evidence to support Gardner's theory (Sternberg, 1991; Waterhouse, 2006). There has also been criticism that Gardner is not expanding the definition of the word 'intelligence', but merely using the word 'intelligence' where people have traditionally used words such as 'ability' (Sternberg, 1991).

EMOTIONAL INTELLIGENCE

Emotional intelligence Capacity of individuals to recognise their own and other people's emotions.

Emotions affect how and what children learn as unchecked emotions raise an individual's stress level and stressed brains find it very difficult to learn (Medina, 2010). Historically, in educational contexts there has been a belief that social, emotional and cognitive learning were separable and that intellectual or cognitive learning was most important. But, as the brain is an interdisciplinary mechanism and information is processed across the brain, children learn through their relationships (social intelligence), their emotions (emotional intelligence) and by making sense of their world (cognitive intelligence). When we consider the maturational timeline of neurodevelopment, the higher cognitive processes we take for granted are the last thing to mature. In other words, the emotional part of the brain (limbic system) should be a consideration in any discussion regarding learning and the social well-being of children. Healthy classroom environments depend on the creation of a classroom culture that allows children to develop emotional intelligence competencies.

Emotional intelligence competencies are said to include the ability to be aware of one's own emotions and patterns of behaviour, to manage negative or destructive emotions effectively and to share in positive relationships and experiences with others in ways that enhance learning and life satisfaction. Mapping out the exact systems and related structures underlying emotional maturation and behaviour is not easily done. This is due to the variability in what can count as emotion and the fact that children, as well as adults, are likely to engage a wide array of neural circuitry simultaneously when processing emotional stimuli (Fries & Pollack, 2007). Emotions are often described as the activation of neurological circuits that prioritise our experiences into things we should pay attention to or things we can safely ignore (Izard, 2007). Feelings, on the other hand, are the subjective psychological experiences (see Chapter 2) that emerge from the activations associated with emotion (Medina, 2010). According to Plutchik (2001), emotions are adaptive and include complexity born of a long evolutionary history. Although we conceive of emotions as feeling states, this feeling state is part of a process involving both cognition and behaviour. He defines eight states of emotions (see also Figure 4.4), each with a specific message for our behaviour:

→ *joy*: to remind us what is important
→ *trust*: to open our hearts
→ *fear*: something needs to change
→ *surprise*: to focus on new situations
→ *sadness*: to connect us with those we love
→ *disgust*: to reject what is unhealthy
→ *anger*: to fight against problems
→ *anticipation*: to look forward and plan (Plutchik, 2001).

Our feelings are a product of how our brain processes and attends to emotional stimulation and children develop their abilities to experience and express different feelings as a result of maturation (Thompson & Lagatutta, 2008). This developmental capacity to experience and express feelings has often been labelled as emotional intelligence and an individual's emotional intelligence is an important component of overall well-being and one's capacity to make sense of, and navigate, social environments (Goleman, 1995, 2006). Again, as with most theories, there is disagreement regarding the definition of emotional intelligence, in both terminology and how it is processed. For example, there are three main models of emotional intelligence:

→ ability model
→ mixed model (usually subsumed under trait)
→ trait model.

See Chapter ❷ for a more detailed discussion of emotions and the development of emotional regulation.

FIGURE 4.4   EIGHT STATES OF EMOTION

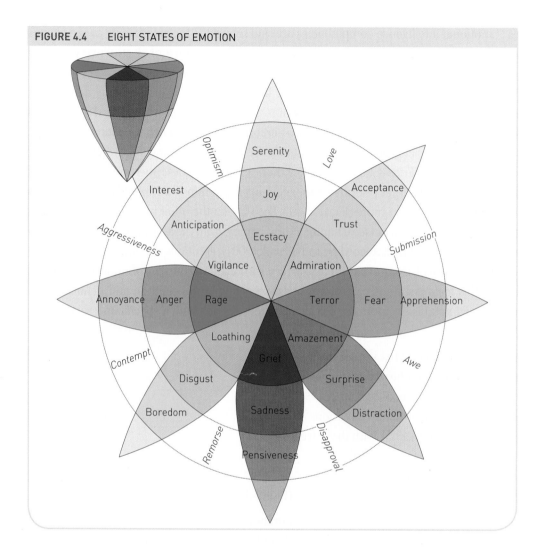

DANIEL GOLEMAN'S MODEL OF EMOTIONAL INTELLIGENCE

The model introduced by Daniel Goleman (1995, 2006) is considered a mixed model and focuses on an array of competencies and skills including five main constructs. These emotional competencies are not innate talents, but rather learnt capabilities.

→ *self-awareness*: the ability to know one's emotions, strengths, weaknesses, drives, values and goals and recognise their impact on others while using them to guide decisions

→ *self-regulation*: involves controlling or redirecting one's disruptive emotions and impulses and adapting to changing circumstances

→ *social skill*: managing relationships to move people in the desired direction

→ *empathy*: considering other people's feelings especially when making decisions

→ *motivation*: being driven to achieve for the sake of achievement (Goleman, 1995, 2006).

Goleman argues that individuals are born with a general emotional intelligence that determines their potential for learning emotional competencies. His model has been critiqued in research literature, due to the difficulty of providing empirical evidence in assessment (Mayer, Barsade & Roberts, 2008). While current theories about and research into emotion might bring up more questions than answers, what is clear is that emotions play an important part in student learning. Having an understanding of the emotion enables teachers to evaluate emerging educational applications. Classroom activities that emphasise social interaction can provide opportunities for emotional support. Games, discussions, field trips, interactive projects, cooperative learning, physical education and the arts are examples of activities that can enhance student learning. As memories are contextual, activities that draw on emotions—such as role playing—may provide important contextual memory prompts that will help students recall the information during closely related events in the real world. We also know that emotionally stressful school environments are counter-productive because they can reduce students' ability to learn (Nagel, 2012a). Even short-term stress-related elevation of cortisol in the hippocampus can hinder our ability to distinguish between important and unimportant elements of a memorable event (Gazzaniga, 1989).

THE NEUROSCIENCE OF INTELLIGENCE

Within the neuroscientific world, the frontal and parietal lobe areas of the brain (see Figure 4.5) are often referred to when talking about thinking and intelligence. This is due to the development of technology that allows non-invasive imaging of the brain. This new imaging shows that many complex mental skills associated with intelligence involve the part of the cortex near the front of the brain. The prefrontal cortex, for example, serves many purposes as it is involved in planning complex cognitive behaviour, decision making, thinking through one's actions or the responsibilities attached to those actions, to abstract thinking, and mediating emotional responses. The term used to refer to the functions carried out by the prefrontal cortex area is executive function, which includes abilities to differentiate among conflicting thoughts and determine good and bad, prediction of outcomes, expectation based on actions, and social control or the ability to suppress urges.

It is the prefrontal lobes that separate humans from all other species. In terms of maturation of a child, it is significant that the prefrontal lobes do not fully mature until the third decade of life (Nagel, 2012a). This is a very important aspect of child development for educators to consider, as the regions of the brain responsible for survival and emotion are in full swing long before the regions responsible for logical and moral reasoning follow suit (see Figure 4.6).

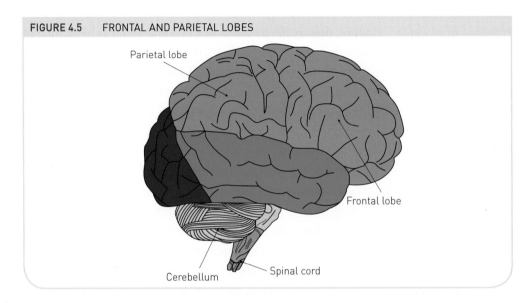

FIGURE 4.5   FRONTAL AND PARIETAL LOBES

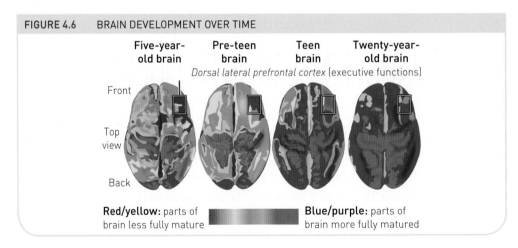

FIGURE 4.6   BRAIN DEVELOPMENT OVER TIME

THE IMPORTANCE OF CONNECTIONS WITHIN THE BRAIN

Haier and Jung (2007) were behind an intelligence-related study that found that regions related to general intelligence were scattered throughout the frontal lobe, suggesting that most of the brain areas thought to play a role in intelligence are clustered in the frontal and parietal lobes, with some of these areas related to attention, memory and more complex functions such as language. In their *parieto-frontal integration theory* (P-FIT), Jung and

Haier (2007) suggest that intelligence levels are based on how efficiently these brain areas communicate with one another. Further studies have gone on to demonstrate how several brain regions, and the connections between them, are what is most important to general intelligence (Basten et al., 2015; Cole, Yarkoni, Repovš, Anticevic & Braver, 2012; van den Heuvel, Stam, Kahn & Hulshoff Pol, 2009). That is, there is emerging evidence that intelligence depends not just on the efficiency or power of various brain regions, but also on the strength of the connections that link them. The fact that the regions of the brain being studied in terms of intelligence are highly malleable suggests that experience and environmental cues may play a very important role in shaping intelligence. Interestingly, they also compared data in men and women with equivalent IQ scores and found that, compared to men, women show more white matter and fewer grey matter areas related to intelligence. Furthermore, men's IQ-to-grey matter correlations are strongest in the frontal and parietal lobes whereas the strongest correlations in women are in the frontal lobe along with the region known as Broca's area. It would appear then that men and women achieve similar IQ results with different brain regions, suggesting that there is no singular underlying neuro-anatomical structure to general intelligence, as different types of brain processing manifest equivalent intellectual performance (Haier, Jung, Yeo, Head & Alkire, 2005).

There are five characteristics of intelligence that have been prominent in discussions and commonly arise in the literature: connectivity, general versus special, modules, development and neuroplasticity (Adey et al., 2007). From an educational point of view, it is the plasticity of intelligence that is both most important and most in need of further understanding. If a general intellectual ability can be itself enhanced by appropriate educational strategies, then the role of the teacher in student learning is critical. When you consider general intellectual processes of the mind are malleable and potentially improved by education, then the construct of intelligence is no longer the ultimate control over our students' ability to learn. Plasticity of intelligence then becomes an explanatory construct and also a construct that may direct interventions. Once one appreciates the plasticity of intelligence and sees it as perhaps the most complete way of accounting for individual differences, intellectual development and learning, it then offers perspectives for raising academic achievement across contexts (Adey et al., 2007).

Perhaps in the near future, neuroscience will provide the opportunity to test whether any combinations of the areas in the brain's processing systems predict something useful for education (Haier & Jung, 2008). For example, take two students who indicate the same IQ but are identified to have different patterns of grey matter areas (one student has more tissue in visual integration regions, the other student more in regions associated with language). Would this have implications for educational pathways or teaching? Perhaps there will be a day when educational research can determine particular brain strengths and subsequently apply more visual hands-on approaches for the former student and a more classic auditory-verbal approach for the latter. If such brain-based knowledge ever becomes available, it would not preclude the importance of environmental, social or cultural contexts (Haier & Jung, 2008). While neuroscience has raised many questions about the exact processing of intelligence, it has also afforded us further understandings about healthy brain development and contributions to intelligence.

THE BEGINNING OF INTELLECTUAL DEVELOPMENT

We all know that a newborn infant appears to have limited intelligent capacities compared to an older child. This can be attributed to differences in 'mental speed', overall neural efficiency and the maturation of the brain's frontal lobes. While an infant is engaged in intelligent activities, the brain has very few neural connections and runs relatively slowly. Newborns can use their senses to recognise a mother's voice and face, to develop the ability to distinguish certain speech sounds and demonstrate aspects of reasoning, categorisation and abstraction before their first birthday. While a newborn's brain responds to sensory stimulation anywhere from three to four times slower than that of an adult does, improvements in cognitive development are evident as the brain becomes faster at mental tasks (Nagel, 2012a). This speed will increase dramatically in the first year when the production of myelin is rampant; there is a two- to threefold increase in the acceleration of neural transmission before a child's tenth birthday (Nagel, 2012a). The increase in speed also means that the brain becomes more efficient as it matures through childhood, in that it will be better equipped to process, store, retrieve and analyse information and burn less energy in doing so (Eliot, 2000). There is a paradox as, in spite of an infant's slower processing speed, an infant's brain uses far more energy than an adult brain. This is likely due to the overproduction and then later pruning of synaptic connections, which in itself contributes to greater neural connectivity, efficiency and overall cognitive abilities and intelligence (Gazzaniga et al., 2010).

Along with changes in speed and efficiency, the maturation of the frontal lobes is also a very important aspect of overall cognitive development and intelligence (Nagel, 2012a). The frontal lobes are one of the last regions of a baby's brain to form while in the womb. During childhood, the frontal lobes form and prune synapses more slowly than any other region of the brain. The frontal lobes, and in particular the prefrontal lobes, do not fully mature until early adulthood. This maturation of the frontal lobes cannot be sped up or advanced, placing limitations on a range of intellectual abilities in children. The frontal lobes play a role across a range of cognitive capacities in reasoning, abstract thought, managing conflict, self-regulation of emotions, working memory, paying attention and concentrating on tasks (Nagel, 2012a). Barring any inherent cognitive impairments or trauma to regions of the brain during normal maturation, there are a few neurologically influenced milestones we would expect to see in children.

Infant milestones (birth to two years)

During the first year of life, children depend on their senses and will learn simply from engaging with the world around them. The frontal lobes then become far more active from around eight months of age, allowing for the development of increased performance in working memory, self-regulation, attention, concentration and greater goal-oriented actions due to improvements in motivation (Nagel, 2012a). Around this time there is an increase in dendritic growth in the left hemisphere of the brain, corresponding with the emergence of expressive language. At around eighteen months of age, language becomes the most obvious change in a child's cognitive capacities and allows for an increased ability to engage independently with the environment. This emergence of language is also a contributing factor to a range of other cognitive abilities, including symbolic thought and a growing sense of self-awareness (Eliot, 2000).

Early childhood milestones (two to five years)

Communication between the hemispheres of the brain improves due to myelination (see Chapter 3) in regions of the brain, resulting in greater crosstalk between the hemispheres as children move from toddlerhood towards their third and fourth birthdays (Berninger & Richards, 2002). In infancy the right hemisphere appears more dominant and, while the left hemisphere becomes more prominent at age two years, it is not until about four years of age that the integration of a child's analytical (left) hemisphere and intuitive/spatial (right) hemisphere takes place, resulting in a brain that resembles that of an adult with regards to hemispheric functionality (Decety & Michalska, 2010). Then, memory improves markedly as children become more aware of their own perceptions and begin to demonstrate a theory of mind, or the ability to understand and predict another person's mental processes, including their thoughts, emotions, motives, beliefs and intentions (McDevitt & Ormrod, 2013). These capacities will continue to mature and develop as a child enters formal schooling.

Middle childhood milestones (six to twelve years)

From when a child is around six years of age, the brain demonstrates a greater degree of sophistication, demonstrating skills such as drawing and language comprehension, and greater powers of attention, concentration, self-regulation and emotional control. This emergence of higher cognitive skills appears to be universal across all cultures, an indicator of innate neurological maturation. This is a time where children begin to move into what Jean Piaget (1954) referred to as operational thinking. Children's thinking and reasoning becomes logical and they begin to demonstrate an enhanced working memory and that they can perform higher order cognitive activities, such as classifying objects mentally. At this time, most aspects of memory improve and children become increasingly more proficient at encoding, storing and retrieving memories whether they be episodic, procedural or semantic (Nagel, 2012a). It is during this time that the vast neural networks across all regions of the brain demonstrate greater efficiency and speed. It is also the beginning of the end of synaptic proliferation; a new phase of development and restructuring takes place roughly at the onset of pubescence.

See Chapter ❷ for a more detailed discussion of Piaget's theories of intellectual development.

An important factor related to cognitive development and intelligence is that children require safe, secure environments and the support of positive social relationships. Key predictors of healthy intellectual development are found in the relationships between children and those responsible for their education, care and well-being. Educators begin to have an increasingly important role in helping children make sense of the world as they grow older.

CONTROVERSIES OVER INTELLIGENCE

IQ TESTING

Intelligence testing is controversial but it has retained its place within education. IQ tests include the Wechsler Intelligence Scale for Children—Revised (WISC-R) and the Kaufmann Assessment Battery for Children (K-ABC). Psychologists use testing methods to measure a child's intellectual capabilities in several specific domains. These domains include verbal comprehension, factual knowledge, abstract reasoning, visual–spatial abilities and short-term memory. While achievement tests are designed to assess students' knowledge or skills in a content domain in which they have received instruction, intelligence tests are broader in scope and are designed to measure the cognitive skills, abilities and knowledge that individuals have accumulated as the result of their overall life experiences, coupled with skills in applying these attributes to solving problems. Psychologists and educators are often divided about the concept of intelligence and the use of intelligence tests, as it is extremely difficult to develop a test that measures innate intelligence without introducing cultural bias.

New theories about the notion of intelligence have been offered over the past twenty years, substantially expanding thinking about intelligence as a much broader construct. Developments on the measurement of such notions of intelligence have not responded to theoretical developments. Sternberg is one psychologist who has tried to change the practice of testing. The Sternberg Triarchic Abilities Test (STAT) is a battery of multiple-choice questions that tap into the three independent aspects of intelligence—analytic, practical and creative—proposed in his triarchic theory, as discussed earlier. Psychologists such as Gottfredson (2003), professor of educational psychology at the University of Delaware, criticise the unempirical nature of triarchic theory, arguing that traditional intelligence tests do measure practical intelligence when they show a moderate correlation with income—especially at middle age when individuals have had a chance to reach their maximum career potential—and that IQ tests predict the ability to stay out of jail and stay alive, qualifying as practical intelligence.

Regardless of where you stand on the intelligence testing debate it is hard to deny the prominence of cultural bias, as most tests reflect what the dominant culture thinks is important (Shiraev & Levy, 2010). While there are attempts to reduce the amount of cultural bias, there are no cultural-fair tests but there are culture-reduced tests (Sternberg, 2011). When languages differ, the same words often have different meanings; when pictures are used as substitutes for words, there is bias against cultures with less experience with drawing and photographs. Research in Africa and Asia has found that people in non-Western cultures often have ideas about intelligence that differ fundamentally from those that have shaped Western intelligence tests (Grigorenko et al., 2001; Sternberg, 2011).

THE NATURE AND NURTURE OF INTELLIGENCE

While the debates continue about the roles of nature and nurture in the development of intelligence, neuroscience provides understandings that demonstrate how closely nature and nurture are intertwined. Neuroscience is offering us evidence of the connection between our genetic make-up, our predetermined neural capacities and the role of the environment in shaping our brains. The building of a child's brain circuitry blurs the boundaries between nature and nurture, as experience plays a pivotal role in 'wiring' the brain (Nagel, 2012a). From this perspective, human development, and indeed intelligence, is a product of both nature and nurture. There appears to be a complex interplay between the genes a child is born with (nature) and the experiences he or she has (nurture), especially in the earliest stages of life (Cirulli, Berry & Alleva, 2003; Felitti et al., 1998; Gluckman & Hanson, 2004; Teicher et al., 2003).

Empirical evidence continues to tell us that the lack of appropriate neural stimulation via experience can lead to alterations in genetic plans (Keuroghlian & Knudsen, 2007; Knudsen, 2004; Shore, 1997). As we learnt from the discussion in Chapter 1 about Maslow's hierarchy of needs, maternal health, stress, nutrition and appropriate stimulation are all environmental factors that can affect brain development, while issues such as socio-economic background (see Chapters 2 and 9) can also affect brain development, learning and ultimately a child's intelligence.

CONCLUSION

In this chapter we have looked at notions of intelligence and the theories that have contributed to our understandings. You may now agree that there is some difficulty defining exactly what intelligence is and how to measure such general cognitive abilities. After reading this chapter, you may have an opinion about whether intelligence is fixed or changeable and the role of genetic inheritance and environmental factors. As we mentioned at the beginning, we suggest you use caution when evaluating theories related to intelligence, and take a nuanced approach with a view that our understandings will continue to be informed by theoretical debates and neuroscience. As notions of intelligence are often associated with a student's ability to learn and what he or she demonstrates in terms of abstract thought, problem solving, memory, planning and logic, as teachers it would be unwise for us to make assumptions or compare children strictly based on test outcomes. As we have discussed, there is more to understanding the story than translating grades into assumptions about IQ. It is a distinctly Western notion to consider intelligence as predominantly involving high levels of competence in literacy, numeracy and technological skills.

The contributions of Charles Spearman, Alfred Binet and Raymond Cattell have influenced our understanding of notions of intelligence through their presentation of more traditional views of intelligence. But traditional notions of intelligence define a relatively narrow set of cognitive capabilities. Sternberg has extended traditional notions to define intelligence as unique mental activity, where the purpose is adaptation to and the selection and shaping of real-world environments relevant to an individual's particular context. Gardner has offered yet a further expansion of cognitive capacities associated with thinking and argues that people have eight frames of mind or specific types of intelligence that include linguistic, logical-mathematical, spatial, bodily-kinaesthetic, musical, interpersonal, intrapersonal and naturalistic intelligences. This model has implications for the classroom, as Gardner views the teacher as pivotal in helping students reach educational goals that are appropriate to their particular spectrum of intelligences. Views about emotional intelligence offered by Goleman are again relevant for educators, as a student's ability to manage his or her own emotions, to navigate negative emotions effectively and to develop positive relationships affects classroom experiences and ultimately learning.

Neuroscientific approaches to understanding intelligence have demonstrated the brain's role in intelligence and factors that enable or constrain the development of such capacities.

Individual differences in general intelligence have been associated with differences in brain structure, neural connectivity, speed and efficiency and overall cognitive organisation for processing. The current era of extensive research on the brain and the underpinnings of cognitive processing continues to provide exciting insights into what is going on in the heads of our students when we ask them to think.

CHAPTER SUMMARY

The chapter looked at the difficulties associated with defining the notion of a general cognitive ability or 'intelligence'. Part of the difficulty in defining intelligence is related to the development of culturally specific abilities. Measuring such an elusive concept is also problematic, particularly as there are debates about whether intelligence is fixed or changeable and the role of genetic inheritance and environmental factors. We considered how intelligence has been defined in different ways according to divergent theories. The traditional theories on intelligence and the works of Charles Spearman, Alfred Binet and Raymond Cattell were reviewed. We then looked at Sternberg's idea that intelligence is more than a static score and his triarchic model that characterises intelligence in terms of distinct components: analytic, creative and practical. The eight specific types of intelligence—linguistic, logical-mathematical, spatial, bodily-kinaesthetic, musical, interpersonal, intrapersonal and naturalistic—proposed by Gardner were discussed. The concept of emotional intelligence was considered, including the influential model of Goleman.

The chapter then focused on neuroscientific approaches to understanding cognitive capacity that involve understanding the brain's role in intelligence. We detailed the early development of the brain and the way that general intelligence involves multiple areas throughout the brain, identifying key regions. Changes in speed and efficiency along with maturation of the frontal lobes are an important aspect of cognitive development and intelligence. The frontal lobes play a role across a range of cognitive capacities in reasoning, abstract thought, managing conflict, self-regulation of emotions, working memory, paying attention and concentrating on tasks. This area does not fully mature until adulthood. Factors that enable or constrain the development of capacities and individual differences in general intelligence associated with differences in brain structure and function were outlined. Links between nature and nurture were discussed.

Implications for Teaching

There is evidence to suggest that the development of general intelligence can be significantly influenced by long-term intervention programs in school. Intervention research designed within the developmental tradition suggests that the central meaning-making mechanisms of the mind can be strengthened, restructured and developed if appropriately influenced (Adey et al., 2007).

The work of Adey et al. (2007) in particular can form the basis of an action plan that teachers can easily put into operation in the classroom to raise the general cognitive abilities of their students.

1 Learning activities need to generate cognitive stimulation and challenge rather than being comfortably within the reach of the learner's current processing capability.

2 Learning should be collaborative in the sense that learners learn to listen to one another, to argue and to justify and become accustomed to changing their position.

3 Teachers need to continually raise awareness in students of what may be abstracted from any particular domain-specific learning:

   a recognising factors in the concept, such as organisation of information that caused difficulties

   b connecting the present concept to other known concepts

   c controlling the thinking and learning processes to transfer mental power from the teacher to the thinker, so the students gradually become self-reliant and self-regulating rather than dependent on the teacher.

4 Learning experiences need to be connected to the concept space and the learning space of the past. That is, have similar concepts already been mastered? How does the present concept relate to them? How was learning of these other concepts in the past handled? Check if these difficulties are specific to this concept, to all concepts similar to it or to any concept.

Ask yourself...

1 In a sense all great teachers have known the strategies in the action plan above but why are they rarely practised?

2 Is teaching for cognitive stimulation more demanding or risky in the classroom than direct instruction on content? If so, why?

3 In Australia, the United States, the United Kingdom and many other Western countries, education has become an important plank in politicians' claims for the way in which they will improve society. This means that schools are typically dictated to by non-professionals who see education primarily as the transmission of information that is valued as culturally important (Adey et al., 2007). What are the implications for teachers?

4 How can you as a teacher contribute to debates about appropriate teaching pedagogies? What kind of teaching pedagogies would you promote: cognitive stimulation or direct teaching? What kind of evidence would you need to back up your claims?

PRACTICAL ACTIVITIES

1   Sternberg's triarchic model of intelligence includes three elements: analytical/componential, creative/experiential and practical/contextual. His view of intelligence revolves around the interchange of analytical, practical and creative aspects of the mind. Develop a profile of yourself and list the capacities that you have under each component of the model. Describe an activity that you do regularly that involves more than one component.

2   The eight specific types of intelligence Gardner proposes are linguistic, logical-mathematical, spatial, bodily-kinaesthetic, musical, interpersonal, intrapersonal and naturalistic. There has also been some discussion about a ninth intelligence—existential intelligence—manifested when an individual is concerned with reasoning about the meaning of life, demonstrating they are spiritually smart or have metaphysical intelligence. Draw a conceptual map and, for each type of intelligence, identify everyday experiences that take place in the classroom that demonstrate it.

3   Evidence tells us that the lack of appropriate neural stimulation via experience can lead to alterations in the way a child's genetic factors are expressed. Develop a list of experiences in early childhood that might affect a child's neural development.

4   Neuroscience is offering us evidence of the connection between our genetic make-up, our predetermined neural capacities and the role of the environment in shaping our brains. Is the nature versus nurture debate still valid? Divide into two groups. Have one group make a list of evidence to support the role of nurture and one group make a list of evidence to support the role of nature. Then have the great debate!

5   Discuss the implications of Western notions of intelligence on classroom practice.

STUDY QUESTIONS

1   According to Spearman, what is general mental ability or 'g'?

2   Cattell refers to crystallised and fluid intelligences: what is the difference?

3   What components make up Sternberg's triarchic model of intelligence?

4   What are the eight intelligences that Gardner describes?

5   According to Goleman's theory of emotional intelligence, what are the five emotional capabilities?

6   What is the role of myelination in developing cognitive capacities in the brain?

7   According to Haier and Jung (2007), what regions of the brain are related to attention, memory and more complex functions such as language?

8   What lobe in the brain is associated with cognitive capacities, is the last to form in the womb and not fully mature until early adulthood?

9   Explain the links between nature and nurture in terms of cognitive capacities.

10   From an educational point of view, what is the significance of neuroplasticity of intelligence?

11   Why is neural efficiency in the brain important for cognitive capacity?

SOMETHING TO THINK ABOUT 4.4

We know that from around six years of age a child's brain demonstrates a greater degree of sophistication and most children demonstrate skills such as drawing, language comprehension and greater powers of attention, concentration, self-regulation and emotional control. Children tend to be better at thinking, and their reasoning becomes more logical as their brains start to demonstrate greater efficiency and speed in the frontal lobe. But, in terms of maturation of a child, the prefrontal lobes do not fully mature until the third decade of life.

Ask yourself...

Q

1   As a teacher, what are the implications of this development at six years if you are teaching five-year-olds?

2   As a teacher, what are the implications of maturation in the frontal lobes in the third decade if you are teaching fifteen-year-olds?

FURTHER READING

Gardner, H. (2011). *The Unschooled Mind: How Children Think and How Schools Should Teach*. New York, NY: Basic Books.

Goleman, D. (1995). *Emotional Intelligence: Why It Can Matter More than IQ*. New York, NY: Bantam Books.

Goleman, D. (2006). *Social Intelligence: The New Science of Human Relationships*. London, UK: Random House.

Nagel, M. C. (2012). *In the Beginning: The Brain, Early Development and Learning*. Melbourne, Australia: ACER Press.

Sternberg, R. J. & Grigorenko, E. L. (2000): *Teaching for Successful Intelligence*. Arlington Heights, IL: Skylight.

VIDEO LINKS

Triarchic Theory of Intelligence
https://www.youtube.com/watch?v=L7C7qIRYiv0

Overview of practical, creative and analytic areas of intelligence proposed by Sternberg.

Massachusetts School of Law at Andover: *What is Multiple Intelligence Theory? Howard Gardner and the Theory of Multiple Intelligicence [sic]*
https://www.youtube.com/watch?v=KEFpaY3GI-I

Discussion about different faculties that may be linked to intelligence.

WEBLINKS

Emily Singer, Brain images reveal the secret to higher intelligence, *MIT Technology Review.*
https://www.technologyreview.com/s/412678/brain-images-reveal-the-secret-to-higher-iq/

Article about how the brain plays a critical role in determining intelligence.

Anatomy and functional areas of the brain
http://www.dana.org/uploadedImages/Images/neuroanatomy_large.jpg

Diagram gives detailed look at areas of the brain and related functions including higher mental
functions associated with the frontal lobe.

5

LANGUAGE DEVELOPMENT AND LEARNING

> The acquisition of language and speech seems deceptively simple. Young children learn their mother tongue rapidly and effortlessly, from babbling at 6 months of age to full sentences by the age of 3 years, and follow the same developmental path regardless of culture. Linguists, psychologists and neuroscientists have struggled to explain how children do this, and why it is so regular if the mechanism of acquisition depends on learning and environmental input.
>
> (Kuhl, 2004, p. 831)

LEARNING OUTCOMES

As you read through this chapter and undertake the exercises at the end, you will gain the ability to complete these tasks successfully:

→ describe and discuss traditional theories of language development offered by behaviourist, nativist and socioculturalists

→ explain the contributions of neuroscience to our understandings of language development and learning

→ understand the complex processes involved in neural fine-tuning associated with language acquisition and how this takes place during periods of high neural plasticity

→ discuss the implications of neuroscientific understandings for enhancing oral language development in the classroom.

KEY TERMS

- language
- literacy
- behaviourist
- nativist
- universal grammar
- socioculturalist
- Wernicke's area
- Broca's area
- telegraphic speech

Peppertree Primary is a small school in an up-market area of a metropolitan city. The school tends to have high-achieving children with very committed parents who like to volunteer at the school. There are high expectations on the teachers to ensure all children are progressing well, particularly in literacy. When a child is struggling academically, it is expected the teacher will deal with the issue immediately and provide any support needed. Jack is a six-year-old boy who appears very quiet and happy but then suddenly becomes very agitated and frustrated when the class is engaged in particular activities. Tom Baker, his teacher, is perplexed by the change in his personality. Tom has tried to have conversations with Jack to try to get to know him and Jack has talked about his love of computer games and watching movies. He has also talked about his three older brothers who also love gaming. But Jack does not seem to enjoy engaging in much conversation, seems to have a very limited vocabulary and often struggles finding the words he wants to say. Tom is reluctant to approach Jack's parents or a school specialist at this stage as he feels that he does not really know what is going on. He does know that Jack is in the lower reading and writing groups but the other boys in these groups do not seem to get agitated. Tom decides to take special note of Jack throughout the day and anecdotally record when he sees Jack become agitated or frustrated. After a week of observations, Tom notices that Jack is happy and engaged in activities such as sport, hands-on mathematics activities and individual work. Jack also seems to love morning tea and lunch break and happily goes to play with friends at these times. He becomes agitated when he is engaged in small group work, reading activities and whole-class discussions. At times he even becomes aggressive.

1   Why do you think Jack is agitated and frustrated during particular activities?

2   Why do you think Jack's attitude and behaviour change?

3   What individual characteristics, classroom, family or peer situations could be contributing to this?

4   What is Tom Baker's role as a classroom teacher?

5   What are some strategies Tom could use to help Jack and how long will he have to implement them?

6   Who should be involved in supporting Jack?

INTRODUCTION

Language
A body of sounds
(phonemes), words,
word order (syntax),
and meaning
(semantics)—
common to people
of the same cultural
tradition.

One of the amazing things about humans is our capacity for language. A constant flow of words appears to stream effortlessly as we choose from a personal lexicon of 60 000 to 180 000 words. Concurrently, we have a remarkable capacity for understanding the enormous amount of language that is part of our everyday lives. As most children appear born to communicate, we often take for granted the complex processes involved in this astonishing phenomenon. Do you remember your own journey developing language skills and the ability to communicate? Most people will not remember, as language appears to develop rapidly; oral language is one of a child's most natural and impressive accomplishments. Most children seem born to speak and to interact socially, with young babies using cries and gestures well before they master words. Babies' first babbles are eagerly awaited by doting parents, who perhaps know their child has just taken a major step towards communicating. Language can be defined as a body of sounds (phonemes), words, word order (syntax) and meaning (semantics)—with systems for their use common to people of the same community, nation or cultural tradition. The capacity for language serves as a cornerstone for human cognition with research demonstrating how the unified nature of human language arises from a shared, species-specific computational ability (Berwick, Friederici, Chomsky & Bolhuis, 2013). While a body of work points to communication used by animals, many researchers argue that animal communication lacks a key aspect of human oral language: that is, the creation of new patterns of signs under varied circumstances (Hockett, 1960). While the term 'animal language' is used, research demonstrates that animal languages are not as complex or expressive as human language (Martinelli, 2010). For example, although songbirds share with humans a vocal imitation learning ability, with a similar underlying neural organisation, researchers believe oral language is uniquely human (Berwick et al., 2013). Studies with primates demonstrate how they have learnt to link visual symbols on keyboards to objects and some can understand sign language but, to date, it has not been possible to teach any other species spoken language (Carter, 2009). As complex oral language is a uniquely human capacity, the nature of language acquisition continues to inspire scholars to investigate this remarkable process.

One of the questions many researchers continue to ask is whether language acquisition is innate or a capacity that is developed during the first stages of life. While the nuances of a specific language appear to be learnt, biology and neuroscience tell us that a significant amount of language acquisition is innate (Nagel, 2012a; Pinker, 2009). Evidence would suggest that our capacities are innate due to the localisation of language in the left hemisphere of the brain; the anatomical differences in the hemispheres that appear in the developing embryo; the ability of newborns to distinguish between sounds; the universality of language acquisition for children of all cultures; and the fact that there is a critical period for language acquisition (Kouvelas, 2007; Kuhl, 2010). It is with great excitement that most children say their first words between twelve and eighteen months of age and develop oral language by age four (Nagel, 2012a). In this way, there are predictable language pathways as children learn to communicate through a native language. By the time a child starts formal schooling, most children know the fundamentals of their language and can converse with peers and adults alike. Significantly, children in every culture master the complicated system of their native language, unless the child experiences severe deprivation or physical problems.

It is important for us to have an understanding of language development, as early language acquisition and development is an essential ingredient for children's ongoing learning and educational achievement. This is particularly important as language facilitates communication, the building of relationships and allows children to engage with and interpret their world. Language, whether it is English, Mandarin or Warlpiri, is therefore crucial in children's development as they learn to competently think and clearly articulate. As you read this chapter, we would like you to reflect on the children's language development you have observed and to thoughtfully acknowledge your own experiences, ideas and knowledge about language and learning. As you participate in the activities and respond to the questions orally and through the act of writing down your thoughts, we would like you to reflect on the significant role of language in your own learning.

LANGUAGE AND LITERACY

Literacy
The ability to use language, numbers, images and other means to understand and use the dominant symbol systems of a culture.

Before we begin, the fundamental differences between language and literacy development should be noted with an understanding that oral language provides the foundation for further literacy skills. While there is a strong link between language and literacy, the terms are often used inappropriately, as if they are synonymous. Language is the ability to acquire and use communication, relying on the context and providing a means of social interaction. This communication involves understanding (receptive language), and our use of language to express ourselves (expressive language). In this way, language offers a means of sharing thoughts, emotions and needs, and participation in the dominant culture (Ahola & Kovacik, 2007). Language development includes acquiring the sounds, meanings, words and sequences of words, volume, voice tone, inflection and turn-taking rules that must be coordinated for a child to communicate effectively in conversations.

Children develop language as they develop other cognitive abilities by actively trying to make sense of what they hear and by looking for patterns and making up rules to put together the jigsaw puzzle of language (Woolfolk-Hoy, 2005). While first developing as a set of oral skills, language can over time then be articulated into written, symbolic and pictorial formats.

Literacy, on the other hand, refers to the capacity to engage with the creation and comprehension of the symbols, pictures and signs used to represent language. While humans have used oral language for around four million years, the ability to represent the sounds of language by written symbols is a relatively recent phenomenon (Kotulak, 1997). While the majority of people around the planet were illiterate until the twentieth century, today it is a general expectation that all members of society should be functionally literate and able to read and write (Kotulak, 1997; Wolfe & Nevills, 2004). Being literate provides access to valued resources, participation in the dominant culture and is a fundamental key to educational achievement. Today in Australia, a repertoire of literacy skills permits access to education, training, employment and participation in local and global economic and cultural exchanges. If you review national and international political agendas, educational policies and national media coverage, you will not be surprised to learn there is currently unprecedented theoretical and cultural concern with literacy embedded in a variety of institutional orders, including economies of knowledge, education, communication, public and private administration and entertainment.

Without a doubt there is a strong relationship between oral language and literacy, as the ability to communicate enables a child to access skills necessary to read, write and interpret in a variety of modes. Simply put, to be literate is the ability to work with language in the non-spoken form. The raw materials of sounds, words, sentences and meaning are all found in oral language. In this sense, oral language provides the building blocks for literate practices. For example, the more complex aspects of oral language, including syntax or grammar, complex measures of vocabulary and listening comprehension are related to later reading comprehension. Significantly, reading comprehension depends on language abilities that have been developing since birth. The early oral development of vocabulary and grammar support comprehension, as each facilitates understanding of words and their interrelationships in and across individual sentences in a text (Kintsch & Kintsch, 2005). Notwithstanding the important links between literacy and a child's future successes across many facets of life, this chapter focuses on the development of language and how this ultimately leads to children becoming literate.

As you work through this chapter, you will look at some traditional theories informed by an understanding that language skills are learnt, and also at more contemporary perspectives informed by what science can tell us about our innate capacities and the contextual influences on language development. These understandings are important as language is the key to communication, learning and thinking.

LANGUAGE DEVELOPMENT IN CHILDREN

One of the interesting things about language is that the vast majority of children learn to speak and communicate articulately without any major difficulties and without any formal training. While there is an array of theories that attempt to explain how this occurs, there is no unified understanding of how humans acquire language and the skills for oral capacities. In the next section, we will consider some of the traditional theories that inform our understandings of language acquisition and reflect on what these perspectives have to offer in terms of contemporary perceptions. While traditionally there has been a nature versus nurture debate—with some researchers emphasising the influences of learning on language acquisition and others emphasising the biological influences—today, most researchers acknowledge that both nature and nurture play a role in language acquisition. After acknowledging the contributions of traditional theories about language acquisition, this chapter will move on to focus more specifically on the contribution of modern neuroscience and developing understandings of the language as primarily a faculty of the mind (Pinker & Jackendoff, 2005).

Over the last decade, there has been a significant increase in neuroscience research examining young children's processing of language at the phonetic (sound), word and sentence levels (Baron-Cohen, 2003; Eliot, 2000; Herschkowitz & Herschkowitz, 2004). This research indicates there are neural substrates for all levels of language identified at early points in development (Nagel, 2012a). At the same time, intervention studies have demonstrated the ways in which the brain retains its plasticity for language processing (Eliot, 2000). While we have been informed by a great deal of empirical research about child development, we are still in the early stages of clearly articulating the neural mechanisms associated with children's innate predisposition to learn when exposed to natural language (Kuhl, 2010). Without adhering to any specific theory of language acquisition, there are some aspects of language development that, for most children, appear universal. If you were to visit a variety of diverse cultures, you would find that children learn language in a remarkably regular way, typically speaking in full and complex grammatical sentences by the age of four or five years (Eliot, 2000). In order to master any language, without much difficulty children will learn the basic components of language:

→ *Phonology* refers to making the meaningful sounds used by a particular language. In English, any word can be broken down into the basic sounds of vowels or consonants or both, which are technically referred to as *phonemes*.

→ *Morphology* refers to the system used to group phonemes into meaningful combinations of sounds and words. Once grouped, these are referred to as *morphemes*, which are the smallest meaningful combinations of sounds in a language. In English, for example, a morpheme may be a word such as 'dog', a letter such as the 's' in 'dogs', a prefix such as 'dis' in 'distasteful' or a suffix such as 'ed' in 'walked'.

→ *Syntax* or *grammar* refers to the rules specifying how words are combined to make meaningful phrases and sentences.

→ *Semantics* refers to the meaning of words or phrases in various sentences or contexts (Nagel, 2012a).

It is important to remember that early childhood is a critical time for children to master language and its interrelated components. It is significant, as by the age of two years most children are beginning to learn to speak; by their sixth birthday, their conversational skills may be as linguistically sophisticated as those of a sixteen-year-old sibling (Blakemore & Frith, 2005; Nagel, 2012a). Equally important is the understanding that, across cultures, children from one to four years of age typically go through predictable phases, as they move towards mastering oral communication. Babbling leads to experimenting with single words to two-word phrases and eventually the ability to engage in increasingly complex sentences (Eliot, 2000; Wolfe & Nevills, 2004). The ease at which most children learn to communicate early in life, compared to the difficulty adults encounter when attempting to learn a second language, suggests that language, in itself, may be innate (Nagel, 2012a).

Ask yourself...

Language is the ability to develop and use communication skills, including how we understand language (*receptive language*) and how we use language to express ourselves (*expressive language*). The development of oral language is one of the most significant factors in children's learning and development and relies on conversations between young children and more competent language users. If indeed language is innate, how would you explain the language abilities of a child who often appears uninterested and tired and lacks the following communication skills:

- uses fewer words or shorter sentences than other children of the same age (expressive)

- points and gestures more than he or she speaks (expressive)

- uses incorrect grammar (for example, I going to school) (expressive)

- has difficulty finding the word he or she wants to say (expressive)?

TRADITIONAL THEORIES OF LANGUAGE DEVELOPMENT

After more than fifty years of research into children's language acquisition, there are still many mysteries about humans' remarkable ability to master complex skills. In this section we will briefly look at some of the traditional approaches to understanding language development offered by behaviourists (Skinner), nativists (Chomsky) and socioculturalists (Vygotsky). You may be familiar with these theorists and they may have influenced the way you currently think about language acquisition. While it is important to acknowledge early theories of language development in children and how our current understandings often build on early work, modern science now affords us opportunities to observe and understand neurodevelopmental processes and how language works in the brain. Human cognitive neuroscience seeks to understand the complex interaction between brain function and behaviours such as language. But first we will consider some of the scholars who have contributed to theories of language development.

SKINNER—BEHAVIOURIST

> The consequences of an act affect the probability of its occurring again. (Skinner, 1957)

Skinner (1957), a behaviourist, provided one of the earliest scientific explanations of language acquisition as he attempted to account for language development due to environmental influences. You may have already read about Skinner's classic studies on pigeon behaviours. Behaviourists, such as Skinner, assume that human behaviours are determined by learning in response to reinforcement. Whether by classical conditioning or operant conditioning, there is a belief that children will acquire new skills as actions produce positive or negative outcomes. Responses that are positively reinforced will be repeated and those that are punished will not. From this perspective, it is believed that correct utterances are positively reinforced when the child realises the communicative value of words and phrases. One such example is when a child says 'up' and a parent smiles and picks a child up; the child will find this outcome rewarding, enhancing the child's language development. While the associations between stimuli, actions and responses have been used to explain many aspects of human behaviour, when it comes to accounting for the prolific language acquisition of a young child, it is problematic. Critics, such as Chomsky (1965), point out that behaviourist explanations are inadequate, as learning language through stimuli, actions and responses cannot account for the rapid rate at which children acquire language. Similarly, with the infinite number of sentences in a language, this acquisition cannot be

Behaviourist Assumes the behaviour of a human is a consequence of reinforcement and punishment.

LINKAGE
See Chapter ❶ for a detailed discussion of classical and operant conditioning.

learnt by imitation. Critics also point out that children appear to acquire language skills even without the consistent correction of their syntax (Ambridge & Lieven, 2011; Chomsky, 1965; Pinker, 2009).

CHOMSKY—NATIVIST

> UG [universal grammar] may be regarded as a characterization of the genetically determined language faculty. One may think of this … faculty as a 'language acquisition device,' an innate component of the human mind that yields a particular language through interaction with present experience, a device that converts experience into a system of knowledge attained: knowledge of one or another language. (Chomsky, 1971, p. 3)

Nativist
Believes biological influences bring about language development.

Noam Chomsky, considered by many as the world's most important linguist to date, was a critic of Skinner's account of language acquisition. Chomsky is considered a nativist and argued that biological influences bring about language development as children would never acquire the skills needed for processing an infinite number of sentences if the language acquisition mechanism depended on language input alone. Noam Chomsky significantly altered our understanding of language in 1957, when he presented a revolutionary theory of language development and coined the term universal grammar. In this theory, he proposed that human brains have a language acquisition device (LAD), an innate mechanism allowing children to develop language skills. According to his theory, all children are born with universal grammar, which makes them receptive to the common features of all languages. Because of this hard-wired background in grammar, children then pick up a language when they are exposed to its particular grammar (Chomsky, 1957). Most linguistic theorists agree with Chomsky's ideas and believe that children around the world acquire language so easily because at birth they possess a 'mental organ' for learning language and a universal capacity for untangling syntax and grammar (Bjorklund, 2005).

Universal grammar
Proposes the ability to learn grammar is hard-wired into the brain: that human brains have a language acquisition device (LAD), an innate mechanism allowing children to develop language skills.

Chomsky (1957) argued that—given the universal nature of language and that all natural languages are similar in structure, function and rules—language must be inherent in the mind. He then extended his theory to include that humans possess a *mental grammar* and an *innate grammar*. Chomsky, who continues to research in this area, suggests that a brain's mental grammar allows it to combine nouns, verbs and objects in an endless variety of sentences, while an innate grammar mechanism that is built into our brains allows us to acquire the complex skills of language very early in life (Bjorklund, 2005; Nagel, 2012a). In this way all the grammatical information needed to combine categories—for example, noun and verb—into simple combinations is provided, with the child's task then to learn the words of his or her language (Ambridge & Lieven, 2011). For example, children instinctively know how to combine a noun (for example, 'girl') and a verb (to skip) into a meaningful, correct sentence (A girl skips) (Ambridge & Lieven, 2011). Chomsky's claim that children universally acquire language easily because at birth they possess a 'mental organ' for learning language and a capacity for untangling syntax and grammar is supported by most linguistic theorists (Bjorklund, 2005). Recent understandings of the brain derived from neuroscientific studies appear to support Chomsky and those who follow his theories (Nagel, 2012a).

The work of Steven Pinker

Steven Pinker (1995, 2009) also argues that humans are born with an innate capacity for language, supporting Chomsky's concept of a universal grammar. He proposes that the human ability to communicate through oral language is evolutionary, in response to the need for communication among social hunter-gatherers. In this way, language is a specialised adaptation with specific structures in the brain that recognise general rules of speech. As evidence of the universality of language, Pinker (1994) notes that children spontaneously invent a consistent grammatical speech, even if they grow up among a mixed-culture population, and that deaf babies 'babble' with their hands as others normally do with voice. He also notes that specific types of brain damage cause specific impairments of language, such as Broca's aphasia or Wernicke's aphasia.

Many will argue that the ability to learn language is the result of innate, language-specific learning mechanisms that can now be monitored due to advances in neuroscience. While mastery of language requires exposure to language during infancy and early childhood, it is proposed that the neural fine-tuning, associated with learning a language's particular parameters, takes place during a period of high neuroplasticity (Eliot, 2000; Nagel, 2012a). There is growing evidence that children have innate mechanisms that predispose them to perceive categorically linguistic stimuli—such as phonemes, words, syntactic categories and phrases—and exposure to these types of linguistic stimuli facilitates the neural fine-tuning necessary for normal language acquisition (Stromswold, 1998).

LEV VYGOTSKY—SOCIOCULTURALIST

> The specifically human capacity for language enables children to provide for auxiliary tools in the solution of difficult tasks, to overcome impulsive action, to plan a solution to a problem prior to its execution, and to master their own behavior. (Vygotsky, 1978, p. 28)

While scholars such as Steven Pinker (2009) have gone on to relate empirical findings to the core of Chomsky's innate propositions, this approach is inadequate for many developmental theorists, as the nativist account does not evolve from observations but from theories of how language *could* be acquired. Moreover, critics surmise that, while innate theories of language acquisition have provided a theory that accounts for the initial and final states of language acquisition, the theory is not developmental and lacks justification about the mechanism of learning (Ambridge & Lieven, 2011). From this perspective, it has been

Socioculturalist
Theory that language
development
depends upon
interactions between
the child and the
environment.

See Chapter ❾ for
more detail on the
sociocultural factors
of learning.

See Chapter ❾
for more detail on
scaffolding and
Vygotsky's theory.

argued that to fully understand early language development there is also a need to consider the nature and function of the mechanism that drives language learning. Socioculturalist approaches provide an explanation of language development emphasising the role of social interactions of the developing child. This approach is based on sociocultural theories of Soviet psychologist Lev Vygotsky.

According to sociocultural theorists such as Vygotsky (1962), the development of language occurs due to a complex interaction between the child and the environment. The sociocultural approach emphasises the role of feedback and reinforcement in language acquisition, and specifically asserts that much of a child's language acquisition develops from modelling and interaction with parents and other adults, who often provide support—*scaffolding*. Language development is then influenced by social and cognitive development; as children develop language, they build a symbol system helping them to understand the world. Vygotsky's theory focuses on interaction and communication with others as key (see Chapter 9 for more detail). While humans are born to speak and appear to have an innate gift for figuring out the rules of the language used in their environment, sociocultural theorists point to the significance of the environment itself. Teachers can help enhance natural language development by providing environments rich in language-development experiences.

In traditional developmental-psychology accounts of language acquisition, the social aspect of the process has often been overlooked. But it has been proposed that, as language is a social behaviour, the associated structures are social conventions (Tomasello, 1992). Children therefore acquire social-communicative functions, including lexical (word) and syntactic symbols, within culturally constituted interactions with others. For example, children begin by experimenting with linguistic rules on their own, saying, 'I goed home' or 'I see your feets', eventually learning through experimentation and feedback the conventional forms of 'went' and 'feet'. As children strive to connect and communicate with others, they learn to make sense of experiences (Wells, 1986).

Social speech, private speech and inner silent speech

Vygotsky (1987) proposed three forms of language development: social speech, private speech and silent inner speech (also see Chapter 9). While the three forms of speech begin as separate systems, they merge at around the age of three. According to Vygotsky (1987), children develop self-regulation as their language moves through a series of stages. A child's behaviour is first regulated by others as a parent or carer uses language and gestures, for example, saying 'No!' when the child moves to touch a hot oven. The child then learns to say 'No!' to another child who, for example, tries to take a toy. Children then move from external social speech to private speech in attempts to regulate their behaviour, saying 'no' quietly to themselves as they are tempted to touch the hot oven. Eventually this private speech is internalised into silent inner speech.

→ *Social speech* (typically from the age of two) refers to external communication as a child talks to others.

→ *Private speech* (typically from two to seven years) is directed to the self and serves an intellectual self-regulation function. It provides a way for children to plan activities and strategies and is a transition point between social and inner speech, helping children overcome task obstacles, and also enhancing thinking and consciousness. Around the age of seven, private speech transforms into silent inner speech. If you have visited a prep classroom you may have heard four- to five year-olds talking to themselves as they work away on projects such as building a block tower: 'Yes, that's the right size. No, that one's too big. Maybe I need some help!'

→ *Inner speech* (typically transition begins from seven years) is thought connected with words. Thought and inner speech become thinking in pure meanings. Inner speech has an important function of its own and, as the child matures, private speech moves from spoken, to whispered speech, silent lip movements and then finally the child just 'thinks' the guiding words (Vygotsky, 1962, 1978).

According to Vygotsky, language development is a process that begins through social contact with others and then gradually moves inwards through a series of transitional stages towards the development of inner speech. In this way inner speech is speech for oneself while external speech is for others. This transition from audible private speech to silent inner speech is a fundamental process in cognitive development, as the child is using language to accomplish important cognitive activities such as directing attention, solving problems, planning, forming concepts and gaining self-control (Berk & Spuhl, 1995). In this way, children tend to use more private speech when they are having difficulty trying to solve a problem or they are feeling confused.

As sociocultural theory proposes that language is learnt through social and cultural interactions, the quality of these interactions is considered significant (Díaz-Rico & Weed, 2010). From this perspective, teachers need to understand the diverse cultural contexts of students' backgrounds to be able to understand how their students' minds have developed. As language plays an important role in human development, and we internalise language that we learn from our social context, language then becomes the basis for our mental tool kit (Díaz-Rico & Weed, 2010).

SUMMARY

As we mentioned earlier, there have been many theories about language development over the years, offering different perspectives. We have looked briefly at a few of the more prominent theories (behaviourist, nativist, sociocultural). While these theories have influenced what we know about language acquisition, contemporary science provides scientific evidence and opportunities to support or question what we have traditionally believed.

What we aim to do in the next section is unpack what we now know about language development informed by contemporary science and understandings about the brain. From this perspective, the contributions of linguists such as Chomsky are built upon and supported by neuroscience, and the contributions of cultural theorists are acknowledged, due to an understanding that, while children may arrive into the world with neural fine-tuning associated with learning language, this acquisition actually takes place in cultural contexts during periods of high neuroplasticity.

Ask yourself...

Noam Chomsky, sometimes referred to as the father of modern linguists, proposed that the principles underlying the structure of language are biologically (nature) determined in the human mind and genetically transmitted. This theoretical perspective is considered *nativist*. Vygotsky proposed that language develops through social interactions (nurture) as humans are driven to communicate. This approach is considered a *sociocultural* perspective.

1 Write a list of factors to support the nativist approach.

2 Write a list of factors to support the sociocultural approach.

3 Discuss your stance on the nature versus nurture debate. Is there still need for such a debate?

4 Reflect on your own language development. What factors enabled or constrained your personal acquisition of language?

5 Vygotsky argued that private speech helps students to regulate their thinking. Teachers who insist on total silence with young students as they are working on problems may make things harder. When you are in the classroom, will you allow or even encourage students to use private speech? If so, how will you facilitate this?

LANGUAGE AND THE BRAIN

The past decade has produced an incredible burst of neuroscience research examining young children's language development. Contributing to advancements in research are rapid advances in safe, non-invasive brain measures that can be used with children. Many people are finding exciting the multiple brain systems that underlie human language capacities that are being revealed by neuroscience. We now know that understanding language development is intrinsically linked to understanding the brain. While we have moved beyond the classic nature versus nurture debates, neuroscientists are still breaking ground about the neural mechanisms that underlie language development (Kuhl, 2010). Concurring with much of the work of Noam Chomsky, who argued that language must be inherent in the mind, contemporary neuroscience is beginning to uncover the structures and processes responsible for receptive and expressive language. While cutting-edge technology now allows us to observe functioning within the brain, it was actually long before modern technology was available that researchers identified regions of the left hemisphere responsible for important functions of language. One of the most apparent reasons to suspect that language derives from an innate and distinct mental organ is how it is physically localised in the brain (Eliot, 2000). While we considered the functions of the brain in some detail in Chapter 3, it is now important to revisit the regions of the brain associated with language.

See Chapter ❸ for more on understanding the brain and neural development.

WERNICKE'S AREA AND BROCA'S AREA

The regions where speech production and language comprehension are processed are usually located in the left hemisphere (half) of the brain (see Figure 5.1).

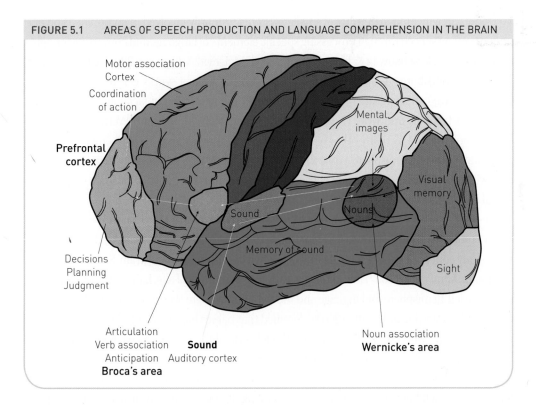

FIGURE 5.1   AREAS OF SPEECH PRODUCTION AND LANGUAGE COMPREHENSION IN THE BRAIN

Motor association Cortex
Coordination of action
Mental images
Prefrontal cortex
Visual memory
Sound
Nouns
Decisions Planning Judgment
Memory of sound
Sight
Articulation
Verb association   **Sound**
Anticipation   Auditory cortex
Broca's area
Noun association
Wernicke's area

While we looked at the functioning of the brain in some detail in Chapter 3, it is important to revisit the regions of the brain that are responsible for receptive language and expressive language. Interestingly, while we now have highly advanced technology that allows us to observe functioning within the brain, early findings about the relationship between the brain and language developed from studies conducted with people of different ages who had suffered some type of brain injury or trauma (Nagel, 2012a). Much of what we understand now about the brain developed from studies with individuals who experienced some sort of impairment. For example, it has been long known that victims of a stroke in the left side of the brain typically suffer some measure of language difficulties, as language centres of the brain are predominantly housed in the left hemisphere. Karl Wernicke and Paul Broca are two researchers who studied language and aspects of brain injury; they found regions of the left hemisphere responsible for comprehension (word recognition) and syntax (and speech production) that now bear their surnames as neuro-anatomical labels.

Wernicke's area

The temporal lobes, located just above the ears, are responsible for processing auditory stimuli and language comprehension and the temporal lobes also include Wernicke's area (Nagel, 2012a).

Broca's area

Wernicke's area includes a number of smaller systems primarily involved in comprehension and understanding speech through processing specific elements of language and converting thoughts into language (Herschkowitz & Herschkowitz, 2004; McDevitt & Ormrod, 2007). Broca's area, which also contributes to our capacities for language, acts like a syntax centre by synthesising language so we can articulate our thoughts through the regulation of facial and hand activity, allowing us to speak and write (Nagel, 2008; Sylwester, 2005). Broca's and Wernicke's work has been complemented by many other types of research acknowledging the left hemisphere as the dominant language hemisphere, while the right hemisphere, with its strong links to emotion and creativity, is responsible for prosody or the inflection and musical quality that lends emphasis to verbal communication (Eliot, 2000; Nagel, 2012a).

The early works of Broca and Wernicke have also been supported by contemporary neuroscientific studies, with one of the most fascinating a study investigating how babies babble. In a landmark study concerning the responsibilities of the two hemispheres of the brain, Siobhan Holowka and Laura Ann Petitto (2002) found that, as early as five months of age, babies demonstrated the use of the left hemisphere for language and the right hemisphere for expressing emotion. As part of the study, Holowka and Petitto (2002) identified that babies babble out of the right side of their mouth and that, when they smile, they use the left side of the mouth. As we know that the left hemisphere controls the right side of the body, while the right hemisphere controls the left, it was determined that if babies babble out of the right side of the mouth then these sounds must be a function of the left hemisphere (Hirsh-Pasek & Golinkoff, 2004). Adults were also found to favour the right side of the mouth when speaking (Hirsh-Pasek & Golinkoff, 2004). The Holowka and Petitto (2002) study was published in the prestigious journal *Science*, and has been supported by numerous other works. It is now widely accepted that the left hemisphere of the brain is the dominant location for language with this lateralisation evident early in life, indicating that we are born biologically primed to learn language.

Wernicke's area
Part of the brain involved in comprehension and understanding speech; processes elements of language, converting thoughts into language.

Broca's area
Syntax centre in the brain synthesising language so we can articulate our thoughts through the regulation of facial and hand activity, allowing us to speak and write.

Connecting pathways

While Broca's area and Wernicke's area have been acknowledged as important in the processing of language, the white matter fibre pathways that connect them are also significant. New advances in technology have uncovered more language networks than originally thought, with pathways believed to specialise in different tasks (Wilson et al., 2011). Dense bundles of nerve fibres link Broca's area and Wernicke's area, connecting them by upper and lower white matter pathways (see Figure 5.2). Brain imaging and language tests show that roles played are different, with damage to the lower pathway producing damage to the lexicon and semantic capacities (Wilson et al., 2011). If you were to lose this capacity you would forget the names of things and meanings of word, while still being able to articulate sentences. Damage to the upper pathway would cause you to understand and remember the names of things but you would have trouble with complex sentences (Wilson et al., 2011). For example, if you were asked, 'A woman was walking in the middle of the highway. She didn't hear the truck coming. What happened to the woman?' You might reply, 'She was hit by the truck' or something similar. A patient with damage to the upper pathway might say something like 'truck, woman, hit' (Wilson et al., 2011).

FIGURE 5.2 BRAIN SCAN SHOWING THE ACTIVATION OF BROCA'S AREA (YELLOW SECTION) AND WERNICKE'S AREA (PINK SECTION) DURING LANGUAGE PROCESSING, AS WELL AS THE ACTIVATED WHITE MATTER PATHWAYS BETWEEN THEM AS REPRESENTED BY THE RED AND BLUE SECTIONS

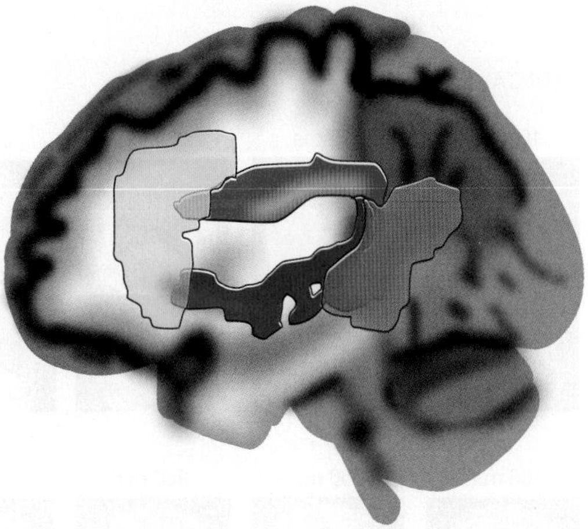

ORAL LANGUAGE

As we have already noted, it is important to recognise that the pathway for learning language for most children includes predictable phases that are similar whether you are born in Brisbane, Barcelona or Brazil.

In utero to six months: recognition

The timetable of language development actually begins long before an infant babbles out of the side of his or her mouth, with studies suggesting that learning the sounds of a language begin in utero, with babies listening in on their mother's conversations a couple of months before birth (Blakemore & Frith, 2005; Nagel, 2012a; Sousa, 2005). Researchers have actually identified that in utero babies tune into and respond to their mother's voice (Fifer & Moon, 1995; Mehler et al., 1988). When mothers speak, foetal heart rates change, and as soon as two days after birth babies show a preference for the sounds of their mother's voice and of their native tongues (Fifer & Moon, 1995; Mehler et al., 1988). These studies imply that children recognise their mother's speech and that they become habituated to their own language while in the womb, listening to Mum's conversations (Nagel, 2012a). Furthermore, researchers who looked at foetal heart rate changes noted that the mother's voice is a naturally occurring and important stimulus during the critical period in which there is significant development in virtually all areas of the brain (Fifer & Moon, 1995).

Modern technology allows us to see images of an infant's brain on hearing the sound of his or her mother's voice. The images in Figure 5.3 show an infant's brain activity while first listening to his mother's voice, and then a stranger's voice. Activation of the left side of the brain, responsible for language learning, is evident in the first instance, and activation in the right side of the brain, responsible for voice recognition, evident in the second instance. The contribution of interactions with mothers and those with close relationships to an infant appear to stimulate areas of the brain responsible for language.

FIGURE 5.3   THE PREFRONTAL LOBES

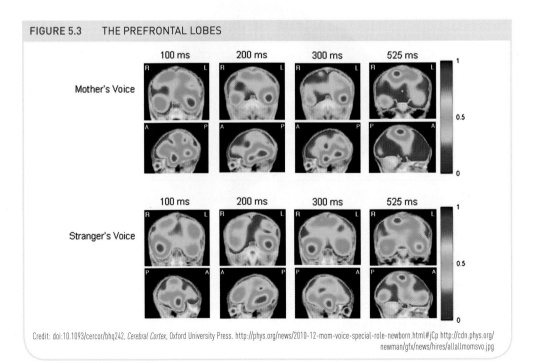

Credit: doi:10.1093/cercor/bhq242, *Cerebral Cortex*, Oxford University Press. http://phys.org/news/2010-12-mom-voice-special-role-newborn.html#jCp http://cdn.phys.org/newman/gfx/news/hires/allallmomsvo.jpg

Given the information we now have available, we have come to understand that sensory stimulation and establishment of the neural architecture of the brain occurs before birth. In this way, babies are already picking up the nuances of language before birth and can identify native speech as soon as 48 hours after birth (Fifer & Moon, 1995; Nagel, 2012a). It is then not surprising that children are born with a keen interest in language and appear predisposed to learn and understand language at a very young age (Blakemore & Frith, 2005; Hirsh-Pasek & Golinkoff, 2004). Before spoken language is evident, many babies are working out words and sentences by listening and identifying language patterns, all without any formal instructions or the help of a best-selling educational DVD!

Six to twelve months: babbling

At about six months of age babies recognise their native language and begin the first stage of expressing oral language: they start to babble (Kuhl, Tsao & Liu, 2003; Plotnik & Kouyoumdjian, 2010). Between six and nine months, infants recognise syllables and begin to develop an awareness of phonetic sequences. By the time they reach their first birthday, infants' perceptions of speech and understanding of language have been dramatically altered by exposure to their native language and by their first forays into communication through babbling (Kuhl et al., 2003; Nagel, 2012a). Babbling, while important, is just one part of the equation related to language development.

Eight to twelve months: first words

While babbling marks the first stage of language acquisition and development, the second stage is evident when a child performs a behaviour that excites its eagerly awaiting parents by saying his or her first words. The transition from babbling begins between eight and twelve months of age when a child begins to form sounds into words. Those initial words, in turn, usually fall into two groups—objects (for example, 'Dada', 'juice', 'cat') and actions or qualifiers (for example, 'up', 'more', 'hot'). Intuitively, adults realise that single words such as 'juice' usually stand for longer thoughts such as 'I want juice'. Language is then further developed when parents take this opportunity to elaborate on their child's single word utterance with responses such as, 'Oh, you want some juice do you? I'll get some for you'. Accordingly, parental interactions take on greater significance and conversations between adult and child begin to emerge.

Two years: combining words

At two years of age, children progress to the third stage of language development and begin to put words together into two-word combinations (Vouloumanos & Werker, 2004). This development gives parents and adults greater understanding of what a child is trying to communicate as well as demonstrating a child's capacity for identifying actions or relationships (for example, 'juice gone'; 'see cat'). It also demonstrates a growing understanding of grammar and expanding vocabulary, which continues to evolve.

Four years: telegraphic speech

By his or her fourth birthday, a child may delight party companions by articulating short sentences with increased grammatical understandings. But, during this time, while a child may be chatting endlessly, he or she will be conveying their thoughts using **telegraphic speech**. Telegraphic speech is a simplified means where only the most important content words are conveyed. Phrases may be devoid of articles (a, an, the), prepositions (in, out) and parts of some verbs (Plotnik & Kouyoumdjian, 2010). While the words give the lexical meaning, the sentences are often shortened. For example 'No, Daddy, no go sleep' will become 'No, Daddy, don't go to sleep'. And 'Mummy give milk me' is the telegraphic equivalent of 'Give me the milk, Mummy'. While 'Nelson make tower' includes the shortening of the verb, the child has used the verb in the correct place, indicating an understanding of subject, verb and direct object sequence.

While telegraphic speech may emerge during a child's second year, around the age of five children transition to speech more reflective of the basic rules of grammar. During these first formative years, language develops rapidly in the brain and a child's vocabulary will grow from 20 to 50 single words—at eighteen months to two years of age—to more than 2000 words by the time they are ready to enter school (Bjorklund, 2005; Plotnik & Kouyoumdjian, 2010). Language acquisition continues through primary and secondary school, and indeed throughout a person's lifetime. As oral language development is ongoing, it would seem that developing language capacities of students in the classroom is the responsibility of all teachers, regardless of the year level taught.

Telegraphic speech
Simplified speech including most important content but combinations may not include articles, prepositions or verbs.

Ask yourself...

Oral language permeates every facet of the school curriculum. The development of oral language is given an importance as great as that of reading and writing. Although the curriculum places a strong emphasis on oral language, it has been widely acknowledged that implementation is challenging for teachers.

- What is the value of promoting oral language with students in the classroom? What developmental and educational outcomes do enhanced oral skills achieve?
- What strategies would you engage to promote oral language in the classroom? How would you promote oral language in these age ranges:
  a   Prep to Year 3
  b   Year 4 to Year 7
  c   Year 8 to Year 12?

MATURATION AND BIOLOGICAL SEX DIFFERENCES

While learning language starts in infancy and can be a lifelong endeavour, it is important to remember that there can be significant variations as individual children mature and move from one stage to the next. Maturation involves the unfolding of changes associated with normal growth; it is a unique and natural process that takes place within the individual. As maturation and learning are inherently linked, many parents become very concerned about whether their child is reaching predefined developmental milestones. Parents, and teachers, can often give many examples of developmental differences in children as they move through the trajectory of language acquisition as children can differ in as much as a whole year in terms of when they pass through a particular stage, depending on the interaction between nature and nurture (Nagel, 2012a).

We now know that the progression of learning sounds, words and then grammatically correct speech is complex and inherently linked with the maturation of Wernicke's and Broca's areas. Wernicke's area, along with other regions of the brain responsible for language comprehension, develops before Broca's area. The neural layers of Broca's area do not mature until roughly four years of age, while full maturation of Wernicke's area is evident by the time a child turns two years of age (Nagel, 2012a). Broca's area also appears to myelinate later than Wernicke's area. Myelin is detectable in all cortical layers of the Wernicke's area by two years of age but not evident in Broca's area until a child reaches four to six years of age (Diamond & Hopson, 1999; Eliot, 2000).

With maturation, increased myelinisation and interconnectivity in the brain produces faster and far more efficient capacities, with this increasing neural speed and efficiency contributing to the child's intellectual development. Synaptic density between regions of the brain related to language and reading allows for increased language skills, improved vocabulary and development of higher order thinking skills (Herschkowitz & Herschkowitz, 2004; Kagan & Herschkowitz, 2005). Increased connections between Broca's and Wernicke's areas enhance language comprehension, syntax and reading potentials (Sousa, 2005).

While some parents and teachers may be concerned about a child who does not seem to be on par with children of the same age, attempts to rush maturation are not helpful. This is especially true in terms of the use of commercially produced products aimed at accelerating a child's intellectual development. One of the reasons attempts at hyperstimulating language and literacy development can be so problematic is that programs and instruments targeting such goals do not account for important neurodevelopmental timelines (Nagel, 2012a). For example, if you consider what we have just said about specific aspects of brain development related to language development, it becomes problematic when a person or product suggests that reading can be achieved by two-year-olds with the correct stimulation.

SEX DIFFERENCES

See Chapter ❾ for more detail on the sociocultural influences on boys' and girls' development.

Many parents and teachers have witnessed differences in the language capacities of boys and girls throughout various stages of childhood. Traditionally, there have been anecdotal illustrations of differences between boys' and girls' language and literacy development but now there are opportunities for these differences to be observed. In this chapter, we talk about biological 'sex' differences and the biological and physiological make-up of males and females; 'gender' usually refers to the socially constructed attributes, including social roles and behaviours. In Chapter 9, we talk about the socially constructed attributes and behaviours associated with gender.

Sex variations in the rates of maturation along with differences in various neuro-anatomical structures and development have been increasingly identified (Baron-Cohen, 2003; Halpern, 2009; Herschkowitz & Herschkowitz, 2004). While research outlining why this might be the case is worth consideration and discussion, it is also important to remember that the neural foundations for sex differences in language are only beginning to be understood. Significantly, we must also remember that there are accounts illustrating how some boys' language skills are exemplary and accounts of some girls who struggle with language and literacy (Scholes, 2010, 2013). Indeed, any discussion or exploration of measurable sex differences in the brain must be tempered with the realisation that questions of differences in language acquisition are still largely unanswered and, importantly, not all boys are the same, nor are all girls (Bjorklund, 2005; Nagel & Scholes, 2014; Scholes, 2013).

There are many anecdotal accounts alike of how people have noticed that the language abilities of girls often appear superior to those of boys, with these abilities and skills evident early in a child's life. Typically, girls will learn to speak earlier and more syntactically and semantically appropriately than boys, produce longer sentences and demonstrate larger working vocabularies at very young ages (Diamond & Hopson, 1999; Eliot, 2000; Nagel, 2012a). With the progression through school, girls will generally outperform boys in many facets of language and literacy, also displaying early advantages in most aspects of communication (Nagel, 2008). These differences may be attributable to the fact that language appears to be processed differently in boys and girls, and regions of the brain responsible for communication not only appear larger in girls but also maintain greater neural density and connectivity (Brizendine, 2006; Kimura, 1999).

A striking difference between boys and girls is that language appears to be lateralised somewhat differently in the hemispheres of females and males (Nagel, 2008, 2012a). While much of our overall language capacities are lateralised in the left hemisphere, language processing tends to be equally distributed between both hemispheres in females, unlike males, who predominantly use the front and back of the left hemisphere (Nagel, 2012a; Shaywitz et al., 1995). Contributing to these differences, the dominant language areas of the brain located in the left hemisphere actually appear to mature earlier in girls (Nagel, 2008). That is, while language may be processed differently in girls and boys, there also appear to be structural differences that affect the processing of language as well as other important functions.

The corpus callosum

If we return to images of the brain, one of the most obvious structural differences between developing males and females is the *corpus callosum*. The corpus callosum is the band of tissue housing a vast array of neural connections linking the hemispheres of the brain, making it the primary pathway for communication between the left and right sides of the brain. Some of the earliest anatomical studies of the brain suggested that the corpus callosum of females appears proportionally larger than that of males (Nagel, 2012a). Contemporary studies have supported that work and have noted that, while the corpus callosum is essentially the same physical size for males and females, greater connectivity between the hemispheres of females is evident. This may be because the brain of a female is physically smaller than that of a male. As the corpus callosum is the same size, females then have greater proportional connectivity. It also appears that the corpus callosum of females is thicker and more bulbous than in males, and synaptically denser, resulting in a greater number of connections between the hemispheres (see Figure 5.4) that facilitates better crosstalk between each hemisphere (Eliot, 2000; Halpern, 2009; Howard, 2006).

FIGURE 5.4   DURING LANGUAGE TASKS, IN MALES MOST CONNECTIONS RUN BETWEEN THE FRONT AND BACK (BLUE LINES); IN FEMALES, THE CONNECTIONS RUN ACROSS THE LEFT AND RIGHT HEMISPHERE (ORANGE LINES)

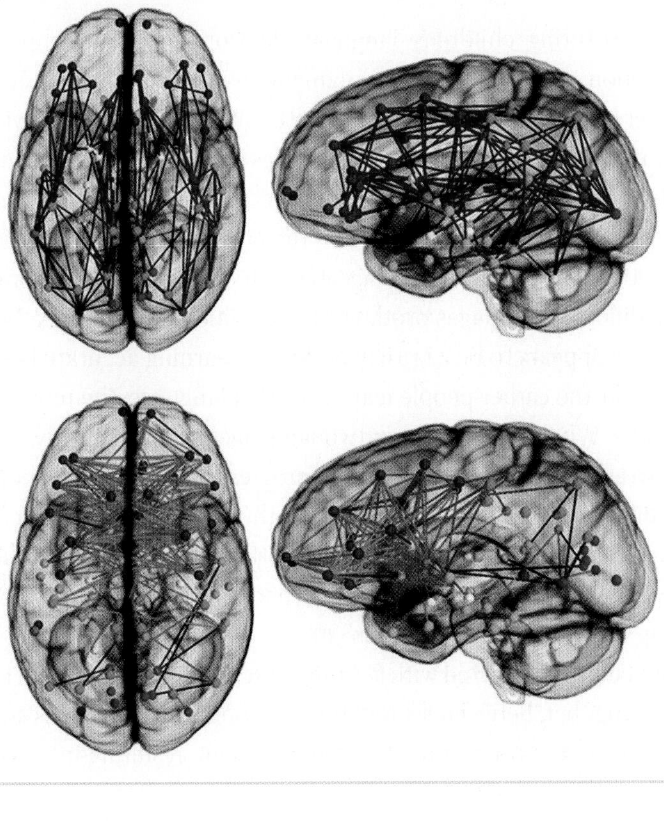

While the proportional size and density of the corpus callosum present differently for males and females, both Broca's and Wernicke's areas appear to be proportionally larger in females. We also know that analyses of Wernicke's area have identified that, in females, the neurons in this region are more densely packed together and have longer dendrites than those in males (Eliot, 2000). If you recall that thicker neural density and greater neural connectivity mean greater proficiency, it would make sense that girls may have greater skills and capacities in areas related to language development and usage as a result of innate sex differences in the brain. If indeed boys and girls do have differences related to language structures in the brain and differences in language development, maintaining unique developmental timelines within and between sexes, attempts to engage in language or literacy activities when the brain is not ready for such endeavours could be equated with having children engage in physical activities when the body is not yet ready (Nagel, 2012a). While brain development does appear to follow a particular trajectory, there are physical anatomical developments that are very important for language to flourish.

ENHANCING LANGUAGE DEVELOPMENT

As we consider nurturing children's language development, it is important to recall Vygotsky's conviction that language is fundamentally a social act. The response a child receives whenever he or she makes a sound, whether it is in the form of crying or babbling, plays an important role. A child's language capacities are shaped by social interactions and from birth to about ten years of age, the daily interactions a child has within social contexts will be fundamental in this acquisition. These interactions are highly significant, with exposure to the subtleties of a particular language in the first year altering the brain to the point that speakers of different languages produce sounds differently (Gopnik, Meltzoff & Kuhl, 1999). That is, there appears to be a critical period for learning accurate language pronunciation. For example, the earlier people learn a second language, the more their pronunciation is near native. When toddlers learn two languages simultaneously, there is a period between ages two and three when they tend to progress more slowly as they figure out the nuances of two different languages. But by age four they generally have the capacity to work out the subtleties and speak as well as natives of both languages (Baker, 2006). As you may be aware from your own experience, after adolescence it is difficult to learn a new language without speaking with an accent (Anderson, 2002).

Part of the difficulties associated with learning a second language later in life is attributed to the understanding that, between six and twelve months of age, babies start to filter out speech sounds not used in their immediate environment, resulting in a loss of sensitivity to speech sounds of foreign languages. In essence, as infants tune into the sounds used in their own homes, they increase their responsiveness to them while at the same time they stop attending to sounds that are not needed for mastering their own language (Faull & McLean-Oliver, 2010). This explanation accounts for the reasons native Japanese speakers struggle greatly with differentiating between an 'r' and 'l' sound; 'l' does not exist in the Japanese language (Nagel, 2012a).

We have considered the importance of hearing the sounds of a language in the first years of life but equally important are the social interactions that take place during the first ten years of a child's life. A child needs to engage in social interactions with others using language in everyday contexts for normal language development to occur. Importantly, the lack of any such activity results in long-term language difficulties or, in an extreme case, can result in the complete inability to speak (Eliot, 2000). One of the most compelling and tragic examples of abuse and the deprivation of language stimulation is that of 'Genie' (Curtiss, 1977; Newton, 2004).

GENIE: A CASE STUDY IN LANGUAGE DEVELOPMENT

Genie (discussed in terms of overall child development in Something to think about 1.2) is also worth considering from the specific perspective of language development. Genie was reportedly developing normally until she began saying her first words at around eighteen months. She was then physically isolated from the family within the house, and not allowed to speak. Her father, who rarely allowed his wife and son to leave the house or to speak, forbade them to speak to Genie. When she did try to vocalise, Genie was beaten with a large stick. Her father was said to bark and growl at her like a dog in order to keep her quiet. By the age of thirteen, Genie was almost entirely mute, commanding a vocabulary of about twenty words and a few short phrases when she was discovered by authorities in November 1970. In spite of receiving several years of training, which resulted in her gaining a larger vocabulary and a good comprehension of conversation, Genie's grammar and communication skills remained limited (Curtiss, 1977; Newton, 2004). Genie's lack of language stimulation during an important developmental time has been supported by other studies; it is now widely recognised that the learning window for language, while seemingly long in duration, requires various types and degrees of stimulation for normal language development to occur.

When the scientists administered tests specifically geared at determining where Genie was processing language, they found more evidence that she was using her right hemisphere for language functions rather than the left hemisphere associated with this function. If humans possess the innate ability to acquire language, Genie demonstrates the necessity of early language stimulation in the left hemisphere of the brain. (To see a documentary about Genie see the Video links at the end of the chapter.)

Ask yourself...

LINKAGE
See Chapter ❶
for more detail on
'Genie'.

Genie is the pseudonym for a feral child who was a victim of severe abuse, neglect, and social isolation.

1   Given what you know so far about language development, with earlier intervention do you think Genie would have been able to acquire language skills comparable to her peers? If yes, at what age and how? If no, why not?

2   What other communication skills could be developed to help Genie overcome her oral language challenges?

3   You may come across children in your class who have what you may consider to be underdeveloped oral language skills. How might that affect their reading and writing literacy skills? What is your role in supporting such a child? Who would you collaborate with to enhance a child's language development?

PARENTESE

The story of Genie highlights the importance of reciprocal interactions for children's language development. An important factor is the response children receive whenever they make any sounds, be they crying or babbling, and much of those responses occur as infant-directed speech called *parentese*. Typically, parents and care-givers naturally talk to their babies along with other immediate family members, relatives and friends. When they do so, they often do so in a way that is unique and specifically aimed at engaging very young children. This sing-songy cadence is not only evident across various ages but also across cultures (Faull & McLean-Oliver, 2010). As parentese is universal and without cultural differentiation, neuroscientists believe that it is innate and plays a special role in a child's language development.

Parentese is recognised by its elongated vowels, repetitions and overpronounced syllables and also by its sound structure and *prosody* (Nagel, 2012a). (Prosody is the emotional quality of speech usually identifiable through intonation and rhythm. It is so important that it can change the entire meaning of a phrase or sentence: 'good for you' conveys different sentiments depending on how it is said or its prosody.) Parentese also provides an infant with the earliest understandings of a language's phonology, morphology, syntax and vocabulary. Steven Pinker, the world-renowned Harvard University professor and expert experimental psychologist, discovered that parentese appears to be far more grammatically correct than normal speech and, as such, offers children the purest form of initiation into their native language (Pinker, 2009). When communicating with infants via parentese, adults also provide important social interactions with their baby, often raising their eyebrows, opening their eyes wide and overemphasising many facial mannerisms

(Faull & McLean-Oliver, 2010). Through these social interactions, infants further enhance their language capacities by watching lip movements, which assist in developing sensitivity to the sounds that accompany those movements.

SOMETHING TO THINK ABOUT 5.2

DEVELOPING A YOUNG CHILD'S VOCABULARY

The attention that the significant adults in a baby's life give to the baby's babbling makes a difference, as two-sided conversations are a fundamental factor in language development (Hirsh-Pasek & Golinkoff, 2004; Medina, 2010). For example, children as young as eighteen months have larger vocabularies than their peers if their parents talk to them about things of interest to the child, and these same children demonstrate larger vocabularies as they enter school, with higher levels of reading and mathematics evident by the time they reach Year 1 (Hirsh-Pasek & Golinkoff, 2004). Facial mannerisms, emotional quality of response and overall social engagement involved in interactions with adults are also an important part of the equation (Faull & McLean-Oliver, 2010). An adult's eye contact and gaze along with verbal tone and prosody assist in a child's overall language development, reminding us that there are more than just words in building meaning and capacities for communicating in the world.

Ask yourself...

1   Increasingly, children appear to spend more time watching television, DVDs, computers and electronic devices. What social interactions could children miss out on if they spend an inordinate amount of time engaged in media? What sort of language skills experiences could be compromised?

2   There are language programs that claim to speed up language acquisition, close the achievement gap in language and improve test scores for students. What are the dangers of some of these highly prescriptive programs? Do they have a place in your classroom? If no, why not? If yes, when and how would you use them?

The provision of language input by adults to children through talking to them, reading to them or telling them stories is an equally important goal of eliciting talk from children. These social interactions cannot be found through television, DVDs or electronic media that are sometimes presented as mechanisms for language and learning enhancement.

Normal and healthy language development is the precursor to developing all aspects of literacy when a child enters formal educational environments. We now know that learning to read depends on well-developed language structures and processes in the brain and early language experiences. In a self-reinforcing cycle, children who are read to from an early age are more successful at learning to read and demonstrate better overall literacy skills as they move through school (Wolfe & Nevills, 2004). Evidence suggests that language development tends to flourish as the brain matures and as it receives stimulation through meaningful human interaction for children across all cultures and all languages, as long as there are no instances of deprivation of stimulation or any innate developmental problems or learning impediments. Teachers, then, have an important role in enhancing children's language capacities through development of conversational skills, increasing vocabulary and indeed listening to children. When teachers read with and to children, there are opportunities for building word banks, extending comprehension and using open-ended questions to expand children's ability to articulate. The teacher's role is significant when you consider that students in the early grades learn up to twenty words a day. As normal and healthy language development is the precursor to developing all aspects of literacy and is achieved through social interactions, talking to children would seem a high priority for parents and teachers alike.

CONCLUSION

Evidence suggests that children are born to communicate, although the process involves complex neural development and social interactions at times of high neuroplasticity. While we have learnt from traditional theories of language development, modern technology has provided opportunities to confirm and further our understandings. While the subtleties of brain functioning involved in language development are still being examined, current knowledge suggests that the language function is based in the left hemisphere of the brain. Sex-based anatomical differences in the hemispheres appear while babies are in utero. There also appears to be universality for the acquisition of language for children of all cultures, with high neuroplasticity at critical stages of development. Within the brain, Wernicke's area and Broca's area contribute to much of the processing involved in language. Wernicke's area is primarily involved in processing specific elements of language and facilitating comprehension and converting thoughts into language, while Broca's area is involved in synthesising language, and facilitating the ability to articulate thoughts. Brain imaging shows us that the dense bundles of nerve fibres that create the pathways to connect these two regions are also important. Maturation for a child includes increased myelinisation and interconnectivity in these areas of the brain, which in turn produce more efficient capacities and increased neural speed.

We also know that social interactions are critical as language development includes acquiring the sounds, meanings, words and communication patterns of a culture. In order to efficiently communicate a child learns meaningful sounds used by a particular language (phonemes); the system used to group phonemes into meaningful combinations of sounds and words (morphology); rules about how words are combined to make meaningful phrases and sentences (grammar); and the meaning of words or phrases in various sentences (semantics). Meaningful social interactions provide stimulation, supporting language development for children across all cultures to flourish as long as there are no innate developmental problems or instances of deprivation. As there is no doubt a strong relationship between oral language and literacy, it seems imperative that classroom teachers understand the processes involved in language acquisition, the implications of maturation and sex differences, and how to facilitate positive language experiences. As almost all classroom-based learning relies on oral language, explicitly supporting children's development in this domain contributes substantially to their learning.

CHAPTER SUMMARY

The chapter explored language development and learning. It considered the importance for teachers to understand language development, as early language acquisition and development is an essential ingredient for children's ongoing learning. Language facilitates communication, relationship building and allows children to engage with and interpret what is taking place in their classrooms. The chapter considered the fundamental differences between language and literacy development with an understanding that oral language provides the foundation for further literacy skills. This chapter also looked at some traditional theories of language development, informed by an understanding that language skills are learnt, and also at more contemporary perspectives informed by what science can tell us about our innate capacities and the contextual influences on language development. In this section we looked at some of the traditional approaches to understanding language development offered by behaviourists (Skinner), nativists (Chomsky) and socioculturalists (Vygotsky).

In this chapter we also looked at how language processes in the brain are predominantly housed in the left hemisphere. It was noted that there are important pathways for learning language for most children that include predictable phases that are similar regardless of what country a child is born in. The contributions of Wernicke's area and Broca's area of the brain to much of the processing involved in language were discussed: Wernicke's area is involved in processing specific elements of language, facilitating comprehension and converting thoughts into language, and Broca's area is involved in synthesising language and facilitating the ability to articulate thoughts. Differences in the brain between the sexes and their implications for language development were considered. The chapter detailed how maturation involves the unfolding of changes associated with normal growth as a unique and natural process that takes place within the individual and how nurturing children's language development is crucial.

Implications for Teaching

Educators draw on a range of theoretical perspectives to inform their practice. Regardless of your theoretical positioning, you can enhance your students' language development by providing learning environments that facilitate this development. For example:

- Research tells us that children who participate in frequent conversations have more advanced vocabulary (Ruston & Schwanenflugel, 2010).

  1 As a teacher, engage in conversations so children will hear and use language.

- We know that language acquisition pathways are not always predictable (Nagel, 2012a). While one child may say their first words at nine months, another may take up to twenty months.

  2 Scaffold language development with an understanding of where students are developmentally and where they are heading.

- Extending conversations by asking open-ended questions provides opportunities for children to expand their vocabulary and language skills (Dickinson & Tabors, 2001).

  3 Don't ask questions that require a 'yes' or 'no' answer, rather ask open-ended questions: 'How do you think that works?', 'How do you think that happened?', 'Tell me more about that.'

- Giving positive reinforcement such as compliments, approval, encouragement and affirmation is considered to be effective in encouraging desired behaviours, such as oral language (based on behaviourist perspectives).

  4 Teachers can make a point of providing lots of positive reinforcement during language experiences.

- Modelling language expands the child's oral language skills and facilitates the development of abstract language (based on sociocultural perspectives). Teachers can engage in this modelling when reading to children, during conversations and when questioning.

  5 Using new and novel words in conversations provides an opportunity for children to learn new words, expanding their vocabulary.

Ask yourself...

1   Given the year level you will be teaching, what kinds of practical strategies can you use every day to enhance language development? Read the following strategies and decided if any are appropriate for you. If so, pick out a number of strategies and detail *how* you would use them in your classroom. If not, explain *why* are they not appropriate strategies.

   a   Read to children every day.

   b   Expose children to a range of texts.

   c   Teach nursery rhymes, poems, songs, chants, raps.

   d   Have a range of books based on children's experiences and interests.

   e   Provide books on children's interests and special topics in learning centres.

   f   Encourage children to initiate and engage in conversations with teachers and peers.

   g   Prompt peer learning and activities that promote talk.

   h   Model using specific language to the children: for example, retelling stories.

   i   Model good listening to the children.

   j   Arrange debates.

   k   Initiate dramatic play.

   l   Facilitate book-sharing.

   m   Set oral reports.

   n   Use storytelling.

   o   Practise questioning and interviews.

   p   Instigate partner and small group work.

2   Wernicke's area includes a number of systems primarily involved in comprehension and understanding speech that process specific elements of language and convert thoughts into language. Broca's area acts like a syntax centre by synthesising language so that we can articulate our thoughts through the regulation of facial and hand activity, allowing us to speak and write. Broca's and Wernicke's work acknowledges the left hemisphere as the dominant language hemisphere. There are a host of left-brain, right-brain activities and exercises available (just look on the internet). Do you think as teachers we should be implementing these types of strategies with our students to enhance left-brain functioning? Why? Why not?

PRACTICAL ACTIVITIES

1   Behaviourists, such as Skinner, assume that human behaviours are determined by learning in response to reinforcement. They believe that children will acquire new skills as actions produce positive or negative outcomes. Responses that are positively reinforced will be repeated and those that are punished will not. From this perspective correct utterances are positively reinforced when the child realises the communicative value of words and phrases. Using behaviourist theory, list and then discuss some of the classroom practices that you have seen that are influenced by the idea that behaviours are influenced by reward and punishment.

2   Now consider nativist theory. Chomsky argued that biological influences bring about language development, as children would never acquire the skills needed for processing an infinite number of sentences if the language acquisition mechanism depends on language input alone. Develop an argument to support this theory and bring in some practical examples of what you have seen in terms of children's language development.

3   According to Vygotsky and sociocultural theory, the development of language occurs due to a complex interaction between the child and the environment. This approach emphasises the role of feedback and reinforcement in language acquisition, and proposes that much of a child's language acquisition develops from modelling and interaction with parents and other adults as they provide scaffolding. Design a classroom activity to scaffold a child's oral language development. Pick a year level that you will teach and then decide what resources, strategies and outcomes you would like.

STUDY QUESTIONS

1   What is the difference between language and literacy?

2   Write a definition of behaviourist theory. What is the name of the theorist associated with this approach?

3   What is the significance of Noam Chomsky's work? What is his theory of language acquisition?

4   Define universal grammar. Who coined this term?

5   According to Vygotsky, how do children acquire language?

6   Explain the processes involved in Wernicke's area.

7   Explain the processes involved in Broca's area.

8   If you were to visit a variety of diverse cultures, you would find that children learn language in a remarkably regular way, typically speaking in full and complex grammatical sentences by the age of four or five. In order to master any language, without much difficulty children will learn what rules of language?

9   An important factor in language development is the response children receive whenever they make any sounds, be they crying or babbling. Many responses occur as infant-directed speech referred to as 'parentese'. Describe the features of parentese.

10 What is the teacher's role in enhancing children's language capacities?

As a teacher, focusing on fostering language is not easy to develop or implement. The interconnected and complex nature of language is influenced by social context, where motivational, behavioural and social factors can affect the learning climate. Children's willingness to engage in language can be affected by their interest in the topic of the conversation, their relationship to the speaker and the classroom setting. The importance of the classroom setting is evident in the Australian Curriculum, Assessment and Reporting Authority's (ACARA) description of oral language development.

Who is responsible for developing a child's oral development? What is the responsibility of parents? Early childhood teachers? Primary teachers? High school teachers?

FURTHER READING

Dickinson, D. & Tabors, P. (2001). *Beginning Literacy with Language*. Baltimore, MD: Paul Brookes Publishing.

Kouvelas, E. (2007) Language and the brain. In A. F. Christidis (Ed.), *A History of Ancient Greek*. New York, NY: Cambridge University Press.

Kuhl, P. (2004). Early language acquisition: Cracking the speech code. *Nature Reviews Neuroscience*, 5(11), 831–843.

Nagel, M. C. (2012a). *In the Beginning: the Brain, Early Development and Learning*. Melbourne, Australia: ACER Press.

Pinker, S. (1994). *The Language Instinct: How the Mind Creates Language*: New York, NY: Marrow.

Pinker, S. (1995). Language acquisition. In L. R. Gleitman & M. Liberman (Eds.), *An Invitation to Cognitive Science* (2nd ed., pp. 135–82). Cambridge, MA: MIT Press.

Tomasello, M. (1992). The social bases of language acquisition. *Social Development*, 1(1), 67–87.

Wells, G. (1986). *The Meaning Makers: Children Learning Language and Using Language to Learn*. Portsmouth, NH: Heinemann.

VIDEO LINKS

A. Raphaeli: *Noam Chomsky vs. B.F. Skinner*
https://www.youtube.com/watch?v=FlyU_M20hMk

Noam Chomsky speaks about universal language acquisition and the biological evidence for his theory.

The Floating University: *Steven Pinker on How Children Learn Language*
https://www.youtube.com/watch?v=ir7arILiqxg

Steven Pinker talks about the process of language acquisition and universal grammar with examples.

M. Mars: *The Brain—Language and Speech, Broca and Wernicke's Areas*
https://www.youtube.com/watch?v=5k8JwC1L9_k

Details how Broca's and Wernicke's areas facilitate language communication with examples of the effects when there is trauma to these areas.

Yuecl: *Theories of Language Development (Nativist, Learning, Interactionist)*
https://www.youtube.com/watch?v=8FhKgzm4Za4

Discusses the main theories of language development.

ApolloEight Genesis: *Genie Wiley—TLC Documentary (2003)*
https://www.youtube.com/watch?v=VjZolHCrC8E

Documentary of the story of 'Genie' who grew up in severe isolation until the age of thirteen and did not learn to talk.

WEBLINKS

Shape of the Australian Curriculum: English (ACARA)
http://www.acara.edu.au/verve/_resources/Australian_Curriculum_-_English.pdf

Document outlining the Australian English curriculum and how oral language proficiency is important in its own right.

English as an Additional Language or Dialect: Teacher Resources (Advice for Teachers)
http://www.acara.edu.au/verve/_resources/EALD_Teacher_Resource_-_Advice_for_Teachers_of_EALD_Students.pdf

Provides a resource for teachers to support ACARA and outlines the development of oral language and influences on such processes.

Promoting Oral Language Development in Young Children
http://www.superduperinc.com/handouts/pdf/120_oral_language_development.pdf

Handy hints for working with young children.

MEMORY AND LEARNING

6

"Learning and memory make each human unique. Even before birth, the human brain takes in sensations, processes them, and begins to encode them into trillions of synapses. Those connections and the electrochemical firing patterns that unite them make the brain an organ different from what it was a moment before. As new connections form in response to stimuli and then become strong through repeated use, the brain integrates new information and stores it until it is needed. *Without learning and memory, the human brain would be little more than clockwork.*"

(Sweeney, 2009, p. 236; emphasis added)

LEARNING OUTCOMES

As you read through this chapter and undertake the exercises at the end, you will gain the ability to complete these tasks successfully:

→ describe and discuss important components of the brain as they pertain to memory formation

→ describe the different systems and stages of memories and give examples of each

→ describe the differences between procedural, semantic and episodic memories

→ describe what can both hinder and enhance memory.

KEY TERMS
- long-term potentiation (LTP)
- affective
- working memory
- long-term memory
- episodic memory
- semantic memory
- procedural memory

Nicholas is struggling with the exam! He studied hard and although he felt prepared for the history test he can't seem to remember all that he has studied over the last few days. He spent hours going over his notes and textbook and now he is finding it difficult to not only answer most of the questions but also to keep his concentration. He knows that he must do well on this last piece of assessment in order to ensure he passes the subject and, as he looks up at the clock, his concerns about passing are exacerbated by the hands on the clock that seem to be moving far too quickly. Only five minutes left and he is now panicking ... it seems like there is nothing he can do now but sign his name to his paper, hand it in and head home given the school day is now done.

On his way home Nicholas can't believe what has just happened. He worked really hard to do well on the exam but this seems to be a reoccurring event for him during tests. As he walks home, he remembers that he has his weekly piano lesson today and his thoughts shift to the new musical piece he learnt last week. He goes over the piece in his mind and visualises which keys he needs to play in order to make the music that he has grown to like very much. He also starts to think of his lead role in the school play next week and mulls over his lines. He really enjoys music and drama and, as his thoughts continue to bring a smile to his face, he suddenly remembers some of the answers to the questions he missed on the test thirty minutes ago. The test answers now seem to be streaming through his mind and he can't believe it ... why now?

Nicholas's predicament is something many students, past and present, have experienced. Many times students draw a blank during tests only to have the answers appear later when relaxed. Some people often think that such occurrences are memory or behavioural problems but, in order to understand why tests and memories don't always work well together, it is important to know some things about the different types of memories we have and how they are formed, retained and retrieved. This chapter explores one of the most complex aspects of the brain and mind: memory. Years of research have illuminated a great number of theories and ideas related to the brain's memory systems; memory research is arguably one of the most expansive areas of neuroscientific study. For teachers, an understanding of memory as it pertains to learning is an important component of pedagogical practice. Before exploring this topic in depth, it is worth exploring your own experiences as they relate to memory by considering the following questions.

1 Have you experienced a similar scenario to Nicholas's? If so, how did you feel at the time? Can you recall how you felt emotionally and physically? What ways to avoid such events from occurring did you or your teachers find to assist you and others in such circumstances? How did they help?

2 On a different note, have you ever considered how you do some things rather seamlessly and without much thought? If you ride a bicycle, drive a car, play an instrument or any number of other activities you are using your memory to do so; indeed, you are using your memory as you read these words without much strain or anxiety. Make a list of ten things you do consciously without much effort and also a list of things you do without even realising it. Keep this list until you have worked through this chapter and see if you can identify what aspects of memory they are related to.

INTRODUCTION

If you recall from Chapter 1, our understanding of learning in educational contexts has changed from being more than the product of some endeavour to a view involving a variety of processes as well. Perhaps this is no better exemplified than when exploring how the brain processes and stores memories. The complexity surrounding memory formation is perhaps one of the most studied areas in the neuroscience and cognitive psychology fields. Aspects of this complexity and an understanding of how memories are formed should be equally important in educational contexts, given that academic success is often based on formal assessment or the demonstration of specific skills, both of which rely on the brain's memory systems. This chapter looks to provide current and future teachers with a better understanding of memory and how the brain retains a variety of information for both short- and long-term usage.

The importance of teachers having a sound understanding of how memories are processed, formed and retained cannot be understated. In terms of brain structures, learning to read differs from learning to throw a ball and associated memory systems rely on different brain systems and develop at slightly different times (Blakemore & Frith, 2005). It is the brain's ability to change with experience that gives us memory; thanks to research, we now know a good deal about what happens when the brain stores facts, experiences and skills in memory and what happens when we recall them. We also know what memories are the most accurate in terms of recall and what might hinder memory formation. Neuroscientists can even map, in some detail, the structures, circuits and molecular processes underlying memory. Yet for all we do know, memory is still misrepresented or misunderstood by many.

It is common for people to think of the brain as having a single unitary recording device, like that of a computer or digital recorder. But the brain is more like an active ecosystem than a static pre-programmed computer, given that there is no single centre for vision, language, emotion, social behaviour, consciousness or memory (Ratey, 2001). Significantly, our collective understanding of how memories emerge into human consciousness as traces of things past is still one of the greatest mysteries of the human mind (Gelbard-Sagiv, Mukamel, Harel, Malach & Fried, 2008). The complexities of memory formation are such that even the shape, smell, colour and taste of a particular food draws on different neural connections and regions of the brain, so that activating these regions simultaneously unites a collection of our experiences, telling us that we are holding and tasting an apple.

Notwithstanding our collective naivety about how the brain forms and stores memories, there are some important things we do know. For example, we know that, while learning and memory are inextricably linked, 'learning' refers to the acquisition of knowledge, information or skills, while 'memory' is the term most often used to describe how and where learning is stored (Nagel, 2013a). We also know that there are different types of memories that in turn engage different regions of the brain. Furthermore, we know that emotions and our experiences are powerful players in the formation of long-term memories and that memory is comprised of three processes: encoding, storage and retrieval. All of these things are explored in greater detail in this chapter but our journey into how learning is retained in the context of memory formation begins at the cellular level.

THE NEUROBIOLOGY OF MEMORY

See Chapter ❸ for details of neurogenesis and synapses.

In Chapter 3, details about the generation of neurons in the developing brain and how neurons communicate with each other were presented. We noted that the passing of information from one neuron to another through synaptic transmission is perhaps representative of the first and earliest stages of learning. This communication is not only representative of learning but also of early memory formation. Thoughts, perceptions, sensory information, emotions and actions are generated as neurons that fire together; in one sense, this represents a measure of encoding in that memories are the patterns this activity leaves behind. Moreover, the encoding and retrieval of experiences via synaptic transmission is also evident in actual physical changes to the brain.

Notions of learning and memory forming real physical changes to the brain go back many decades but the work of Canadian neuropsychologist Donald O. Hebb during the mid-twentieth century is particularly noteworthy. In the absence of the technology available today, Hebb proposed that the repeated and persistent transmission of signals from one neuron to another was not only a sign of learning and memory at the cellular level but also an example of synaptic neuroplasticity resulting in physical changes to the brain (Hebb, 1949). Hebbian theory, as it has come to be known, was strengthened with hard evidence in 2007 when researchers demonstrated concrete changes in the synapses of regions of a rat's brain that are critical to learning and memory (Sweeney, 2009). Such changes become evident when neurons are frequently activated, which in turn has the potential to create network systems for long-term storage.

At a cellular level, the physical process of storing a memory is incredibly complicated. There are many different types of storage systems or memory mechanisms distributed throughout the brain, which can be used in multiple ways with multiple retrieval cues. Ultimately, memory is a series of molecular events in a neural micro-architecture (Berninger & Richards, 2002). Forming memories requires many steps that lead to the chemical storage of information through the manufacture of proteins that make certain synapses more likely to fire thereby creating patterns of neural networks (Sweeney, 2009). This continuous activation of neurons leading to the establishment of neural networks has been referred to as **long-term potentiation (LTP)** (Ratey, 2001). While LTP was first researched in numerous other mammalian species, there is now ample evidence supporting such processing in the human brain (Cooke & Bliss, 2006). In terms of learning, LTP reminds us that continued practice of something leads to that thing becoming a more permanent part of memory that is easily available when needed and that new learning requires a considerable amount of practice (Doyle & Zakrajsek, 2013). In other words, the growth and maintenance of synaptic connections make memory persist or, perhaps more simply, practice makes permanent (Kandel, 2006). LTP also helps to reinforce the widely accepted view that the brain does change through experience and that neuroplasticity is an important aspect of learning and memory.

Long-term potentiation (LTP) The continuous activation of synapses leading to the hard-wiring of neural connections.

THE HIPPOCAMPUS

While the plasticity of the brain's neural networks allows us to store and retrieve fragments of information, some neurons appear to be specialised for different types or pieces of memories and it seems likely that some structures of the brain play a role in such processes (Ratey, 2001). One such structure, the *hippocampus* (see Figure 6.1), resides in the limbic system and appears to act as a filter and temporary stopover for processing short-term memories into something more permanent.

There are actually two hippocampi, located within the temporal lobes of both the right and left hemispheres. Scientists and medical practitioners have identified that the hippocampus is an important structure for processing memory in that, if it is damaged, our ability to learn and remember certain things diminishes markedly (Dudai & Morris, 2013; Morris, 2006; Shapiro, 2001). A good example of this is found within those who

See Chapter ❸ for an overview of the limbic system and its primary structures.

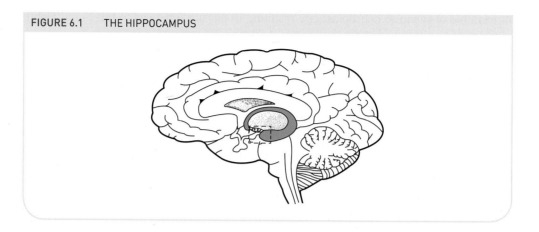

FIGURE 6.1   THE HIPPOCAMPUS

suffer from a particular type of amnesia resulting from injury to their hippocampus; they are unable to undertake further learning but their older memories remain intact (Geake, 2009). Interestingly, age can also play a role in memory formation via the hippocampus. The hippocampus often shrinks in size in older adulthood and older adults with small hippocampi volume struggle with certain types of memories (Zimmerman et al., 2008). It also appears that the hippocampus plays a role in responding to the here and now. In one sense the hippocampus could be described as a moment-by-moment whiteboard of the mind, determining what is important to remember and shifting those memories into storage; it acts as a mechanism of the mind that teaches the cortex (Shapiro, 2001; Nagel, 2014).

THE AMYGDALA

With regards to learning, the hippocampus also determines what is worth paying attention to by determining the inherent novelty of a situation. The hippocampus works in concert with the amygdala to determine what is worth remembering. The amygdala plays an important part in creating permanent memories (Bermudez-Rattoni, 2010). The amygdala sits next to the hippocampus (Figure 6.2) and, while it plays a role in many aspects of emotion, it also helps to determine what is worth remembering, due to the fact that emotional arousal activates the amygdala thereby attaching an emotional tag to events and experiences (McGaugh, 2004; McGaugh, Cahill & Roozendaal, 1996; Nagel, 2014). So powerful are emotions that people may remember emotionally significant material even when their initial processing of that material was not engaged in a deeply significant manner (Ritchey, LaBar & Cabeza, 2011).

Perhaps one of the reasons the amygdala plays such an important role in deciding what is to be remembered lies in the fact that it is the amygdala that helps to drive our innate

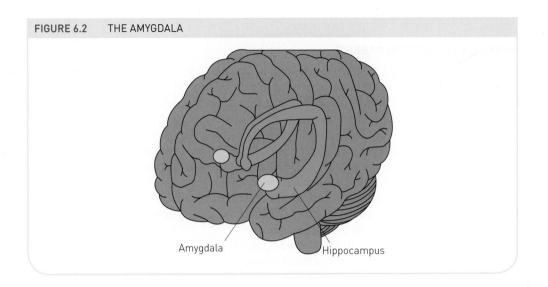

FIGURE 6.2   THE AMYGDALA

Amygdala   Hippocampus

fight-or-flight responses. The amygdala has also been described as the part of the limbic system that serves as the neural basis of emotion and, as it takes in sensory data from the thalamus, it seems to attach affective value to that information (LeDoux, 2000, 2002; McGaugh, 2004). Taken in its entirety, and at the risk of oversimplification, the amygdala works in concert with the hippocampus to give experiences emotional value. New and novel experiences, or those that excite these important structures of the limbic system, are more likely to engage an affective response and be deemed worth remembering in other regions of the brain.

Affective
Of or having to do with emotions or the feeling of emotion.

SUMMARY

It should appear evident from this discussion that the limbic system plays an important role in determining the pieces of experiences and events that we store. But where these pieces are dispersed and how they are reconnected is still something that is not well understood (Ratey, 2001). Indeed, an understanding of the neural mechanisms for encoding, storing and retrieving traces of memory or determining how such activities culminate in long-lasting biochemical and structural changes in the brain represents a grand challenge for neuroscientists (Morris, 2006). One thing that is somewhat clearer is that many researchers prefer thinking of memory within the brain as more of a process than a collection of storage devices and that there are a variety of different types of memory (Morris, 2006; Tulving, 2000). Those that are significant in terms of learning in an educational context are explored next.

NEUROPLASTIC LONDON CABBIES

In terms of memory, one of the brain's most important capacities is that of neuroplasticity or its ability to reorganise neural pathways via new experiences. This topic was explored in Chapter 3, but a fascinating group of studies in London help demonstrate the remarkable changes a brain can undergo due to particular stimulation.

In London every driver of a black cab is required to be completely familiar with a memorised map of this capital city, including some 25 000 streets and thousands of landmarks. This information—commonly referred to as 'The Knowledge'—can take years to develop and culminates in the completion of a final test known as the Knowledge of London Examination System. Candidates often take twelve attempts in order to pass, given the sheer volume of information. Interestingly, it appears that the preparation leading up to the test and its completion changes the brains of trainee cabbies.

In a lengthy study published in 2000 and led by the University College London's Professor Eleanor Maguire, researchers found that those trainee cabbies who managed to pass the Knowledge Exam had discernible differences in brain structures associated with memory and in particular regions of the hippocampus. Simply stated, these areas were larger in the successful cabbies than in the controls or non-trainees (Maguire et al., 2000). As the trainees took to the streets and started driving, the researchers found further evidence of change, resulting in better performance on memory tasks compared to non-drivers. In order to help substantiate their findings, a later study by Maguire and others in 2006 compared the brains of London taxi drivers and bus drivers to determine if other factors such as driving experience might contribute to enhanced memory (Maguire, Woollett & Spiers, 2006). The researchers found that, compared to the bus drivers who follow the same route on a daily basis, taxi drivers continued to show greater changes to the structures and regions associated with memory than their bus-driving counterparts. A significant caveat derived from these studies is that London taxi drivers have been found to have significantly more knowledge about London landmarks and their spatial relationships, suggesting that certain aspects of cognition also improved during the training. Taken in their entirety, these studies remind us that the environment can change the brain due to its neuroplasticity and the tremendous potential to improve memory and cognition through practice.

Ask yourself...

1   Drawing from the findings of the studies above, what might this mean in terms of helping students remember the important concepts and information they encounter in the learning and teaching enterprise?

2   Practice makes perfect: how can you apply this phrase to various subjects you might be teaching? Too often the phrase is considered for physical endeavours only, but given that memories are the residue of thought what might you, as a teacher, do to help students remember those things deemed important aspects of the curriculum? You may wish to revisit this question once you have a better understanding of the systems and stages of memory.

SYSTEMS AND STAGES OF MEMORY

Thoughts, perceptions and actions are generated by neurons firing together; memories are the patterns this activity leaves behind. There appear to be two systems to preserve such neural networks along with a series of possible stages leading into placing information within these memory systems (see Figure 6.3). Importantly, different stages of memory rely on different parts of the brain; at this moment, your brain is using a number of these structures in a variety of ways. Paying attention to the text you are reading is one way you are remembering something but there are also a number of other things going on within your mind that will engage a memory system, allowing you to focus on the words in front of you.

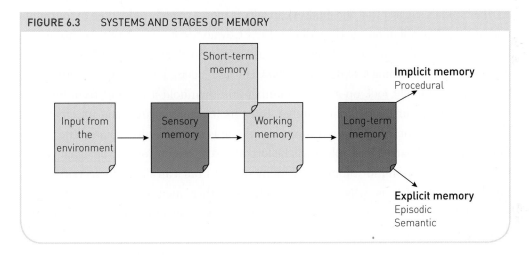

FIGURE 6.3   SYSTEMS AND STAGES OF MEMORY

SENSORY MEMORY

The human brain takes in a great deal of sensory information each second. If we had to attend to all of this stimulation, we would simply lose our minds. Fortunately, all sensory information—with the exception of smell—is processed through the thalamus, which acts as a type of stopover for determining what is important to attend to or ignore, and shifting this information to regions of the cortex for conscious perception (Sherman, 2005; Sweeney, 2009). It appears that the fundamental purpose of *sensory memory* is to give the brain's cognitive areas time to choose which information is important and worthy of attention (Bloom, Beal & Kupfer, 2006; Nagel, 2014). Sensory memory stores incoming sensory information in detail but only for an instant and such memories are not under conscious control. In other words, we cannot actively try to remember through our senses; instead our senses tell our brain what needs our attention.

SHORT-TERM MEMORY

The next stage of memory is one that most people are familiar with, and sometimes frustrated by. *Short-term memory* (sometimes abbreviated to STM) is a type of memory that allows us to store information for immediate or short-term use but the memories will decay quickly, usually lasting only for a few minutes, seconds or less (Berninger & Richards, 2002). We often use short-term memory when making brief mental notes from information in the external environment. Short-term memory not only has limitations in duration but also in storage capacity. The seminal work of George Miller (1956) suggested that people learn and remember information most efficiently in units of seven, plus or minus two, or that the capacity of short-term memory works best when information is presented in chunks based on the magical number of seven, as it has come to be known. Further studies suggest that the limit in capacity is more typically only three or four units and may be dependent on age (Broadbent, 1975; Cowan, 1998, 2001, 2008). An interesting feature of short-term memory is that information stored will fade away unless rehearsed or consolidated (Berninger & Richards, 2002; Howard, 2006). For example, in ordering a pizza a person might look up a phone number and then hold it in short-term memory when initially dialling the phone number. But this information may end up creating a degree of frustration if the pizza restaurant's phone is engaged, given that, if the phone number is not rehearsed mentally, it will be forgotten and require looking up again. Short-term memory is useful for moment-by-moment tasks but can decay in seconds when not rehearsed. This is why we must rely on other memory systems, including working memory (sometimes abbreviated to WM) and long-term memory (sometimes abbreviated to LTM).

Working memory
A memory system that both stores and manipulates information and is important for reasoning, comprehension, learning and processing information into long-term storage.

Long-term memory
As evident in the term, this type of memory stores information for a long period of time.

WORKING MEMORY

Historically, the terms 'working memory' and 'short-term memory' were often used interchangeably. Within recent literature, there is still considerable confusion regarding each; this confusion may be due to semantics (Cowan, 2008). Subsequently, it is perhaps best to consider that WM is not completely distinct from short-term memory. Indeed, it does appear that short-term memory is a subset of working memory, given that working memory is often considered a more holistic conceptualisation of memory in that it consists of a number of components *working* together (Cowan, 2008). Early theoretical understandings of this memory system often suggested the existence of a single unitary and temporary memory storage. Recent research suggests that there is much more at work in a system that effectively forms the interface between perception, attention, memory and action and as such the term working memory is preferred (Baddeley, 2007; Cowan, 2008; Nagel, 2014).

Components

The theoretical framework underpinning and identifying the existence of working memory emerged from research in the 1970s (Baddeley & Hitch, 1974). Importantly, while definitions of working memory have varied since, there does seem to be a consensus that working memory encompasses both storage and processing functions (Cowan, 1998; Cowan & Morey, 2006; Goldman-Rakic 1996; Li, Christ & Cowan, 2014). These functions are represented in a model of working memory that consists of three components (Figure 6.4): the *phonological loop*, the *visuospatial sketchpad* and the *central executive* (Baddeley, 2003b).

FIGURE 6.4   COMPONENTS OF WORKING MEMORY

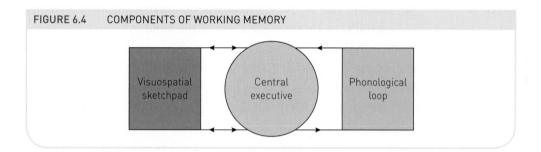

The phonological loop is a limited capacity system that encodes auditory information and is active when we remember words through reading them, speaking them or repeating them (Gazzaniga, Heatherton & Halpern, 2010). This system is also evident when we talk to ourselves using our 'inner voice'. As you read these words, it is your phonological loop that is engaging your inner voice as your mind recites what you see.

The visuospatial sketchpad is also a limited capacity system but it processes visual and spatial information rather than sounds. It is the visuospatial sketchpad that enables people to create and manipulate objects in their mind or plan spatial movements, such as deciding one's way through a complex building. Similar to the inner voice of the phonological loop, the visuospatial sketchpad provides an 'inner eye' when we plan how we might move from place to place or when visualising the layout of our home if asked how many windows it has. Being able to hold and manipulate visuospatial representations is an important aspect of memory and cognition for architects and engineers and likely played an important role in Einstein's development of a general theory of relativity (Baddeley, 2003b).

The final component of working memory that appears to preside over the actions of the phonological loop and visuospatial sketchpad is the central executive. As the name implies, it oversees the general functions of working memory. Importantly, the central executive is an active system that appears to be able to work at different speeds depending on the task (Cervone, 2015). Taken together, the central executive, phonological loop and visuospatial sketchpad underpin the functionality of working memory as a collection of mental processes that permits information to be held for a period of time in service of some mental task. Due to the underlying dynamics of the components, it is also evident that working memory is related to cognitive aptitude and relies on attention (Cowan, 2008; Vergauwe & Cowan, 2014). Listening to a speaker while writing down notes of what might have been said some seconds earlier is one example of how attention and working memory are connected.

Development of working memory

Given the structure and function of the components of working memory, it is not surprising that it is a critically important mechanism of the mind in terms of language development and reading. Problems with working memory have been associated with a number of learning disabilities (Baddeley, 2003a; Breznitz & Share, 1992; Gathercole & Baddeley, 1993; Jeffries & Everatt, 2004). Working memory also serves a number of other important functions, including being part of high-level cognitive activities such as thinking (Berninger & Richards, 2002). Because it is involved in higher order functions, it also should not be surprising that the brain's frontal lobes play a role in the storage and processing of working memory. Other areas of the brain, including the cerebellum, seem to be involved in supporting working memory, depending on the demands of the particular task, but it is the frontal cortex that appears to be of most importance; individual differences in frontal cortical structures have been shown to correlate positively with differences in working-memory capacity (Geake, 2009). It also appears that converting working memory into long-term memory involves a complex interplay between the frontal lobes and hippocampus (Geake, 2009; Ratey, 2001). It is also worth noting that working memory improves with age and becomes active when children can store information in their mind and perform rudimentary executive functions (Goldman-Rakic, 1993). Generally speaking, working memory is very poor during infancy, improves markedly from four to eight years of age and then shows gradual improvement through adolescence, when performance begins to mirror adult capacities (Ben-Yehudah & Fiez, 2007; Gathercole, 1999; Nagel, 2012a).

While working memory matures and improves with age, it is also important to note that it is limited by the workload it can handle and it is very effortful and attention demanding. Working memory is linked with many important cognitive functions, including paying attention, thinking, following instructions, reasoning, social interactions and complex learning (Gathercole, 1999). Over the course of development and as working memory improves, children can handle increasing workloads, but throughout development the workload of any task may exceed working-memory capacities (Berninger & Richards, 2002). One way of reducing the workload of working memory is to build the automatic nature of certain low-level functions in order to free up capacity for higher level cognitive activity. For example, helping children develop their rote capacities for spelling or number facts or both in the early primary years allows them to devote greater time and energy later to more advanced aspects of writing and solving problems.

This description of working memory is supported also by numerous studies noting that learning is based not only on cognitive mechanisms that draw on information with emotional significance but also on automatic responses associated with rote memory (Berninger & Richards, 2002). As noted earlier, the amygdala plays an important role in memory formation and—because of its role and function in the limbic system—it appears ideally suited for processing emotionally charged information, thereby helping to determine what is important to pay attention to and remember. But, once some measure of stimuli is attended to and recognised as important or worthy of remembering for more than a short period of time, the brain shifts this information into long-term memory.

LONG-TERM MEMORY

Understanding long-term memory and how learners might store information in it to use on later occasions to solve problems is arguably a major goal of most educational endeavours. In itself, long-term memory provides a system for permanently storing, managing and retrieving information for later use, some of which may be available for a lifetime. But, as simple as it may sound, long-term memory is actually a multi-stage process involving many regions of the brain. It appears that, while the amygdala and hippocampus play important roles in shifting working memory into long-term memory, the temporal and frontal lobes also assist in this process (Kandel, Kupfermann & Iversen, 2000). When the brain converts data and information from the environment into mental representations—what is known as *encoding*—the process of strengthening these representations for long-term memory—otherwise known as *consolidation*—requires various actions. Repetition, practice and linking information to previous memories are examples of how the brain consolidates mental representations into long-term memory. During consolidation, the brain reorganises and stabilises its memory traces. Consolidation may occur over several hours or longer. It involves deep processing of material via a number of brain regions but most importantly the frontal lobes and regions of the limbic system (Berninger & Richards, 2002; Brown, Roediger & McDaniel, 2014; Sweeney, 2009). The process of consolidation establishes memories more firmly for later retrieval when needed, making them less subject to misremembering or forgetting. But not all long-term memories are the same and, while thoughts, perceptions, emotions and actions are both the product and process of neurons firing together, there seem to be two systems of long-term memory that influence and are influenced by such neural networks—*implicit* and *explicit* memories.

EXPLICIT MEMORIES

Explicit memories, sometimes referred to as *declarative* memories, engage the hippocampus, thalamus and regions of the frontal cortex, and are those memories that we recall consciously and describe verbally (Frackowiak, 1994). Explicit memory involves *knowing that*, for example, Canberra is the capital of Australia, kangaroos are marsupials and you had a wonderful time during your last holiday. Explicit memory is the foundation for factual knowledge, involves a degree of conscious effort to bring to mind and, to add to its complexity, can be broken down into two further subgroups: episodic memory and semantic memory.

Episodic memory
A type of explicit memory where we recall things said or done over time.

Semantic memory
A type of explicit memory related to factual information and knowledge.

Episodic memories

Episodic memories seem fairly self-explanatory, given that they refer to the memories of specific experiences in our lives that generally have strong emotional value. They are the memories of the things we have seen or done, and we have the capacity to place facts and events in time and refer to them freely (Nagel, 2012a). Episodic memories are very strong, given they are shaped by emotion, but they are also rather fallible. We tend to assume that the memories of important episodes in our lives remain consistent and stable over time, yet we often add to these memories, change subtle details within them and each time recall a memory we integrate whatever details we do remember with our expectations for what we should remember (Chabris & Simons, 2010). Two individuals can have very different recollections of the same event; this is one of the reasons why eyewitness testimony to a crime can be problematic without corroborating evidence or why personal tales of fishing adventures from one group of friends to another can see the size of catch increase without scrutiny.

Notwithstanding the potential inconsistencies associated with episodic memories, they also play a significant role in the encoding and consolidating of long-term events and experiences. When an event evokes a strong emotional response, a person is more likely to remember many, but not all, aspects of the event. This is another reason the limbic system can play such a significant role in memory formation and should always be a considered aspect in the design of any formal learning experience; emotions can play a powerful role in retaining what has been learnt.

Semantic memories

While it is clear that episodic memories may not always be as accurate as we like, semantic memories do not share such inconsistencies. Semantic memories are those memories about information and knowledge of the world around us and generally deal with facts such as names, dates and places (Howard, 2006; Nagel, 2012a). Semantic memories also differ from episodic memories in that they are devoid of any emotional content. Semantic memories are those that students rely on when they do exams and attempt to recall information such as the date Japan bombed Pearl Harbor. Interestingly, the interplay between semantic and episodic memories and how we rely on each for different things presents various challenges for teachers when it comes to pedagogy and assessment.

It should now be apparent that emotion and the limbic system play a significant role in our capacity for forming long-lasting memories. While episodic memories are not difficult to recall, given that they tend to be emotionally laden, the same cannot be said for semantic memories. For many, trying to remember specific dates or various other types of factual content found in curriculum can be a challenge. Semantic memories focus on facts and verifiable information, yet they are exceedingly difficult to draw upon, particularly in stressful situations such as exams. It is not uncommon for students to draw a blank when they are being tested; if that same student has previously found the context of examinations to be a negative experience, then his or her episodic memory of such events can actually impede the capacity for recalling semantic information.

A further challenge regarding memory that teachers must always bear in mind is that the memory distortions often associated with episodic memory are exacerbated in a young, developing brain. Most people will have very few, if any, memories of their lives before the age of three or four, given the immature nature of the brain and the lack of experiences to coherently tie events together; all aspects of a child's memory system simply improve with age (Bauer, 2005; Davis, Gross & Hayne, 2008; Howe & Courage, 2004; Munkata, 2004; Nagel 2012a, 2014; Neisser, 2004). As children mature, their working-memory capacity improves as does their ability to shift important information into their long-term memory; teachers who are able to limit stress and develop pedagogical strategies that use emotions as a catalyst for learning are more likely to assist students in their ability to recall all aspects of explicit memories. Fortunately, implicit memories are not often as laborious to place into long-term storage.

IMPLICIT MEMORIES

In contrast to explicit memories, implicit memories relate to those things we do without thinking or without typically putting into words. Implicit memories are knowing how to do something, and can also be referred to as *non-declarative* memories. Implicit memories include habits and conditioned reflexes along with automatic actions acquired through practice and repetition. The most common manifestation of implicit memory is procedural memory and refers to those things we perform or proceed to do automatically. Riding a bicycle or driving a car requires procedural memory to balance and pedal or switch smoothly from accelerator to brake without conscious effort. Procedural memory is called upon regularly through the course of any day and is evident when we tie our shoes and brush our teeth with little or no awareness of the skills involved.

One of the most interesting aspects of implicit memory is that it does not appear to reside within a particular structure of the brain but rather reflects a general principle of neuroplasticity in that it operates as a complex system of neuro-circuitry (Reber, 2013). This may help to explain the automatic nature that can be obtained but also serves to remind us that two important keys to forming long-term implicit memories are practice and repetition. This is true of the skills we need to rehearse when learning how to ride a bike or practising the alphabet to a point where each letter can be rapidly stated without having to pay serious attention to it. While rehearsing such skills over and over again, the brain is going through a continual process of shaping and reshaping until such actions become a hard-wired platform of the mind.

A final important point related to procedural memories, and in contrast to explicit memories, appears to be that procedural memories are not stored and retrieved but instead are used. This explains why procedural memories do not reside in particular structures but rather work as a system of motor pattern generation and feedback processes that can be activated and deactivated according to necessity and context. For example, riding a bicycle involves numerous regions of the brain to facilitate balance and coordination. The visual system is also engaged in an effort to respond to oncoming objects while automatic motor reflexes, such as compensating for objects that might influence the steering, are engaged without conscious thought. All of these activities use a number of systems and regions of the brain in a moment-by-moment skill set for bicycle riding.

Notwithstanding the distributed nature of procedural memories, it is clear that the prefrontal cortex and cerebellum—as well as another area of the brain known as the basal ganglia—are significant regions of activity when procedural memories are called upon. They appear to learn from each other and work together to facilitate the numerous skills we often do not think about and learn to take for granted, given the automaticity that evolves over time. To that end, it is important to remember that the neural basis of procedural memory operates as a system that makes use of almost the entire brain with different regions specialising for different aspects of procedural learning (Reber, 2013). This may be one reason procedural memories are not easily forgotten, while other types of memories can fade, be hindered or appear lost.

Procedural memory
A type of implicit memory that is used to do things automatically and without conscious effort.

MEDITATION, MINDFULNESS AND MEMORY

Schools are busy places! You will hear teachers and students describe their days as hectic and sometimes chaotic. Unfortunately, chaos is not a great foundation for memory formation and learning. Increasingly, schools are looking for ways to calm the minds of their students and there is a growing body of research noting how incorporating mindfulness programs as part of the curriculum has significant benefits for student mental health and scholastic endeavour. For example, a recent study found that students assigned to a mindfulness meditation program showed improvements in memory (Quach, Mano & Alexander, 2015).

From March to July of 2013, 198 middle school students from a school in southern California were randomly divided into three groups: mindfulness meditation, hatha yoga or a waitlist. The students were from low-income households and completed memory assessments before engaging in the study. The meditation and yoga groups met with trained instructors for forty-five minutes twice a week for four weeks and those doing meditation focused on breathing techniques, posture and wandering thoughts. While measures of stress and anxiety decreased in all three groups, including the 'waitlist' control group, working memory scores only improved in those students who engaged in the meditation sessions. Importantly, the researchers note that the practice of meditation, which requires sustained attention while simultaneously redirecting waning attention to the meditative experience, is closely related to the function of working memory. It is equally important to remember that working memory is involved in many aspects of learning like reasoning ability, reading comprehension and solving mathematical problems, suggesting that meditation may be a useful tool for helping students with various scholastic endeavours.

The Quach, Mano and Alexander (2015) study is one of a growing number looking at the benefits of mindfulness, meditation and yoga programs for behaviour, learning and productivity. Such studies are also finding benefits in attention, concentration, emotional regulation and numerous other processes of the mind related to behaviour and learning. Concurrently, organisations as diverse as Google, General Mills, the Seattle Seahawks (an American gridiron team) and branches of the United States military have embraced mindfulness programs as a means of boosting productivity and performance. Given the scientific evidence and the willingness of such enterprises as Google and the military to use mindfulness programs to get the best out of their personnel, perhaps schools might embrace such ideas with a view to improving memory, attention and concentration and, by association, behaviour and learning.

Ask yourself...

1   Drawing from the findings of the studies above, what might this mean in terms of helping students in your classroom perform better?

2   Reflect back to Chapter 1 and the brief discussion of teacher burn-out. Given the potential benefits from 'mindfulness' programs, what might you do to assist yourself in remaining attentive, calm and at your best in the often-hectic environment you are planning on working in? What could you and your students practise together? What steps would you need to take to develop and implement such practices in your class or school?

WHAT HINDERS MEMORY AND WHY WE FORGET

Not too dissimilar to understanding the complexity of how memories are formed, why we forget seems equally multifarious. Certainly any damage to regions of the brain associated with memory formation could result in problems with both short-term memory and long-term memory. One of the most famous examples of this in scientific literature, first reported in 1957 by Scoville and Milner, is the case of Henry Gustav Molaison who, until his death in 2008, was only referred to as HM to protect his privacy. His story began when he received major trauma to his head in a bicycle accident at seven years of age. After his accident, Molaison suffered from partial epileptic seizures that increased in number and severity as he aged. By age twenty-seven he could no longer earn a living; large doses of anti-seizure medication were ineffective so radical surgery was recommended. This surgery was performed on various regions of his temporal lobes but also resulted in the removal of large sections of his hippocampi and amygdala. Although Molaison's seizures disappeared, an unexpected result of his surgery was that he could remember much of what happened before the surgery but he could not form new memories. Molaison's language and perceptual skills were intact and his attention and working-memory capacity were normal but he could not consolidate and store information into long-term memory. For example, he could carry on a conversation proficiently but only a few minutes later would be unable to remember the exchange or whom he had spoken with (Annese et al., 2014). Interestingly, Molaison's ability to form long-term procedural memories was left unimpaired; he could learn new motor skills, despite not being able to remember learning them.

The results of Molaison's surgery revolutionised our understanding of the organisation of human memory and provided the basis for the study of human memory and disorders (Sweeney, 2009). His surgery also provided the first conclusive evidence that the hippocampus is fundamental in the formation of memories and paved the way for research into this important region of the brain. Fortunately, most people will never share Molaison's experience given the advancements in technology and surgical procedures.

While Molaison's story provides us with a concrete example of how memory can be impaired due to brain injury or trauma, we also know that the consolidation of memories can be impeded through much less tragic means. Decay, or the fading of information from memory, is one way that we forget (Cervone, 2015). One prominent theory of forgetting linked to decay is found in the phenomenon known as *interference*, whereby our memories of certain bits of information are hampered by the presence of other information. McInerney (2014) provides a great example of how interference occurs at the beginning of every year with teachers when the need to learn the names of their new students is often hampered by memories of the names of their students from the year before. Eventually the teacher will come to remember the new names but ironically may now struggle to remember the students they taught previously. This example also demonstrates how interference can be either *proactive* or *retroactive*. While trying to remember new names, proactive interference results from old memories and later retroactive interference occurs when the memory of new names inhibits the recollection of the names of past students. Importantly, both phenomena possess implications for all kinds of human learning.

ATTENTION AND ASSOCIATIONS

While interference can hamper memories, we may often forget things due to other problems in encoding. Attention is crucial to the encoding of memories and, as such, learning new information can be impeded when we are distracted. It is significant to note that attention improves with age; as the brain matures, our capacities for maintaining attention increase. But, no matter what our age, we will pay more attention to something if it interests us and we will remember much better if what we are trying to remember has meaning or cues previous memories: thus your memory is a product of what you think about (Willingham, 2009).

The importance of attention to memory, and by association learning, cannot be understated. Attention refers to the processing or selection of some information at the expense of other information (Pashler, 1998). Attention helps to determine which information is encoded into short-term memory from sensory memory and, in a cyclical fashion, our memory systems influence what we pay attention to (Cervone, 2015). Attention is also important for the encoding and manipulation of information in working memory; things cannot move into long-term memory unless they have first been in working memory (Fougine, 2008; Willingham, 2009). This is why paying attention to something is important for learning and why distractions can hinder what we remember. Distractions, in effect, work to decay memories. In the absence of any distractions, we may not make enough associations with new information, which also leads to an inability to retrieve such information later.

Making associations with new information is an important component of remembering. In an educational context, making associations serves as a constant reminder of the importance of understanding a student's prior knowledge and interests. Making associations also helps to reinforce that learning and remembering new information is intimately linked with prior-to-class learning both inside and outside school (Geake, 2009). Association, along with other parameters around how to enhance aspects of memory, are explored later, but one final point related to forgetting is significant here.

THE NECESSITY OF FORGETTING

While it may sound educationally antithetical, forgetting is not always a negative. Given the nature and underlying structures of our memory systems, we actually forget most of what impinges on our everyday lives. Our senses take in thousands of bits of information every second and our short-term memory systems hold information momentarily for good reason: not doing so would create chaos in our mind if our brains attended to and remembered every minute detail of the day. In this sense, forgetting is a necessary mental activity that may actually serve as an adaptive feature of the mind (Bannon, 2006; Geake, 2009). It is important to note that while forgetting may be an important process for effective functioning of the mind, the intent of much educational endeavour is about remembering information and acquiring various skills. From pre-school to tertiary settings, educators want students to remember many things and the success of any educational endeavour is often based on how well students can demonstrate what they have remembered and learnt. This necessitates some insights into what may not only hinder memory but also what might be done to help students remember.

ENHANCING MEMORY: EDUCATIONAL AND PEDAGOGICAL CONSIDERATIONS

An important demand often made of students in an educational context is the retrieval of information as a means of demonstrating that learning has occurred. This retrieval of information can take many forms and be expressed in a number of ways but is usually couched within a framework of assessment. In itself, assessment in an educational context is a complex enterprise (aspects of assessment are explored in Chapter 10). Our focus here is on what can be done to enhance memory or, more succinctly, what are the key factors and strategies for helping students retrieve information or remember.

See Chapter ⑩ for more detail on problematic assessment practices.

Before we look at specific strategies for enhancing the retention of skills and information, it is significant to note that a number of factors will influence long-term memory retention and retrieval. For example, the intersection of the degree of organisation and structure of material being learnt with a student's prior knowledge and instructional techniques is an important consideration for facilitating retention (McInerney, 2014). Such factors are part of a teacher's pedagogical practice and, importantly, will vary depending on age and background of students, context, subject content, curriculum demands, time and assessment strategies. Throughout *Understanding Development and Learning*, references have been made to pedagogy in a variety of ways but it is noteworthy that a template for successful pedagogical practice is arguably a bridge too far to offer in theory or in practice. 'Good' teaching has often been described as an art or science but it is likely both; 'good' pedagogy is a fluid enterprise that is not solely the product of any one thing. To that end, what follows is a list of strategies that have been shown to facilitate better encoding and retrieval of information.

REPETITION AND PRACTICE

It should not be surprising that perhaps the foremost mechanism for enhancing some aspects of memory is through repetition and practice. But there are some important considerations for each strategy that are often forgotten or misunderstood. First, repetition in itself does not lead to greater retention; a belief that if students do something often enough they will catch on or remember something is erroneous (McInerney, 2014). What is important in terms of repetition is that it is most useful if it has the interest and attention of the learner, is used to recall material already learnt and is associated with meaningful thinking (McInerney, 2014; Willingham, 2009). For example, students can write out spelling words over and over again but still not remember them if simply writing them out is the way the task is performed. If students are required to articulate the actual meaning of each word and use them in a personally meaningful sentence each time they are written then the likelihood of remembering the spelling is enhanced. It is always important to remember that what you think about is what you remember or, more aptly put, that memory is the residue of thought (Willingham, 2009). Significantly, providing students with specific tasks that will encourage them to think about meaning will not only assist in retaining information but also make retrieval of that information easier in the future (Pressley & El-Dinary, 1992).

Second, practice must also be meaningful but it is more effective when it is spaced out or distributed over time. This is true of all types of memory. For example, encoding procedural memories often takes multiple instances of practising a particular skill before automaticity is reached, while cramming for an exam will yield a poorer result than studying material in multiple sessions over time. There is an extensive amount of research noting that the most efficient way to learn is to study for shorter periods but spread these out over several days or weeks (Gazzaniga et al., 2010). Studying a few spelling words each day for a week will ensure better mastery than a large number bunched into one lesson (McInerney, 2014). Importantly, practice must also be meaningful given that we will attend to information more deeply if we are interested in it or see it as having a purpose.

Finally, retention of information through repetition is enhanced through feedback. Learning to ride a bicycle requires the brain to process information related to balance, speed, the environment and spatial awareness; constant feedback is provided as one sits on a bike and tries to move it forward without falling over. The spelling of words can easily be remembered incorrectly if feedback is not provided; if practised, over time incorrect spelling can be ingrained in the neuro-circuitry of the brain as easily as those words spelt correctly. In this sense feedback is not a summative endeavour but is part of an ongoing dynamic used to enhance what needs to be remembered and retained for future use. Indeed, frequent formative assessment and corrective feedback are integral tools for not only promoting long-term memory, but also for developing the executive functions of analysis and reasoning (Willis, 2010). Executive functioning and memory are also enhanced through reflection, elaboration and overlearning.

OVERLEARN, REFLECT AND ELABORATE

Closely linked to repetition and automaticity is the concept of *overlearning*. When people have material in front of them or when they think that they have mastered something, they may become overconfident that they will remember things later. To overlearn means to practise beyond the level of mastery and suggests that rehearsing material even after one believes it has been learnt will further enhance retention (Gazzaniga et al., 2010). Improving memory through the rehearsal of material is also enhanced when we *reflect* and *elaborate*. Thinking about the meaning of what we are trying to learn and then using those reflections by organising that information in a way that makes sense or putting it into our own words is highly beneficial. For learners, this is about using working memory to carve out a deeper understanding of material. For teachers, this suggests that helping students to process material more deeply by looking for relevance and thinking about meaning should be an important goal whenever applicable and appropriate (Willingham, 2009). To achieve such a goal, learners can be asked to treat new information actively rather than passively: for example, by asking questions about it, diagramming it, outlining it or presenting it in some other format. Learners could also be asked to look for relationships or differences between new information and what is already stored in their long-term memory. The key point here is that long-term memory retention and retrieval is improved when learners actively interact and think about the information in working memory.

CHUNKING AND MNEMONICS

Working memory is an important component for shifting information into long-term memory for later retrieval. Chunking and mnemonics are strategies that can assist this process and also aid retrieval of what is stored in our long-term memory. Because working memory has limitations in terms of capacity, duration and processing, chunking is useful for increasing the amount of information to be used in working memory. As the name suggests, chunking is a strategy whereby different pieces of information are put together into one memorable piece. For example, read the line of letters below and then quickly cover up the line and see how many you can remember:

TQLASDSAVNICSW

What you are likely to find in remembering the random letters is that you may recall the first few or the last few but not the middle. This is because the randomness of the letters, on the surface, does not present any pattern and there are too many to be remembered. You may remember the first bit or the last bit due to phenomena known as the *primacy* and *recency effects*; items at the beginning (primacy) of the list or end (recency) are not interfered with by other information and thus are recalled more easily than those in the middle (Cervone, 2015). But what happens if you group the letters as follows?

TAS QLD SA VIC NSW

The letters are no different from those presented earlier, but they are now in five easily recognisable chunks of information representing five of the states in Australia. If you were asked to remember the letters now, you would find it much easier. Presenting materials in a way that promotes chunking or looking for ways to chunk information provides a tool for assisting working memory and long-term retention, as do mnemonics.

Mnemonics are useful tools for organising information in memory and the use of mnemonics in encoding can enhance retrieval and the transfer of knowledge (McInerney 2014; see also Carney & Levin, 2000). The word 'mnemonics' is derived from the Greek word *mnēmonikós* meaning 'of or relating to memory' and refers to using strategies for organising information for easier recall. Almost fifty years ago, a ground-breaking study found that students who regularly used mnemonic devices increased test scores up to 77 per cent (Miller, 1967). Mnemonic devices can take many forms. For example, music mnemonics have been used by generations of teachers to help children remember the letters of the alphabet by singing the ABC song. Acronyms employ mnemonics, which is why the word UNICEF can be easily unpacked as the United Nations International Children's Emergency Fund if such information is needed. And name–phrase mnemonics can be employed to remember ordered lists. The colours of the rainbow or visible spectrum—red, orange, yellow, green, blue, indigo, violet—become ROY G. BIV, while 'Kids play catch over Farmer Grey's stable' helps us remember the animal classification system of kingdom, phylum, class, order, family, genus, species.

There are many different types of mnemonic devices that can be employed for remembering various things. It is worth noting that the use of such devices is limited and depends very much on what is to be learnt and remembered.

HOW AND WHEN TO PRACTISE FOR BEST RESULTS

Practice makes perfect—but how much practice and how often? Some would have you believe that in order to master any field you need ten thousand hours of 'deliberate' practice (Gladwell, 2008). That idea has now been widely debunked with evidence noting that the amount of time required to achieve mastery depends on the type of field or activity, that a number of variables influence mastery and that practice only accounts for a small percentage of any performance outcome (Macnamara, Hambrick & Oswald, 2014). In an educational context, an important question for teachers is how much practice students need to learn a given body of knowledge or group of facts. Interestingly, an important part of that answer was uncovered more than one hundred years ago by Hermann Ebbinghaus, a psychologist often credited with the first scientific study of memory in 1885. In an experiment that would test the patience and endurance of many, Ebbinghaus tested his ability to learn hundreds of lists of meaningless syllables under different conditions and found that, if he distributed his practice over a period of time rather than trying to cram the information in quickly, he achieved better results, often cutting his study time in half (Ebbinghaus, 2011).

Since Ebbinghaus published his work, his 'spacing' effect has held up across many other studies with the end result being that massed practice, or what many students, parents and teachers call 'cramming', is less effective than distributed practice. In other words, trying to cram as much study into your brain the night before an exam is far less effective than short periods of study over time leading towards the exam. It is significant to note that distributed practice appears most advantageous for learning simple motor skills and learning new facts but not necessarily for highly complex skills; as such its effects will vary (Donovan & Radosevich, 1999). But the effect of distributing practice holds true for adults and school-age children alike and this is an important consideration when it comes to planning learning and teaching activities and designing assessment items and frameworks.

Ask yourself...

1   Aside from discouraging students from cramming for exams, how else might the phenomenon of distributed practice be used in an educational context? Consider homework, for example.

2   Students often have some 'down time' during the school day. What strategies can be used for distributed practice during the day when students are not engaged in specific classroom endeavours?

EMOTION

Not all that long ago, and indeed in some classrooms today, teachers focused on cognitive objectives at the expense of affective considerations, yet we now know that emotions play a vital role in learning, given that positive emotional arousal affects the strength of encoding long-term memories (Erk et al., 2003; Immordino-Yang & Faeth, 2010). This should not be surprising given that we are more likely to remember something if we pay attention to it and we generally pay attention to things that interest us with some measure of emotional arousal. Furthermore, our levels of motivation are influenced by emotion, we typically recall things that have the greatest emotional impact and separating our thoughts and emotions is arguably impossible (Nagel, 2013b; Zull, 2011). The importance of emotion as it pertains to motivation is explored in further detail in Chapter 7, but one final point about emotion deserves attention.

When we consider the important role emotions play in learning and memory, it is easy to focus on content. It is true that when students find content meaningful and relevant, they are more likely to engage with it, as this will evoke a level of emotional appeal. New or novel experiences may also foster a level of emotional engagement that helps to encode information into long-term memory. But one of the most important affective aspects of learning and memory, for better or for worse, is the emotional bond between students and teachers (Willingham, 2009). Effective teachers are able to connect personally with students and numerous studies across a number of disciplines tell us that positive relationships between teacher and student are a crucial factor in learning (Cozolino, 2013). Many competent teachers know this; those who don't would do well to remember that, when it comes to learning and memory, our memory systems do not operate like the emotionally devoid hard drive inside a computer, but function in the social emotional milieu of the environment around us.

CONCLUSION

Why and how we retain information and skills in our mind is a key consideration for educators. For optimal learning to occur, an understanding of how the brain changes with experience to give us memory should be a cornerstone of any teaching agenda. Thanks to more than a hundred years of research and recent advances in technology, we know a good deal about what happens when we store facts, experiences and skills in memory and what happens when we recall them. We also know what can hinder the formation of memories and what can be done to enhance them. Furthermore, we can ensure that students receive the best information and optimal conditions for memory and learning to occur, given that some long-standing notions of memory are misplaced or poorly understood.

In many schools past and present, students have been asked to memorise lengthy poems or passages of writing. The value of doing so is not in question here but one tangential benefit often provided to students for undertaking this endeavour is worthy of scrutiny. In order to justify the activity itself, some teachers have suggested that this activity is akin to exercising and strengthening the memory systems of the brain like lifting weights strengthens the body; memorise a long passage of writing, do so repeatedly and this will make your memory better for similar tasks in other subjects or contexts. While it may sound like a plausible theory, the fundamental ideas behind it are completely false: memorising one type of material may help improve performance on similar lists or materials but the benefits of such practice will not generalise to other materials (Roediger, 2013). There are methods that can be used to help students remember information and skills but we cannot strengthen memory systems in the same way we might strengthen our bodies.

Notwithstanding the important message in the preceding example, we can enhance the retention and retrieval of skills and information. An important component of doing so is the need to ensure that students look to find meaning in what it is they are attempting to remember. The brain is quite adept at storing meaningful information that can lead to neurochemical changes that produce emotional reactions resulting in the likelihood of that information being stored in memory and more easily retrieved (Gazzaniga et al., 2010). Teachers should be clear about what they want their students to remember, along with the how and why of doing so. The information in this chapter has been presented to give teachers a foundation for doing just that by explaining how the brain remembers through learning and how enhancing the retention and retrieval of information may be achieved.

CHAPTER SUMMARY

This chapter focused on the links between memory and learning or, perhaps more succinctly, explored memory systems of the brain as both a process and product of learning. The chapter opened with a look at the physiology of memory formation in the brain with a detailed look at the role of the hippocampus and amygdala in forming memories. The important role of emotions in memory formation was also explored before engaging in an examination of particular memory systems and stages. Working memory and long-term memory were considered along with a detailed look at episodic, semantic and procedural memories.

Given that memory plays such an important role in determining what, if any, learning has occurred, the chapter then shifted its emphasis by looking at what contributes to the hindering of memories or why things may be forgotten with a particular interest in how this might happen in an educational context. Importantly, the chapter concludes by providing some insights into strategies and approaches for enhancing memory formation in the classroom. The final emphasis focuses on broad strategies for encoding, consolidating and retrieving information and skills rather than a pedagogical panacea for enhancing memories across all ages and year levels. This approach is purposeful in that the range of differences within individuals and across educational contexts is far too expansive to offer a template for working on aspects of memory in all students.

Implications for Teaching

While human memory systems appear complex and have often been described as one of the brain's most mysterious features, it is clear that memory and learning are inextricably linked. In order for learning to occur, the brain receives information and encodes or creates meaningful representations of these experiences. For those experiences we wish to remember, there must be a measure of consolidation whereby the brain reorganises and stabilises the information received. Finally, when necessary, the information is retrieved. Encoding, consolidating and retrieving are arguably the systemic framework for memory and learning. As a future teacher, your goal is to engage this system most effectively. This section outlines some key considerations to both help reinforce the content of this chapter and provide a succinct template to keep in mind when planning learning and teaching experiences.

Encoding happens all the time as we gather information from the environment through our senses and experiences. Consolidation, on the other hand, requires more effort along with a degree of prior knowledge. Consolidation is about the mind pulling fragments of information together from the past and present and organising that information so that it moves from the working memory to long-term storage. As noted throughout the chapter, many things can both assist and hinder consolidation and, by association, influence the retrieval of that information.

Retrieval, therefore, best occurs when memory formation results from the consolidation of knowledge, skills and experiences that are particularly vivid, meaningful and practised. That means that we are more inclined to remember and learn those things that have interest and meaning to us, given that we will pay more attention to what we are doing or need to do. Retrieval can be impeded or overridden by other memories or past experiences. Context plays a key role in retrieval, and the social and emotional environment of a classroom is an important consideration when it comes to memory and learning. For example, it is significant to remember that emotional memories such as a fear or anxiety about remembering dates can impede the retrieval of historical facts for a test, as experienced by Nicholas at the opening of this chapter.

Ask yourself...

1   If a student's emotions can play such a powerful role in memory and learning, what might this mean in terms of how you interact with students in a classroom? What are some important considerations in terms of how teachers engage with students? How would engagement differ across year levels?

2   The consolidation process in memory formation is something that can be readily influenced by the teacher. What strategies or approaches are important to consider when helping students learn new information? Is this the same for all ages of students? If not, why? You may wish to revisit Chapter 2 to answer this question.

PRACTICAL ACTIVITIES

1 *While on practicum*, keep a record of the strategies for promoting the memory of skills or information as used by your mentor teacher or other teachers you observe. If possible, try using some of the strategies from this chapter with your students to help them in their learning.

2 *While on practicum*, note the study skills used for test preparation by students or promoted by teachers. Where possible, develop and implement a plan of distributed practice as a means for test preparation. You may need to refer to *Understanding Development and Learning* to support what you intend to do and assist in your decision making and planning.

STUDY QUESTIONS

1 Describe the process of long-term potentiation in simple terms and note what that might mean in terms of learning and teaching in an educational context. Provide some examples of how teachers can enhance long-term potentiation.

2 What two structures in the limbic system are important in terms of memory formation? Why are they significant?

3 Describe and give examples of each of the following: episodic, semantic and procedural memories.

4 List some positive examples of how to use repetition and practice in a classroom context without creating situations that are monotonous or boring.

5 What are five things that may hinder consolidation or retrieval of information in an educational context? As a teacher, what can you do to limit the impact of such things in your practice?

FURTHER READING

Baddeley, A. D. (2007). *Working Memory, Thought and Action.* Oxford, UK: Oxford University Press.

Berninger, V. W. & Richards, T. L. (2002). *Brain Literacy for Educators and Psychologists.* San Diego, CA: Elsevier Science.

Brown, P. C., Roediger, H. L. & McDaniel, M. A. (2014). *Make It Stick: The Science of Successful Learning.* Cambridge, MA: Belknap Press.

Chabris, C. & Simons, D. (2010). *The Invisible Gorilla and Other Ways Our Intuitions Deceive Us.* New York, NY: Crown Publishers.

Cowan, N. (2008). What are the differences between long-term, short-term and working memory? *Progress in Brain Research, 169,* 323–338.

Immordino-Yang, M. H. & Faeth, M. (2010). The role of emotion and skilled intuition in learning. In D. A. Sousa (Ed.), *Mind, Brain and Education* (pp. 69–83). Bloomington, IN: Solution Tree Press.

Neisser, U. (2004). Memory development: New questions and old. *Developmental Review, 24*(1), 154–158.

Willingham, D. T. (2009). *Why Don't Students Like School: A Cognitive Scientist Answers Questions about How the Mind Works and What It Means for the Classroom.* San Francisco, CA: Jossey-Bass.

VIDEO LINKS

TVO Parents: *Working Memory and Learning*
https://www.youtube.com/watch?v=F5Ehe3KVGmY

This video is produced by a parenting organisation and provides a good discussion of working memory and learning along with ideas to help children improve their working memory.

L. Loar: *Enhancing Memory: The Role of Emotion*
https://www.youtube.com/watch?v=D2yE2uK_jB8

A fascinating look at the interplay between emotion and memory with a vivid explanation of the role of the amygdala in forming memories.

WEBLINKS

Educationworld: *Brain Friendly Teaching: Strategies to Improve Memory*
http://www.educationworld.com/a_curr/profdev/profdev156.shtml

A useful website for teachers in terms of exploring issues and challenges around teaching along with strategies and ideas for improving one's practice. In this part of the site, there is an interesting look at how to enhance student memory.

HelpGuide.org: *How to Improve Your Memory*
http://www.helpguide.org/articles/memory/how-to-improve-your-memory.htm

This website is developed by a non-profit organisation that focuses on mental health and well-being. In this part of their website, they offer some great ideas for improving and enhancing memories that can be applied in any context and practised with students.

7

MOTIVATION AND LEARNING

> The importance of student motivation has varied from peripheral to central in psychological and educational research over the years. Currently, research on student motivation seems to be central to research in learning and teaching contexts. Researchers interested in basic questions about how and why some students seem to learn and thrive in school contexts, while other students seem to struggle to develop the knowledge and cognitive resources to be successful academically, must consider the role of motivation.
>
> (Pintrich, 2003, p. 667)

LEARNING OUTCOMES

As you read through this chapter and undertake the exercises at the end, you will gain the ability to complete these tasks successfully:

→ describe and discuss important components of the brain as they pertain to motivation

→ describe important concepts of motivation and in particular the differences between extrinsic and intrinsic motivation

→ describe various theoretical understandings of motivation

→ develop strategies for engaging students and enhancing motivation in the classroom.

KEY TERMS

- motivation
- extrinsic motivation
- intrinsic motivation
- states
- traits
- anxiety
- arousal
- self-efficacy
- flow

Engaged students present fewer behavioural problems! This was expressed a great deal to Ms Weston when she was studying education at university. Now in her third year as a Year 7 teacher, Ms Weston is finding that ensuring students are always engaged in their work is not as easy as it sounds. Indeed, it is not uncommon for certain students to complain that what they are doing is boring and as such Ms Weston is concerned with her students' levels of motivation, and in particular with Tyler's seemingly endless desire to do nothing at all. Tyler's apparent lack of motivation, which Ms Weston believes borders on complete apathy towards school, has been exacerbated by his increasingly poor behaviour as he disengages from most tasks. In an attempt to remedy the situation, Ms Weston decides to develop a reward system for the whole class but with her own hidden agenda of changing Tyler's behaviour. The class has been informed that whenever they finish any in-class work ahead of time they will collectively earn extra free time at the end of the week. This free time, in turn, can be used to go outside, play games, watch a movie or any other activity that Ms Weston and the class can mutually agree on. The plan starts off well and all students, including Tyler, are enthusiastic and seem motivated to do their work when they need to in order to get their weekly reward. After three weeks, the apparent novelty wears off with Tyler and he is back to his old ways, only now his peers are blaming him for the dwindling lack of weekly free time as Tyler reverts to not completing his work when required. Unfortunately, his behaviour becomes worse as he rebels against some of his classmates, who continually deride him for not staying on task and helping the class win free time.

Tyler's behaviour is not uncommon, nor is the approach Ms Weston takes to try to remedy the situation. Unfortunately, the overall results are also not so terribly uncommon, given the complexities surrounding motivation, behaviour and learning. The following chapter sets out to explore various theories of motivation as they relate to learning and teaching but it is first advantageous to consider the following questions related to the scenario above and then revisit those questions later.

1   From your own experience in school, can you remember and note how teachers may have tried to motivate you or your peers?

2   Of those strategies, which seemed to be most positive and productive? Why might they have worked?

3   How might you look to motivate students in your classroom? What strategies would you implement?

INTRODUCTION

There is little denying that motivation is a key factor in learning and behaviour. People learn better when they are highly motivated as opposed to when they have little or no motivation (Reeve, 2015; Tokuhama-Espinosa, 2011). Generations of teachers know that motivated students typically do better academically and present fewer problems behaviourally. Students of all ages who arrive at school ready and eager to learn are often described as a 'joy to teach', while those who are less enthused can be labelled as 'unmotivated', 'lazy' or 'difficult'. But theories and ideas around motivation are expansive and far more complex than these simplistic descriptors of students. What drives one student into doing something may be completely different from what might drive another and how teachers contribute to student motivation is an equally important consideration. This chapter explores such issues and challenges around motivation by looking at the links between the brain and motivation and by examining various theories of motivation as they relate to learning, behaviour and educational contexts. Such an exploration is very important to teachers, given that any understanding of how learning works in an educational context has to have an understanding of what motivates students to learn (Mayer, 2008).

Students will do many things simply because they want to do them but, in an educational context, students may also need to do things for a number of other reasons that may conflict with their own desires and wishes. In this sense, understanding motivation and finding ways to motivate students is integral to most aspects of any classroom endeavour and useful for enhancing one's pedagogical practice. And while teachers have been exposed to various theories and research about this important topic, many of these theories have been developed around cognitive frameworks. Learning itself has often been deconstructed by psychologists as having three distinct components: cognition, emotion and motivation (Hidi, 2006; Meyer & Turner, 2002). This chapter does not aim to follow such practice and instead recognises the intimate links between cognition, emotion, motivation and their interrelated roles in learning.

Aspects of cognition have been explored throughout *Understanding Development and Learning* but, while they play a part in this chapter as well, the principal focus will be on emotion and motivation. Such an approach aligns with most theories of motivation, given that they are generally concerned with energising and directing behaviour in the knowledge that motivation links emotion to action (Pintrich, 2003; Ratey, 2001). Equally important to this approach is the recognition that there are a number of ways to describe and define motivation but the term itself is derived from the Latin verb *movere*, meaning 'to set in motion'. Broadly defined, motivation is a person's internal instigation and direction that influences behaviour. Motivational theories attempt to answer questions about what gets

individuals moving towards various activities or tasks (Nagel, 2014; Pintrich & Schunk, 2002). And while theories of motivation are important, our understanding of motivation, like our understanding of memory, begins by looking at the brain.

THE NEUROBIOLOGY OF MOTIVATION

It is important from the outset to note that concepts around motivation emerging from neuroscience can be quite different from those in education (Howard-Jones, 2010). Neuroscientists focus on the inner workings of the brain that facilitate particular behaviours while educators focus on behaviour and how to change it when necessary. But the insights into motivation derived from neuroscience provide educators with a deeper understanding of motivation that in turn may influence their practice and pedagogical decision making. By understanding how the human brain works to motivate students, educators have a starting point for thinking about how to enhance motivation. For example, an understanding of the reward systems of the brain is important in understanding the differences between intrinsic and extrinsic rewards and the pedagogical value of each. The following information related to the inner workings of the brain focuses on the most useful aspects for learning and the educating of young minds. This is purposeful given that mapping out all of the structures and their associated functions related to motivation is highly complex and beyond the scope of *Understanding Development and Learning*. For example, there appear to be sixteen structures associated with motivational and emotional states and each of these is influenced by a range of hormones and neurotransmitters (Reeve, 2015). It also appears that there are significant neural differences in the activation of various structures depending on whether motivation is a product of intrinsic desires or extrinsic factors (Lee, Reeve, Xue & Xiong, 2012).

See Chapter ❸ for an overview of the limbic system.

See Chapter ❻ for more information on the link between the limbic system and memory.

Notwithstanding such complexities, it should not be surprising that exploring the links between motivation and learning might initially focus on the limbic system. Chapter 3 provided an overview of the limbic system while Chapter 6 provided insights into the links between the limbic system and memory. Within these chapters it was noted that the limbic system is integral in the control and regulation of emotional responses and is an important region for working and long-term memory formation. The limbic system is also linked to the brain's pleasure centre, survival mechanisms and the prefrontal cortex. From a neurobiological perspective, feelings of pleasure and our innate drive to ensure survival (avoidance of pain) are arguably the brain's key instigators for action or, more succinctly, the brain's primary motivators (Esch & Stefano, 2006). Pleasure and survival as motivators are also evident in neuroscientific research that tells us that the brain has a set of hard-wired neural systems designed for either the avoidance of or approach to particular stimuli and that these systems involve regions of the limbic system and activities of particular neurotransmitters (Cervone, 2015).

THE HYPOTHALAMUS

Of the key elements associated with motivation, the most influential may be the hypothalamus. The hypothalamus (Figure 7.1) is not much larger than the end segment of the little finger and comprises only 0.4 per cent of total brain volume, but it controls and regulates a number of important functions and could be considered a 'motivational giant' (Carter, 2009; Reeve, 2015). Aside from controlling the autonomic nervous system, which regulates a number of important bodily functions, and also regulating the endocrine system, it is the hypothalamus that drives key biological functions including hunger, thirst and sex (Reeve, 2015). When we are motivated to eat, drink and seek intimacy, it is our hypothalamus that is playing a key role in these desires.

FIGURE 7.1   THE HYPOTHALAMUS

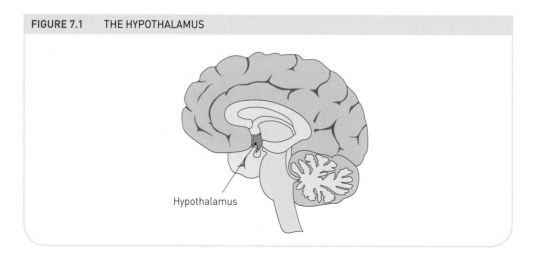

Hypothalamus

THE AMYGDALA

While the hypothalamus seems to drive pleasurable pursuits, the amygdala acts to ensure our survival. As noted in Chapter 6, the amygdala helps drive our fight-or-flight responses and plays an important role in emotional processing and memory. The amygdala also acts in concert with other regions of the brain to ensure our survival by detecting environmental threats and generating defensive responses (Cardinal, Parkinson, Hall & Everitt, 2002). Another important function of the amygdala is that it detects, responds to, and learns about rewarding and beneficial properties of various environmental stimuli and events (Baxter & Murray, 2002; Reeve, 2015). If you are thirsty—as mediated by the hypothalamus—and you see a cold drink, it is the amygdala that associates a stimulus-reward response and helps drive you to have a sip of that drink. This stimulus-reward principle is part of the amygdala's overall threat-and-reward detecting function and a key motivator for particular behaviours.

VENTRAL TEGMENTAL AREA

The amygdala is a key player in detecting potential rewards and it is important to remember that, at a neurobiological level, rewards are fundamental to motivation (Reeve, 2015). One region of the brain that is practically synonymous with the experience of reward is known as the *ventral tegmental area* (see Figure 7.2), which includes the *ventral stratium* and *nucleus accumbens* (Cardinal et al., 2002; Nagel, 2014; Reeve, 2015). The ventral tegmental region is one of the most primitive regions of the brain, containing a collection of neurons that synthesise dopamine (Nagel, 2014). As you recall from Chapter 3, dopamine is often referred to as the pleasure chemical. This is likely due to the fact that it is dopamine that allows communication between the brain structures involved with reward and pleasure (Daw & Shohamy, 2008). Some level of dopamine is always present in the brain but during pleasant or emotionally arousing experiences the ventral tegmental region facilitates the release of greater levels of dopamine into the nucleus accumbens, which in turn tells the prefrontal cortex that such experiences are pleasurable and worth acting on or seeking out (Nagel, 2014; Reeve, 2015). The nucleus accumbens is active not only during pleasant sensory experiences but also through social acceptance and inclusion and via several addictive drugs (Reeve, 2015; Sabatinelli, Bradley, Lang, Costa & Versace, 2007; Wise, 2002). It is through the activation of the ventral tegmental region and its associated structures that we learn what to like, what to prefer and what to want (Reeve, 2015).

FIGURE 7.2   THE VENTRAL TEGMENTAL AREA AND NUCLEUS ACCUMBENS

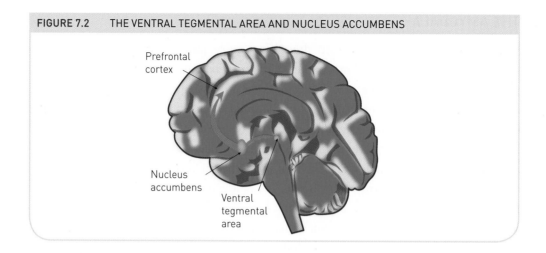

SUMMARY

It is worthy noting here that while regions of the limbic system have earlier been discussed as separate components, they work in an interrelated fashion to help drive the neurobiology of motivation. For example, people associate a reward value of any object or event via the amygdala and ventral stratium; then, through the release and interplay of dopamine, the ventral tegmental region and nucleus accumbens send excitatory signals to other regions of the brain for further action (Hampton & O'Doherty, 2007; Hayden, Nair, McCoy & Platt, 2008; McClure, York & Montague, 2004; O'Doherty, 2004; Reeve, 2015). Importantly, while it is the extent and volume of dopamine release that is the essence of reward-related information and provides sensations of pleasure or excitement or both, it is the prefrontal lobes that underlie affect (emotion), goals, personal strivings and what, if any, action is to be taken (Reeve, 2015).

Chapter 3 presented some background on the prefrontal lobes and identified them as the regions where executive functioning occurs and where much of our higher cognitive functions such as abstract thought and analytical reasoning take place. The prefrontal lobes are also significant in processing emotions and making decisions, and as such help facilitate mental events associated with planning goals, strategies, values and beliefs. It could be argued that the prefrontal lobes provide conscious and cognitively rich motivations as opposed to the unconscious, automatic and impulsive motivators like hunger, anxiety and fear found in the limbic system (Reeve, 2015). Of significance here is that, when it comes to motivation, the prefrontal lobes operate in a very interesting fashion. Activity in the left prefrontal lobe is associated with calmness, positive affect, group-oriented desires such as affiliation and a 'go' approach to motivation, while right prefrontal lobe activity is associated with arousal, danger, negative affect, individual-oriented desires such as personal protection and a 'no go' approach to motivation (Davidson, 2004, 2012;

Harmon-Jones, 2011; Reeve, 2015). In other words, right activations of the prefrontal cortex signal negative emotion and avoidance motivation and left activations facilitate positive emotion and approach motivation (Davidson, 2012). Moreover, biological basic personality differences exist and people with sensitive left prefrontal lobes approach tasks like thinking and planning with greater optimism and positive affect while those who have sensitive right prefrontal lobes may show avoidance behaviours, negativity and pessimism (Gable, Reis & Elliott, 2000). In an educational context this serves to remind teachers that no two children are the same and differences go beyond appearance, gender, ethnicity and culture; different neurobiological activations precipitate different approaches to learning and behaviour.

The differentiated activities associated with the left and right prefrontal lobes and motivation are representative of what have been labelled as behaviour approach systems (BAS) and behaviour inhibition systems (BIS) (Smillie, Pickering & Jackson, 2006). The BAS involves regions of the limbic system, dopamine and the left prefrontal lobe and is dedicated to producing pleasure states that drive people to pursue rewarding stimuli. In contrast, the BIS also involves regions of the limbic system but these areas work in concert with serotonin and the right prefrontal lobe to increase levels of negative affect, anxiety and arousal that causes people to stop pursuing rewards and attend to environmental threats (Cervone, 2015). In terms of motivation and learning, these neurobiological systems further emphasise that the human brain maintains innate differences in aspects of personality and also that the environment can act as a catalyst for engaging such systems; rewards and punishment can drive aspects of motivation at a neurological level. These systems also coalesce nicely with psychological notions of motivation and the various theories of motivation discussed next.

THE PSYCHOLOGY OF MOTIVATION

While neuroscience is interested in the mechanisms of the brain, psychology is generally interested in how the mind works and how this influences our thoughts and actions. The field of psychology is also very diverse; such diversity means different approaches and theories related to behaviour, emotions and thinking processes. But, in spite of the differences in approach, all branches of psychology are underpinned by a commitment to scientific methods requiring researchers to collect evidence, take observations systematically and record how observations were made in order to assist in replication en route to verifying results (Cervone, 2015). It is such an approach that allows us to look at motivation through various lenses and use the most applicable components of each theoretical lens within educational contexts. In order to begin such an exploration it is important to examine a few important concepts in motivation and then unpack particular orientations to motivation derived from psychology.

IMPORTANT CONCEPTS IN MOTIVATION

While various orientations to motivation focus on different factors, there are a few important concepts in motivation that are worth consideration by future teachers. The complexity associated with motivational theories dictates that aspects of these concepts may overlap with one another or be associated with different orientations to motivation. But what is important for future teachers is a basic understanding of each of these concepts and how they can affect the motivation, behaviour and learning of students. The first of these concepts is covered in greater detail when examining behaviourist orientations to motivation but it does deserve some initial mention here given its pervasive nature in society.

Extrinsic and intrinsic motivation

An important concept in terms of motivation that is quite prevalent in many of the things we do or avoid is that of extrinsic and intrinsic motivation. Extrinsic motivation arises from external sources, usually in the form of rewards or punishment. For example, parents may bribe their children with dessert if they finish their meal or teachers may provide gold stars or praise to students for completing a task. While the use of extrinsic motivators is quite common, they are not without controversy and for some people they are not as effective in the long term as intrinsic motivators. Intrinsic motivation refers to behaviour that arises from within the individual allowing for action without any obvious rewards. Intrinsic motivation is often associated with doing something for enjoyment or as an opportunity to explore, learn or arrive at a number of positive emotional states, while most of the activities we might think of as work are extrinsically rewarded (Baard, Deci & Ryan, 2004; Coon & Mitterer, 2010; Ryan & Deci, 2000). Extrinsic and intrinsic motivation are evident in many aspects of schooling and receive greater attention later in this chapter but for now it is important to note that they are intimately connected to the next important concept around motivation.

States and traits

In terms of motivation, aspects of states and traits often intertwine and it is sometimes difficult to distinguish between the two. Generally speaking, states refer to temporary conditions or feelings that might drive an individual's behaviour, while traits are stable and long-lasting dispositions. For example, being thirsty or hungry would drive one to seek water or something to eat while one's sex drive may be considered as a long-lasting disposition. It is important to note that traits can be a product of nature (innate predispositions) or nurture (learnt) and as such are linked to intrinsic and extrinsic motivation. Sex drive can be considered an innate trait, while a drive to achieve a good grade is something that is learnt. In an educational context, learnt traits may be the product of various needs including a need for affiliation, power, approval or achievement (Vialle, Lysaght & Verenikina, 2005). This links well with the work of Jere Brophy (1987) in terms of learning and classroom endeavour, for he identified that, while trait motivation is not overly influenced by environmental or situational factors, state motivation is highly variable and modifiable by external factors such as teacher behaviours and expectations. In this sense, it is important to remember that most states are temporary and can be adjusted but, if left unchecked, may result in the manifestation of an undesirable learnt trait. Perhaps a good example of this can be seen when students experience some measure of test anxiousness, which might initially be a state but, if not mediated, could present as a personality trait over time.

Anxiety and arousal

Many of us have experienced some measure of anxiety and arousal, but they are not the same thing. Anxiety is a generally considered a negative emotional state with feelings of worry, self-doubt, nervousness, apprehension and tension that can often engage the body's stress-response systems. Arousal, on the other hand, involves both physical and psychological reactions that can lead to positive behaviours and performance. It is this type of positive arousal that allows performers and athletes to excel at their chosen craft and may drive an individual to complete a task that might initially appear daunting; public speaking is a good example of a task that can exert some level of arousal on students so that they can perform when needed.

Understanding the links between anxiety and arousal and their relationship to motivation and performance has a long research history but one of the most commonly referred to theories is that of the inverted U theory, developed by Yerkes and Dodson (1908). Referred to as the Yerkes–Dodson Law, the balance between a state of arousal and performance is illustrated through the use of an inverted U, as shown in Figure 7.3.

Anxiety
A negative emotional state that can impair performance and engage the body's stress-response system.

Arousal
A physiological and psychological reaction that allows for enhanced alertness, attention and, at times, performance.

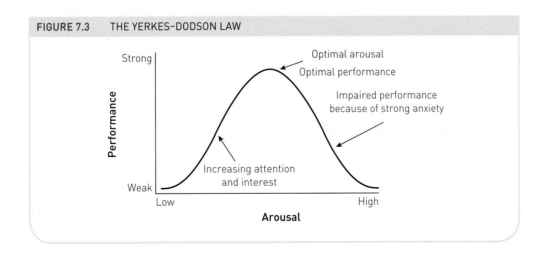

FIGURE 7.3   THE YERKES–DODSON LAW

The Yerkes–Dodson Law (Yerkes & Dodson, 1908) stipulates that a level of arousal can rise only so high before performance begins to diminish due to increased levels of anxiety associated with excessive arousal. It is noteworthy that, while there has been a fair degree of critique of the Yerkes–Dodson Law and subsequent models (see, for example, Hancock & Ganey, 2003; Hanoch & Vitouch, 2004), it is still widely regarded as an important, albeit simplistic, framework for understanding the relationships between anxiety, arousal, motivation and performance. In an educational context, for example, excessive arousal associated with anxiety can lead to poorer performances academically as evident in test anxiety. Anxiety can be very problematic in terms of learning, particularly in competitive environments where there is pressure to perform and severe consequences, perceived or actual, for failure (Wigfield & Eccles, 2002). An understanding of the role of arousal and anxiety in motivation is an important factor for enabling development and learning in a positive manner.

Affect and interest

Given the significance of the impact of anxiety and arousal on motivation, it should be equally apparent that affect and interest are important concepts when it comes to motivation. *Affect* or *affective* is a psychological term used to describe the experience of feelings, emotions or emotional states (Hogg, Abrams & Martin, 2010). At the same time, emotions have motivational power and interest is one emotion that increases motivation (Cervone, 2015; Lazarus, 1991). In itself, interest can be both a cognitive process pertaining to attention and concentration, as well as an affective state associated with positive feelings and a heightened state of arousal (Krapp, Hidi & Renninger, 1992). In an educational context, and in simpler terms, students tend to be motivated by things that interest them, whether such interest is aroused through internal states such as curiosity or via special characteristics of a situation such as a subject topic or lesson (Ainley, 2006). The role of affect and interest in terms of motivation and classroom endeavour cannot be understated. Triggering interest activates systems that generate positive feelings, focus attention and prompt cognitive activity (Ainley, 2006), but the methods used for triggering such interest are important considerations occupying various theoretical orientations: behaviourist, humanist, cognitive and social cognitive.

BEHAVIOURIST ORIENTATIONS TO MOTIVATION

See Chapter ❶ for detail on behaviourist orientations to learning.

Behaviourist views on motivation align closely with behaviourist views on learning (see Chapter 1). For behaviourists, motivation to do something is derived from past experiences and is generally shaped by rewards and punishment (Nagel, 2013b). In this context various types of reinforcements can be given to increase the likelihood of desirable behaviours. Enhancing motivation, in turn, is achieved primarily through using extrinsic reinforcement to stimulate a desired outcome. Extrinsic reinforcement can take many forms. In educational settings, extrinsic reinforcement can be used to help develop skills, enhance motivation or manage behaviour and can include positive feedback, praise, gold stars, a smile or the loss of privileges such as missing out on a desirable activity (Krause, Bochner, Duchesne & McMaugh, 2010). It is significant to reiterate that extrinsic reinforcement is not always positive and can include negative reinforcement or punishment. In this sense, rewards and punishment effectively operate in the same manner and, although they may use different behavioural means to an end, they function on a 'do this and you get that' principle.

The interrelated nature of rewards and punishment are indicative of a number of debates regarding the use of extrinsic reinforcement as motivational devices. While it is true that rewards might make an individual feel good and experience pleasure via the release of dopamine in the brain, and punishment may lead to negative affect and avoidance behaviours, there are some issues and challenges associated with extrinsic reinforcement. For example, researchers have found that the use of extrinsic motivators may undermine intrinsic motivation (Deci & Ryan, 2000; Deci, Koestner & Ryan, 1999, 2001). Intrinsic motivation is best defined as a desire to engage in activities because they are personally interesting, enjoyable and challenging (Gazzaniga, Heatherton & Halpern, 2010; Ryan & Deci, 2000). Surprisingly consistent evidence has shown that an interesting feature of intrinsic motivation is that rewards from others can actually decrease, rather than increase, motivation. A classic study conducted with children in the 1970s provides an excellent example of why this might be so and why teachers should think carefully about how, when and why they use rewards.

SOMETHING TO THINK ABOUT 7.1

EXTRINSIC MOTIVATION: A VICIOUS CIRCLE?

Stanford Professor of Psychology Mark Lepper and his colleagues conducted a fascinating experiment that involved drawing and pre-school children (Lepper, Greene & Nisbett, 1973). In this study, three groups of children were given the opportunity to draw with coloured marking pens. One group was extrinsically motivated with a 'good player award'. The second group of children were rewarded unexpectedly after the task, while the third group was neither rewarded nor led to expect that a reward was forthcoming for doing the task. During subsequent playtime the children who were offered the 'good player award' spent considerably less time playing with the pens than the children who never received a reward or received one unexpectedly. In essence the children who received the extrinsic motivation were less motivated to draw in their free time and would not do so unless they were 'paid' to do so. Importantly, subsequent years of research have replicated similar results showing that when people are intrinsically motivated to do something and then provided an extrinsic reward, their intrinsic motivation goes down (Deci, Koestner & Ryan, 1999; Cervone, 2015).

Ask yourself...

1   What might be some of the potential consequences for students of diminished intrinsic motivation?

2   Given the potential problems associated with rewards, what are some ways teachers can facilitate intrinsic motivation?

Further compounding potential problems with rewards is the fact that a reward, and punishment for that matter, is generally out of one's personal control. Whenever a reward is used, it is the person offering the extrinsic motivator that decides how, when or why it is given. Once again extrinsic rewards may diminish intrinsic motivation because they undermine a person's feeling that they are choosing to do something for themselves (Deci & Ryan, 1987). This is covered in greater detail later in this chapter but, for the moment, it is important to note that what Lepper and his colleagues found presents interesting considerations for any classroom. While there is evidence to suggest that rewards may increase or decrease the frequency of certain behaviours, they may also diminish intrinsic motivation that in itself appears to be an important component of any successful learning endeavour. This is most evident when exploring the humanist view of motivation.

HUMANIST ORIENTATIONS TO MOTIVATION

As you will recall from the discussion of humanist orientations to learning in Chapter 1, the core of humanist educational endeavour focuses on student needs, desires, personal values, self-perceptions and motivations. Humanist views of motivation, in turn, view the learner as a whole person and explore experiences of, and relationships among, physical, emotional, intellectual and aesthetic needs. There is also a focus on choice, creativity and self-realisation as part of developing one's individual potential, which is viewed as essentially good (Woolfolk & Margetts, 2013). Maslow's hierarchy of needs (see Figure 1.1 in Chapter 1) once again provides an appropriate foundation for examining aspects of humanism as applied to an understanding of motivation.

The first two levels of Maslow's hierarchy represent primary motivators for human survival. Food, water, warmth, rest, safety and security are essential needs, while the next two levels represent important psychosocial needs. Remember, the limbic system and the more primal regions of the brain are responsible for driving the behaviour, or motivating one's actions, to meet these needs. These needs are sometimes referred to as deficiency needs, because they motivate people to act only when they are unmet to some degree

(Snowman et al., 2009). Importantly, each of the lower needs must be met before the next higher need can be tackled; Maslow found that people were limited in their personal growth when deprived of needs or satisfaction at any level (Woolfolk & Margetts, 2013). Personal growth is where the limbic system and prefrontal lobes work in tandem, as they process emotion and engage higher order thinking and abstract reasoning. This type of neural activity is what one would expect moving up Maslow's pyramid, where it becomes evident that what might motivate an individual to go beyond deficiency needs are those needs associated with self-esteem, competence and autonomy as noted earlier. Indeed, Maslow's theoretical framework sits nicely with that of self-determination.

Self-determination theory

Self-determination theory is another humanist approach to motivation and suggests that a need for autonomy, whereby individuals strive to be in charge of their behaviour, is a critical component of intrinsic motivation. Autonomy involves volition and means moving away from the control of others and towards an increasing capacity to depend on one's self and to regulate one's own thoughts, feelings and behaviours (Deci & Ryan, 2000; Reeve, 2015). So strong is the human need for autonomy that it will always override any aspect of external control, even when this control is mediated by rewards (Reeve, Deci & Ryan, 2004). Significantly, numerous studies demonstrate that the more autonomous a person's motivation is, the more positive the person's functioning, the more effort a person puts forth, the more freely and willingly that effort is exerted and the more positive a person's outcomes are in terms of learning, performance and achievement (Reeve, 2015). It should be self-evident that self-determination plays an integral role in any educational endeavour and that a humanist approach to motivation in the classroom maintains important positive benefits. Classroom environments that support and foster self-determination and autonomy are associated with greater curiosity, student interest, creativity, conceptual learning, use of self-regulated learning strategies, sense of competence, school attendance, preference for challenge and psychological well-being; when students make choices, they are more likely to believe the work is important, even if it is not 'fun' (Woolfolk & Margetts, 2013).

Summary

To sum up: behaviourist approaches to motivation using rewards appear to have a number of limitations in terms of learning and behaviour and are likely best used for short-term purposes only, while humanist approaches appear to offer far greater benefit and positive outcomes. Cognitive views on motivation, given their emphasis on intrinsic motivation, seem to align somewhat with humanist views and also provide further insights into what drives an individual into action.

COGNITIVE ORIENTATIONS TO MOTIVATION

Cognitive orientations to motivation, like those of humanism, developed as a reaction to behavioural views (Krause et al., 2010; Woolfolk & Margetts, 2013). Some of the most well-researched and discussed theories of motivation have arisen from cognitive explanations of motivation (Krause et al., 2010). Cognitive orientations emphasise that a person's behaviour, and by association motivation, is determined by their thinking and not necessarily strengthened by the use of rewards and punishment (Snowman et al., 2009).

Like cognitive orientations to learning, definitions and meanings surrounding cognition and motivation can vary. As an umbrella term, 'cognition' unites a number of mental constructs including beliefs, expectations, goals, mindsets, plans, judgments, self-concepts and values that collectively function as determinants to action, or contributors to motivation (Reeve, 2015). In an educational context cognitive theories generally accept that children are innately active and curious, and there is a strong emphasis on intrinsic motivation (Pintrich & Schunk, 2002). Arguably, one of the most important theories to be found within a cognitive orientation to motivation is attribution theory.

Attribution theory

Attribution theory may best be encapsulated with the word 'why'. Students will often ask why they failed or succeeded in something and search for explanations or causes. The explanations for such outcomes can be considered as examples of attributions—and attribution theory is concerned with the way explanations of success and failure influence motivation and behaviour (Weiner, 1979). Such explanations are pivotal in educational settings, given that learners may attribute success or failure to different causes depending on their beliefs about who or what is in control of their success or failure (Krause et al., 2010). Importantly, classrooms are arenas for motivations beyond scholastic achievement and students may also ask questions related to interpersonal rejection or acceptance (Weiner, 1979). Perhaps the underlying constructs of this theory can be found in the realisation that positive and negative outcomes influence positive and negative emotions, promoting a causal search (Weiner, 2000, 2010).

The work of the esteemed American social psychologist Bernard Weiner has been some of the most influential for understanding attributes to success or failure in schools. According to Weiner (1979, 2000, 2010), the most important factors affecting attributions are ability, effort, task difficulty and luck, and the majority of attributed causes of successes or failures exist within three causal dimensions: *locus, stability, controllability*. Locus refers to when a learner has a tendency to attribute success or failure to internal (controllable) or external (uncontrollable) factors. For example, ability and effort could be considered as internal loci while luck or poor teaching may be positioned as external to the learner.

Stability, on the other hand, refers to whether an attribute stays the same (stable) or can change (unstable). Effort is something that can change, while talent may be considered a stable attribute. Finally, controllability is linked to whether the learner can control the cause of the success or failure. Effort is certainly controllable, while innate talent in music, for example, is not.

These causal dimensions play integral roles in motivation in schools, due to the fact that they often shape the reasons learners give for succeeding or failing at a task. Students with a history of success often attribute such success to effort and ability and any failure to lack of effort. Conversely, those students who struggle with aspects of school may attribute success to luck or ease of task and failure with a lack of ability (Snowman et al., 2009). Citing effort as a factor in success or failure is therefore likely to be more motivating than citing ability, because effort is something that can be modified, while ability can be demotivating in that it is a stable attribute and viewed as unchangeable.

An important feature of the attribution model and its causal dimensions is the recognition of both cognitive and affective influences on motivation (Krause et al., 2010). The internal influence of emotions on perceptions of causality are key to how students often view themselves and others. For example, the internal–external locus seems closely related to feelings of self-esteem in that, if success or failure is attributed to internal factors, success will foster pride and increased motivation while failure will diminish self-esteem. Controllability can be related to feelings of anger, pity, gratitude, guilt or shame. Failing a task due to lack of effort may elicit a sense of guilt while failing due to a lack of ability can lead to shame or anger (Weiner, 2010). In this sense, a student who feels guilty may take more responsibility for their effort, engage with future tasks more effectively and look to improve their performance, while a student who is angry or ashamed due to a perceived lack of control due to ability or talent may just give up. Such approaches to a task are closely related to another theory of motivation that focuses on expectations of success or value.

Expectancy-value theory

From the outset it is important to note that expectancy-value theory has been derived from various other theories and is closely related to individual notions of ability and attributes. Early work in this area identified that individual dispositions to success and failure are influenced by the environment and, as such, the value of a specific task and the expectation of success have an influence upon individual motivation (Atkinson & Feather, 1966; Atkinson & Raynor, 1974). Research has extended early notions of success and value, and identified that expectancies and values are assumed to not only influence achievement choices but also performance, persistence and effort (Eccles & Wigfield, 2002; Wigfield, 1994; Wigfield & Eccles, 2000; Wigfield, Eccles & Rodriguez, 1998; Wigfield, Tonks & Eccles, 2004; Wigfield, Tonks & Klauda, 2009). A key aspect of expectancy-value theory identifies that individuals tend to strive for successes and avoid failures. In an educational context this suggests that a student's expectations of success juxtaposed with their perceived value of the task influence the academic choices they make, the goals they set and ultimately their level of motivation. The value of a task, in itself, has been explored further (Eccles et al., 1983) with four components of value identified:

→ *attainment value*: the personal importance of doing well on a task
→ *intrinsic value*: the inherent, immediate enjoyment derived from performing the activity
→ *utility value*: the perceived importance the task has for current and future goals, even if there is no interest in the task for its own sake
→ *cost*: the negatives associated with engaging in a task, which can include anxiety, fear, amount of effort or lost opportunities with other activities (adapted from Eccles et al., 1983).

While the value of a task is a significant factor in an individual's motivation and choice of activities, it appears that the expectation of success is more important. It also appears that expectations of success are influenced by ability beliefs (Wigfield & Eccles, 2000), which are often an aspect of affect (emotion) and related to an individual's sense of self.

SOCIAL COGNITIVE ORIENTATIONS TO MOTIVATION

Paralleling the negative reaction to behaviourist views of motivation as set out by humanistic and cognitive orientations, social cognitivists also question the value of extrinsic sources of motivation (Krause et al., 2010). Social cognitivists are interested not only in the relationship between thinking and motivation but also how feelings of self in particular contexts influence motivation. Social cognitive orientations to motivation and learning, therefore, often focus on individual feelings of personal effectiveness or **self-efficacy**. It is important to note that self-efficacy is not the same as ability but rather it is a generative capacity in which a learner improvises ways to best translate personal abilities into effective performance (Reeve, 2015). Self-efficacy is future-oriented and context specific. To emphasise, context is important and a learner's motivation can be influenced by their own beliefs regarding their capability of completing specific tasks, which in turn can influence their perseverance or willingness or both to accept challenges. Self-efficacy can also influence a learner's approach to various tasks along with the types of learning goals a learner chooses. The work of Albert Bandura (see Chapter 1) once again plays a significant role here.

Self-efficacy

Professor Albert Bandura of Stanford University has shed considerable light on learning and, in particular, in relation to social learning theory. Bandura (1997) has also helped shape our understanding of the pervasive role of self-efficacy in learning, personal development

Self-efficacy
An individual's perceptions of ability of success in valued tasks.

See Chapter ❶ for more detail on social learning theory.

and change. According to Bandura (1977, 1997, 2006), efficacy beliefs affect whether learners think optimistically or pessimistically—or in self-enhancing or self-debilitating ways—and such beliefs influence goals, aspirations, outcome expectations, perseverance and, by association, motivation. For example, learners with low efficacy beliefs may give up on a task, particularly if they view the pathway to attaining success as one with insurmountable impediments and beyond their abilities.

A learner's sense of self-efficacy can very much influence their views of success or failure. Self-efficacy also plays a role in goal-setting behaviours; research evidence suggests that students will choose a variety of goal-setting approaches depending on their self-efficacy beliefs (Snowman et al., 2009; see also Harackiewicz, Barron, Pintrich, Elliot & Thrash, 2002; Obach, 2003; Pintrich & Schunk, 2002; Urdan, 2004; Urdan & Midgley, 2001; Wolters, 2004). For example, some students may exercise performance-avoidance goals such as avoiding novel or challenging tasks, cheating, putting off homework or projects until the last minute or other similar behaviours in order to avoid looking less capable than other students (Snowman et al., 2009). Importantly, how a learner exercises a sense of self-efficacy by setting goals and approaching tasks is also a product of experience; success can raise self-efficacy beliefs while failure can lower efficacy (Bandura, 1997). Along with past experiences, other sources and influences of self-efficacy include vicarious experiences, verbal and social persuasion and somatic (bodily) and emotional states (Bandura, 1997). Learners' self-efficacy beliefs and motivation can be influenced by watching others, encouragement from others or by physical and emotional states caused by thinking about undertaking new tasks or behaviours. In this sense, self-efficacy aligns with self-concept, which refers to our knowledge, ideas, attitudes and beliefs about ourselves and is formed through interactions within our environment and the people in it (Krause et al., 2010).

It is important to note that self-efficacy and self-concept are not the same thing, but that self-efficacy could actually be a component of self-concept (Woolfolk & Margetts, 2013). Both are shaped by experience, and vary according to age; research evidence tells us that in an educational context, learners often construct their academic self-concept on the basis of beliefs about how others appraise their academic ability (Cozolino, 2013). Learners' self-concept and self-efficacy beliefs will fluctuate and they will work up or down depending on the level of perceived expectations of others: they will see their academic abilities as they believe their teachers and parents see them (Cozolino, 2013; see also Bong & Skaalvik, 2003; Troullioud, Sarrazin, Bressoux & Bois, 2006; Troullioud, Sarrazin, Martinek & Guillet, 2002). Indeed, studies show that positive self-concept and self-efficacy beliefs generate many desirable outcomes and often lead to students setting challenging yet attainable goals, feeling less anxious in achievement settings, enjoying their school work more, persisting longer on difficult tasks and, perhaps most importantly, feeling better about themselves as a person and as a student (Bong & Skaalvik, 2003). This has a number of implications for educators in that a positive learning environment juxtaposed with how a teacher designs a learning experience or presents a task and how well he or she knows the students works hand in hand in terms of influencing a learner's self-concept, self-efficacy and level of motivation. Furthermore, feelings of self-efficacy and self-concept also play a role in shaping a student's goals.

Goal theory

Goal theories of motivation share similarities to expectancy-value theory in that both can be described as achievement goal theories. Research has clearly demonstrated that achievement goals influence motivation and performance (Pekrun, Elliot & Maier, 2009; see also Dweck, 1986; Elliot, 1997; Nicholls, 1984). In an educational context, goal theories examine the purposes that students have in different situations that guide their behaviour, affect and cognition. These theories generally focus on two facets of achievement strivings: mastery and performance (Hullemon, Schrager, Bodmann & Harackiewicz, 2010). Performance goals are those set by students in order to demonstrate their abilities and ultimately to outperform others, while the point of mastery goals is to improve and learn, and thereby achieve mastery. Performance goals, by their nature, are driven by extrinsic rewards such as good test scores. Mastery goals, on the other hand, are intrinsically driven and as such share similar positive attributes in terms of learning, as described earlier in the chapter.

The relative merits and limitations of both mastery and performance goals have been widely debated, resulting in further conceptualisations of each by linking the words 'approach' or 'avoidance' to both (Elliot & McGregor, 2001; Hullemon et al., 2010; Pintrich, 2000a). A performance approach focuses on outperforming others and being superior; performance avoidance is about avoiding looking stupid or losing. A mastery approach is about mastering a task or skill, while mastery avoidance focuses on avoiding any misunderstandings and not mastering the task or skill (Pintrich & Schunk, 2002).

The complexity surrounding definitions and the associated research surrounding performance and mastery goal theories should be self-evident but the implications of each in the classroom is important for teachers. Performance goals present similar difficulties to those identified earlier when looking at behaviourist orientations to motivation. Performance goals often rely on others and, while striving to outperform one's peers can have advantages, a performance approach can also turn into performance avoidance if a student is not successful, leading some to suggest that teachers should avoid trying to motivate using competition and social comparison (Brophy, 2005). Research in performance-oriented goal structures has also demonstrated a substantive number of negative outcomes and maladaptive behaviours such as cheating (Anderman, Cupp & Lane, 2009; Anderman & Midgley, 2004; Murdock, Hale & Weber, 2001), decreases in self-efficacy (Pintrich, 2000b), avoidance of seeking assistance or help (Ryan, Gheen & Midgley, 1998; Ryan & Pintrich, 1997) and academic self-handicapping (Urdan, 2004). Mastery goals, conversely, are driven by intrinsic desires to do well and improve and there is a substantive body of evidence showing positive academic and socio-emotional outcomes associated with a mastery-oriented climate (Rolland, 2012).

SOMETHING TO THINK ABOUT 7.2

I THINK I CAN, I THINK I CAN, I THINK I CAN ...

Of the hundreds of studies conducted by Albert Bandura, the Bobo doll studies discussed in Chapter 1 that established social learning theory tend to stand out above all others. But Bandura's work goes beyond that; for example, he discovered the importance of various behavioural models while working with patients with snake phobias (Bandura & Adams, 1977; Bandura, Jeffery & Wright, 1974). In this work Bandura found that patients' observations of former patients handling snakes were a more effective treatment than treating phobias using persuasion and observing a psychologist handling snakes. In other words, the patients he treated were more likely to consider their own behaviour when they observed information from others who were like them. Bandura expanded this work in a number of domains but of interest here is the work he conducted around self-efficacy and in particular in relation to motivation and learning. For Bandura (1986, 1993), student beliefs about their efficacy to regulate their learning and master activities are important factors in determining their aspirations, level of motivation and effort towards academic achievements. Importantly, teachers' self-efficacy beliefs in terms of their abilities to motivate students and promote effective learning have an impact on the types of learning environments they create and the academic progress their students will make. In a school context, therefore, Bandura's work suggests that perceptions of success at an activity raises efficacy beliefs and future expectations while negative perceptions lead to decreased efficacy beliefs. Moreover, and as alluded to throughout this chapter, physiological and emotional states can add to feelings of mastery or failure.

Ask yourself...

1 How might self-efficacy and goal theory be related and how might this influence pedagogy?

2 What are the implications regarding the provision of feedback in terms of individual student self-efficacy beliefs?

3 What might be some strategies for teachers in terms of ensuring their own self-efficacy beliefs are such that they positively influence the learning environment and student achievement?

The theory of flow

Flow
A state of intense
concentration
that supersedes
other affective and
cognitive processes.

Mastery goals and their intrinsic nature may facilitate the final theory of relevance here: that of **flow** (Eccles & Wigfield, 2002; McGregor & Elliot, 2002; Mustafa, Elias, Roslan & Noah, 2011). The term 'flow' is derived from work focusing on happiness, positive psychology and optimal experience as developed by the psychologist Mihaly Csikszentmihalyi (1975, 1982, 1988, 1990). Flow is often characterised by emotional rewards and pleasurable feelings; it is the result of an intense attentive focus on a particular task. Importantly, this intense attentive focus has also been linked to intrinsic motivation and has gained a great deal of support through research and literature noting the problems associated with extrinsic rewards and reinforcement-base theories (Weber, Tamborini, Westcott-Baker & Kantor, 2009). In essence, flow describes a state of 'being' whereby an individual is so immersed in an activity that they can lose track of time and events occurring around them. Athletes often describe flow as 'being in the zone', a time when their focus was so intense they did not have to consciously think through their actions.

Flow is a distinctive state of consciousness. One of its important aspects is that, when in this state, individuals are motivated yet they are not focusing on any rewards or inducement but rather on the activity itself (Weber et al., 2009). Csikszentmihalyi (1990) has also identified that flow can be characterised through the following traits:

→ intense concentration so no attention is given to anything irrelevant
→ a transformation into a state of holistic consciousness
→ a distortion of time
→ the pleasantness of the experience
→ a sense that one's skills are balanced with the challenge that is presented.

The final point is worthy of further explanation in that it appears that, when challenges and skills are high, then flow is more likely to occur than when a challenge is low and deemed boring or when a person does not have the skills to engage effectively in the activity (Csikszentmihalyi 1975, 1982, 1990; Csikszentmihalyi & LeFevre, 1989). Furthermore, clear task goals and immediate and repeated feedback also appear as necessary ingredients to being in a state of flow (Csikszentmihalyi, 1990). People may experience all of the above elements, and by association experience flow, when they are playing an instrument, working on a craft or hobby, and engaging in sports activities, art or other creative endeavours. Recently there has also been much interest and research in how technology and various forms of media elicit flow given that individuals can become fully immersed in video games, lose track of time and seemingly stimulate neural processes responsible for flow (Weber et al., 2009). The neural substrates of flow are currently an intense area of research interest; as you will recall from the opening of this chapter, the neurobiology of motivation is highly complex and very individualistic. Perhaps the most important contribution the theory of flow gives educators is the importance of setting challenging and attainable tasks to enhance motivation and learning. In order to do so, teachers must be very aware of the attributes, skills and knowledge that their students possess. Indeed, a deeper understanding of the students who enter a teacher's classroom is perhaps the key factor in understanding motivation and learning.

UNDERSTANDING CONTEMPORARY LEARNERS

Chapter 6, which focused on memory, noted the importance of relationships for enhancing attention, memory and learning and alluded to the importance of knowing one's students. The beginning of this chapter also placed much emphasis on how an understanding of motivation and how to motivate students can influence classroom behaviour and academic outcomes. Such understandings of motivation must also take into account the fact that enhancing motivation in a positive manner requires some knowledge of those who enter a classroom each and every day. In this sense, motivation, attention, memory and learning share an important consideration: the need for developing some knowledge of the background and interests of the very students one is going to teach. Perhaps at no other time in the history of 'schooling' and education is such a claim more important given the changes in technology and information accessibility that have occurred since the onset of the twenty-first century. A brief look at some recent history helps to shape this position.

As discussed in Chapter 1, our understanding of learning and teaching has evolved over time. Indeed, a great deal has changed since the early days of schooling. Remember that it was not that long ago that the challenge of mass education led to a system of teaching and learning analogous to mass production in factories, in which children were regarded as raw materials to be processed by technical workers (teachers) to reach an end product (Bransford, Brown & Cocking, 2000; Nagel, 2013b). In such a system, parents, teachers and books were the main sources of information and support as teachers went about administering any curriculum to school-aged children as they progressed from one year to the next. Students in classrooms today, however, can go well beyond their homes and classroom environments to source information, engage with people globally and operate in a media-rich, socially manipulated, 24/7, technologically driven world. Importantly, this seemingly brave new world of information and technology is relatively new but may be more pervasive in terms of learning than current generations of teachers and parents are aware.

Every generation likes to think that the current younger generation is different, sometimes deficient in some ways. Labels such as 'baby boomers', and 'gen X' have been

See Chapter ❶ for more detail on the history of education.

used to attach particular times and events to previous generations and three of the newest labels include 'gen Y' and 'millennials'. Gen Y refers to those individuals born between 1980 and 2000, while millennials are those born from the year 2000 onward. Many of these individuals currently make up much of the current educational population across all sectors and they have also been described as 'digital natives', for they are the first to grow up in a digital era and have never known a world without computers, the internet, 24-hour news and mobile phones (Prensky, 2001). Digital natives are likely to find their mobile devices of greater use for gathering research and information compared to what is available in their local library. They have replaced encyclopaedias with Google, Yahoo and Wikipedia and now create their own information entries and contribute to global information through blogs, interactive media and social networking sites (Dannar, 2013; Small & Vorgan, 2008). With each passing year, conservative estimates of the time digital natives spend using technology seemingly grows exponentially and digital natives tend to describe learning as something that occurs in bytes and nanoseconds as they multitask across an ever-increasing array of technological gadgets (Nagel, 2013b).

EFFECT OF TECHNOLOGY ON THE BRAIN

The potential impact of technology on human development and learning is explored in greater detail in Chapter 10. What is important to emphasise here is that, given the arrival of technology and the digital age, the world of today's learners is vastly different from that of any previous generations. This is not to say that technology is a panacea for solving any challenges facing education. Instead, technology is recognised as a tool in the classroom but also a mainstay in the lives of the students who enter those classrooms. Young people of all ages are texting, blogging, tweeting, shopping, gaming and socialising in ways that continue to change rapidly. There is also growing evidence suggesting that technology may be affecting the human brain in ways that no other cultural or social mechanism ever has. Given the neuroplastic nature of the brain, it should not be surprising that the meshing of young maturing brains and minds with a virtual and digital world may be altering aspects of attention, concentration and numerous other neurophysiological processes. For example, research has identified that, while the internet may be shaping the minds of digital natives to better filter information and make snap decisions in a virtual world, it may also be diminishing their capacity for reading facial cues or picking up on subtle physical gestures or aspects of body language in the real world (Small, Moody, Siddarth & Bookheimer, 2009). Numerous other studies further demonstrate that long-term exposure and experience with particular stimuli and training trigger changes in related brain regions and brain physiology (see, for example, Gaab & Schlaug, 2003; Gaser & Schlaug, 2003; Maguire et al., 2000; Nigmatullina, Hellyer, Nachev, Sharp & Seemungel, 2015; Trainor, Shahin & Roberts,

2003). Importantly, not all changes are deleterious in nature; there is also evidence some that technology may be improving some cognitive abilities (Flynn, 2000; Kearney, 2007).

While there seems to be growing consensus that technology is having an impact on the minds of young people, the question for teachers is what might that mean in terms of motivation, pedagogy and engagement. For example, in a world of multitasking, what might traditional notions of 'time on task' actually mean? Perhaps there needs to be greater recognition that today's students may attend and work through tasks and activities very differently from their twentieth-century counterparts. In terms of motivation, hyperlinked minds that spend much time in virtual worlds where success, gratification and pleasure may have very different views on extrinsic and intrinsic motivation (Nagel, 2103b). Nonetheless, we also have a fairly substantive body of research that sheds some important light on what may enhance and hinder motivation in educational contexts and, in spite of the advances in technology, aspects of each of the orientations towards motivation noted earlier still play an important role in a teacher's repertoire of motivational practices.

MOTIVATION IN SCHOOL: AFFECTIVE AND EFFECTIVE CONSIDERATIONS

The heading for this section is suggestive and purposeful. Earlier in the chapter, we briefly looked at the concepts of affect and interest as they pertain to motivation. Those insights are extended here by first reiterating that the word 'affective' refers to emotion, while 'effective' means producing the intended or expected result. Given these definitions, it should be apparent, once again, that emotion is an integral component of motivation towards attaining particular results. In the context of schooling, the intended results are not necessarily academic per se but we argue that engagement is perhaps the most important result linked to motivation. Students who are engaged with the content or learning activities or both are generally motivated; in a cyclical fashion, motivated students are generally engaged with the material or task at hand. Engagement is not only a precursor to the desired classroom behaviour of most teachers but is also an important consideration in terms of overall school performance. But, while most would agree that engagement is important, finding a consensus regarding the meaning of the word 'engagement' is not as easily attained.

In the research literature, engagement has been described as 'multidimensional' with substantial variations in how it is operationalised and measured (Appleton, Christenson & Furlong, 2008; Fredericks, Blumenfeld & Paris, 2004; Furlong & Christenson, 2008).

See Chapter ❷ to review social and emotional development.

See Chapter ❸ for the structure of the brain responsible for emotions.

Various typologies associated with engagement have also been offered and focus on a variety of contextual factors. For example, Furlong and Christenson (2008) note that engagement can be contextualised as academic, behavioural, cognitive or affective engagement. We believe all of these are important but, in terms of motivation, will focus on those factors related to positive affect and its associated behavioural desires. The purpose for such an approach is twofold. First, aspects of positive affect such as a strong sense of belonging or positive relationships have been linked to better overall motivation (Osterman, 2000) and better scholastic performance (Willms, 2003). Second, taking such an approach aligns well with contemporary understandings of social or affective neuroscience and with aspects of self-determination theory that have been identified as key components of motivation. Overall, we believe that emotion is integral to motivation and this link is well established in most areas of motivation research (Reeve, 2015), and as such is most appropriate for developing the skill sets of new, and existing, teachers.

Positive affect refers to positive emotions but more succinctly is associated with feelings that reflect a level of pleasurable engagement with the environment such as joy, happiness, excitement, contentment and enthusiasm (Cohen & Pressman, 2006). In an educational context it should be self-evident that positive affect is a desirable mental state in terms of desirable behaviours, motivation and engagement. Positive affect also appears to broaden attention and cognition as well as build physical, intellectual and social resources and contribute to personal and professional success later in life (Frederickson, 2001; Frederickson & Joiner, 2002; Lyubomirsky, King & Diener, 2005). Conversely, behavioural problems in students along with student disengagement have been associated with negative affect, particularly situational threats to feelings of competence, self-determination or value to others (Deci & Ryan, 1985; see also Cohen & Steele, 2002; Deci & Ryan, 2002). Under such circumstances negative affect may narrow thoughts and behaviour, whereby disengagement can be internalised as boredom or distress or externalised as misbehaviour, fight or flight, truancy or many other associated negative outcomes (Reschly, Huebner, Appleton & Antaramian, 2008).

THE ROLE OF TEACHERS IN MOTIVATING STUDENTS

For teachers, the key for motivation and engagement lies in developing structures and practices that accentuate positive *affect*, thereby limiting negative *effect*. Before looking at proactive strategies for enhancing positive affect, it is timely that we look at what might hinder motivation in the school context and also scrutinise some practices that have endured for generations. The first of these is to reconsider extrinsic motivators found in practice and structures.

As noted earlier, extrinsic motivators such as rewards and punishment have a long history in school and indeed in Western society. Incentive plans, gold stars and prizes are not uncommon rewards in many classrooms while loss of free time and other privileges, isolation and negative critique are examples of punishments meted out by teachers and parents alike. Importantly, even grades have been used as rewards and punishment. Behaviourism suggests that people will do things to obtain rewards and avoid punishment but the immediate effects of using such reinforcers are usually limited to very specific behaviours, provide short-term solutions, may diminish student engagement, are in the control of another person and may actually impede intrinsic motivation. Moreover, the desired effects of extrinsic motivators may not be ample enough to get the desired results and too often may cast the teacher in a negative light or damage student–teacher relationships and interactions. There is considerable evidence to suggest that extrinsic motivators should be used cautiously and no more than necessary, given the desirable outcomes are often superficial and hinder deeper notions of motivation and engagement (National Research Council, 2004). It is important to remember that, while there are times that rewards and punishment may be effective for short-term behavioural change, an over-reliance on reinforcers is not likely to positively engage student motivation and learning. Instead, recognising that many students will do things in lieu of any extrinsic motivator and using strategies for engaging intrinsic motivation will provide better long-term outcomes in terms of engagement and scholastic success.

Teachers' beliefs about students and themselves

In order to effectively use particular strategies for fostering intrinsic motivation, it is important for teachers to consider some bigger-picture ideas regarding human behaviour and learning. First, let's start with the teacher. Too often much of the discussion around student motivation does not give enough attention to teachers' beliefs about their students' abilities or their own sense of self-efficacy. Students who appear both highly motivated or display low levels of motivation will be influenced by what they think their teacher believes they will achieve (Tokuhama-Espinosa, 2011; Wentzel, 2002). Concurrently, a teacher's own beliefs in how effective he or she is in terms of achieving a teaching task is often judged positively or negatively by students, which will also influence students' motivation to learn (Tokuhama-Espinosa, 2011). Future and current teachers would benefit from remembering that, while teacher self-efficacy and a sense of confidence usually come from experience, the more confidence and enthusiasm shown, the more confidence the students will have in their teacher, which, in a cyclical fashion, positively enhances a teacher's confidence and self-efficacy beliefs (Reeve, 2015; Tokuhama-Espinosa, 2011).

A teacher's beliefs about students' abilities and capacities will also influence students' motivation. This relates to students' sense of belonging and self-concept and, as noted earlier, students will come to see their abilities as teachers see them and work up or down to the level of perceived expectation (Bong & Skaalvik, 2003; Troullioud et al., 2002;

Troullioud et al., 2006). This suggests that teacher attitudes and beliefs regarding student ability are as important to student motivation as is each individual student's attitude and beliefs. It also reminds us that teachers must act as positive role models when it comes to learning, be supportive of their students' needs and work to develop positive relationships with their students. Indeed, building positive relationships may be the cornerstone to enhancing motivation.

Importance of the teacher–student relationship

Positive relationships between teachers and students have been shown to have numerous benefits in terms of affect, motivation and school success (Cozolino, 2013; Marsh, Clarke & Pittaway, 2014; Tokuhama-Espinosa, 2011). And while there is no template for how to build relationships per se, there are some important considerations for doing so that will prove beneficial. First, teachers who display warmth and enthusiasm towards their students and their teaching and who never ridicule a student for lack of knowledge or mistakes build better relationships and enhance intrinsic motivation (Marsh et al., 2014; Snowman et al., 2009). Praising students for effort and when they do well, while arguably an extrinsic motivator, also helps to foster positive relationships. Teachers must also ensure that they are fair and accepting of all students' varying levels of ability, commitment and personality traits to instil a sense of equity in their practice and a sense of safety, security and belonging in their classroom. They must also develop their understanding of particular strategies that enhance motivation.

A FRAMEWORK FOR MOTIVATING STUDENTS

In planning pedagogical strategies with enhancing motivation in mind, it is almost impossible to provide a template for all. Motivation is a deeply personal affair and is influenced by innumerable factors; it is intimately linked with individual or situational interests, attributes and abilities (Nagel, 2013b). There is unlikely ever to be a magic formula for motivating all students all of the time but there are some important considerations that can help shape the decisions we make about motivation and learning. First, it is important to remember that most of us value feeling competent, successful and a degree of self-determination and, as such, planning with motivation in mind should include these ten components:

1 learning experiences that are challenging, specific and at an appropriate level of difficulty

2 opportunities for demonstrating the value of learning tasks in terms of immediate and long-term outcomes or benefits, and the provision of short-term goals that are achievable

3   ongoing and immediate feedback that is respectful and always focused on the task and opportunities to clarify student perceptions of any problems or misconceptions

4   strategies and ideas for students' success and to scaffold learning when necessary to ensure successful outcomes are attainable

5   opportunities for students to self-reflect and articulate their own ideas related to their learning

6   opportunities for students to make choices and exercise degrees of autonomy with a view to enhancing their beliefs that they have a measure of control over their learning

7   clear outcomes to ensure students know what is expected

8   minimal or no threats to students' feelings of competence

9   a means of ensuring that students feel accepted by their teacher and peers

10 a means of ensuring that students perceive the learning environment as their space for learning and that that space is comfortable, orderly, safe and secure (adapted from the works of Marsh et al., 2014; Nagel, 2013b; Walker-Tileston, 2004).

These ten points place a degree of onus on the teacher but this is purposeful. Such an approach emphasises that motivation is not the sole responsibility of the students themselves and instead acknowledges that teachers are responsible, whether consciously or not, for student motivation (Tokuhama-Espinosa, 2011). It also serves as a reminder that in spite of the many theories of, and about, motivation, teachers can exercise a degree of agency towards enhancing positive affect in the classroom and positively affecting motivation. Finally, focusing on enacting the ten points listed in practice serves to remind teachers that motivation and learning takes place within and between individuals in a web of social relationships. Fostering positive relationships using the ideas above is integral to this enterprise.

SOMETHING TO
THINK ABOUT
7.3

DEALING WITH DISENGAGED STUDENTS

Let's revisit Ms Weston's approach to motivation and Tyler in the opening of this chapter. If you recall, Ms Weston attempted to re-engage Tyler through a whole-class reward system. This approach seemed to work in the short term but in time faded in its efficacy with Tyler. Making things worse, Tyler's behaviour progressively worsened as his peers became frustrated with him. It is clear that Ms Weston is struggling to engage Tyler in a positive and meaningful way. Given what you have covered in this chapter, identify some key considerations and strategies for alleviating the situation if you were Ms Weston. It may help to answer the following questions first.

Ask yourself...

1   What might be some of the potential reasons for Tyler's boredom or lack of engagement?

2   Is Tyler's behaviour related to self-efficacy beliefs and how might you determine this?

3   How can you use the ten points listed above to plan a lesson or series of lessons that may enhance Tyler's motivation?

CONCLUSION

Understanding motivation is a complex endeavour. Numerous theories about what drives one person to do something while another might avoid the very same activity are testimony to such complexity. At a neurological level, regions of the limbic system and frontal lobes are associated with motivation ranging from survival instincts associated with hunger and survival to pleasurable pursuits. Interestingly, when most people think of the brain, they focus their attention on its cognitive and intellectual functions without realising that it generates wants, appetites, urges, needs, rewards, desires, cravings, feelings, pleasure and mood with the full range of associated emotions (Reeve, 2015). It is important for teachers to be aware that at the core of much of our motivations are those activities found predominantly in the limbic system and associated with emotion.

Given the links between motivation and emotion, it is evident that any decisions related to motivation, pedagogy and didactic endeavour do well to consider what contributes to positive affect and drives intrinsic motivation. Historically, schools tended to focus on behaviourist notions of motivation and operated with an emphasis on extrinsic motivators. Gold stars, incentive plans, grades and other reinforcers were used to help drive students towards desirable outcomes. While such reinforcers are still used today, it is also now widely recognised that extrinsic motivators have some strengths but many limitations. Arguably the greatest limitation in using extrinsic motivators is that they can undermine intrinsic motivation and ultimately prove to be of limited value over the long term. This is also an important consideration for teachers, given that their students may be quite different from those of previous generations of learners.

The changes in technology coupled with the exponential growth of information have had tremendous influence on most aspects of society. Students today are able to access information in an unprecedented way and appear to have learnt to learn differently.

Motivation is likely also influenced by technology, given the powerful influence of social media, video games and other technological arenas on the minds of young learners. There is growing evidence that various forms of technology have both positive and negative effects on the neurobiology of the brain. Given the 24/7 availability of mobile technology in the hands of young learners, it should not be surprising that the extrinsic motivators of the past may be of little value for contemporary educational endeavour. But one thing that has not changed is the impact and influence of a teacher.

Teachers are motivators! How they present themselves and how they conduct their professional practice influences student motivation. It is important for future and current teachers to always remember that motivation and engagement work in tandem and that teachers are integral in that equation. Great teachers find ways to reach the hard-to-reach learner, and by developing positive relationships that allow students to feel safe, secure, competent and autonomous. In terms of motivation, that should be the principal motivator for all educators: the knowledge that they can positively influence what drives their students.

CHAPTER SUMMARY

This chapter has explored the complex topic of motivation. An exploration of how the neurobiological processes of motivation work within the brain was followed by an exploration of the psychology of motivation. As research and technology progress, we are gaining a far greater understanding of the many processes within the brain implicated in motivation and how they affect behaviour. Importantly, there are multiple overlapping layers between motivation and behaviour, illustrating how interconnected they are and emphasising that an understanding of both is important for teachers in terms of better understanding the links between motivation, engagement and learning.

This chapter also provided a detailed look at key concepts related to motivation and a broad look at particular orientations to motivation and key theories associated with each. These theories were then followed with a look at the students of today given the nature of the contemporary world they are immersed in as they grow, develop and learn. This is an important consideration for teachers in that they cannot look at their students in the same way they may have perceived themselves as students; perhaps more succinctly, they must, where applicable, avoid teaching as they were taught and recognise that technology and advances in science have changed much of our lives. Finally, the chapter concluded with a look at the important links between motivation and emotion as they relate to engagement and learning, and offered a framework for developing strategies to engage students and learning in the classroom and school environs.

Implications for Teaching

Throughout this chapter, we have referred to the individualistic nature of motivation. For example, self-efficacy beliefs are highly individualistic in nature as are individual goals, aspirations and perceptions of challenge. This means that it is important for teachers to know their students. A classic experiment related to motivation provides further food for thought and consideration.

In the mid-1960s, world-renowned psychologist Professor Martin Seligman and colleagues identified an interesting learnt condition in animals that is also evident in human beings. Coined 'learned helplessness' (Seligman, 1972), Seligman found that he could teach dogs to be helpless (Seligman & Maier, 1967; Seligman, Maier & Geer, 1968). In the controlled experiments conducted by Seligman and his colleagues, dogs were put in situations where they received punishment in the form of electric shocks that they had no control over and could not escape from. Later, and after repeated exposure to the electric shocks, the situation was modified: the dogs could escape or turn off the mechanisms that provided the shock but they did not bother trying either. Instead the dogs gave up; they had learnt to be helpless victims. Seligman's work has been transferred into studies of human behaviour, albeit without electric shocks, with similar results. We now know that what a person thinks plays a role in behaviour and it turns out that this can have a tremendous impact on a student's motivation and learning. When learning experiences contribute to low self-esteem or when effort goes unrewarded, a student may begin to believe that no amount of effort will lead to any measure of success, so why bother; in the end 'learned helplessness' is adopted.

Ask yourself...

1 Given the findings of the work of Seligman and others, what might this mean for teachers in terms of planning learning experiences and providing feedback?

2 How might an over-reliance on rewards contribute to a sense of learnt helplessness in some students?

3 How can a teacher ensure that students achieve some measure of success?

PRACTICAL ACTIVITIES

1   List some of the activities, experiences or events that motivate you. Plot them on a continuum with intrinsic factors at one end and extrinsic factors at the other. What distinguishes the activities that are motivated intrinsically from those that are motivated extrinsically?

2   *While on practicum*, discuss with your mentor teacher(s) what strategies they use to motivate their students. Ask your mentor how they enhance positive self-efficacy beliefs or if they use any aspect of setting goals with their students. Using the same format as in Question 1, identify which strategies focus on extrinsic motivation and which focus on intrinsic motivation. Is one more prevalent than the other and if so, why do you think that is? Given what you have learnt about extrinsic and intrinsic motivation, what will you do to take advantage of the research?

STUDY QUESTIONS

1   Write a definition for the word 'motivation' and list as many factors as you can think of that influence motivation, whether positive or negative.

2   What are the differences between intrinsic and extrinsic motivation?

3   What are the positives and negatives around using rewards and punishments as tools for motivating students?

4   What is the significance of Maslow's hierarchy of needs in an educational context? What strategies can you employ at each level to help your students move up the hierarchy?

5   Emotions are critical elements to motivation and engagement. What does this mean in terms of your role as a teacher? What will you do to avoid the emergence of 'learned helplessness' in any of your students and promote positive states of affect?

SOMETHING TO THINK ABOUT 7.4

The concept of 'states' as discussed in this chapter is an important aspect of motivation but also of one's inner feelings and associated behaviours. It is significant to remember that the human brain always reacts to the environment, leading to various emotional manifestations or states. Such states could include fear, boredom, interest, enthusiasm, disengagement or any number of feelings or more succinctly, 'states of mind' (Zull, 2011).

Zull encapsulated this poignantly: 'our environment always influences the "state" of our mind. These states of mind depend on our experience, and thus will be different in detail for each of us. But the potential for engagement and motivation is a feature of every brain. In education, the challenge is not to create emotions but to unearth them' (2011, p. 61).

Reflect on your own experiences in school and note the times you remember when you were most motivated. What elements of your experience(s) can you translate into your craft as a teacher? What do you think you might do to 'unearth' emotions towards engaging in positive affect with your students?

FURTHER READING

Bransford, J. D., Brown, A. L. & Cocking, R. R. (2000). *How People Learn: Brain, Mind, Experience, and School*. Washington, DC: National Academy Press.

Cozolino, L. (2013). *The Social Neuroscience of Education: Optimizing Attachment and Learning in the Classroom*. New York, NY: W.W. Norton.

Csikszentmihalyi, M. (1990). *Flow: The Psychology of Optimal Experience*. New York, NY: Harper & Row.

Daw, N. C. & Shohamy, D. (2008). The cognitive neuroscience of motivation and learning. *Social Cognition, 26*(5), 593–620.

Deci, E. L., Koestner, R. & Ryan, R. M. (2001). Extrinsic rewards and intrinsic motivation in education: Reconsidered once again. *Review of Educational Research, 71*(1), 1–27.

Deci, E. L. & Ryan, R. M. (2002). The paradox of achievement: The harder you push, the worse it gets. In J. Aronson (Ed.), *Improving Academic Achievement: Impact of Psychological Factors on Education* (pp. 62–90). San Diego, CA: Academic Press.

Nagel, M. C. (2014). *In the Middle: The Adolescent Brain, Behaviour and Learning*. Melbourne, Australia: ACER Press.

National Research Council (2004). *Engaging Schools: Fostering High School Students' Motivation to Learn*. Washington, DC: The National Academies Press.

Pintrich, P. R. & Schunk, D. H. (2002). *Motivation in Education: Theory, Research, and Applications* (2nd ed.). Upper Saddle River, NJ: Prentice Hall.

Reschly, A. L., Huebner, E. S., Appleton, J. J. & Antaramian, S. (2008). Engagement as flourishing: The contribution of positive emotions and coping to adolescents' engagement at school and with learning. *Psychology in the Schools, 45*(5), 419–431.

Walker-Tileston, D. (2004). *What Every Teacher Should Know about Student Motivation*. Thousand Oaks, CA: Corwin Press.

Wentzel, K. R. (2002). Are effective teachers like good parents? Teaching styles and student adjustment in early adolescence. *Child Development, 73*(1), 287–301.

VIDEO LINKS

A. Kohn: *It's Bad News If Students are Motivated to Get A's*
https://www.youtube.com/watch?v=EQt-ZI58wpw&list=PL1C90B066832A4033&index=4

Alfie Kohn is a prolific author and his book *Punished by Rewards* makes for interesting reading for any teacher.

Reading Horizons: *7 ways to increase student engagement in the classroom*
https://www.youtube.com/watch?v=TjADkTe5upA

An interesting video with seven strategies that provide a good framework for working with students in a classroom context and applicable to all ages.

WEBLINKS

Vanderbilt University Center For Teaching
https://cft.vanderbilt.edu/guides-sub-pages/motivating-students/

A useful website that provides some great examples of motivation and how to motivate students.

Teach Hub
http://www.teachhub.com/learned-helplessness-and-how-we-can-overcome-it

This site explains how to recognise and alleviate 'learned helplessness' in the classroom.

INCLUSIVE LEARNING

8

> Inclusion depends on teachers' attitudes towards students with special needs, on their capacity to enhance social relationships, on their attitudes towards differences in classrooms and their willingness to deal with those differences effectively.
>
> (Hyde, 2014a, p. 355)

LEARNING OUTCOMES

As you read through this chapter and undertake the exercises at the end, you will gain the ability to complete these tasks successfully:

→ describe and discuss your beliefs about inclusive learning

→ define the role of the teacher when facilitating experiences for diverse learners

→ explain some of the struggles students with special needs might face in schools

→ discuss the role of neuroscience in our current understandings of diversity

→ understand how learning difficulties may affect children's cognition.

KEY TERMS

- inclusion
- disability
- special needs
- gifted and talented
- learning difficulties

SETTING THE SCENE

Mrs White has been teaching for thirty years in large metropolitan schools. Recently she has been transferred to Tuharma Road Primary School in regional New South Wales. Year 5 is her favourite class to teach and she was happy she had been allocated this year level at her new school.

The year had started well and most of the children in her class seemed to be meeting the academic requirements that she expected. But there was one boy, Matt, whom she was particularly worried about. On her arrival she had been told that Matt had attention deficit hyperactivity disorder (ADHD). She had noticed that indeed he did seem easily distracted, fidgety, talked excessively and was impulsive—acting without thinking. He often disrupted the class when she was trying to teach her planned lessons. Additionally, Matt was not meeting the year level expectations academically and Mrs White thought some sort of intervention was needed.

Mrs White believes that she had been very lucky at her previous schools, as there had been special classes to cater for children like Matt, who did not appear to cope in the mainstream class. The special education program had provided a modified curriculum with smaller class size to allow for more individual attention. She thinks it would be good for Matt to be in a special education class to allow the other children to concentrate. But Tuharma Road Primary School has no such option. This seems very unfair on everyone, she thinks, as it is more work for her to try to manage the class, Matt is not learning, and it is distracting for the rest of the class.

1   Debates about the advantages and disadvantages of inclusive education for children with special needs are ongoing. What are the positives and negatives of integration of students with special needs into regular classes?

2   What are some of the typical indicators of attention deficit hyperactivity disorder (ADHD)?

3   In some instances children with ADHD are on medications such as Ritalin and Adderall to increase dopamine and strengthen weak dopamine signals in the brain. Parents who have chosen not to medicate their children have reported being pressured by teachers to put their children on such medications. If a teacher is having trouble managing a child with ADHD, does he or she have the right to pressure parents to medicate their child? If yes, why? If no, why?

4   ADHD is a neurological condition that needs to be accurately identified and diagnosed. It is considered a debilitating developmental disorder marked by inability to self-control behaviour. Should teachers be diagnosing ADHD in the children in their class? What are the dangers associated with teachers diagnosing children?

5   What specific strategies can teachers put in place to support a child with ADHD in their class?

INTRODUCTION

Chapter 7 considered motivation for learning, relevant theories and the neurobiological underpinnings of motivation of the brain for contemporary students. While we talk a lot about the brain and we are beginning to get a better understanding of the daily functioning of this most complex organ in our body, just what is a *normal* brain? Do you have a normal brain? Do I have one? If we accept that a child's brain, and indeed an adult's brain, is influenced by a host of experiences including genetics, relationships, socio-economic background, siblings, material health and exposure to toxins, we also need to acknowledge that each brain is unique. We now know that the brain makes physical changes in response to environmental and social experiences. This implies that each and every child is on an ongoing journey of crafting his or her own brain, and that anyone with an interest in education has an important part to play in contributing to this unique development. Depending on whom you refer to, 30–50 per cent of a student's performance can be attributed to genetics or IQ. That being said, there is a lot of leeway in terms of the impact of experiences! Given any classroom context will include children with inherently different genetic make-up and a variety of environmental experiences, educators are challenged to provide an inclusive classroom that facilitates optimum learning for all.

WHAT IS INCLUSIVE EDUCATION?

Inclusive education is a more recent concept that presumes that all students attend schools in age-appropriate, regular classes and are supported to learn and participate in school life (Hyde, 2014b). An understanding of inclusion is often confused by earlier notions such as *mainstreaming* and *integration*. Mainstreaming traditionally referred to placing children from special schools into regular schools while integration implied including children with disability into a mainstream class when their ability for placement warranted. Inclusion assumes that children with difference should be included from the beginning in education

Inclusion
All students attend and are welcomed by schools in age-appropriate, regular classes and are supported to learn, contribute and participate in all aspects of the life of the school.

Disability
Consequence of an impairment that may be physical, cognitive, mental, sensory, emotional or developmental.

and that, in a just and fair society, educational institutions will provide practices that support and accommodate such differences (Allen & Schwartz, 2000; United Nations Educational, Scientific and Cultural Organization—Unesco, 2009). Inclusion in a general sense refers to the right to active participation and achieving equity through engagement in all aspects of daily life (Hyde, 2014b).

An inclusive school provides an environment where every child belongs, is accepted and is supported by the school community to ensure his or her needs are met (Stainback & Stainback, 1989). The concept of inclusion reflects human rights principles and is evident in many of the international agreements to which Western countries such as Australia have made a commitment (Hyde, 2014b). Policies define inclusion as a process of considering and responding to the diversity of needs of all learners and reducing exclusion (Booth, 1996; Unesco, 2009). Schools are therefore expected to develop and design classrooms, programs and activities so that all students learn and participate together. Our current understandings of inclusive education reflect the principles first adopted by Unesco at the Salamanca World Conference on Special Needs Education, Spain, in 1994. To this end educators are required to make changes and modifications in content, approaches, structures and strategies, with a common vision to provide a system to educate all children (Unesco, 1994).

As educators we therefore need to have a comprehensive understanding of the term 'inclusive education', the potential outcomes of inclusive education and barriers to, or facilitators of, inclusive education. While there is a tendency to think about inclusive education as referring to the system of programs and services traditionally offered for children considered to have special needs and learning difficulties, inclusion is also about providing appropriate learning for gifted and talented students through differentiated curricula that are both enriched and accelerated. This enrichment is often accomplished through segregated programs but the reality is that learners with special needs and gifted students continue to spend the majority of their education in general classroom settings. Debates about the advantages and disadvantages of inclusive education for children with special needs are ongoing, although community acceptance has increased and the integration of students with disability in regular schools is occurring more regularly.

Special needs
Educational requirements due to learning difficulties, physical disability or emotional and behavioural needs.

Gifted and talented
Broad term for those who demonstrate outstanding levels of aptitude or competence in one or more domains.

FORMAL AND INFORMAL CONSIDERATIONS

Australian society has a commitment to the World Declaration on Education for All, adopted in Jomtien, Thailand (World Conference on Education for All, 1990) that sets out an overall vision of access to education for all children and youth, and the pursuit of equity. This means being proactive in identifying the barriers that many children encounter when accessing educational opportunities in schools and identifying the changes needed to overcome those barriers. International policies clearly outline that there should be a general understanding that inclusive education is a pivotal human right (Unesco, 2009). Many schools and teachers successfully facilitate an inclusive community, directing resources and developing staff skills to support greater participation for diverse children. For other schools there are still major obstacles in terms of providing inclusive communities with new attitudes and resources needed (Hyde, Carpenter & Conway, 2014).

As a society we have a need for an ongoing cycle of reflection to consider which individuals and groups actually need recognition. Increasingly, modern neuroscience is providing us with insights about what is happening in terms of brain functioning for children with individual differences and special needs. These insights provide further understandings about what teachers can do in the classroom to facilitate learning. Schools typically have students with a range of special needs, requiring teachers to provide experiences for children from those considered exceptionally gifted in terms of academic, artistic, musical or athletic abilities to children considered as having a disabling condition. Children with disabilities may have high or low support needs. You may be aware of some of the more common special needs teachers need to support, such as children who have learning difficulties, dyslexia, attention deficit hyperactivity disorder (ADHD) and autistic spectrum disorder (ASD), including Asperger's syndrome. Giftedness is also recognised as a special need, as these children also require special educational programs or services.

One of the most notable groups that need to be considered in the future is children living in *disadvantaged* environments who may be experiencing *poverty* (Hyde et al., 2014). These children are often disadvantaged in many ways, resulting in reduced participation and lower educational outcomes in schools. We have talked previously about the ways that environmental influences affect the brain development of children living in disadvantaged situations, who are more at risk of poor health, low nutrition, stress, parental instability and unemployment, and lack of emotional and educational support, to name a few factors. While it is important not to overgeneralise, children from lower income or disadvantaged families tend to have lower educational outcomes at school and have more difficulties on standardised tests (Jensen, 2013). It is a concern that one of the biggest single correlating factors with poor literacy and numeracy skills is poverty (Hyde et al., 2014). As we know the brain is responsible for cognition and behaviour, it is believed there must be some differences in the brains of children living in poverty.

THOSE WHO CAN, DO

Healthy brains lead to healthy learners and with the addition of healthy learning environments we have a good chance of achieving positive educational outcomes for children in classrooms. To be specific, there are some universal stages involved in learning and *typically* many children in any given class will be ready and willing to learn. When we talk about children who have not been exposed to chronic stress, trauma or significant differences in their brain development, we are talking about the typical child in the class, or the majority. While every child's path of development is unique, resulting from the incredibly complex processes in the brain, the underlying processes and conditions needed for successful brain development are the same for all children.

TYPICAL MATURATION

Many children do follow a typical pathway and reach universal milestones of development within an expected time frame. For these typical children, with maturation, neural networks form and a child learns academically, emotionally and socially (Gazzaniga & Mangun, 2014; Nagel, 2012a). As maturation of the brain influences readiness, external experiences influence development. A healthy brain is preconditioned to enjoy learning and learns best when exposed to an array of ideas, experiences, skills and materials (Nagel, 2012a). As a teacher, your role is to challenge and nurture children so they benefit from the experiences facilitated. Learning experiences that are aimed too far above or below the maturity level of a child are not appropriate and can also lead to disengagement and behaviour problems in the classroom (see Chapter 7; Semrud-Clikeman & Ellison, 2009). That being said, when experiences are facilitated at the level appropriate for a child, in most cases children flourish and learn.

At first, this learning is rote in nature with skills, over time, becoming more automatic and requiring less attention. Initially, rote learning is the most efficient way for a child to learn concepts such as right and left. When a child does not learn this concept, he or she may be less able to determine the differences between *b* and *d* or 17 and 71 later on. Repetition, repeat and review are also necessary for initial learning of concepts such as letters and numbers. Once children automate initial understandings, they can focus on more complex tasks requiring more attention and processing, such as skills required for reading and writing (Semrud-Clikeman & Ellison, 2009).

With maturity a child then moves from rote learning to more inferential thinking. This shift in focus is facilitated by increased connectivity in the brain, including chemical changes in the neuronal pathways that support short- and long-term memory (Gazzaniga & Mangun, 2014).

MATURATION AND EDUCATION

At every stage of development it is important to give children experiences that include tasks that match their needs and provide enrichment in terms of their learning (Semrud-Clikeman, 2006). Educational programs can provide enhancement for children's learning through repeated practice and progressively increase the challenge to develop skills such as creativity, flexibility, self-control and discipline (Diamond, 2012; Diamond & Hopson, 1999). A child may be ready to learn a specific skill but the learning environment determines much of the opportunity for hard-wiring of the brain for further development of that skill. For example, a child may be ready to learn to read when his or her auditory system is developmentally ready to distinguish one sound from another but if parents do not read to their child or reading tuition is not provided, learning to read may be delayed (Semrud-Clikeman & Ellison, 2009). On the other hand, if a child's auditory system is not ready and reading instruction is pushed, there may be a delay in learning to read. It is therefore important for teachers to understand key predictors of reading readiness such as a child's ability to understand rhyming (Semrud-Clikeman, 2006).

For teachers it is important to understand the maturation of the brain and how this influences learning readiness. This is especially true for teachers interested in providing an inclusive classroom and designing learning experiences and facilitating appropriate strategies for such a classroom. While learning involves maturation of the brain and readiness, there are also differences in brain development that influence children's capacities to engage with and accomplish skills as readily as their peers. We will briefly look at some of the more prominent influences on brain functioning that can subsequently create special needs in the classroom.

DIFFERENT BRAINS, DIFFERENT LEARNERS

Modern neuroscience demonstrates the differences that can be found in brains and how this can lead to differences in learning for children in the classroom (Armstrong, 2008; Baron-Cohen, Tager-Flusberg & Lombardo, 2013). Traditionally, there has been a preoccupation with defining a 'normal' brain, 'normal' developments and the 'average' child, while the reality is that there may be great variation in children's abilities to engage with learning. A further consideration also revolves around those children who are considered outside the typical or majority boundaries. As educators, it is important to consider what happens when a learner is affected by conditions that challenge learning. The impact of developmental delays, environmental influences and biological conditions that precede variation in neural development all present challenges that require greater knowledge of the brain and development, fine-tuned teaching skills and enriched teaching resources. While some learners may appear harder to reach academically, and at first demonstrate some behavioural challenges, these children are reachable once you master the necessary skills and strategies (Jensen, 2000).

Learning a new language is one example of how an endeavour can be experienced by individuals at different rates, given their brain capacities, and how the experience itself changes the brain's network both structurally and functionally. In this way, the efficiency of brain networks is defined by the strength and direction of connections between brain regions. A recent study of thirty-nine young adults (average age twenty years) learning a foreign language demonstrates the differences inherent in different brain structures and an individual's ability to learn (Li, Legault & Litcofsky, 2014). These thirty-nine young adults underwent an MRI before and after a six-week period of learning Chinese vocabulary. The participants who were more successful in attaining learning the information were found to have a more connected brain network before and more increased connectivity after the program in contrast to the less successful participants and those who did not learn at all (Figure 8.1). It was concluded that a better-integrated brain network is more flexible and efficient, making the task of learning a new language easier (Li et al., 2014: Yang, Gates, Molenaar & Li, 2014).

FIGURE 8.1   CONNECTIVITY IN THE BRAIN BEFORE AND AFTER LEARNING A LANGUAGE:
A) THE CONNECTIVITY OF A SUCCESSFUL LEARNER; B) THE CONNECTIVITY OF
A LESS SUCCESSFUL LEARNER; C) THE CONNECTIVITY OF A NON-LEARNER

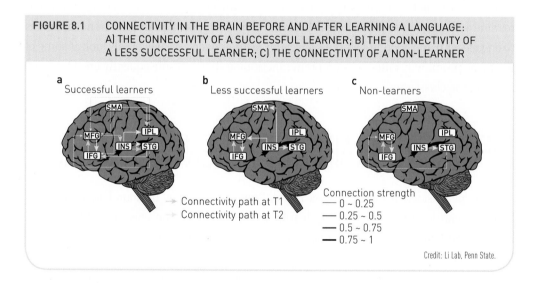

Credit: Li Lab, Penn State.

Li and colleagues' study (2014) suggests that success in learning in this endeavour (learning a second language) reflects individual differences in learners' capacities. For teachers this is significant, as facilitating experiences for children in the classroom requires an understanding of the range of different connective capacities and an understanding that the experiences provided potentially change or develop neural pathways. If different learners have different brains and capacities, it makes sense for educators to have some idea of what these differences might look like. The following sections look at some of the differences in relation to those who experience various learning difficulties.

LEARNING DIFFICULTIES

Functional magnetic resonance imaging (fMRI) findings demonstrate how children with learning difficulties process information differently from children who are not struggling (Baron-Cohen et al., 2013; Breier, Simos & Fletcher, 2002; Schlaggar et al., 2002). For example, as children develop, their frontal brain regions become more active and efficient in varying ways (see Chapter 3). While activation of the brain is more fragmented when children are beginning to learn to read efficiently, the left hemisphere becomes more specialised as reading improves. Fluent readers appear to activate this area more than children with reading difficulties (Schlaggar et al., 2002). What MRIs also show is that children with reading problems demonstrate more activity in the 'wrong' places (Breier et al., 2002). For example, poor readers show more activity in the right hemisphere than the left and their parietal and occipital areas are more active. In contrast, children without reading problems activate the frontal regions and the left hemisphere with less activation in the right hemisphere. For example, when asked to read single words, typical readers show left hemispheric activation, whereas those with dyslexia show more right hemispheric activation (Breier et al., 2002; Papanicolaou, 2003).

Learning difficulties
Challenges associated with processing information.

Dyslexia

Dyslexia is a complex learning disability in reading, characterised by difficulties with accurate word recognition, poor spelling and decoding abilities (Lyon, Shaywitz & Shaywitz, 2003). Dyslexia is an often-misunderstood word for reading problems. The term 'dyslexia' is made up of two different parts: *dys* meaning not or difficult, and *lexia* meaning words, reading or language, literally meaning difficulty with words (Catts & Kamhi, 2005). Dyslexia can include the inability to interpret spatial relationships or to integrate visual and auditory informing and does not encompass all reading problems (Jensen, 2000). One of the most common misunderstandings is the assumption that dyslexia is based on a problem of letter or word reversals (b/d, was/saw) or of letters, words or sentences seemingly mixed up on the page (Rayner, Foorman, Perfetti, Pesetsky & Seidenberg, 2001). Teachers need to use caution in labelling children as dyslexic, because writing and reading letters and words backwards are common in the early stages of learning to read and write among average and dyslexic children. Dyslexia is a specific learning disability that is neurobiological in origin, characterised by difficulties with accurate and fluent word recognition, poor spelling and decoding abilities. These difficulties typically include problems with phonological components of language while other cognitive abilities appear uninhibited (Lyon et al., 2003).

Once again MRIs allows us to learn more about the differences in the brains of children with dyslexia and demonstrate how the brain area involved in matching sounds and letters is found to be compromised in children with this disability (Maisog, Einbinder, Flowers,

Turkeltaub & Eden, 2008). There are changes from right hemispheric processing to left hemispheric processing when children improve their reading and language skills but these changes do not take place for children with dyslexia. Neuro-imaging in children with dyslexia reveals reduced engagement of the left temporo-parietal cortex for phonological processing of print and altered white-matter connectivity (Gabrieli, 2009). It appears that the brain of a child with dyslexia has a different distribution of metabolic activation from a child without reading problems, so, when faced with the same language task, a child with dyslexia experiences failure of the left hemisphere rear brain systems to function optimally (see Figure 8.2).

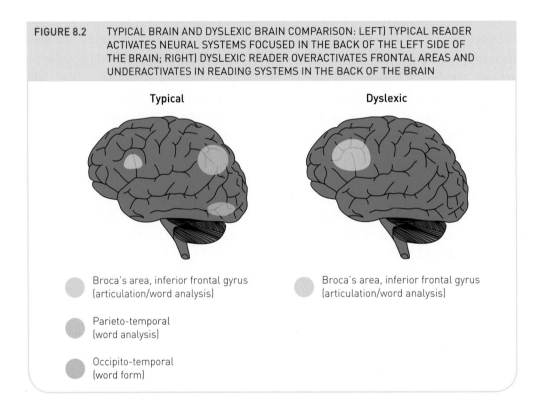

FIGURE 8.2   TYPICAL BRAIN AND DYSLEXIC BRAIN COMPARISON: LEFT) TYPICAL READER ACTIVATES NEURAL SYSTEMS FOCUSED IN THE BACK OF THE LEFT SIDE OF THE BRAIN; RIGHT) DYSLEXIC READER OVERACTIVATES FRONTAL AREAS AND UNDERACTIVATES IN READING SYSTEMS IN THE BACK OF THE BRAIN

Typical   Dyslexic

Broca's area, inferior frontal gyrus (articulation/word analysis)

Parieto-temporal (word analysis)

Occipito-temporal (word form)

Broca's area, inferior frontal gyrus (articulation/word analysis)

Dyslexia appears to run in families and is influenced by both genetic and external factors. The dyslexic brain is less energy efficient with underactivity in Wernicke's and Broca's areas (Jensen, 2000). Smaller brain areas have also been found for children with dyslexia that correlate with poorer skills for reading, word deciphering and naming ability of letters, numbers and objects (Gabrieli, 2009). Furthermore, the corpus callosum has also been found to differ in dyslexics, with differences in connectivity in regions involved in language and reading (Fine, Semrud-Clikeman, Keith, Stapleton & Hynd, 2007). While it is believed these differences are due to decreased rates of apotosis (see Chapter 3) during the fifth and seventh months of gestation (Paul, 2011), children who are identified early and receive intense instruction can minimise the severity of their problems. While there is still a lot to learn about dyslexia, early accurate identification and the implementation of appropriate strategies in the classroom are necessary steps in an inclusive classroom.

See Chapter ❸ for details on the parts of the brain.

SOMETHING TO THINK ABOUT 8.1

INDICATIONS OF DYSLEXIA

Dyslexia is a complex condition with many indicators across a range of ability areas. Those who have dyslexia may show just a few of these signs or several. While the list below is made up of common indicators of dyslexia, there may be others—and having a single indicator does not necessarily mean dyslexia. For example, with growing use of digital devices, messy, poorly spaced handwriting is almost more common than not. These are some common indicators of dyslexia (adapted from Jensen, 2000).

Memory

→ Quick learner, quick to forget
→ Weak role memorisation and rapid oral retrieval
→ Difficulty memorising non-meaningful facts
→ Difficulty following directions and remembering instructions
→ Memory instability for spelling, grammar, maths, days of the week, months of the year

Visual processing

→ Reversal of characters such as *b* and *d*, 6 and 9, 16 and 61
→ Letter and word blurring, doubling, scrambling
→ Tendency to skip letters
→ High distractibility, light sensitivity, delayed visual and phonetic processing

Phonological processing

→ Takes longer to catch subtle differences in sounds and words
→ Mixes up sounds in multi-syllabic words ('am-in-nall' for 'animal'; 'lower' for 'lawn mower')
→ Inability to rhyme by four years
→ Inability to correctly complete phonemic awareness tasks

Writing

→ Messy, poorly formed, spacing and letter-sequencing errors
→ Motor coordination problems

Reading

→ Slow and easily fatigued
→ Compensates with head tilting, rapidly alternating between near and far focusing, and finger pointing
→ Sequencing difficulties
→ Difficultly with multiple-choice questions and long reading passages

▶

▶ **Cognition**

→ Problems generalising and applying new information to situations
→ Difficulty learning the names and sounds of letters
→ Inability to be playful with words and make up sounds and rhymes

Speech

→ Slurring, articulation errors
→ Auditory input–output: speech lags with noticeably slower enunciation than peers
→ Delayed speech
→ Lack of timing precision in motor actions

Kinaesthetic processing

→ Difficulty learning ordered tasks, such as tying shoelaces
→ Confusion between left and right, over and under
→ Lack of dominant handedness; switching between hands for tasks

Ask yourself...

1 Read through the list above. Are there some indicators that may be evident that are not necessarily indicators a child has dyslexia? For example, a young child may have trouble tying his or her shoes due to lack of experience.

2 Highlight indicators that on their own may not indicate dyslexia. For example, if a child becomes tired and fatigued during reading, does that automatically indicate dyslexia? What else could be the problem?

3 If you had a child who was demonstrating a number of the indicators, how would you ensure that you were not prematurely labelling the child?

4 As a teacher, what are some of the strategies you would use to support a child who has been diagnosed with dyslexia? Brainstorm some strategies to support each of these areas:

   a memory

   b visual processing

   c phonological processing

   d writing

   e reading

   f cognition

   g speech

   h kinaesthetic processing.

A framework for assisting students with dyslexia

It is important for teachers to be cautious of labelling children but they do need to provide additional support for children who are having problems associated with dyslexia or reading difficulties. Phonemic awareness games and rhyming games are especially important for the early years of schooling. Phonological awareness is a key factor in some reading problems, with a range of programs and strategies available that can be incorporated in the classroom and at home with parents. Schools usually have access to a range of specialists who can support a struggling child and you as a teacher in the classroom.

WHAT TEACHERS CAN DO

These are some practical strategies to make the classroom environment supportive for students with dyslexia.

→ Give individual instruction.
→ Provide intensive phonics instruction in a fun way.
→ Have positive expectation of children.
→ Develop a long-term approach to supporting children.
→ Balance the reading program with whole language and phonetic awareness.
→ Read books aloud.
→ Make reading fun.
→ Teach songs and make up rhymes with children.
→ Evaluate hearing and vision and seek professional support.
→ Communicate with parents and families.
→ Have learners break reading into small chunks.
→ Practise sequencing.
→ Practise breaking instructions into chunks.

Attention deficit hyperactivity disorder

Attention deficit hyperactivity disorder (ADHD) is a neurological condition that needs to be accurately identified and diagnosed. It is considered a debilitating developmental disorder marked by inability to self-control behaviour (Barkley, 2006). While we do not know specifically what causes ADHD, the condition appears early in childhood and is one of the most commonly diagnosed conditions, with more boys than girls typically diagnosed (Howard et al., 2011). Researchers have implied there are links with genetics, diet, heavy metal exposure and prenatal exposure to tobacco smoke and alcohol, among others (Thompson & Carpenter, 2014). That being said, it is also a condition that is over-diagnosed due to broad symptoms that can be observed in many children at particular times. The condition generally involves problems with information processing such as inattention, impulsiveness and problems with self-regulation that can be coupled with other learning difficulties. In some cases hyperactivity is not present.

MRI images demonstrate a link between a child's ability to maintain attention and the level of activity in the brain with various areas involved in a child's ability to concentrate

(National Institute of Mental Health, 2006). These areas may be less active and develop more slowly in children with ADHD. Structural imaging shows that brains of children with ADHD are significantly smaller, with the prefrontal cortex, basal ganglia and cerebellum being differentially affected, and there is some reduced connectivity in white matter tracts in key brain areas (National Institute of Mental Health, 2006).

Educators need be cautious in labelling children as having ADHD, as not every child who is overly hyperactive, inattentive or impulsive has an attention deficit disorder. Most children will at times seem to flit from one task to another, or become disorganised and forgetful. Diagnoses of ADHD require expertise from specialists as not every child is exactly the same and some afflicted children do not have the typical behaviours of ADHD, such as inattention (see Figure 8.3).

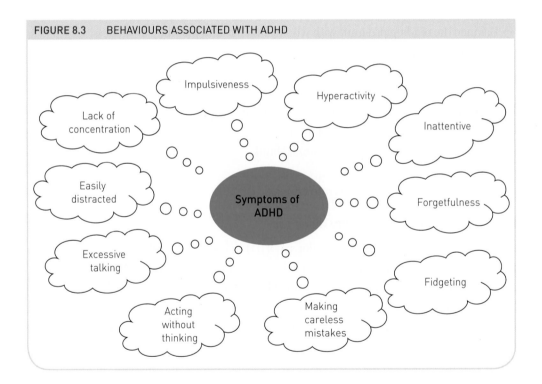

FIGURE 8.3   BEHAVIOURS ASSOCIATED WITH ADHD

While the condition is confusing, we are learning more about what is happening in the brain for children who are accurately diagnosed using brain scans based on blood flow and brainwave activity. Children with ADHD appear to have brains that tend to mature more slowly and, when asked to perform a task, certain areas of their brain are more or less active compared to people who don't have ADHD (see Figure 8.4). For example, functional neuro-imaging illustrates a view of the brain when a person is doing a task and shows lowered activation in the regions of the frontal lobe and caudate nucleus when a child with ADHD is asked to inhibit a response (Pliszka et al., 2006). This lowered activation suggests the brain is making fewer connections between neural networks, generating poorer attention to detail.

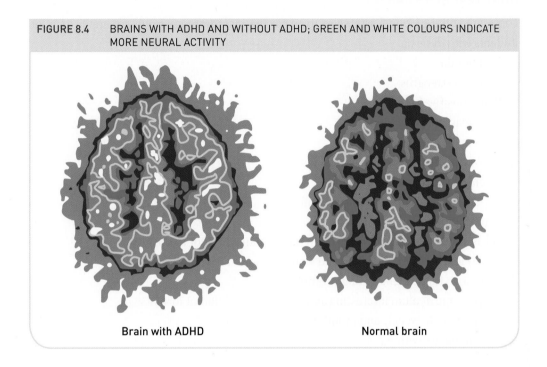

FIGURE 8.4   BRAINS WITH ADHD AND WITHOUT ADHD; GREEN AND WHITE COLOURS INDICATE MORE NEURAL ACTIVITY

Brain with ADHD   **Normal brain**

Another important aspect of ADHD is the role of dopamine dysregulation. Dopamine, as noted in previous chapters, is an important chemical in terms of pleasure and motivation and has also been linked to many other functions, including movement, sleep, mood, attention and, by association, learning (Jensen, 2000). Differentiation in dopamine receptors in the brain has been believed to be associated with ADHD, which is why ADHD medications are stimulants such as Ritalin and Adderall that increase dopamine, strengthening weak dopamine signals in the brain. While many researchers believe abnormalities in dopamine transmission are the main cause of ADHD, new research at Cambridge University suggests that the crux of the disorder may lie instead in structural differences in the grey matter in the brain (del Campo et al., 2013). In this study, adults with and without ADHD were given Ritalin. Patients with ADHD, who had significant loss of grey matter in the brain, showed significantly improved attention performance on Ritalin but there was also an increase for patients without ADHD. As Ritalin also improved attention performance in some healthy individuals, findings suggest the need to consider further the significance of the loss of grey matter in the brain. Research into the area of ADHD continues.

A framework for assisting students with ADHD

Students with ADHD present their own challenges to teachers. But they are challenges, not impossible barriers.

WHAT TEACHERS CAN DO

These are some practical strategies to make the classroom environment supportive for students with dyslexia.

→ Set boundaries.
→ Focus on strengths.
→ Praise positive behaviours.
→ Have realistic expectations.
→ Implement peer tutoring.
→ Encourage healthy peer relationships.
→ Establish predictable routines.
→ Divide tasks into manageable sections.
→ Repeat and remind instructions.
→ Tell them what you want them to do rather than what not to do.
→ Move closer to the child when you want his or her attention.
→ Work with the student through complex tasks.
→ Keep the curriculum interesting and presented in different formats.
→ Maintain daily, weekly and monthly goals.
→ Communicate with parents.

Autistic spectrum disorder and related disorders such as Asperger's syndrome

Autistic spectrum disorder (ASD) is another neurodevelopmental disorder first evident in early childhood. ASD is referred to as an autistic *continuum* or autistic *spectrum* due to the range of autistic disorders. Autism is often referred to as a more severe aspect of ASD, although disorders can vary for individuals. There are many symptoms associated with autism, including impairments in social interaction and communication, restricted interests and repetitive behaviours (Hadwin, Howlin & Baron-Cohen, 2008). Individuals will typically display difficulties in three areas including communication, social skills and behaviour, although the severity depends on the individual (Carpenter, 2010). Children with autism have social challenges, and lack the intuition or empathy exhibited in typically developing children (Baron-Cohen, 2009). This lack of social skills is attributed to poorly working empathy circuits in the brain (Baron-Cohen, 2012). The label 'autistic spectrum disorder' is more common among boys than girls, and these children often demonstrate social withdrawal, cognitive processing problems and language disorders as early as two years of age (Baron-Cohen, 2009). At some point during a child's developmental trajectory, autistic children start to demonstrate different social, communication and behavioural patterns. These differences appear in response to different brain structures and functions in the brain (Baron-Cohen, 2009; Belmonte & Bourgeron, 2006).

ASD is believed to share some similarities with ADHD such as inattentiveness, impulsiveness and distractibility, leading to some children mistakenly being diagnosed with ADHD rather than ASD (Carpenter & Thomson, 2010). One of the earliest indicators of autism appears when a child demonstrates a 'sticky' attention style and does not become disengaged as quickly as non-autistic children, preferring instead to become narrowly focused on one particular object as opposed to many different objects (Belmonte & Bourgeron, 2006). Preoccupation with objects, a narrow range of interests and difficulty with change are all associated with this disorder (Adreon & Stella, 2001). While children do not outgrow disorders such as autism, their symptoms can be lessened over time with appropriate interventions (Adreon & Stella, 2001; O'Donnell et al., 2012).

There is ongoing research to establish just what is happening in the brain of an autistic child. Traditionally it was believed that children with autism were characterised by weakly connected brain regions, but more recent images (see Figure 8.5) show overly connected regions compared with the brains of typical developing children (Keown, Shih, Nair, Peterson & Müller, 2013; Supekar et al., 2013).

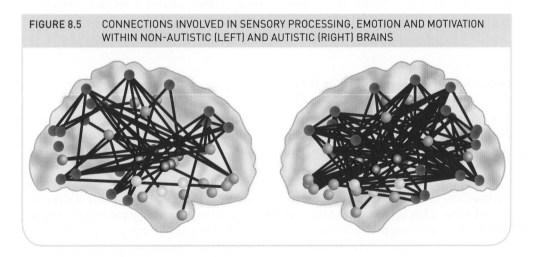

FIGURE 8.5   CONNECTIONS INVOLVED IN SENSORY PROCESSING, EMOTION AND MOTIVATION WITHIN NON-AUTISTIC (LEFT) AND AUTISTIC (RIGHT) BRAINS

ASPERGER'S SYNDROME

Asperger's syndrome is one of the disorders included on the continuum of ASD. Asperger's syndrome is present in more capable children who may function in the average or above-average range of cognitive functioning, yet have some learning disabilities; such children can be highly talkative and may display socially odd behaviour (Carpenter, 2010; Jordan, 1999).

These children are more able to function within a classroom setting and are considered to be on the more able end of the spectrum. That being said, children with Asperger's, as it is commonly referred to, will have trouble with social interactions and can sometimes demonstrate behaviours such as repetition of actions and attachment to certain routines. While these symptoms can overlap with children with autism, children with Asperger's tend to show language and cognitive development closer to those of typically developing children (Belmonte & Bourgeron, 2006). The key difference between autism and Asperger's syndrome is that an autistic child will learn to talk at a very late stage, often not saying any words before the age of two, while demonstrating a range of learning difficulties and exhibiting developmental delays (Belmonte & Bourgeron, 2006). In contrast, a child with Asperger's syndrome will typically talk as expected and will not demonstrate learning difficulties, although they will still find socialising challenging and often be obsessed with narrow topics of interest (Baron-Cohen, 2009).

A triad of impairment—in social skills, communication and behaviour—is typically present in children considered autistic (Carpenter, 2010). Difficulty with social skills and lack of empathy are often associated with our understanding of ASD and this is how the condition is represented in popular culture and the media. Psychologists are particularly interested in how autism and Asperger's syndrome sufferers' lack of social skills is linked to working empathy circuits in the brain. Children who lack empathy tend to have poor ability when it comes to attributing mental states to others and inferring what someone else is thinking (Baron-Cohen, 2009). This area of research is related to 'theory of mind'.

SOMETHING TO THINK ABOUT 8.2

INDICATORS OF AUTISM SPECTRUM DISORDER

Popular culture is surprisingly fond of depicting characters with autism, perhaps more so than other physical disabilities. The best-selling Australian novel *The Rosie Project* features a protagonist with Asperger's syndrome, as does the British international best-seller *The Curious Incident of the Dog in the Night-time*, which was adapted for the stage and became a Broadway award-winner. Dustin Hoffman won an Oscar in 1989 for his depiction of an autistic man in *Rain Man*, while *What's Eating Gilbert Grape*, *The Black Balloon* and even the clay-mation film *Mary and Max* have also been among the many films to have autistic characters. The accuracy of some of these depictions has been much debated, but the many and varied indicators of ASD are possibly what makes it appealing to film-makers and writers: a person with ASD can appear 'normal' and it can be simply through their behaviours that their differences manifest themselves.

A medical diagnosis is a more complex situation. For ASD to be considered, children must show indicators in at least three domains (Carpenter, 2010). Autistic children tend to have difficulty with social skills, communication and behaviours, shown in a range of indicators.

Social

→ Aloof, indifferent, inappropriate or repetitive styles of social interactions
→ Difficulties due to inability to empathise with others
→ Child can't imagine how others feel and are unable to respond appropriately

▶

▶ **Language and communication**

→ Lack of communication skills, lack of interest in communicating

→ Echolalia speech—repeating the vocalisation of others

→ Difficulty understanding jokes due to tendency to take things literally

Rigidity of thought and behaviour

→ Repetitive behaviours

→ Lack of imaginative play

→ Ritualistic behaviours and focus on minor details such as one part of a toy

→ Obsessive interests to the point of excluding other interests

Ask yourself...

Teachers can help autistic children by implementing strategies to manage their learning.

1   What specific strategies would help resolve difficulties children may have with social interactions?

2   What specific strategies would help resolve difficulties children may have with language and communication?

3   What specific strategies would help resolve difficulties children may have with socially rigid thoughts and behaviour?

By understanding autistic tendencies, teachers can gain insight into how to support students who have special needs. Teachers can help by creating a calm, stable and predictable classroom environment and give children extra time to respond to questions, adapt to changes in classroom routines and work towards assisting children to manage their learning (O'Donnell et al., 2012).

Disadvantage

Poverty arising from lower socio-economic backgrounds has been associated with differences in students' cognitive development and educational outcomes. Increasingly, risks for students living in poverty are recognised as influences on students' learning. Although we need to be careful about negatively stereotyping children from lower socio-economic backgrounds, research provides information that paints a broad picture of what goes on for children living in disadvantaged environments. For example, the lower a child's socio-economic status, the greater the health risks (Sapolsky, 2005). These children are also less likely to exercise or have proper health care and more likely to have poor nutrition. Poverty is also associated with lower standards of living and less community infrastructure. While each health-related factor affects cognition and behaviour, we are still learning how experiences of advantage and disadvantage translate into brain structuring.

A recent study by Noble and colleagues (2015) investigated the possible relationship between socio-economic factors and brain morphometry (the measurement of brain structures and changes) independent of genetic origin. The researchers studied nearly 1,100 individuals who were between the ages of three and twenty years, collecting data on their socio-economic background, conducting MRI brain scans and cognitive tests (Noble et al., 2015). They found a strong positive association between family income and brain surface area, largely in brain areas linked to skills instrumental in learning and academic success. They also found that a child living in the United States in a home with a family income of less than $25 000 was likely to have 6 per cent smaller surface area than their more advantaged counterpart living in a home with a $150 000 income. This relationship between family income and brain surface area was most dramatic at the lower end of the socio-economic spectrum. After accounting for genetics, the advantage observed in children from higher-income families was attributed to exposure to better nutrition, health care, schools, play areas, air quality and other environmental factors known to play a role in brain development (Noble et al., 2015).

As discussed throughout *Understanding Development and Learning*, environmental experiences affect the way the brain wires itself through childhood and adolescence. The good news for teachers is that improving a disadvantaged child's environment through healthy school lunches, engaging curriculum, quality teaching, innovative after-school programs and other nurturing initiatives can have a long-lasting positive effect on a child's brain development, cognition and educational outcomes (Jensen, 2013; Noble et al., 2015). While students from lower socio-economic backgrounds may provide challenges to teachers, teaching quality can offset the devastating effects poverty has on students' academic outcomes (Hanushek, 2005).

REACHING THE HARD-TO-REACH STUDENT

We have talked about only a few of the most common conditions that might challenge learners, although there are a range of situations when differentiation will be needed that are beyond the scope of this work. As an educator you will encounter children who do not fit into any list of symptoms and who will not necessarily respond to typical teaching tips. When we are in any given classroom, there will be a percentage of children who will need differentiation to accommodate their learning needs and who require special consideration for engagement. When the majority of children in the class are not identified as needing special support, there can be a tendency for teachers to 'teach to the middle'. Curriculum guidelines and supporting documents appear to be aimed at this middle group of students.

While you probably agree it would be impossible to individualise every lesson for every child, research has shown that teaching to the middle is ineffective (Tomlinson, 2000). Teaching to the middle ignores the needs of advanced students, leaving them unchallenged and bored, and can intimidate and completely confuse lower-functioning learners. Differentiated instruction is an approach that can be used for the diversity of learners in a classroom so that learners can be reached through a variety of methods and strategies (Tomlinson, 2000). Students are more successful when they are taught based on their own readiness levels, interests and learning. Inclusive practices (see Figure 8.6) require teachers to develop skills, knowledge, and pedagogical and teaching expertise to deal with such diversity.

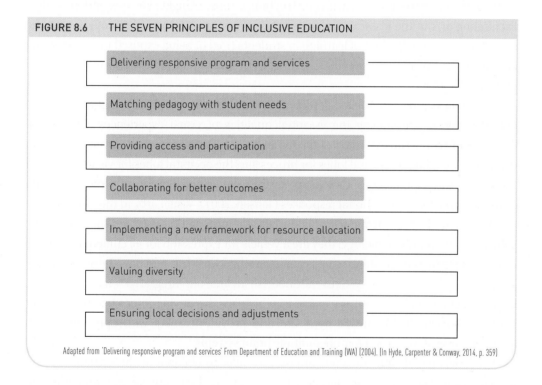

FIGURE 8.6   THE SEVEN PRINCIPLES OF INCLUSIVE EDUCATION

- Delivering responsive program and services
- Matching pedagogy with student needs
- Providing access and participation
- Collaborating for better outcomes
- Implementing a new framework for resource allocation
- Valuing diversity
- Ensuring local decisions and adjustments

Adapted from 'Delivering responsive program and services' From Department of Education and Training (WA) (2004). (In Hyde, Carpenter & Conway, 2014, p. 359)

Providing appropriate learning experiences for individual learners includes teachers scaffolding learning in an inclusive environment. Differentiation offers opportunities for a class lesson with provisions for supportive practices such as peer tutoring, small group work and one-on-one time with students.

THE ARTS

Student-focused planning in collaboration with multidisciplinary teams and family involvement may be an ongoing process for some of the children in your class. Looking for students' strengths and delivering curriculum that provides enriched experiences for all the children in your class is optimum. There are many ways to engage students with different needs and a host of resources available. Of interest, the arts are one area of the curriculum that has been suggested as a way of engaging students not ordinarily reached (Fiske, 1999; Jensen, 2001; Upitis, 2011). Indeed, some have argued for more endorsement of the arts in education (Scholes & Nagel, 2012). Highlighting the arts connects learners to the world of real work through theatre, music, and production of works. Through this medium students learn to become sustained, self-directed learners rather than recipients of facts from direct instruction for the next high-stakes test (Jensen, 2001). Students of lower socio-economic status gain as much or more from arts instruction as those of higher socio-economic status. Facilitating arts in the classroom changes the environment to one of discovery with the potential to reignite the love of learning in students tired of being exposed to rote learning and facts. Specifically, arts provide challenges for students at all levels, from delayed to gifted (Fiske, 1999).

The brain is a pattern seeker, detecting contrast and movement. Visual arts provide opportunities for developing the essential qualities of visual experiences. One of the functions of art is as an extension of the visual brain with all areas of the brain involved in cognition, including the frontal lobes for processing, the occipital lobes for visual input and visualising, the parietal lobes for sensory sorting, the cerebellum for movement, and the mid-brain area for our emotional responses (Jensen, 2001). Visual arts, in this way, provide an efficient tool for academic learning. In fact, the arts can be used for such academic subjects as anatomy and biology; they are a vehicle for expression for all students. Theories of the brain help us understand what is going on when we do art and how the arts enhance the process of learning. The systems they nourish include our integrated sensory, attentive, cognitive, emotional and motor capacities, which are the driving forces behind all other learning (Jensen, 2001). Furthermore, the arts provide learners with opportunities to simultaneously develop and mature multiple brain systems.

The labels 'gifted' and 'impaired' are used to refer to children at the extreme ends of a continuum. These extremes are used to identify children with unique strengths and weaknesses. There is a remarkable phenomenon when these extremes are present within one child, a condition known as being an autistic savant. Let's look at the case of Nadia as an example.

SOMETHING TO THINK ABOUT 8.3

GIFTED YET IMPAIRED: NADIA, AN AUTISTIC SAVANT

An autistic child, Nadia, was born in England with virtually no spoken language yet by her third birthday she was producing drawings with astonishing detail and perception (Selfe, 1985, 2011). At the age of six years, Nadia had a vocabulary that consisted of only ten one-word utterances and it was believed that this lack of language was coupled with a severe degree   ▶

▶ of literal-mindedness. But Nadia's art still had remarkable realism and she was producing amazing sketches. Though many of her other brain functions were impaired, her brain's visual-spatial areas were apparently enhanced to the point that one of her drawing parallels one by Leonardo da Vinci (Selfe, 2011). Although autistic children are known for attention to detail, it is still amazing that Nadia with her underdeveloped language, weak cognitive skills, a lack of traditional communication skills and no artistic training demonstrated phenomenal skill and realism in her drawings.

Nadia drew instinctively without the usual need to understand or interpret what she was seeing (Selfe, 1985). While Nadia's autism compromised functioning in her brain precluding her from engaging in a range of typical activities, the right parietal lobe—the part of the brain concerned with sense of artistic proportion—was not affected (Ramachandran, 2004).

For a review of Nadia's case and to see her outstanding drawings, see Lorna Selfe's book *Nadia Revisited* (2011).

Opportunities for making music also contribute to the development of essential cognitive systems, including reasoning, creativity, thinking, decision making and problem solving (Jensen, 2001). Music helps with thinking by activating and synchronising neural firing patterns that orchestrate and connect multiple brain sites (Catterall, Chapleau & Iwanaga, 1999). The neural synchrony ensembles increase both the brain's efficiency and effectiveness with these systems connected and located in the frontal, parietal and temporal lobes and the cerebellum. In this way, making music supports spatial reasoning, creativity and generalised mathematical skills. It is noteworthy that introducing students to music has been associated with increased maths scores (Catterall et al., 1999).

EXTENDING THE EXCEPTIONAL LEARNER

A gifted and talented child has special needs in a similar manner to a child with a learning disability. Once again, educators need to meet and facilitate appropriate learning experiences for these diverse children. Approaches to educating gifted and talented students vary between schools with many children incorporated in regular classroom and others involved in extension programs that withdraw children as part of the process. Processes to identify gifted and talented students rely on definitions of intelligence and the capacity to test ability to excel. Giftedness is perceived through various definitions that include combinations of abilities, talents and exceptional capacities (Milne, 2010). We talked in detail about constructions of intelligence and different perspectives in understanding intelligence in Chapter 6. While gifted and talented children are identified across cultures, as well as among individuals with disabilities and special needs, we need to be careful about

See Chapter ❹ for more detail on defining intelligence.

labelling these children (Milne, 2010). Definitions of giftedness are complex, reflect social values and change over time.

Gifted and talented children experience a sense of well-being and engagement when teachers provide supportive and challenging learning environments. They need opportunities that are responsive to their individual strengths and interests. Classrooms should respond to each individual child's learning needs. For the gifted individual, this may require modifying the curriculum or planning a differentiated curriculum that is stimulating. Gifted and talented students are often different from their age-peers in terms of their abilities and learning needs. They have particular learning needs that require specific strategies and approaches that include daily challenge in their specific areas of ability or interest; learning experiences that reflect a range of learning styles; opportunities to socialise and learn with peers of like-ability as well as work independently on areas of interest; and connections to people and opportunities beyond the early childhood setting or school that support their particular passions and talents while connecting to the curriculum (Rogers, 2007). Education for the gifted and talented requires specific curriculum, assessment and teaching methods. Teachers also need to be aware of gifted and talented students' socio-emotional development, as some students may be sensitive and perfectionists. When students' abilities are not recognised and supported, students may demonstrate boredom, frustration and lack of motivation. Responding to gifted and talented students is the responsibility of teachers and schools.

Giftedness is complex; individuals who advance quickly or who appear promising in a particular domain can often be labelled 'gifted'. Identifying giftedness can be challenging with 10 to 20 per cent of the school population qualifying as gifted (Renzulli, 2005). These children will generally demonstrate above-average ability identified through testing methods but must also demonstrate task commitment, perseverance, endurance, dedicated practice, self-confidence and the ability to carry out the task in one's area of interest (Renzulli, 2005). Meeting the needs of these children presents a challenge as misrecognition can lead to behaviour problems as boredom and disengagement set in. Meeting the needs of gifted children requires a constructivist approach to provide effective and flexible options.

All children have gifts and talents

All children have strengths. Nadia, in Something to think about 8.3, provides an exciting illustration of how a child may struggle profoundly with specific academic capacities but also bring into the world an amazing gift through her perceptions of the world.

Talent requires practice, and practice plays a large role in any accomplishments arising from underlying talent (Bailey, Morley & Dismore, 2009). Students' desire to increase their talent may stem from enjoyment, process flow and external support. Process flow happens when a child wants to improve a skill in a domain for its own sake, such as shooting goals to become a better basketball player. The incentive to practise and improve a talent such as shooting goals is intrinsically motivated (Bailey et al., 2009). In this way, repeated practice can alter a student's capabilities. As a teacher, you will notice that children will enter school with different skills and talents; some students will appear naturally better at language or you may have a child who appears to be a star athlete. While some believe talent is genetic, individual capacity is also based on dedication to practice and experiences that improve skills. One important thing to remember is that all children have strengths and indeed talents!

CONCLUSION

Inclusion involves educating students in regular classrooms regardless of their special needs. Within schools, the way that inclusion is interpreted, and how children with diverse needs are provided for, varies. Meeting the needs of children with special needs requires teachers to have expertise, special skills and access to professional support. There are challenges for schools, teachers, students and indeed parents in terms of providing the support and educational experiences required for diverse students. But there is generally an acceptance that all children have the right to equal and appropriate education. That being said, there continue to be ongoing debates about the advantages and disadvantages of inclusion and the impact this model has on children and teachers alike. As a teacher, you will be challenged to develop an informed opinion about your thoughts on inclusion and to develop the skills and knowledge you will need to support the children in your care. Through your recognition, caring and support, you can make a difference in the lives of all children and indeed the development of brain capacities and wiring of neural pathways! Insights from modern neuroscience suggest that teachers have an important role to play in facilitating lasting positive effects on children's brain development, cognition and educational outcomes.

Given we know a child's brain is influenced by environmental experiences that include relationships, environmental stimulations, experiences that facilitate the development of neural pathways and the impact of quality education, teachers have a significant role to play in the life of a child experiencing difference. We also know that the brain makes physical and neurological changes in response to environmental, social and educational experiences.

As you look around, you will see that many schools and teachers successfully facilitate an inclusive community, putting students centre stage and enlisting the help and assistance needed to support participation for diverse children. If you encounter schools where there are major obstacles in providing inclusive communities, there are resources, research and new attitudes that can help lay down the groundwork for supporting students with diverse needs.

CHAPTER SUMMARY

In this chapter we discussed the concept of inclusive education and how some schools still find obstacles associated with providing a truly inclusive school community. Inclusive practices require teachers to develop skills, knowledge, pedagogical and teaching expertise to deal with such diversity. While there are universal stages involved in learning that children will typically demonstrate in a class, there may be a number of children who struggle due to their special needs. 'Typical' children experience maturation as their neural networks form and they learn academically, emotionally and socially. When children do not demonstrate expected milestones of development within an expected time frame, there may be a need to further investigate. But teachers need to be careful about labelling children and need to be part of a multidisciplinary team that includes specialists and the child's family if any assessments are to be conducted.

We considered the complex difficulties associated with dyslexia and how this learning disability in reading is characterised by difficulties with accurate word recognition, poor spelling and decoding abilities. The chapter also discussed attention deficit hyperactivity disorder (ADHD) and how this neurological condition needs accurate identification. Autistic spectrum disorder (ASD) was also defined, including why this neurodevelopmental disorder is referred to as a continuum and spectrum due to the range of autistic disorders. Poverty associated with lower socio-economic backgrounds has been associated with differences in students' cognitive development and educational outcomes and is an increasing risk.

Of interest in this chapter was how the arts are one area of the curriculum that has been used to engage diverse children with different needs. Gifted and talented children and their special needs were discussed. Approaches to educating gifted and talented students vary between schools with many children incorporated in regular classrooms and others involved in extension programs.

Finally, it was concluded that classrooms need to respond to each and every child's learning needs.

Implications for Teaching

Brain research gives us insight into how to develop teaching experiences that help children grow synapses and for learning to occur.

Teachers need to be able to take on these responsibilities:

- understand the memory system and how students transfer new information into long-term memory

- recognise types of memory as a basis for using strategies to build recall of content

- use strategies that tap into emotions to improve memory

- activate students' prior knowledge.

Furthermore, teachers can ensure that they put in place these strategies:

- use children themselves as a guide for shifting the lesson focus to retain interest, encourage movement, and allow for processing of content

- use novelty to improve recall and engage students

- make the first and last parts of a lesson highly meaningful for students.

Additionally, teachers can ensure that these practices are reflected in their classrooms:

- incorporate music and movement to enhance recall

- teach to the naturally social brains of learners to engage them

- understand that stress and failure in the classroom inhibit learning.

Brain-based learning is a focus on improving the efficiency of the brain's processing. Processing efficiency is how the brain functions to support learning and intellectual activity, including memory, attention, processing rate and sequencing. Teachers can help students to process more effectively by having an understanding of how the brain works and providing appropriate strategies (Armstong, 2008).

PRACTICAL ACTIVITIES

1   Draw a plan of an inclusive classroom. What features would you need to include?

2   *While on practicum*, discuss with your mentor teacher(s) what concerns you might have if you had a child with an intellectual disability in your class. Would you be concerned about behavioural/social issues? Would you be concerned about your own professional competence?

3   Where do you stand on the debate? What do you personally think are the advantages and disadvantages of inclusion? Do you have experiences or examples to back up your thoughts?

4   What behaviours and characteristics can you identify in a child you have known who would have benefited from attending an alternative school with a modified curriculum, smaller class size and more structured environment?

5 Write a list of the experiences a child in a class or school devoted solely to children with special needs might miss out on.

6 Differentiation is when a teacher adapts what they teach (content), how they teach what they teach (process) and how the student demonstrates what they have learnt (product). Choose a year level and a subject you are familiar with. Give an example of how you would differentiate a learning experience for a child with ADHD.

STUDY QUESTIONS

1 Write a definition of an inclusive school environment.

2 Explain the indicators of dyslexia.

3 List some strategies teachers can use with children who have dyslexia.

4 What is ADHD?

5 How would you help a child with ADHD in your class?

6 Autistic spectrum disorder (ASD) is a neurodevelopmental disorder. Why is it referred to as a continuum or spectrum?

7 What is the difference between gifted and talented?

8 How can the arts be used to engage children with different needs?

SOMETHING TO THINK ABOUT 8.4

POVERTY AND SPECIAL NEEDS

There are established links between poverty and disability. Children living in poverty often do not have access to the health care they need and are also less likely to exercise and receive adequate nutrition. While health-related factors affect cognition and behaviour, we are still learning how experiences of advantage and disadvantage translate into brain structuring.

Ask yourself...

1 How might lack of health care and nutrition impact on children in the classroom?

2 Can schools address some of the issues for children who do not have adequate health care or nutrition?

FURTHER READINGS

Armstrong, S. (2008). *Teaching Smarter with the Brain in Focus: Practical Ways to Apply the Latest Brain Research to Deepen Comprehension, Improve Memory, and Motivate Students to Achieve.* New York, NY: Scholastic.

Baron-Cohen, S., Tager-Flusberg, H. & Lombardo, M. (Eds.) (2013). *Understanding Other Minds: Perspectives from Social Cognitive Neuroscience* (3rd ed.). Oxford, UK: Oxford University Press.

Carpenter, L. (2010). Understanding autism spectrum disorder. In M. Hyde, L. Carpenter & R. Conway, *Diversity and Inclusion in Australian Schools* (pp. 267–279). Melbourne, Australia: Oxford University Press.

Diamond, M. & Hopson, J. (1999). *Magic Trees of the Mind: How to Nurture Your Child's Intelligence, Creativity, and Healthy Emotions from Birth through Adolescence.* New York, NY: Penguin Putnam.

Fiske, E. (Ed.). (1999). *Champions of Change: The Impact of the Arts on Learning.* Retrieved from Arts Edge: The Kennedy Center: http://www.artsedge.kennedy-center.org/champions/

Hyde, M., Carpenter, L. & Conway, R. (Eds.) (2014). *Diversity, Inclusion and Engagement* (2nd ed.). Melbourne, Australia: Oxford University Press.

Jensen, E. (2000). *Different Brains, Different Learners: How to Reach the Hard to Reach.* Thousand Oaks, CA: Corwin Press.

Unesco (1994, June). *The Salamanca Statement and Framework for Action on Special Needs Education.* World Conference on Special Education Needs for Education: Access and Quality, Salamanca, Spain.

VIDEO LINKS

Roger Slee Education and Inclusive Communities—Article 2
https://www.youtube.com/watch?v=Hjc4430D8As

A speech given in New Zealand by Professor Roger Slee, who is the director of the Victoria Institute for Education, Diversity and Lifelong Learning; simultaneously signed.

Principals Australia Institute: *How Inclusive Is Your School*
https://www.youtube.com/watch?v=F2-FjRBjGx0

Overview of inclusion and diversity.

WEBLINKS

Australian Advisory Board on Autism Spectrum Disorders
http://www.autismadvisoryboard.org.au/

Information on autism spectrum disorders from the websites of the Advisory Board's member organisations.

Children and Young People with Disability Australia (CYDA)
http://www.cda.org.au/

CYDA is the national peak body that represents children and young people (from birth to 25 years) with disability.

Gifted and Talented Education
http://www.curriculumsupport.education.nsw.gov.au/policies/gats/index.htm

Support for teaching gifted and talented students from the New South Wales Department of Education.

9

SOCIOCULTURAL FACTORS OF LEARNING

> ' Learning and development are facilitated by the participation of the developing person in progressively more complex patterns of reciprocal activity with someone with whom that person has developed a strong and enduring emotional attachment and when the balance of power gradually shifts in favour of the developing person. '
>
> (Bronfenbrenner, 1979, p. 60)

LEARNING OUTCOMES

As you read through this chapter and undertake the exercises at the end, you will gain the ability to complete these tasks successfully:

→ describe and discuss sociocultural factors that affect learning

→ discuss the importance of language in Vygotsky's theory of learning and development

→ explain the zone of proximal development and how you can scaffold learning for children in your class

→ understand the importance of immediate and broader sociocultural contexts according to Bronfenbrenner

→ discuss how gender, socio-economic background and culture can affect children's learning.

KEY TERMS

- zone of proximal development
- scaffolding
- guided participation
- enquiry learning
- ecological systems theory
- bio-ecological theory
- gender
- culture
- culturally responsive teaching

Sara Wilson completed her university degree in a metropolitan city and has spent her whole life living in Australia. She is now enjoying her first year of teaching in a primary school and she has a Year 3 class. She was very excited when she was offered a teaching position at Tangerine Primary School and also a little apprehensive as the school is situated 45 minutes outside a metropolitan city within a disadvantaged community. The student population is a mix of children from English-speaking and non-English-speaking backgrounds. The school is coeducational, catering for 534 students from Prep to Year 6. Established in 1910, the school has welcomed children and families from many countries, with more than forty nationalities represented. Approximately 20 per cent of the students are learning English as a second language and the Aboriginal and Torres Strait Islander community is growing, with 6 per cent of students identifying with this group. Recently there have been a number of children attending the school from immigrant Vietnamese families who have just relocated into the area.

Sara's class includes a mixed range of abilities and she needs to cater for diverse learners. The room is big enough to have the children's desks arranged in small groups, a carpeted area for whole group work and four computers along the back wall. Sara likes to use a lot of hands-on resources and has collected many handy bits and pieces for small group activities. She also enjoys doing a lot of artwork with her class and has access to paints, oil pastels and collage materials. Books and reading are part of her daily program as she believes that literacy is very important.

Sara has two new Vietnamese boys, Danh and Xuan, in her class, who have very little English, are very shy and reluctant to interact with her. She is concerned because they do not seem to be making friends with the other children. The two boys tend to gravitate together and do not engage with others in group work. She is also concerned because they do not seem to be improving in their oral language or literacy skills. They seem to wait for her to direct all their learning. Each day Sara hopes their parents will come to the class so she can talk with them but so far she has not seen them. The Vietnamese culture is not something she knows very much about. With so many children from different cultural backgrounds, sometimes she thinks it is too much to expect teachers to understand each child's situation.

Earlier in the year Sara had a lot of success developing a relationship with Ameena, who had just arrived from Nigeria. Ameena was very bright and much more interested in making friends and learning. She worked hard and her oral language and literacy skills improved quickly at school and at home with help from her parents. Ameena is very polite, outgoing and quickly became popular with the other girls. Sara is not sure why Danh and Xuan are so hard to engage.

Sara decided to do some research about the Vietnamese culture and traditional approaches to learning. She found out that Vietnamese culture is very much a 'villagers' culture', focused on collective good rather than individual competition. She found out that *collectivism* refers to a value system in which a person's identity, attitudes and actions are determined to a large degree by the groups to which he or she belongs. In this way children feel more comfortable working as a team member. Sara also found out that traditional learning methods are often teacher directed, about translation of information and rote memory. This implies children are dependent rather than independent learners. This is disturbing to Sara as she likes to facilitate a child-centred classroom with opportunities for children to construct their own knowledge. She also likes the children to discuss their learning as part of the process.

1 Is it Sara's role as a teacher to find out about Danh's and Xuan's background? If yes, why? If no, why not?

2 What sorts of difficulties could be faced by Danh and Xuan as learners and by Sara as a teacher given the cultural differences?

3 What information about the two boys would inform Sara and her teaching practices? What information does she need to enhance learning opportunities?

4 What specific strategies could Sara implement to try to involve Danh and Xuan in oral language opportunities and experiences? What resources could she use and how could she arrange her classroom environment?

5 What specific strategies could Sara implement to enhance Danh's and Xuan's learning in general?

6 Why haven't Danh's and Xuan's parents been to visit the classroom? What can Sara do to facilitate a relationship with the children's parents?

INTRODUCTION

The significance of sociocultural factors and how they affect learning will be discussed in this chapter. While the previous chapters have focused on individuals and learning, this chapter considers the broader influences of schools, families and communities on learning. Increasingly, sociocultural perspectives are becoming more visible within psychology, with the understanding that cognition, memory, emotion, personality, identity and other psychological constructs develop within particular social and cultural environments. A diverse group of psychologists and social researchers have contributed to our understandings of contemporary sociocultural theories, as they have articulated the interplay between psychological and sociocultural domains. But, despite the contribution of these researchers over time, recognition of the significance of sociocultural influences in the study of psychological phenomena has been underdeveloped.

It is important to note that currently there are changing perspectives in psychology as we move from individualistic developmental explanations of learning towards theories that consider socially and culturally constructed contributions to this process. Learning and development are then considered intertwined and embedded in contextual processes; in essence, learning occurs at the nexus of nature and nurture. Contributing to the move from binary understandings of psychology and sociocultural processes has been the development of new ways of conceptualising children and the sociology of childhood. When children are considered active participants in the social construction of childhood and contributors to shared culture, children are understood to have agency and power within their own right (Prout & James, 1997). The child's contextual world, including class, gender, race and ethnicity, are therefore seen as interpreted, defined and actively mediated by children.

Traditionally, cultural psychology and neuroscience inhabited opposite ends of the scientific spectrum. In the past cultural psychology has been characterised by *ethnographic holism*—focusing on the whole rather than individual parts—while neuroscience has been characterised by *biological reductionism*, or a belief that human behaviour can be explained by breaking it down into smaller component parts (Ames & Fiske, 2010). But these two approaches to understanding people are related. Recently, the emerging fields of social cognitive neuroscience and cultural neuroscience have combined the theories and methods of these two disciplines (Ames & Fiske, 2010; Han & Northoff, 2008). Social cognitive neuroscience emerged to investigate cognition in a way that considers the social contextual factors which cognition likely evolved to manage (Ochsner & Lieberman, 2001). Cultural neuroscience is a relatively new interdisciplinary field that investigates the relationship between culture (for example, value and belief systems and practices shared by groups) and human brain functions (Han et al., 2013).

Cultural neuroscience has the potential to explore the ways that sociocultural systems structure the developmental experiences of individuals and also the content and process of experience, thought and behaviour in everyday life in ways that have a recognisable trace at the neural level (Ames & Fiske, 2010). As culture is stored in people's brains, human brains are biologically prepared to acquire culture. As human beings we have evolved neurobiologically to acquire basic cultural capabilities—such as language—ensuring the ongoing functioning of our culture.

Neuroscience has established that human brains are a work in progress and that early experiences affect brain development and long-term learning (Shonkoff & Phillips, 2000). While there is growing recognition of fields such as cultural neuroscience, this chapter aims to provide an overview of the contributions of prominent researchers in terms of sociocultural theory and how contextual factors can affect students' experiences. By understanding broad sociocultural influences, teachers are then placed to help change the course of inequitable trajectories by providing more resources, more time and nurturing learning environments.

See Chapter ❸ for an overview of neurological development

Specifically, the impact of immediate and wider social and cultural environments on learning will be considered with specific attention on the influence of the classroom, family and wider community. To this end, in the following sections we will revisit some of the theorists briefly noted in Chapter 1, with a focus on Lev Vygotsky, Urie Bronfenbrenner and Jerome Bruner. We will highlight their contributions to understandings about how sociocultural factors influence students' learning and development. Then, we will identify some of the key broader contextual factors that may affect the students you will teach in terms of the social, economic and cultural environments in which they interact on a daily basis. As teachers have ongoing daily contact with the children in their care, understanding the diverse social and cultural contexts in which a child is developing is essential. These understandings can then inform your teaching practice and the curriculum and pedagogical decisions you make continually throughout your teaching day.

See Chapter ❶ for more information about social constructivist theorists.

SOME BACKGROUND

So what is sociocultural theory and what does it have to do with learning? Increasingly, educators are challenged to enter dialogue about theoretical perspectives that define the cultural and socially constructed nature of learning (Anning, Cullen & Fleer, 2004). We now know the importance of the social and cultural processes associated with learning and we cannot separate and compartmentalise the process of learning from the intertwined and embedded context of the learning environment. Contemporary understandings of children acknowledge that they are active participants, are competent beings, have agency and contribute to the learning environment in which they participate (Corsaro, 1997; Prout & James, 1997). Thinking about children in this way involves viewing children as social beings who actively influence and are actively influenced by the cultures in which they live. Taking a sociocultural perspective also involves being aware of the diversity among children and taking into consideration gender, ethnicity, the influence of children's family and how cultural expectations form part of children's daily lives and influence their learning.

VYGOTSKY

Understandings about sociocultural perspectives associated with learning are often attributed to the work of Russian-born psychologist Lev Vygotsky (1896–1934), who built on the work of collaborators in Russia during the 1920s and 1930s. Primarily, Vygotsky was a developmental psychologist who proposed a theory linking the development of higher cognitive functions in children to interactions in their social environment. Cognition, as previously discussed in Chapter 2, is mental activity and behaviour that allows us to understand the world and includes functions of learning, perception, memory, thinking and reasoning. While many psychologists were developing theories associated with explanations of human learning that removed the child from the learning context, Vygotsky, significantly, developed a theory that accounted for the richness associated with children's lives. His work was suppressed by the Soviet Communist Party from 1936 to 1956, only coming to prominence in the 1950s and 1960s. He has since been recognised as making a noteworthy contribution to contemporary sociocultural approaches to learning and his work has been built upon by many scholars. While Vygotsky's work has been influential in

Western countries, there are limitations, as his work has had to be translated into English and he died at a relatively young age. But a selection of his writings in *Mind in Society* (Vygotsky, 1978) proved influential. Vygotsky offers us the opportunity to conceptualise the interplay and interdependence of social and individual processes and consider the implications for facilitating children's learning.

There are some similarities between the work of Piaget (see Chapter 1) and Vygotsky as both were interested in psychological research that came about due to a request to replicate Binet's intelligence test in Russia. Both Piaget and Vygotsky proposed that humans construct their own knowledge through a series of stages, often through interactions with others. There are major differences, as Piaget focused on the individual and Vygotsky was focused on learning within socio-historical and sociocultural contexts, proposing that interactions between the child and the environment produce cognition in culturally specific ways. Vygotsky was concerned with the interdependence of learning and development, in contrast to prevailing views of his time in which learning was regarded as an external process (Wertsch, 1991). Vygotsky critiqued Piaget's theory, in which maturation was a precondition of learning, but never the result of it (Vygotsky, 1978). Specifically, Piaget proposed that children moved through developmental stages preceding their learning, while Vygotsky articulated the ways that social learning preceded development. Significantly, Vygotsky's work is mainly associated with the sociocultural and socio-historic origins of cognitive development and language as a mental tool.

SOCIOCULTURAL THEORY OF COGNITIVE DEVELOPMENT

According to Vygotsky, children's thinking develops as a result of their social knowledge, which is communicated by language and cultural tools, such as counting systems and art. Learning takes place through a process that involves interactions between a child, carers and the environment, mediated through language. While thought and language are initially separate domains in the beginning of life, they merge around three years of age. The role of language is then significant because when children begin to use *social speech*, *private speech* and *inner speech*, they learn to communicate, form thoughts and regulate intellectual functions. Social speech is external communication that involves talking with others and develops from around the age of two, while private speech serves an intellectual function and involves conversations with the self. Private speech typically develops from the age of three. Private speech is considered the transition point between social and inner speech, where language and thought unite to constitute verbal thinking (Vygotsky, 1987).

Private speech becomes a tool used by the child to facilitate cognitive processes, to overcome task obstacles, and to enhance imagination, thinking and conscious awareness.

Children use private speech most often during tasks of intermediate difficulty as they attempt self-regulation, verbally planning and organising their thoughts (Winsler et al., 2007). Private speech takes on an important self-regulation function around the age of seven, developing into silent inner speech. Silent inner speech has its own function, as children's monologues internalise, and becomes thinking in pure meanings, driving cognitive development (Vygotsky, 1962). The role of language is significantly highlighted in Vygotsky's work as he argues that children can solve practical tasks with the help of their speech, as well as their eyes and hand.

The elementary mental functions of attention, perception, sensation and memory also work to develop new concepts with a combination of biological and psychological factors contributing to cognitive development (Vygotsky, 1978). As children interact within their sociocultural environment, these functions develop into more sophisticated higher mental functions. Higher mental functions develop through social interactions with significant people in a child's life, such as parents and teachers. Through these interactions, a child learns the habits of mind of the specific culture, including speech patterns, written language and other symbolic knowledge that develop as a consequence of interactions that involve historical elements of the culture. Historical elements may include cultural symbols involved in language, art and mathematics or material artefacts involved in literacy and technology. For example, memory can be an elementary mental function involved in storing initial images and impressions of events. Higher mental functioning develops as a child uses literate practices of the culture, such as symbolic signs, paper or technology to extend the natural memory function. Mnemonics or learning ways to cue and remind oneself and assist memory are also cultural strategies taught to children. Cultural signs and tools mediate children's mental functions as they develop understanding of the cultural usage of signs and tools through social interaction.

See Chapter ❷ for a neuroscientific view of cognitive development.

See Chapter ❺ for an overview of language development.

VYGOTSKY'S ZONE OF PROXIMAL DEVELOPMENT

The interdependence between individual and social processes in the construction of knowledge was highlighted by Vygotsky (1978) when he introduced the construct of the zone of proximal development (ZPD). Cognitive development, according to Vygotsky, is a process of increased mental sophistication mediated through social interactions within the ZPD. The ZPD was a fundamentally new approach to matching learning with the child's level of development, based on the need to recognise the actual and the potential levels of development. First, there is a need to identify what the child can accomplish independently; second, there is a need to recognise what the child can do when assisted (see Figure 9.1). The distance between what the child can demonstrate alone and what the child can

Zone of proximal development Difference between what learners can do without help and with help.

accomplish under guidance or collaboration with someone more capable is referred to as the ZPD. Specifically, the ZPD refers to the distance between the actual developmental level as determined by independent problem solving and the level of potential development determined through problem solving under adult guidance or in collaboration with more capable peers (Vygotsky, 1978). Therefore, the ZPD refers to the ways in which the acquisition of new knowledge depends on previous learning, as well as the availability of guided instruction. This zone becomes the space where the child is cognitively prepared but benefits from social interactions.

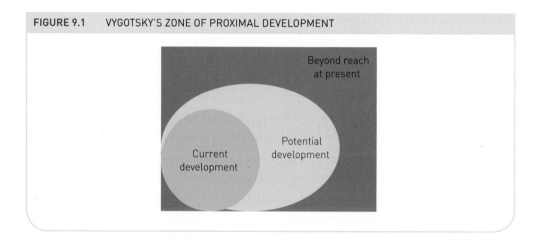

FIGURE 9.1   VYGOTSKY'S ZONE OF PROXIMAL DEVELOPMENT

BRUNER AND SCAFFOLDING

Scaffolding
Guidance received from an adult or more competent peer.

An understanding of the ZPD is significant for teachers who wish to scaffold children's learning. Scaffolding, associated with the work of psychologist Jerome Bruner (1978, 1983), describes what takes place in the ZPD, due to the process of temporary support provided by the teacher, adult or peer, for the learner. Bruner also emphasised social environments, highlighting the important role of adults in assisting children's learning. Significantly, scaffolding has been translated into educational contexts; teachers can take an active role in this process, determining what a child can do alone and what he or she can do with help. By providing assistance, resources and questioning, the teacher can scaffold learning, contributing to the child's understanding of more complex knowledge domains and his or her development of more sophisticated skills. If a child is having difficulty in social situations, the teacher may step in and model how to use language to engage peers. For example, four-year-old Max walks over to the block corner and steps on Jordan's block construction. Ms Watson says, 'Max, you could use some blocks to build a garage for Jordan's truck factory.' This gives Max a way to enter Jordan's play, encourages Max to interact with Jordan and ultimately creates a more rewarding experience for the boys while modelling social interactions. This process includes careful observation and assessment of a child and the development of curriculum experiences that facilitate and support emerging learnings. The challenge for educators is defining the limits of the zone, matching adult support and scaffolding the learning to a point beyond the child's current capabilities.

ROGOFF AND GUIDED PARTICIPATION

While sociocultural theory developed from the seminal work of Vygotsky, contemporary theorists similarly attest to the importance of social and cultural processes in learning (Bronfenbrenner, 1989; Bruner, 1996; Rogoff, 1990). The concept of the ZPD has been extended by theorists to include understandings of guided participation (Rogoff, 1990). In guided participation, children's cognitive development is considered an apprenticeship that occurs through guided participation in social activity, supported by individuals who stretch children's understandings and skill in using the tools of the culture (Rogoff, 1990). In this case, guided participation focuses on the interrelatedness of children's and teachers' interactions without the need for the face-to-face didactics highlighted by Vygotsky. The guidance can be from a distance and include non-verbal forms of communication, broadening sociocultural influences beyond language-based interactions as the primary source of learning (Rogoff, 1990). Guided participation can include scaffolding but extends to broader views of supportive context for learning and development beyond the adult or more experienced partner. Within the classroom context, the teacher may structure tasks into different levels or sub-goals. Sub-goals are broken down further or changed as the child and adult are engaged in interaction or in exploring the ZPD. Often the teacher will have a skill in mind that is within the child's cognitive reach and offers support by helping the child define sub-goals and providing resources. The significant role of information technology and communication (ICT) currently in schools provides opportunities for students to work under the guidance of teachers towards goals without necessarily having face-to-face instruction.

Guided participation Builds on the concept of the zone of proximal development to include broader support such as structuring tasks and ICT.

ENQUIRY LEARNING

More recently, Vygotsky's ZPD has been proposed as a space that provides an opportunity for teachers and students to work collaboratively, moving away from traditional authoritarian pedagogies, towards an inter-subjective space for both students and teachers to learn from each other (Scholl, 2014). In this way the ZPD becomes a space for mentor and mentee to engage in enquiry learning together, reflecting Dewey's notions of freedom, shared authority and openness to experience as a means of learning (cited in Scholl, 2014). In this way, the teacher moves from being a guide to the role of co-enquirer or co-constructor with

Enquiry learning Problem-based learning with co-enquiry by student and teacher.

the student. This starts by the teacher posing questions, problems or scenarios and may include these activities:

→ identifying real-world questions and issues
→ identifying controversies that need researching
→ solving problems and creating a solution
→ individual and group collaborations
→ investigations
→ fieldwork
→ case studies
→ research projects.

Children then need to be provided with rich environments to explore knowledge domains in collegial ways with mentor and mentee both bringing particular expertise to the learning experience. Through mutual questioning, discussion, collaborative problem solving and reflection, teachers and children can create a learning environment that scaffolds children's evolving understandings and cognitive growth.

SUMMARY

Vygotsky's theory of cognitive development has been influential in educational settings with his work reflected in teachers' work as they scaffold and facilitate learning experiences to support the development of children's cognitive capacities. His work has been built upon by others who have proposed the value of guided participation and collaborative or enquiry learning. In summary:

→ children learn within social contexts, through interactions with others
→ cognitive development is an outcome of interaction between a child, his or her carers and the environment
→ interactions within sociocultural environments contribute to the development of sophisticated cognitive functions, thinking and reasoning
→ memory is an example of a mental function that is predetermined by biological factors, while culture determines the type of memory strategies developed
→ the zone of proximal development is the space between the child's current knowledge and potential learning
→ more advanced learners (teachers, peers) can scaffold a child's learning by providing assistance, resources and questioning
→ guided participation includes opportunities to enhance student learning beyond face-to-face experiences
→ the zone of proximal development can also provide a space for mentor and mentee to engage in collaborative enquiry learning.

BRONFENBRENNER

So far in this chapter we have been discussing how sociocultural theorists perceive the distinct processes of learning and development as inextricably intertwined and embedded in the context in which they occur. Urie Bronfenbrenner (1917–2005), an American developmental psychologist born in the Soviet Union, provides a framework that clearly situates individual learning and development within immediate contexts such as the school and home, broader contexts of the local community and in wider society. His framework is referred to as ecological systems theory (Bronfenbrenner, 1989) and highlights how children's experiences always take place within an environment that includes external dimensions. The child then learns and develops as a result of interactions and reciprocal relationships within immediate and broader contexts. The framework provided a lens for developing understandings about the multiplicity and interconnected nature of contextual influences on children's learning.

Bronfenbrenner is widely recognised for his early contribution to Head Start, an intervention program in the United States aimed at improving the educational outcomes of young children living in poverty, and his (1979) approach is evident in a wide range of policies and practices today. Ecological theory advanced by Bronfenbrenner is evident in current research in many fields including educational psychology, human development, child welfare and protection, health, work–family relations, families dealing with incarceration, after-school programs and academic performance, and literacy development.

Ecological systems theory
Posits reciprocal relationships within immediate and broader contexts.

ECOLOGICAL SYSTEMS THEORY

Bronfenbrenner first articulated the original ecological model of human development in 1979. The model consists of hierarchical, nested structures that constitute the layers of environment affecting a developing child (see Figure 9.2) and are referred to as the *microsystem, mesosystem, exosystem* and *macrosystem* (Bronfenbrenner, 1979). Four elements influencing learning and development in these series of contexts are the person, process, context and time. First, we will look in some detail at the hierarchical layers of the environment that affect learning. Then we will consider how the person, process, context and time can influence this learning and, finally, we will consider the implications for teachers.

MICROSYSTEM

The developing child is at the core of the microsystem of the inner circle of Bronfenbrenner's (1979) model and the microsystem includes the child's experiences and interactions

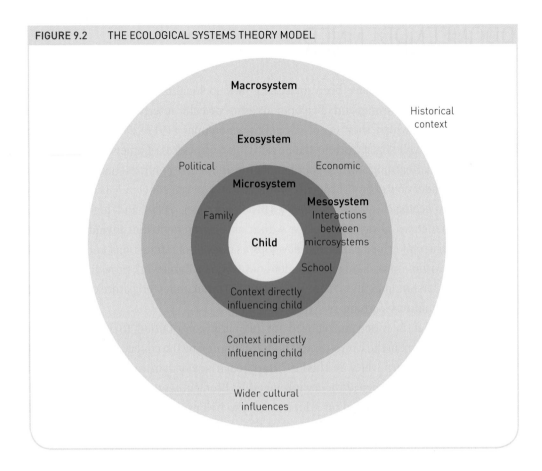

FIGURE 9.2   THE ECOLOGICAL SYSTEMS THEORY MODEL

within everyday environmental settings such as the home, school and neighbourhood that construct the world of the child. These progressively more complex interactions can directly inhibit or enhance the child's development and learning. As the child's social, emotional, cognitive and physical characteristics develop, relationships within the environment change and the developing child constructs the microsystem as much as he or she is shaped by it. The impact of poverty can be influential at this level as social disadvantage can affect a child in terms of the quality of relationships, levels of stress in the home and language interactions with significant adults.

An example of children's learning at the microsystem level is evident in young children's reading development. A child's reading development is influenced by the literacy experiences and interactions with significant others in the immediate environment. Positive, ongoing pre-literacy practices in the home prepare children for more formal literacy experiences in the classroom. Parental skills, beliefs and attitudes about reading are communicated through everyday literacy interactions while the child's attachment with care-givers and the nature of ongoing interactions have been found to be important for literacy development (Yont, Snow & Vernon-Feagans, 2003). Similarly, teachers' beliefs and attitudes about reading are conveyed to children in everyday classroom interactions (McNaughton, 1995). As children progress, they internalise external experiences and develop personal beliefs and attitudes about reading that influence participation in literacy activities.

Reluctance to read on the part of child may influence educational outcomes as negative attitudes affect reading ability, due to lack of engagement and practice (McKenna, Kear & Ellsworth, 1995; Sainsbury & Schagen, 2004). Reluctance indicates that children may be missing out on the cumulative influence that exposure to print has on the accelerated development of reading processes (Freebody, Maton & Martin, 2008; Stanovich, 1986). It is argued that, as these students have increasingly less exposure to text, the gap between skilled and unskilled readers will be compounded (Cunningham & Stanovich, 1997).

Interactions within the immediate environment that encourage and support reading on a daily basis contribute to cumulative development of reading skills and expertise (Freebody et al., 2008; Stanovich, 2000). Practices that engage students in authentic everyday reading and develop associated skills are essential, when understanding language and literacy as a disciplinary knowledge that develops over time is conceptualised in terms of 'cumulative learning' (Freebody et al., 2008; Maton, 2009). When knowledge builds over time, there is an integration and subsuming of previous knowledge and a *segmented learning*, where new ideas or skills are accumulated alongside past knowledge (Maton, 2009). There is also a need for students to transfer knowledge between contexts and to build knowledge over time (Freebody et al., 2008; Maton, 2009).

MESOSYSTEM

The mesosystem consists of the relationships and interactions between significant people in the child's microsystem. These interrelationships make up the second level of the ecological system theory model and include relations between home and the school, and home and the workplace environment of carers. While the child may not be directly involved in these relations, interactions between the child's parents and the school, for example, indirectly influence daily experiences.

Significantly, parent–teacher relationships can influence learning in profound ways. Teachers' perceptions of parents and their beliefs about parental values can contribute to educational outcomes in both positive and negative ways. Teachers working in disadvantaged communities have been found to work with very limited expectations of both parents and children, culminating in relatively low-level, repetitive and unchallenging activities in the classroom (Anyon, 1997; Connolly, 2004; Freebody, Ludwig & Gunn, 1995). These stereotypical views resonate with the findings of others and have been referred to as 'middle-class bias' (Alloway, Freebody, Gilbert & Muspratt, 2002; Lott, 2001). This bias, based on teachers' perceptions of parents, can result in low expectations of children and less daily classroom instruction in higher level skills in low socio-economic schools (Connolly, 2004; Greenwood, 1991). Connections between familial socio-economic background and school academic achievement have been reported in Australia and other Western countries (Australian Council for Educational Research, 2010; Organisation for Economic Co-operation and Development, 2014). Social discrimination and unsupportive classroom environments, in response to children from lower socio-economic backgrounds, are continuing realities influencing children's academic achievement (Anyon, 1997).

As a teacher, you are particularly positioned to enhance classroom experiences by implementing socially just practices that consider the powerful influence of wider environments. Strengthening the home–school relationship with a focus on the facilitation of common core values is an imperative that needs to extend beyond the early primary years of school. There is also a critical need to encourage parents to form partnerships within low socio-economic communities where tensions are often reported due to teachers' lowered perceptions and belief that that these parents do not value schooling (Anyon, 1997; Connolly, 2004; Freebody et al., 1995).

EXOSYSTEM

The exosystem comprises the links and processes that take place not directly involving the child but indirectly influencing the child through the family, educational environment and community. Government initiatives, educational policy and local community stratification and structures are significant at this level. Attending school in a low socio-economic community would be one example of this relational system, as the implications of disadvantage influence daily experiences at home and at school, exacerbating inherent educational injustices within and also beyond the contexts of schooling.

If we consider literacy development at this level, we could say that educational policies are influential as they mandate the school starting age in association with national curricula, influencing the timing and acquisition of reading skills. In Australia, policies governing national benchmark testing in years 3, 5, 7 and 9 influence curriculum, school policies and classroom assessment. The current dominant culture of performativity, obsessed with academic outcomes and the measurement of specific and easily quantifiable aspects of education (Keddie & Mills, 2007), filters into students' everyday realities. Educational policies also indirectly influence teacher training, classroom curriculum and pedagogy, critically shaping children's schooling experience.

Curriculum is another influence that can be considered a social and cultural construction at the exosystem level, as it is value-laden and developed at a particular time with purpose. Curriculum developers bring to the role particular values, attitudes and priorities. Valued knowledge is portrayed as worthwhile while the knowledge of marginalised groups is often invisible. The construction of curriculum influences children's experiences within the classroom, as the implications become part of their daily practice. What children learn or do not learn about at school is dictated by external forces.

A *deficit-oriented* perspective of children from lower socio-economic backgrounds has led to the belief that these children require direct instruction and basic skills, while more advantaged children should be involved in rich, integrated, experiential, enquiry-based approaches. The current government mandate on accountability and standardised testing has resulted in children from disadvantaged homes often being subjected to endless rounds of pre-test preparation as schools try to increase their test scores. High-stakes tests generally do not assess higher order thinking or reasoning. This can result in disadvantaged children spending a disproportionate amount of time practising multiple-choice and standardised tests and being taught low-level curriculum as educators teach for the test (Anyon, 1997; Feinberg, 2012). This dumbing-down of the curriculum, and teaching rote drill and test practice, ensures these children will fall further behind their peers in terms of learning.

MACROSYSTEM

The macrosystem consists of the dominant cultural, political and economic environments of the time in a particular society. Valued knowledge, available resources, cultural practices, workplace demands and lifestyle opportunities indirectly influence a child's experiences at home, in the community and at school. Western cultures such as Australia participate in the Organisation for Economic Co-operation and Development's (OECD) Programme for International Student Assessment (PISA) that has a range of indicators used for comparative measures of education and training systems across its member nations. The latest PISA, for 2012, included sixty-five countries and almost half a million students (OECD, 2014). Nations participated in tests of students in particular curriculum strands such as literacy, numeracy and science, demonstrating the significance of global spaces of equivalence and commensuration of school performance. These measures are often used comparatively at an international level. Australian children's performance on this international stage has indications for national priorities and the level of concern for particular academic domains and associated outcomes.

Governments use international benchmarking to evaluate their country's standing, with teachers often held accountable for children's academic levels. The global emphasis on skills such as literacy contributes to the high status of this proficiency and the associated privileges (Barton, 2007; Wilkinson & Pickett, 2009). Furthermore, globalisation affects local lives and identities as literacy becomes a benchmark for success, influencing educational programs within the classroom (Barton, 2007; Lingard, Martino & Mills, 2009). Australia is not alone in making explicit the perceived economic implication of low literacy skills for economic development. Authorities such as the OECD have made the relationship between literacy skills and employment a powerful and dominant discourse. Underachievement in literacy is therefore a concern for nations seeking to add to the economic value of people and increase their value in the labour market (Black, 2004). This mindset has led to a focus on literacy in classrooms as a set of technical skills to be acquired and assessed using standardised measures (Black, 2004).

This can be problematic, as literacy is more than a set of technical skills; from a sociocultural perspective, literacy is defined by social and communication practices in which children engage in their everyday lives (Barton, 2007).

BIO-ECOLOGICAL MODEL

After publication of the original ecological model, studies concerning children in real-life settings became common in the research literature on human development, prompting Bronfenbrenner to protest that 'in place of too much research on development "out of context" we now have a surfeit of studies on "context without development"' (Bronfenbrenner, 1989, pp. 287–288). The bio-ecological model of human development subsequently proposed by Bronfenbrenner (2001, 2005) endeavoured to extend and redefine several of the key assumptions of the original. With the introduction of the **bio-ecological theory**, human development was subsequently defined as the phenomenon of continuity and change in the bio-psychological characteristics of human beings, both as individuals and as groups (Bronfenbrenner, 2005). This phenomenon is understood to extend over the life course of an individual through historical time. Within the bio-ecological model there are four interrelated components: process–person–context–time (Bronfenbrenner, 2001):

Bio-ecological theory
A refinement of the ecological systems theory model, incorporating bi-directional influences between individuals' development and their surrounding environment.

→ the developmental *process* involves the dynamic realities of the individual and the context
→ the *child*, with an individual repertoire of biological, cognitive, emotional and behavioural characteristics
→ the *context*, conceptualised as the nested levels or system of the ecology of human development (Bronfenbrenner, 1979)
→ and *time*, conceptualised as involving the multiple dimensions of temporality— ontogenetic time, family time, historical time—moderating change across the life course.

The characteristics of the child appear twice in the bio-ecological model. First, as one of the four principal elements (process, person, context and time), as the child influences the form, power, content and direction of the proximal processes. The child then appears again as the developmental outcome, as the developing person's changes over time. The characteristics of the child function as indirect producer and the product of development (Bronfenbrenner, 2001).

Two propositions suggested by Bronfenbrenner (2001) are central to the bio-ecological theory. The first proposition suggests that human development takes place through progressively more complex reciprocal interactions between a child and the people, objects and symbols in the environment. Interactions that occur regularly over time are the proximal processes and include child–teacher activities. The second proposition advocates that the influence of the proximal processes vary due to the bio-psychological characteristics of the child, the environmental context and the nature of the developmental outcome considered.

The bio-ecological paradigm draws on the theoretical assumption that genetic material interacts with environmental experiences to determine developmental outcomes (Bronfenbrenner & Ceci, 1994). In terms of reading development, for example, the environmental influences are initially external and include significant adults, print in various forms (books, newspapers, magazines, multimedia, environmental print) and the dominant alphabetic symbols (English). These external influences become internal as a child interacts in literacy experiences with significant adults over time. The individual characteristics of the child influence the nature of the literacy experiences, with adults demonstrating the possibility of internal characteristics affecting external contexts. These bi-directional interactions occurring slowly over time are referred to as proximal processes. Effective proximal processes are evident in reading when genetic potential is actualised and the necessary knowledge and skill are acquired to interpret the symbolic environment necessary in reading. Variation in outcomes is taken to be due to the joint function of the proximal processes (teacher/child, parent/child), their stability over time (frequency of reading activities), the environmental context (value and beliefs about reading, resources), the characteristics of the child (bio-psychosocial characteristics, attitudes and beliefs about reading) and the learning outcome considered (reading) (Bronfenbrenner & Ceci, 1994).

SUMMARY

Bronfenbrenner's work spanned six decades and offers educators ways to consider the implications of developmental psychology and the interdisciplinary domain of the ecology of human development. His original work was contrary to the predominant view at the time that child development was purely biological, with no influence of experience or environment. Ecological perspectives provide a lens for developing more nuanced understandings about the multiplicity and textured nature of children's experiences. One of the main concepts evident in Bronfenbrenner's work has been the need to understand the immediate and wider environmental influences and to include the child's parents and community in any intervention. This was evident in the direction of the Head Start program in the United States, when he developed methods to improve education outcomes for children in poverty with a view of providing equal educational experiences and outcomes to those of more advantaged children. The focus of Head Start to this day remains on building relationships with families and communities that support well-being, strong relationships and ongoing learning and development for parents and children. As teachers, you are well placed to consider how you can contribute to enhancing learning for the children in your care by understanding and then building upon a child's contextual world.

SOMETHING TO THINK ABOUT 9.1

One of the main concepts evident in Bronfenbrenner's work has been the need to understand the immediate and wider environmental influences and include the child's parents and community in any intervention. This model has been used to develop programs for successful interventions with children from disadvantaged communities in the United States, such as Head Start. Bronfenbrenner's work helped form the Head Start Program in 1965 with his research and his theories key in changing the perspective of developmental psychology by calling attention to the large number of environmental and societal influences on child development.

You may have heard about Head Start; if not you can find plenty of information about the programs that are still running today.

For now let's go back to our opening story about Sara, the Year 3 teacher and her two new Vietnamese students, Danh and Xuan.

Ask yourself...

1   What interactions within the immediate environment (microsystem) might be constraining Danh's and Xuan's experiences learning English and engaging with other children in group work?

2   What interactions or lack of interactions between Sara and the boys' parents (mesosystem) might be constraining their learning? We know that parent–teacher relationships can influence learning in profound ways. Teachers' perceptions of parents and their beliefs about parental values can contribute to educational outcomes in both positive and negative ways. What stereotypical views might Sara hold and how can she engage the parents to enhance learning for the boys?

3   There are lots of things that might be indirectly affecting the boys' educational experiences (exosystem) such as government initiatives for immigrants, educational policies for children for whom English is a second language, local community stratification and the effect of attending a school in a low socio-economic community. Can Sara do anything about these influences? Should Sara find out more about these influences? If yes, why? If no, why not?

4   Dominant Western cultural, political and economic environments of the time in society also affect the boys' experiences at school (macrosystem). Valued knowledge, available resources, cultural practices, workplace demands and lifestyle opportunities will indirectly influence Danh's and Xuan's experiences. What wider contextual influences might be constraining for the boys? How can Sara take into account different valued knowledge and cultural practices in ways that enhance learning? Provide an example.

GENDER, SOCIO-ECONOMIC BACKGROUND AND CULTURE IN THE CLASSROOM

The impact of factors such as **gender**, socio-economic background and culture on children's learning is often interdependent and interrelated. For example, the notion of gender is significant in children's daily life from when they start school at four or five years of age (Jordan, 1995). School peer groups and the desire for group belonging then become significant in the construction of masculine and feminine stereotypes (Connell, 2009; Keddie 2006). Social constructions of masculinity and femininity stereotypes, however, is never just about gender but is a reflection of the many different ways gender combines with socio-economic background and ethnicity to produce differing and enduring forms of identity (Connell, 2005; Connolly, 2006). It is problematic to homogenise boys and girls as two binary entities, as exploring differences among groups of boys and girls makes visible difference not always accounted for. To this end there is growing acknowledgment of the salience of social class, or social and economic status, the influence of boys' and girls' experiences at school and the interactional complexities associated with educational outcomes (Keddie & Mills, 2007; OECD, 2010; Scholes, 2011; Scholes & Nagel, 2012).

To try to understand how boys' and girls' experiences at school affect learning, we need to understand how notions of gender have been shaped by the societies and cultures in which we live and how they are intertwined with, and mediated by, socio-economic status. Understandings about the complexities associated with gender, socio-economic status and achievement are entering educational enquiry and discussions at the policy level, but the general implications of these dialogues have not filtered down into schools. There are barriers, as recognition of differences among groups of boys and girls is not always evident in schools among staff who have been socialised by past generalisations made by educators and policy-makers about all boys and girls as two homogenous groups (Read, Francis & Skelton, 2011).

We now understand that both boys and girls attending schools in disadvantaged communities are more likely than their counterparts from higher socio-economic communities to position themselves in opposition to schooling and underperform (Australian Council for Educational Research, 2010; Scholes, 2013). But there are also performance differences according to the nature of the subject: it is boys who underperform in literacy, compared to girls, at all levels of socio-economic status, while boys from low socio-economic backgrounds make up the lowest group (Australian Council for Educational Research, 2010; OECD, 2010).

Gender
Range of characteristics pertaining to, and differentiating between, masculinity and femininity. May be based on social and gender identity.

Discrimination according to race or culture is also a factor that interplays with gender and socio-economic status to influence children's learning experiences at school. For children from culturally diverse backgrounds, the issue of whiteness is significant (Martino, 2003). Racist whiteness mentality can drive bullying, harassment and physically abusive practices at school, although for boys the threats may be physical violence and for the girls more about bitchiness, taunting and intimidation (Martino & Pallotta-Chiarolli, 2005). Physical and non-physical forms of discrimination and bullying are equally detrimental to boys' and girls' psychological well-being and, in turn, well-being influences learning.

While we may consider Australia to be an egalitarian society in many ways, within schools some groups do not have the same experiences, opportunities or equal outcomes. In Australia inequality and class exclusion are continuing realities and formative influences on education (Connell, 2005; Wilkinson & Pickett, 2009). There is therefore a need to consider which boys and which girls are actually struggling in terms of their learning and educational outcomes (Australian Council for Educational Research, 2010; Lingard et al., 2009). Within the context of social justice, envisioning institutional reforms to recognise notions of gender redress and distribution of resources requires understanding of the complexities and interactional influences of disadvantage, school experiences and gender (Fraser, 2007; Lingard et al., 2009). Classroom teachers are in a unique position, with abilities to ensure children have access to opportunities, and to learn in an inclusive and supportive environment. Significantly, sociocultural understandings can inform teaching and learning with considerations necessary in planning, pedagogy and assessment.

GENDER

One of the most obvious differences you may notice between children when you enter a classroom is the physical distinction between boys and girls. Differences will be highlighted by uniforms, hairstyles, behaviours, and so on. Much of what we have traditionally heard and read about boys and girls has portrayed these differences in simplistic, binary terms. While neurological sex differences in cognition and emotion have been considered in Chapter 5 and there are obvious physical differences, much of what we perceive as dissimilar derives from society and culture. From sociocultural perspectives, 'gender' encompasses both biological and cultural influences and thus recognises the interdependence of biological and cultural sources of difference. Children pick up messages from social interaction with others in their immediate environments. From the moment they are born, girls are equated with pink and boys with blue. They are read stories with masculine heroes and feminine damsels in distress. Particular types of play are deemed appropriate with assertiveness often encouraged for boys and compliance valued for girls. Parents and teachers provide gender role models that serve to reinforce gender roles in children. Social experiences at school further homogenise and stereotype boys and girls, with gender stereotypes affecting both boys' and girls' daily lives, creating a narrowing of opportunities for engagement and marginalising some students.

While gender has been a topic of discussion in Australian education since the nineteenth century, it was particularly stirred up by the publication of *Girls, school and society* by the Schools Commission in 1975. This report highlighted poorer achievement and participation of girls in traditionally male-dominated subjects such as mathematics and science. Resulting strategies culminated in girls now participating as well or better in the targeted subjects. Attention then turned to boys after *Boys: Getting it right*, an inquiry into boys' education by the House of Representatives Standing Committee on Education and Training in 2002. Lower literacy rates and lower matriculation results for boys were highlighted in association with higher rates of disengagement with schooling and lower retention rates to Year 12 for males. These differences were more significant for boys from lower socio-economic backgrounds, boys attending schools in rural area and Indigenous boys (Australian Council for Educational Research, 2010; Collins, Kenway & McLeod, 2000).

See Chapter ❺ on sex differences in language development

Boys

Educational outcomes for boys are of ongoing concern in Europe (European Commission, 2010), the United Kingdom (Younger et al., 2005) and Australia (Australian Council for Educational Research, 2010), with gender differences in particular educational outcomes recognised more globally by the OECD (2010). Stereotypical images of boys' underachievement that have been illustrated and reinforced in educational policy and practice are now being questioned. Many generalisations about boys' underachievement are not representative of particular groups of boys and focus on narrow constructions of masculinity that perpetuate a binary divide between boys and girls, positioning young males as a homogenous group. Furthermore, there is growing impetus to consider the differences among boys and how 'being a boy' is performed by different groups with recognition of the interactional influence of school cultures.

MASCULINITY

There are many types of masculinities that boys perform in the classroom, or ways of being a 'boy' (Mac an Ghaill, 1994; Martino & Pallotta-Chiarolli, 2005). Being a boy is influenced by how students act, talk and look, and friendship groups. Within the school context a hierarchy or pecking order is created between groups of boys. For boys, these social orders are influenced by one's perceived popularity and attributes such as 'doing' heterosexuality, athletic ability, 'coolness' and 'toughness' (Adler, Kless & Adler, 1992; Pratt & George, 2005). For many boys, subjects such as literacy become a criterion for benchmarking or demarcating 'uncool' students with a boy's commitment to reading and schoolwork challenging his masculinity (Gilbert & Gilbert, 1998; Martino, 2003). As boys make choices about educational endeavours and engagement, they are often influenced by social orders that put boundaries around what they do. Boys spend considerable time monitoring one another, deciding what is appropriate or inappropriate, and who should be included or excluded. Relationships are reinforced by powerful boys' dominance in opposition to less influential boys' subordination. Dominant forms of masculinity are often associated with strength and power, while subordinate masculinities are associated with feminine characteristics.

Acting cool at school often involves boys acting tough, impressing mates, using put-downs and making fun of boys' feminine traits (Martino & Pallotta-Chiarolli, 2005). As working hard at school has been viewed as a feminine practice, by association, boys who strive to achieve educationally may be perceived as feminine (Skelton, 2001). As students fail, they may seek other means to validate their identity and reclaim some power (Connell, 2005). Some boys have also been found to create a culture of physicality within school settings, with this form of masculinity often accentuated by boys from lower socio-economic communities (Connolly, 2004). Schools create spaces, such as the playground and sports field where specific behaviours are considered normal. An acknowledgment that notions of masculinity may be diverse and influential in the positioning of educational pursuits in students' gendered identities is needed to make visible the inflections of boys' experiences at school.

UNDERACHIEVEMENT IN SCHOOL

There are many explanations for boys' underachievement and lack of engagement at school. Biological and role model theories are often quoted in the popular media, while educationalists debate teacher quality and sociocultural explanations. Traditional explanations include a focus on biological explanations (essentialist), ones that claim schools now favour girls (feminine schools), ones that blame boys' lower education attainment on poor or mediocre teaching (failing schools), ones that focus on the adverse effects of wider changes within society on boys (crisis of masculinity), ones that cite the impact of feminism and the increase in girls' aspirations (feminism) and ones that identify boys' laddish behaviour (working-class masculinity) as the principal cause of boys' lower performance (Connolly, 2004).

Furthermore, boys tend to represent the lowest achievers in schools and are over-represented in terms of disabilities relating to education, including mental health, intellectual and physical or sensory disabilities (Collins et al., 2000). Boys are also more likely to have auditory-processing problems that can affect learning and behaviour (Rowe & Rowe, 2002). Boys have also been described as systematisers with preferences for analytical modes of learning and girls described as empathisers, preferring open-ended discussion-based learning (Baron-Cohen, 2003). But we must exercise caution in making broad assumptions about the learning of boys and girls, as many boys in fact excel in literacy and the humanities, achieving high academic outcomes. Similarly, many girls struggle and do not represent a typical female student excelling in the humanities. While girls may have an advantage over boys in early language-related skills such as literacy, this advantage generally evens out by age six (Bornstein, Hahn & Haynes, 2004). We need to be mindful that many explanations of boys' underachievement do not consider the socialisation of boys that alienates them from schooling and how masculinity is constructed among diverse groups of boys, affecting education and learning.

There are many accounts of the dangers for boys who are marginalised in their masculinity in the school context (Epstein & Johnson, 1994; Mac an Ghaill, 1994; Martino, 1997). Some researchers point to the hetero-normative privilege many boys have historically been granted and suggest that white, middle-class high school boys intentionally define and redefine masculinities through counter-hegemonic practices (Francis & Skelton, 2005; Martino, 2001). It has been noted that it is boys from marginalised backgrounds who are more likely to develop anti-school cultures to compensate for their relative lack of success in education in attempts to gain status through the construction of hegemonic forms of masculinity (Connolly, 2009; Mac an Ghaill, 1996).

WHAT TEACHERS CAN DO

Teachers who challenge stereotypical versions of gender and disrupt taken-for-granted ways of being a 'boy' can make visible alternatives that are more inclusive of difference (Keddie & Mills, 2007; Martino & Pallotta-Chiarolli, 2003). Creating a classroom culture where children value all subjects, without distinctions between traditional masculine and feminine pursuits, is a step towards equity. Planning experiences that account for all students' learning is also necessary. Furthermore, expanding the repertoire of experiences for boys involves engaging in ways that do not conflict with desirable constructions of masculinity but instead provide relevance, meaning and avenues for boys to expand the boundaries of their constructions and performance of being a male student. Teachers can explore traditional feminine pursuits, such as reading, as human endeavour and re-engage boys in a broad range of possible ways of being male, replacing dominant forms of masculinity to develop a sense of being male that boys find inspirational (Gilbert & Gilbert, 1998). This would involve positioning reading within masculine identities that are admirable, desirable and equitable through experiences that draw together and explicitly build upon desirable core values within the peer group, home, community and wider society. A significant consideration in deconstructing dominant forms of masculinity in the classroom is the need to expand being a boy to encompass visions of learning and a sense of manhood that young males can aspire to and value (Gilbert & Gilbert, 1998).

Fostering connected classrooms that encourage respectful relations within peer groups and enabling 'experiences of others' is also important for teachers who want to challenge dominant forms of masculinity that position particular endeavours as 'nerdy' and 'uncool'. These challenges must be explicit, as teachers build social environments by working with boys individually and within peer groups to develop democratic communities that strengthen opportunities for relating to others as learners. As identities are shaped and policed within peer group communities, teachers' work here is critical in developing male peer groups that challenge the potent and restrictive versions of masculinity often reported (Connell, 2000; Martino, 1999; Keddie & Mills, 2007). Masculinising practices that cause some boys to struggle with communication and also endorse harmful and ineffective modes of relating based on physical or verbal communication may require explicit teaching of skills (Keddie & Mills, 2007).

Girls

Popular media often positions girls as winners within the educational system but there are many schoolgirls, irrespective of social class and ethnicity, who have problems coping with the expectations of academic success placed upon them by parents, teachers and themselves (Skelton, Francis & Read, 2010). Indeed, many of the challenges that girls face involve societal expectations and reinforcement of gender roles. If we are to move beyond normative gender configurations and consider differences within students' experiences, we need to disrupt taken-for-granted notions shaped by the societies and cultures in which we live. This includes disrupting the naturalness of girls' engagement with typically feminine educational pursuits and the idea that all girls are predispositioned to schooling.

FEMININITY

For some girls, there can be a preoccupation with stereotypical images linking popularity and niceness, and with goodness, creating impossible images of femininity for girls (Read et al., 2011). Girls' popularity at school has been linked to being kind, friendly or helpful to peers (Read et al., 2011). Shyness, on the other hand, has been socially stigmatised as a characteristic of unpopular students, especially by those deemed popular (Read et al., 2011). Friendships and their importance on girls' identities and practices have been explored by researchers with recognition of the influence of peers on presentations of self (Adler et al., 1992; Read et al., 2011). Complex patterns of popularity have often focused on a girl's need to be perceived as pretty, fashionable and attractive (Currie, Kelly & Pomerantz, 2007; Read et al., 2011) within the dominant construction of femininity associated with feminine 'goodness' (Walkerdine, 1990).

While boys develop a hierarchy of social superiority of masculinity by devaluing what is feminine, many girls contribute to this subordination in the roles they take up in schools.

Girls find themselves caught within a dichotomy: they can reinforce what is perceived as feminine as they contribute to the classification often related to body image and sexual expression (Martino & Pallotta-Chiarolli, 2005). As two fourteen-year-old girls explained: 'Girls are expected to look pretty, be thin and have a large chest. Girls are very sensitive about what others think of their weight. Some go anorexic over the issues of being told they're fat by peers' (Martino & Pallotta-Chiarolli, 2005, p. 96).

For girls who do not conform to accepted notions of being a girl, there can be ramifications. Loud and assertive behaviour by girls can be interpreted by teachers as unfeminine (Francis, 2010). Girls who do not invest in feminine aesthetics, sociality and the maintenance of the heterosexual matrix can be subject to marginalisation, contributing to underachievement and disengagement (Francis, 2010). Recent research highlights that there are differences among girls, suggesting that masculine and feminine dichotomies are premised on simplistic notions that attribute masculinity to male bodies and femininities to female bodies (Francis, 2010; Halberstam, 1998). Increasingly, there are visible descriptions of girls' gendered diversity and differences emerging in the literature (for example, Allan, 2010; Francis, 2009; Jackson, 2006).

When girls do not conform to stereotypical expectations by resisting or reworking their image, they can be marginalised by teachers and or their female peers. Traditional discussions about girls and schooling do not allude to the possibility of girls acting like boys, or masculine girls. When girls reject the expected way of being a girl, they often take on what are perceived as masculine traits, thereby denigrating the constructs of femininity and valorising the traditional normative forms of masculinity (Martino & Pallotta-Chiarolli, 2005; Scholes, 2013). Emerging more recently are female students who describe anti-school peer groups and preferences for doing 'bad things', as they are more fun (Scholes, 2013). Coupled with girls' descriptions of fighting and anti-reading cultures, there were also descriptions of enjoyment of competition, a socially masculinised construction (Francis, 2000; Merten, 1997; Read, 2006). When girls valorise being naughty, they potentially create tensions between their peers and with their teachers.

A framework for disrupting gendered disadvantage

Pedagogical practices can enhance learning and engagement for boys and girls alike. These are some strategies teachers can implement to militate against harmful gender roles:

→ identifying which boys and which girls are most at risk of exclusion, marginalisation and disengagement. Getting to know these students well and develop learning experiences in which they can excel and then be challenged is a proactive way to meet student needs.
→ modelling and ensuring respect for all students regardless of gender and background. Teachers are role models and how they engage with students sends important messages to students.

→ challenging gender inequity. It is important to challenge any student interactions that do not support an inclusive classroom environment or that marginalise students regardless of gender.

→ developing student's cooperative working skills where appropriate. Creating a classroom culture where students work cooperatively requires implementing strategies to model, practise, reflect and refine group work skills and the recognition that boys and girls may differ in how they relate to others.

→ identifying which boys and girls exert power over peer groups due to their physical presence, manner or behaviour. Remember both boys and girls are capable of bullying but may engage in different behaviours to perpetuate bullying. Working with influential students to disrupt taken-for-granted behaviours related to bullying and fostering those students to be key leaders in terms of including marginalised students is not only effective for those at the risk of marginalisation but also for building leadership skills in others.

→ remembering the importance of context and the influence the teacher has in creating a learning environment that recognises individual student needs, while keeping abreast of the research related to gender and schooling and trialling different strategies when possible (adapted from Nagel & Scholes, 2013).

SOMETHING TO THINK ABOUT 9.2

Let's revisit the chapter opening scenario about Sara and her student Ameena. Sara believed that she had a lot of success developing a relationship with Ameena. She was also very happy that Ameena tried hard, was polite and made friends with the other girls. It would appear that Sara's expectations for Ameena were being met.

Ask yourself...

1   What kind of stereotypical expectations might Sara have had for Ameena?

2   Do you think Sara may have had different expectations for Danh and Xuan? If so, what would they be?

3   How can Sara challenge stereotypical versions of gender and disrupt taken-for-granted ways of being a boy or a girl in her classroom?

4   What pedagogical strategies could Sara use to provide equal opportunities for boys and girls in her classroom?

Summary

Discussions in educational contexts related to gender and schooling often invoke strategies that are debated in the popular media, including catering to particular learning styles, single-sex schools or classes, increasing the number of male teachers, and others. The complex nature of gender as noted throughout this section suggests that any single strategy presented as a panacea for engaging all boys and girls would be simplistic and not cognisant of the immediate and broader social and cultural issues.

SOCIO-ECONOMIC BACKGROUND

Children growing up in lower socio-economic homes or disadvantaged environments may be adversely affected in a number of ways. Australian and international research has found correlations between poverty and behaviour, finding that being born into deprived circumstances has negative effects on children's outcomes and life chances (Shonkoff & Phillips, 2000). Family characteristics correlated with income and parenting styles are said to make the difference (Lexmond & Reeves, 2009). Indeed, the striking differences connected with levels of household wealth and status predict how well children develop and succeed (Shonkoff & Phillips, 2000). The development of skills that predict later success (including literacy, numeracy and character capabilities) are influenced by socio-economic background, and the home learning environment (Winter & Luddy, 2010).

Non-genetic influences contribute to these differences, indicating that interventions to help shape children's brain development and function are critical (Shonkoff & Phillips, 2000). Early disadvantage, associated with poverty, can have a significant influence on children's future progress and development (Siraj-Blatchford & Woodhead, 2009). While brain adaptation and learning is lifelong, a child's capacity to learn when he or she enters school is strongly influenced by the neural wiring that takes place in the early years of life (McCain, Mustard & Shanker, 2007). While parents of higher socio-economic status have been found to use more developmentally enhancing activities with their children, some of the risk factors associated with disadvantage include emotional and social challenges; acute and chronic stressors; cognitive lags; and health and safety issues (Jensen, 2009).

Brain development is influenced by the nature of children's engagement in relationships with parents and carers. Research shows that young children in loving, caring relationships have a lower stress response than children in less secure relationships (Juffer, Bakermans-Kranenburg & van Ijzendoorn, 2012; Shonkoff & Phillips, 2000). A strong bond with a caregiver increases a child's attachment. Attachment, in turn, has been found to lower levels of cortisol, a stress hormone that can disrupt brain development and function. Children growing up in environments characterised by consistent, predictable, nurturing, rich experiences will develop neurobiological capabilities that will increase the child's chance

See Chapter ❷ on socio-economic influences on intelligence.

for long-term health, happiness, productivity and creativity (Winter & Luddy, 2010). On the other hand, if early nurturing relationships are compromised, long-term deficits in neurodevelopment may develop (Perry, 2002).

Children who experience disadvantage may develop neural networks needed for survival in adverse situations, as growing up in lower socio-economic homes may include overwhelming challenges on a daily basis that require brain adaptation to suboptimal conditions in ways that undermine school performance (Jensen, 2009). Unpredictable environments and finding ways to adapt to them may contribute to the development of neural systems and functional capabilities that reflect disorganisation (Perry, 2002). As discussed in Chapter 3, neuroscience says much about conditions that negatively affect the developing brain. But we cannot assume that more of the opposite will lead to enhanced or accelerated brain development. In fact, a child, in a 'normal' child-oriented environment, is unlikely to be deprived of sensory input, with any normally stimulating human environment sufficient for human infant development (Blakemore & Frith, 2005). While an impoverished environment may deprive the child of the richness required for optimal development we cannot contented that extra stimulation leads to increased synaptic connections as over-stimulating babies has been found to have the opposite effect (Mitchell, 2009). Appropriately stimulating activities may enhance development by helping children with specific skills (for example, linking letters to sounds), and developing the child's ability and motivation concerned with learning generally (Winter & Luddy, 2010).

The Longitudinal Study of Australian Children found that children living in the most disadvantaged communities have lower socio-emotional and learning outcomes than children living in more affluent communities, even when family income, parents' employment status and mother's education were taken into consideration (Edwards, 2005). A combination of risk factors (depressed mothers, mother's low educational attainment, lack of social support) rather than one factor alone appeared to have a negative effect on children's outcomes. Additionally, children living in lower socio-economic communities are more likely to have lower quality social and local services, and are more likely to be living in areas with higher crime rates. Often, these children will have less access to cognitively enriching experiences with fewer books in the home and less cultural capital than their more affluent counterparts (Kumanyika & Grier, 2006). While children bring to school diversity and differences influenced by economic disadvantage, as a teacher, you are in a position to enhance children's learning and engagement when they are in your care.

What teachers can do

As discussed earlier, teachers can bring a bias, based on their perceptions of parents, that can result in low expectations of children from low socio-economic backgrounds (Anyon, 1997; Connolly, 2004; Greenwood, 1991). Overcoming social discrimination and responding to the needs of children from lower socio-economic backgrounds can influence children's academic achievement (Anyon, 1997). Having a positive attitude towards parents and students, building relationships of respect, engaging children in meaningful activities, preparing well-developed educational experiences and demonstrating your passion that makes students curious, excited and even inspired are all ways forward (Jensen, 2013).

CULTURE AND ETHNICITY

Culture and *ethnicity* are often used interchangeably to refer to people from diverse ethnic groups who share a particular race, nationality, language or religious background. Culture can extend to systems of belief, knowledge, values and behaviour shared by members of a group with the potential for cultural differences to exist between people of the same ethnic backgrounds, social classes and gender. As Australia becomes increasingly multicultural, differences in beliefs, language and learning processes can influence children's classroom experiences. While Australia continues to receive immigrants from the United Kingdom and New Zealand, more recently at least half of the top ten countries for immigrants have been Asian (Australian Bureau of Statistics, 2015).

Australia is a country that has traditionally been influenced by the settlement of immigrants and this socio-ethnic diversity continues to rise. Teachers therefore require understanding of the ethnic and cultural differences of the children in their class to facilitate optimal learning. Culturally responsive teaching (Gay, 2000) is based on a genuine interest and awareness of different cultural backgrounds of the students in your class. Moreover, this involves fostering a mutual respect for the values, beliefs and practices of diverse cultural groups, including emerging minority groups. When we are identifying culturally diverse groups, it is important to remember that no group is homogenous and there are in fact subgroups with diverse characteristics. For example, among Indigenous people there are hundreds of communities that have their own language, territory and attributes (Fryer-Smith, 2002).

Culturally responsive teachers will use cultural knowledge, prior experiences, frames of reference and performance styles of ethnically diverse students to make learning encounters more relevant and effective (Gay, 2000). Students' cultural identities are complex and are influenced and formed in response to a range of experiences. Getting to know students as individual cultural identities requires taking into consideration these factors:

→ ability and disability (see Chapter 8 for a more detailed discussion)
→ age
→ ethnicity and nationality
→ geographic region
→ health
→ language
→ race

Culture
Knowledge, beliefs, values, morals, laws, customs traditions and artefacts common to members of society.

Culturally responsive teaching
A genuine interest and awareness of different cultural backgrounds of the students.

→ religion

→ sex, gender and sexuality

→ social class and social status (Cushner, McClelland & Safford, 2000).

Student–student and student–teacher misunderstandings may appear on a number of levels (Bennett, 2003). Traditional Western views, values and practices embedded in mainstream teaching and learning practices tend to disadvantage minority students. Getting to know students on a personal level is therefore important for teachers, as is building teaching around the students' interests when possible, highlighting students' talents and using those students' gifts as teaching tools (Bennett, 2003).

What teachers can do

Teachers can work to ensure curriculum content is engaging and relevant to students' lives and cultures. This can be enhanced through the integration of art, music and movement and making learning visible through photographs and children's work. There will be a need to work in partnership with families and to have high expectations, demonstrating to children and their parents that you perceive them to be capable learners and communicators. There are numerous activities that can support multicultural diversity by highlighting the customs and traditions of a family, and enhance extended conversations:

→ Star of the Day (or Week), which encourages parents to help children fill out a questionnaire about their life, likes and dislikes

→ Family Treasure Box, which encourages children to bring a shoebox filled with examples of favourite things, family artefacts and family celebrations

→ Family of the Week, which provides opportunities to invite family members to come and share a family photo album or a favourite book with the class.

LINGUISTIC DIVERSITY

As Australian communities become increasingly diverse, with people from more than 200 ethnic backgrounds, linguistic diversity is one factor that may affect the children you teach. The Longitudinal Study of Australian Children (Australian Institute of Family Studies, 2015) found that of the 5,104 children in the study, for 12.8 per cent English was not the first language they spoke at home. Furthermore, for these children, 20 per cent of their primary care-givers were born overseas. Supporting students' first language in the classroom is significant, as it conveys value and respect for a child's cultural and ethnic background. There are challenges for children as they arrive at school with particular backgrounds where culture is transmitted through language. There are also challenges for teachers as children arrive with particular views about learning and behaviour, reflecting their carers' parenting styles and educational goals. While there may be group generalisations that can be made about a particular ethnic group, it is important to keep in mind that all children are individuals and bring with them experiences that also reflect their own development in terms of cognition, memory, emotion, personality, identity and other psychological constructs.

See Chapter **5** for an overview of language development.

A large group approach to learning using direct instruction is not desirable for children from diverse backgrounds or mainstream Australian children alike. Hands-on learning, small group work, cooperative learning, discussion and solving problems are more favourable (Matthews, 2002). To enhance the learning process, visual imagery and drawing to represent knowledge and reflective cognitive styles are also advocated (Osborne, 2003). Cognitive styles influence individuals' approaches to thinking strategies in problem solving, decision making and conceptualising. Children may need step-by-step instructions; some are impulsive and make many mistakes, whereas reflective children work more slowly and make fewer errors.

Racism is a form of discrimination that has the potential to affect children's well-being and subsequently their learning at school. Racism in schools is experienced by children directly and indirectly, through harassment, abuse and prejudice. For children from diverse backgrounds the issues of whiteness are a significant influence driving the marginalisation they may encounter from other students (Martino & Pallotta-Chiarolli, 2005). As racism can be destructive to children's emotional well-being and educational outcomes, teachers need to be proactive in terms of challenging racist behaviour such as teasing and providing a culturally sensitive curriculum. Teachers need to be aware of the transition from an acceptance of diversity to inclusion (see Figure 9.3). Some of the things teachers can deal with include providing content that includes examples from diverse cultures, facilitating equity for students from diverse groups, providing an empowering classroom culture, challenging cultural assumptions and directly disrupting prejudice as it arises (Banks & Banks, 2004).

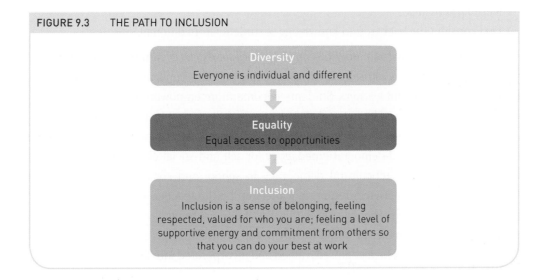

FIGURE 9.3   THE PATH TO INCLUSION

Diversity
Everyone is individual and different

Equality
Equal access to opportunities

Inclusion
Inclusion is a sense of belonging, feeling respected, valued for who you are; feeling a level of supportive energy and commitment from others so that you can do your best at work

Framework for supporting multiculturalism and ethnically diverse students

Some areas for teachers to consider when supporting children's learning include awareness of the child's verbal communication, non-verbal communication, time orientation, social values and learning processes (Bennett, 2003). Differences in experiences may predispose some children to be reluctant to speak up in a group or ask questions. In many Asian countries, it is disrespectful for children to ask questions or voice opinions. Similarly, children from Asian or Indigenous backgrounds may not look directly at the person or make eye contact when speaking as this is considered defiant. While some cultures are not as time conscious, such as Indigenous Australians, they may also not give credence to mainstream values such as competition and individualism (Bennett, 2003). Facilitating learning for children from diverse backgrounds may require flexible teaching formats and consideration of children's out-of-school learning experiences.

Your ability, as a teacher, to provide a culturally inclusive learning environment will be influenced by your beliefs. It is important to look at your own cultural or racial biases and how these may influence your teaching practices. You might ask yourself:

→ Do I have particular beliefs about different groups—Indigenous, Muslim and African?
→ Do I feel comfortable around children who have a different background from me?
→ Do I expect students from minority groups to need extra help?
→ Do I believe Indigenous students will participate less than others?
→ Do I expect Asian students will be smarter and work harder than others?
→ Do I believe Asian girls will be quieter and more submissive?
→ Do I believe different cultural values and knowledge should be recognised in my classroom?
→ Do I incorporate multicultural examples, materials and visual aids in my classroom and learning activities?
→ Do I consider the background knowledge of students from different cultures?

A multicultural classroom provides opportunities for exciting learning opportunities for you and your students. Culturally sensitive teaching provides opportunities for students to become more successful learners. Students become more empowered academically, have improved self-efficacy and learn to take more initiative. Students must first believe they can succeed in learning tasks and have the motivation to persevere. Empowering education is characterised by critical-democratic pedagogy for self and social change. It is a student-centred program for multicultural democracy in school and society (Shor, 1992). The learning process is negotiated, requiring leadership by the teacher, and mutual teacher–student co-construction of knowledge. In this way children's strengths and accomplishments are built upon. For example, the verbal creativity and storytelling that is unique among some Indigenous cultures can be recognised, valued and incorporated into literacy experiences.

See Chapter ❼ for an overview of student motivation.

Linking back to the class introduced in the chapter opening scenario, describe a literacy lesson that Sara could facilitate in her classroom that caters for her Year 3 class and also supports the needs of Danh and Xuan. Describe a lesson where the learning experience is challenging with Year 3 literacy level in mind, considers the needs of Danh and Xuan, where the diverse cultural backgrounds of the children are recognised and the resources and physical environment enhance the experience.

Ask yourself...

1 Describe your lesson plan, including objectives, strategies, resources and special considerations.

2 To whom would you go for support with this type of planning?

3 How could you draw on the knowledge and expertise from the children in your class in your planning?

4 How would your planning be different for Danh and Xuan if they were in Year 9?

CONCLUSION

As noted in this chapter there are a range of sociocultural factors that can potentially affect children's learning and development. As sociocultural perspectives become highlighted in psychology, complexities associated with understanding cognition, memory, emotion, personality, identity and other psychological constructs are evident. As teachers come to understand the child's contextual world, including class, gender, race and ethnicity, understandings about ways to enhance individual children's learning can become part of daily curriculum and classroom pedagogy. While in the past cultural psychology and neuroscience where perceived as binary sciences, these two approaches to understanding learning offer teachers contemporary perspectives. In this chapter we aimed to provide an overview of the contributions of scholars to our understanding of sociocultural theory and how contextual factors can affect students' learning. The impacts of immediate and wider social and cultural environments on learning were considered including the influence of the classroom, family and wider community. While contributions of theorists such as Vygotsky, Bronfenbrenner and Bruner have influenced how we understand social and cultural influences, contemporary understandings of children also acknowledge that they are active participants, competent beings who have agency and contribute to the learning environment. The significant role of socio-economic background, gender and cultural diversity were also considered. As educators, part of our challenge is to enter into discussions about theoretical perspectives that define the cultural and socially constructed nature of learning.

CHAPTER SUMMARY

The chapter explored the significance of sociocultural factors and how they affect learning in the classroom. As sociocultural perspectives are becoming more visible within psychology, there is increased understanding that cognition, memory, emotion, personality, identity and other psychological constructs develop within social and cultural environments. To this end this chapter considered the broader influences of schools, families and communities on learning. In this way learning and development are embedded in contextual processes and children are considered active participants in the social construction of their experiences. The child's contextual world, including class, gender, race and ethnicity, are interpreted, defined and mediated by children themselves.

In this chapter we provided an overview of the contributions of prominent researchers in terms of sociocultural theory and discussed how contextual factors can influence students' experiences. The chapter looked as sociocultural theorists such as Lev Vygotsky, Urie Bronfenbrenner and Jerome Bruner. It highlighted their contributions to understandings about how sociocultural influences affect children and subsequently their learning and development. It is important for teachers to have this understanding as they are well placed to help change the course of inequities and promote social justice by providing resources and sensitive learning environments. We also identified some of the key broader contextual factors that affect students such as social, economic and cultural influences. The significant roles of socio-economic background, gender and cultural background were detailed.

Implications for Teaching

VYGOTSKY'S ZONE OF PROXIMAL DEVELOPMENT

Vygotsky's concept of the zone of proximal development (ZPD) proposes that learning is defined by what a child can do independently and by what a child can do with assistance from a teacher or a more advanced peer. This means a teacher needs to know two levels of learning for a child: what the child can do now; and what the child can do with support. Only activities and experiences that fall within the zone promote learning. Lessons can be planned to provide practice in the ZPD for individual children or for groups of children. Additionally, cooperative learning activities can be planned with groups of children at different levels who can help each other learn.

If you are teaching letter–sound recognition and a child cannot identify the sounds in a word even after many prompts, the child may not benefit immediately from instruction in this skill. Practice of previously known skills and introduction of concepts that are too difficult and complex have little positive impact. Scaffolding becomes a major part of teachers' work.

Scaffolding

As discussed in this chapter, the role of the teacher in scaffolding is to provide support and feedback to meet children's individual needs. Scaffolding facilitates opportunities for children to learn at a higher level than they would independently.

Wood, Bruner and Ross (1976) identified six features of effective scaffolding:

- create children's interest in the task
- simplify the task: for example, breaking it down into stages
- keep children on track by reminding them of the goal
- point out the key task or show the child other ways of doing parts of the task
- control the child's frustration during the task
- demonstrate an idealised way of doing the task.

As a teacher you can scaffold learning in these ways:

- question children about their processes and work
- provide hints when children struggle to understand concepts
- encourage children to use additional resources to help them understand concepts
- offer alternative answers or choices for children when they need extra support
- answer questions
- encourage children to use additional resources to help them understand concepts.

The teacher's role is to design steps to scaffold student learning. For example, in a high school science class, a teacher might provide scaffolding by first giving students a very detailed guide about how to carry out experiments, then give brief outlines that they might use to structure experiments, and finally ask them to set up experiments entirely on their own.

Ask yourself...

Given the year level you think you will be teaching, how important is the role of scaffolding? Provide an example of how you will scaffold a small group activity.

1 What learning is taking place?
2 What resources will you need?
3 How will you facilitate the environment?
4 What questions will you ask?

PRACTICAL ACTIVITIES

1   Using Bronfenbrenner's ecological systems theory diagram in this chapter, create your own ecological systems and fill in details about the four systems that affect your learning and development. Consider influences in the microsystem, mesosystem, exosystem and microsystem levels.

2   Now consider Sara's Year 3 class from the chapter opening scenario, and draw an ecological systems theory diagram identifying the possible influences on the children in her class. For example, at the microsystem level how might the socio-economic background of the school community and the multicultural nature of her cohort influence everyday experiences?

3   As a pre-service teacher how would you define your experience as a tertiary student? In your own context are there issues associated with student difference and disadvantage that impede social justice and might influence learning? What differences are there in your peer groups that need to be taken into consideration? How will they impact on your learning?

4   Now reflect on a classroom context familiar to you (day care, kindergarten, prep, primary or high school). This classroom may be one you visited on practicum or a classroom you remember from your own schooling. Map out obstacles that might impede equal participation for some of the children in the class. Discuss how these obstacles will impact on learning.

5   Think about some of the questions you might ask your mentor teacher when you are on practicum about the students you will be teaching. For example, how does your mentor teacher identify difference?

STUDY QUESTIONS

1   Write a definition of sociocultural theory. What factors may influence learning?

2   What is the significance of Bruner's work? What relevance does this have to your work as a teacher?

3   According to Vygotsky, children's thinking develops as a result of their social knowledge, which is communicated by language and cultural tools such as counting systems and art. What is the role of language in this learning and how would you describe the differences between social speech, private speech and inner speech?

4   How would you describe the zone of proximal development? What is your role as a teacher?

5   Bronfenbrenner proposed a model that consisted of hierarchical, nested structures that constitute the layers of environment affecting a developing child. Describe these four environmental systems.

6   Bronfenbrenner then went on to develop the bio-ecological model. What were the four elements in this model influencing learning and development?

7 What are some of the educational risks for children coming from lower socio-economic backgrounds?

8 List some of the stereotypes perpetuated about boys and girls at school.

9 If you want to be a culturally sensitive teacher, what are some of the things you would take into consideration and practise in your classroom?

SOMETHING TO THINK ABOUT 9.4

If a teacher wants all students, regardless of gender, to develop emotionally, socially and academically, are there times when splitting boys and girls for a particular learning experience may be appropriate? What would be the pros and cons?

Some schools have trialled different approaches to working with boys and girls in a number of subject areas. Reflect on your own understandings of gender. Can you identify where the separation of boys and girls might be advantageous? Why?

FURTHER READING

Campbell, S. R. (2012). Educational neuroscience: Motivations, methodology, and implications. *Educational Philosophy and Theory, 43*(1), 7–16.

Carew, T. J. & Magsamen, S. H. (2010). Neuroscience and education: An ideal partnership for producing evidence-based solutions to guide 21st century learning. *Neuron, 67*(5), 685–688.

Claxton, G. (1999). *Wise Up: The Challenge of Lifelong Learning*. New York, NY: Bloomsbury Publishing.

Darling-Hammond, L. & Bransford, J. (Eds.) (2005). *Preparing Teachers for a Changing World: What Teachers Should Learn and Be Able To Do*. San Francisco, CA: John Wiley & Sons.

Donovan, M. S., Bransford, J. D. & Pellegrino, J. W. (Eds.) (2000). *How People Learn: Brain, Mind, Experience and School*. Washington, DC: National Academy Press.

Lee, H. S. & Anderson, J. R. (2013). Student learning: What has instruction got to do with it? *Annual Review of Psychology, 64*, 445–469.

Martinez, M. E. (2010). *Learning and Cognition: The Design of the Mind*. Boston, MA: Allyn & Bacon.

Nagel, M. C. (2012a). *In the Beginning: The Brain, Early Development and Learning*. Melbourne, Victoria: ACER Press.

Robinson, K. (2011). *Out of Our Minds: Learning to Be Creative* (2nd ed.). West Sussex, UK: Capstone Publishing.

Tokuhama-Espinosa, T. (2011). *Mind, Brain, and Education Science: A Comprehensive Guide to the New Brain-Based Learning*. New York, NY: W.W. Norton.

VIDEO LINKS

Charlie demonstrates Vygotsky 0001
https://www.youtube.com/watch?v=ibEP4xBdJco

Charlie practising counting—demonstrates how learning takes place in the zone of proximal development.

Zone of proximal development
https://www.youtube.com/watch?v=qSSVgrxdpM0

Ben teaches his brother Tom his times tables.

High Resolves: *Sydney Boys High School Gender Equality Project*
https://www.youtube.com/watch?v=JgIg6z5nXGI

High school boys talking about their gender equality project.

K. Knight: *HSIE Cultural Diversity—Multicultural Australia*
https://www.youtube.com/watch?v=NyjHNppTXjI

An overview of cultural diversity in Australia.

WEBLINKS

ACARA: Student diversity
http://www.acara.edu.au/curriculum/student_diversity/student_diversity.html

Examine how ACARA defines diversity and how it fits within the new curriculum.

NDT Resource Centre: Appreciating and valuing diversity
http://www.ndt-ed.org/TeachingResources/ClassroomTips/Diversity.htm

This site explains the term 'diversity' in great detail and also has many different resources and ideas for teachers on this topic.

GIHE Good Practice resource booklet: *Creating Culturally Inclusive Classrooms*
https://www.griffith.edu.au/__data/assets/pdf_file/0011/184853/Creating-a-Culturally-Inclusive-Class-room-Environment-mcb2.pdf

Tips for creating cultural inclusion.

NURTURING
LEARNING

10

> Today the world is in the midst of an extraordinary outpouring of scientific work on the mind and brain, on the processes of thinking and learning, on the neural processes that occur during thought and learning, and on the development of competence. The revolution in the study of the mind that has occurred in the last three or four decades has important implications for education ... a new theory of learning is coming into focus that leads to very different approaches to the design of curriculum, teaching, and assessment than those found in schools today.
>
> (Bransford, Brown & Cocking, 2000, p. 3)

LEARNING OUTCOMES

As you read through this chapter and undertake the exercises at the end, you will gain the ability to complete these tasks successfully:

→ describe some of the challenges associated with systemic approaches to education

→ describe the potential problems associated with standardised testing and homework

→ describe how stress can shut down learning and affect behaviour and cognition

→ describe how the creative arts and physical activity can play an important role in fostering healthy development and by association, positive learning outcomes.

KEY TERMS

- NAPLAN
- standardised testing
- hyperstimulate
- downshifting

It's that time of the year again and Ms Raine's Year 3 class is just a few days away from having to do NAPLAN testing. As a new teacher, last year was Ms Raine's first experience with NAPLAN and she was surprised at how some of her students and parents reacted to the testing. For some parents NAPLAN was something they believed their children should excel at and they spent weeks before the tests practising questions at home using resources purchased at the local bookshop. Interestingly, their children often arrived on the days of testing looking very anxious and worried about how things might progress. Two girls even broke down in tears last year and struggled to get through the range of questions being asked of them.

Some parents, on the other hand, found NAPLAN to be 'over the top', as they said, and they questioned why the principal made so many references to its importance in newsletters leading up to the prescribed days of testing. These views were vocalised and shared by a number of parents at monthly parent community meetings, which often turned into highly contested debates of opposing views on the merits and problems with NAPLAN. For the principal, there was concern over last year's results where numerous children did not perform as well as those at some of the other local schools.

For Ms Raine, NAPLAN seemed like an important activity but, given it lasted such a short time, she wondered why so many people had such strong feelings about it and why it seemed to cause so much angst in many of her students. She could clearly see the stress it was creating and was unsure how to combat her students' anxieties or concerns but she reconciled in herself that it would soon be over and she would be able to get back to her students in more productive and positive ways. She was unaware that the principal had decided to pay close attention to not only the students who did not do well but also the teachers in charge of those classes. NAPLAN was about to become as stressful for teachers as it was for some parents and students.

1   Can you recall a time in your life as a student when you felt some measure of anxiety associated with assessment? If so, how do you think it affected your performance on that assessment?

2   Education has many sacred cows and taken-for-granted beliefs as to what constitutes good practice. Other than standardised testing, can you list other aspects of educational endeavour that are rarely questioned in spite of unintended negative consequences?

3   As you progress through this chapter keep the following statement and questions in the back of your mind. Stress is the brain's, and by association learning's, worst enemy. What things do you think stress students? As a teacher how can you alleviate that stress? Conversely, what things do you think enhance learning and how can you positively influence learning in lieu of any stressors?

INTRODUCTION

The quote at the start of this chapter is intended both to provoke thought and be contentious. Written almost twenty years ago, the sentiment suggests that significant changes can, and should be, made within the contexts of 'schooling' and learning. We have learnt a great deal about the brain and mind and continue to do so. But, in spite of a great deal of evidence, many systems, processes and structures of and within schools are not too dissimilar to those of the nineteenth and twentieth centuries. For example, in most instances the school day and school year is no different than that experienced by the parents, grandparents and great-grandparents of today's students while many classrooms still mirror practices of many bygone days. This is not to say that all things must change but rather it is wise to scrutinise many taken-for-granted beliefs and practices in an effort to improve what is done to and with students. This chapter is an attempt to provide an avenue and dialogue for such scrutiny.

There are many things that happen in schools that should continue to be valued and maintained. For many students, school is a place of safety, security and belonging—and, as such, we would never want to do anything that might change that—but we may be able to do things that make things better in terms of all avenues of development and learning. In order to do so we must be open-minded and consider that past practices may need changing and that many of the educational sacred cows often held so dear may need slaughtering. That may sound a bit harsh but there are indeed a number of practices that are worthy of such critique and this chapter hopes to shed some light on these. In taking such an approach we accept that we are also open to scrutiny in terms of the ideas presented but we welcome such debate that aims at improving what happens in schools and educational systems. The overall intent is to start you thinking about your practice as an educator and also have you think about the bigger picture of education itself, so that you can make sound decisions in terms of your students' learning, well-being and development. This journey starts by looking at how some contemporary practices purported to enhance learning and achievement may actually be doing more harm than good.

THE PERILS OF STANDARDS AND TESTING

We need to raise standards! This phrase is often used as a catchcry for improving education whenever students appear to be underachieving and, in particular, when achievement is framed using comparisons across other countries. For example, since the year 2000 many countries around the globe, including Australia, have participated in the Programme for International Student Assessment, or what has now become more commonly referred to as PISA. PISA is a worldwide study of fifteen-year-old students' scholastic performance in maths, science and reading, repeated every three years by the Organisation for Economic Co-operation and Development (OECD). The intent of this major assessment is to improve education policies and outcomes. Arguably, there are also other unintended consequences arising from PISA.

AUSTRALIAN PISA RESULTS

In the first iteration of PISA in 2000, Australia ranked 6th in maths, 8th in science and 4th in reading out of a group of forty-one nations, but in 2012 those rankings dropped and saw Australia ranked 19th, equal 16th and equal 13th in each respective category. And while the number of participating countries had increased, there was and continues to be great concern about Australian standards. Notwithstanding the overall intent of improving educational outcomes for students, there are inherent difficulties in comparing test results across vastly different social, cultural and economic settings. While there is currently substantive research looking into the disparities between countries, comparatively low scores often bring on much discussion and debate about how school systems should be changed to improve their rankings. Worryingly, that earlier catchcry becomes a mantra for 'standardisation', which can also be exacerbated by internal political objectives such as those that can be found in NAPLAN.

NAPLAN
The National
Assessment
Program—Literacy
and Numeracy is a
set of standardised
tests administered
annually to
Australian children
in Years 3, 5, 7 and 9.

NAPLAN

At the turn of the twenty-first century a number of important initiatives were happening in Australian education circles. In 1999, Australian state ministers for education released the Adelaide Declaration on National Goals for Schooling in the Twenty-First Century or what became known as the 'Adelaide Declaration'. Within this declaration was an agreement to use national key performance measures as a mechanism for reporting on progress towards the achievement of national goals. In order to measure student achievement in relation to such national goals, ministers agreed to a program, called the National Assessment Program (NAP), to collect, analyse and report nationally comparable data on various aspects of student achievement. Later, in 2008, the Adelaide Declaration was superseded by the Melbourne Declaration on Educational Goals for Young Australians. Among many other things, the Melbourne Declaration helped establish an annual assessment of students in Years 3, 5, 7 and 9 within the National Assessment Program—Literacy and Numeracy or what is more commonly referred to as NAPLAN.

The genesis of PISA and NAPLAN may not necessarily be problematic in their intent but too often a push for some measure of standards creates more problems than it sets out to solve. A lengthy history of standardised testing suggests as much, and importantly, standardised testing has a history that goes beyond that of both PISA and NAPLAN. This history is rife with negative outcomes and concerns (Erlauer, 2003). To that end and regardless of name or prescribed intent, standardised tests should be critiqued and analysed in terms of any deleterious effects to learning, students or broader educational agendas.

Standardised testing
A systemic approach to testing students in predetermined areas of importance.

PROBLEMS WITH STANDARDISED TESTING

In terms of learning, one of the most significant outcomes of standardised testing can be found in the belief that an overemphasis on such devices may, paradoxically, be lowering standards. The reasons for this are threefold. First, standardised tests are limited in their capacity to determine what a student actually knows or has learnt and provide a rather shallow overview of learning. Standardised tests tend to reveal what information has been memorised rather than how well a student can apply knowledge, draw conclusions, create models or engage in solving problems, thinking critically or using creative endeavour (Caine & Caine, 2001; Erlauer, 2003; Kohn, 2000). By their nature, standardised tests can show how students compare to other students but they tell almost nothing about an individual's learning and progress, given that they are only a snapshot in time and not a complete picture of a student's capacities or overall understanding of material learnt (Erlauer, 2003).

Second, standardised tests can quickly become a high-stakes endeavour whereby they end up as a forum for competition and an inaccurate barometer for accountability (Amrein & Berliner, 2002; Au, 2009; Nichols & Berliner, 2007; Popham, 2007; Sahlberg, 2010). In Australia, NAPLAN acts as a standardised instrument; results are published on the *MySchool* website each year, where comparisons between so-called 'like' schools may be freely drawn by parents and anyone who views the site. 'Like' schools are those schools with similar socio-economic student populations and, while some similarities within this broad parameter may exist, it is also evident to anyone who has worked in education that no two children are alike, let alone any two schools. Importantly, one of the unintended outcomes of comparisons between 'like' schools is the ill-advised conclusion about the academic prowess of one school over another, leading to misguided assertions about why some schools may be outperforming others. Following on from such assertions are notions related to teacher efficacy and accountability; surely, if students in 'like' schools are getting very different results, then the fault of poor results lies with the underachieving schools and their teachers. This creates a high-stakes environment for teachers, which can then lead to a disproportionate amount of time being used to prepare for the impending tests or, in some cases, accusations of institutionalised cheating to ensure the best results possible. Such measures are hardly conducive to promoting positive associations between 'schooling' and learning. Moreover, increased attention to improving scores on a standardised test can also lead to the eradication of many exceptional pedagogical practices as teachers or schools or both, either willingly or through systemic pressure, expend too much energy and time focusing on improving test scores (Caine & Caine, 2001).

Finally, it is important to note that any notion of issues and challenges around high-stakes assessment are not confined to teacher attitudes and beliefs or perceptions of particular schools. For example, a recent study in Australia found that NAPLAN causes high anxiety in some students and that many parents are confused about its purpose (Wyn, Turnbull & Grimshaw, 2014). Too often the guidelines and information for administering standardised tests place students in contexts vastly different from mainstream classroom endeavour and, in conjunction with the build-up for performing well, can evoke negative reactions such as anxiety and stress (Nagel, 2013b). Anxiety and stress-related issues are frequent outcomes for many students exposed to standardised tests. Students have reported experiencing stress-related conditions such as insomnia, hyperventilation, profuse sweating, nail-biting, headaches, stomach aches and migraines leading up to, or during, test periods (Wyn et al., 2014). This begs the question as to whether standardised tests are actually in the best interests of students or are indeed the best method for determining what students know or have learnt.

TESTING AND ASSESSMENT

Notwithstanding the potential pitfalls associated with standardised tests, it is important to note that assessment is an important component of educational endeavour. But assessment and tests are not necessarily the same things. There are many different ways to determine what students know and have learnt other than subjecting them to standardised tests. For example, students in Finland, which has consistently ranked in the top ten countries in the PISA surveys, are not tested using a standardised instrument. Instead, a wide array of assessment practices, including some forms of testing, are used to make determinations related to student learning but this is done in a manner that proactively avoids imparting anxiety and stress and embodies trust in the skills and capacities of teachers while operating in the best interests of students (Sahlberg, 2010). Interestingly, Finland also seems to adopt a similar approach to another problematic educational sacred cow deeply embedded in many Western countries: namely *homework*.

NAPLAN: A BRIEF HISTORY

Schoolchildren in Australia began sitting the NAPLAN tests from 2008. Initially, NAPLAN was administered to Year 3, 5 and 7 students; later, Year 9 students were included. Importantly, the testing of literacy and numeracy was occurring before the nationwide implementation of NAPLAN but there are significant differences in previous models of testing. Perhaps the two most prominent differences are testing students at the young age of Year 3 and making results available to the general public, through the publication of results online. In 2007/2008, the desire to publish the results online was premised on the Labor federal government's questionable notion of promoting quality education through promoting accountability and transparency (Rudd & Gillard, 2008). Such an approach made NAPLAN an inherently high-stakes assessment item and, worryingly, the government of the time appeared to either wilfully omit or tacitly neglect an examination of the research noting the inherent difficulties in using standardised testing as an accountability mechanism or as any real instrument for improving learning and academic outcomes. Now, after a number of years of implementation, student achievement results have been mediocre at best, with little or no improvements in the achievements of Indigenous or remote students and no statistically significant improvement in the number of students achieving the minimum standard across Australia, with evidence of a decline in some areas tested (Thompson, 2013). NAPLAN appears to have created more problems than solutions.

In their analysis of teacher perceptions of NAPLAN, Thompson and Harbaugh (2013) cite a multitude of studies of standardised tests across a number of nations that highlight numerous unintended negative consequences of such approaches. These consequences vary but tend to include teaching to the test, narrowing the curriculum focus, increasing teacher and student anxiety, a decrease in student motivation, the promotion of direct teaching methods and the creation of classroom environments that are less, not more, inclusive. These unintended consequences have also been observed in Australia through multiple sources (see, for example, Dulfer, Polesel & Rice, 2012; Thompson, 2013) and now include accusations of cheating whereby teachers manipulate results or how the test is conducted in order to attain better scores for their students (Thompson & Cook, 2014). Such findings and results appear to diminish any notion of meaningful learning and call into question any government agenda to improve standards through standardised tests and through publishing results that lend themselves to such desperate measures as cheating or any other unintended negative consequences.

Ask yourself...

1   One of the inherent difficulties within the teaching profession is evident when teachers encounter policies and practices that may be in conflict with their own beliefs and philosophies associated with learning and teaching. Given NAPLAN is a nationwide systemic apparatus, what might you be able to do to help you and your students work through this testing regime when encountered? For example, what messages would you give your students and the parents?

2   One of the greatest unintended consequences of standardised testing is test anxiety in students. As a teacher, what steps can you take to help alleviate any notion of text anxiety and help your students perform to the best of their ability?

3   Refer back to the discussion in Chapter 2 of studies noting the impact of socio-economic standing on vocabulary development. How might the disadvantages noted in families with low socio-economic status affect any measure of standardised testing?

HOMEWORK: A NECESSARY EVIL?

Too much or too little? Too easy or too difficult? Nightly or weekly? Enhances or hinders learning? Debates surrounding many aspects of homework have existed for years. Indeed, one of the most predictable and consistent aspects of school on which almost every adult has an opinion and can attest to experiencing is homework (Nagel, 2013b). Homework is a polarising topic for many and one of the most sacred of educational sacred cows. Today, homework is often a taken-for-granted notion of productive schooling and considered one of education's necessary evils. Interestingly, this was not always the case and there is much to question about homework's purported benefits to learning and scholastic endeavour.

BACKGROUND

A full history of homework in Western countries is beyond the scope of this chapter but it is interesting to note that before the end of the Second World War, homework was not held in very high regard. For some, homework was seen as nothing less than 'legalised criminality' (Nash, 1930) and early research concluded, with few exceptions, that homework had little or no positive effect on achievement (Otto, 1941). But, from the mid-twentieth century, opinions on the value of homework began to shift; homework was increasingly seen as an important component of any educational endeavour. The reasons for this are multifarious but one thing that does stand out as a catalyst for pushing the homework agenda forward is concern over declining educational standards (Gill & Schlossman, 2004). As noted earlier, global comparisons as reported through instruments such as PISA play a role in setting educational agendas and policies and are often used as a platform for advocating many things, including the perceived value of doing homework. But a key question is this: what does the research on homework actually say?

RESEARCH FINDINGS

Research summaries regarding homework's efficacy and impact on student achievement are far from conclusive and often contradictory. It is a truism that doing good research necessitates accounting and controlling for as many variables as possible, yet homework research is rife with difficulties in this regard. Much of this can be attributed to the many variables associated with homework, including a concise definition of the term, types of homework and home support, differences in how teachers use and assess homework, socio-economic demographics, amount of homework and standardised versus classroom assessment results to name a few (Baker & LeTendre, 2005). From the outset it is apparent that arriving at any cause-and-effect relationship between homework and achievement is inherently problematic. Perhaps this is why research on homework has a long history of being characterised as political, contradictory and often inconclusive; for every advocate expounding homework's merits, there is a critic stating its disadvantages (Nagel, 2013b). This does not stop homework proponents from pushing the homework agenda, often under the belief that surely doing more work is better in the long term.

CURRENT POLICIES

Perhaps the notion that 'more is better' is at the heart of misguided beliefs about the advantages of homework. Homework policies are evident in government websites, school-based documents and on the walls of many classrooms, while parents often judge the effectiveness of a teacher or school by the volume of homework given. Government policies focusing on education, achievement, standards and global comparisons are often premised on notions that doing more would surely facilitate doing better. This belief creates a trickle-down effect as schools look to improve their standing and parents seek out what they perceive to be sound educational practice. Of importance here is that more does not always equal better! In examining homework policies around the world, researchers have concluded that the relationship between patterns of homework and achievement suggests that more homework may actually undermine achievement (Baines, 2007; Baker & LeTendre, 2005). Using international benchmarks, those schools that consistently rank among the highest achievers in literacy, mathematics and science set the least amount of homework while those doing consistently wanting more work at home perform worse (Baker & LeTendre, 2005). This suggests that, if international benchmarks are to be used to enhance educational standards at a national level, then perhaps some notice should be given to the tangential factors potentially underpinning excellence. It seems that homework is not one of the positive contributors.

PROBLEMS WITH ARGUMENTS FOR HOMEWORK

Aside from the evidence drawn out of international comparisons, there are other important challenges associated with claims about the benefits of homework. The two claims that are most often presented as homework positives are that homework improves academic outcomes and that homework enhances various future life skills, such as the development of time-management skills or the fostering of a positive work ethic. At the time of writing and after many decades of research, there exists scant, if any, empirical evidence to support homework as a significant mechanism for improving scholastic achievement and no evidence that it is somehow character building or an instrument for improving any measure of life skills (Barber, 1986; Hattie, 2009; Kohn, 2006; Kravolec & Buell, 2000; Trautwein & Koller, 2003).

A second important concern surrounding homework is that, although homework may be assigned with the best intentions, teachers, parents and students alike frequently cite it as a source of difficulty, frustration, conflict and stress at school and at home (Bennett & Kalish, 2006; Buell, 2004; Kohn, 2006; Kravolec & Buell, 2000; Warton, 2001). Too often there can be a mismatch between a teacher's or a school's expectations and parental input that can inadvertently create tension between teachers and parents, parents and children, and teachers and students (Nagel, 2013b). Such tensions can contribute to anxiety and stress in many students and parents alike, negating any perceived positive benefits of doing work at home. Indeed, a study of high school students in Victoria, Australia, found a direct relationship between how much time students spent on homework and the levels of anxiety, depression, anger and other mood disturbances they experienced (Kouzma & Kennedy, 2002). Given the negative effect homework can have on learning, it seems that homework may not be an entirely positive contributor to learning. In addition, given the potential for various mood disorders such as anxiety and stress, it seems that any claims or discussions about homework should not be taken seriously if they fail to consider its impact on students (Kohn, 2006).

THE ARGUMENTS AGAINST HOMEWORK

Stress and tension resulting from homework are frequent and arguably indicative of another important consideration regarding homework. It is widely accepted that homework affects people differently and, most significantly, affects people of different socio-economic standing differently. Students are not a homogenous group and too often there is an assumption that all students have the same and equal opportunity in educational contexts. In terms of homework it may be that not all students will have the time or opportunity to do homework in an environment conducive to such work. Homework may be a positive activity for one set of students but completely disastrous for another; research does suggest that students from families who have more resources surge ahead of their classmates who have less (Kravolec & Buell, 2000). In the end sociocultural factors may negatively affect students and their homework practices or lack thereof, given that, for some students, life outside the confines of a school may not be conducive to hours of homework (Buell, 2004; Nagel, 2013b).

A further important consideration regarding homework in the context of human development and learning is that homework studies often confuse grades, achievement and test scores with learning. In an educational climate of increased accountability and raising standards, it appears that children are having to do more: one way of ensuring that more is done is to do so at home. Homework, therefore, becomes a direct insertion of school authority, with its emphasis on achievement, into the daily lives of families; for some, such a push may be detrimental to any child's intrinsic desire to learn (Baker & LeTendre, 2005; Buell, 2004). As you will recall from earlier chapters, learning is much more than a product or score: it is a process that is influenced by a number of factors including age, motivation and context. The prescription of any measure of homework must therefore take into account many factors, perhaps all of which would require more time than homework is actually worth.

One final point worthy of consideration regarding homework can be found at the nexus of human development and the brain. While it is true that our understanding of memory reminds us that a great deal of practice and repetition are necessary to retain the skills for reading, writing and basic mathematical computations associated with the early years of schooling, it is also important to bear in mind that children learn different skills at different times. In an effort to enhance academic performance, schools may be pushing students beyond what is developmentally appropriate in the classroom and with their homework. No parent or teacher wants a child to fall behind but increasing the demands of homework may also negatively affect that very child. Because the research is so inconclusive, we cannot rule out that homework may assist some students in terms of reviewing or consolidating some aspects of learning and it may provide communication platforms between teachers and parents. But homework should always be scrutinised in its intent and never taken for granted as integral to learning.

ENRICHMENT DOES NOT MEAN MORE!

Paralleling the issues and challenges associated with standardised education and a proliferation of homework in the lives of children has been a gradual, yet incessant, movement for younger and younger children to do more and do it earlier in life. This agenda has often been couched under the term of *enrichment*, with a view that doing more, earlier, ensures that no child is left behind. Historically, the push to hyper-educate children seems to have gained momentum somewhere between the late 1970s and into the 1980s with parents trying to create super-babies by exposing newborns to significant amounts of advanced mathematics and other languages (Hupp & Jewell, 2015; see also

Clarke-Stewart, 1998). In the 1990s and early part of this century, popular media and educational entrepreneurs advocated listening to Mozart to improve intelligence and using educational and cognitively stimulating videos to help produce geniuses (Hupp & Jewell, 2015). Underpinning much of this hyperbolic pathway to higher IQs and better life chances is a long-standing belief—some would argue a truism—that early experiences shape human potential. But agendas for child improvement and enhanced academic prowess under the guise of enrichment are highly problematic and arguably harmful.

The idea that early experience is important in shaping one's potential is not new and is widely accepted; what is new is the quantifiable evidence provided by neuroscience that early experiences play a role in shaping the brain and mind (Clarke-Stewart, 1998). Indeed, the late 1990s witnessed a number of prominent media outlets, including *The New York Times*, *Time Magazine* and *Newsweek*, publish articles emphasising the important links between brain development, neuroplasticity and experiences in the first few years of life. But too often such reporting and the use of scientific evidence has been misread or misused for promoting questionable educational products and practices. Parents and educators alike have often been led to believe that, because early experiences are so important, surely more education, sooner, would be better. Indeed, many parents do believe that their children can become smarter using various so-called educational videos or products (Ryan, 2012; Zimmerman, Christakis & Meltzoff, 2007). While giving children the best possible chance in life is something all parents aspire to and something that underpins educational practice, such ideals are best achieved using the best evidence and a greater understanding of how the brain matures and develops. Each of these is worthy of further elaboration, starting with a quick review of brain development.

BRAIN DEVELOPMENT

See Chapter ❸ to review the concepts of experience-expectant and experience-dependent stimulation.

Hyperstimulate Trying to enhance a child's intellect or learning by providing numerous extracurricular activities or learning programs, or through the provision of a multitude of so-called learning toys.

As outlined in greater detail in Chapter 3, maturation of the human brain is a complex endeavour but underpinned by some important principles. First, the brain expects and depends on various types of stimulation; the first few years of a child's life are indeed important for hard-wiring the brain. But the brain also undergoes a process known as myelination, which is a lengthy journey that is not fully complete until the third decade of life. Stimulation and myelination work in tandem to help produce the brain's interconnected superhighway and to date there isn't any evidence to suggest we can somehow **hyperstimulate** or advance this process. Perhaps what is most important is ensuring that children are not *deprived* of important stimuli. For example, in the earliest days of life, the brain *expects* to see things and subsequently hard-wires for sight; depriving a child of such experiences could lead to impaired vision or complete blindness, as shown in many animal studies and infant cataract research.

In terms of the types of stimulation the brain depends on for development, these are best described as the day-to-day learning experiences a child encounters. Reading to a child, for example, is an important learning experience for helping to develop oral language skills. Significantly, it is the nature of these types of experiences that are of most importance and the science is fairly conclusive in noting that 'cognitively stimulating videos', language DVDs, 'smart baby' products and products marketed as improving cognitive development do not magically boost intelligence or facilitate enhanced academic prowess or success. In fact, there is an abundance of evidence noting that, in terms of development, nothing really beats positive relationships with parents and care-givers along with interactions with other human beings in real life, usually through exploration and play behaviour (Brown, 2009; Hirsh-Pasek & Golinkoff, 2004; Hupp & Jewell, 2015; Kolb, 2009; Nagel, 2012a; Shonkoff, 2010).

As alluded to above, the pathway of typical brain development is more a marathon than a sprint and it is important to remember that education is not a race. This is very important in terms of how the word 'enrichment' may be misused with a view to increasing academic demands on children at younger and younger ages. It is not uncommon to see pre-school children receive extra tuition and educational prepping before entering formal school environments but it is worth noting that any agenda that forces learning upon young children may actually be doing more harm than good.

For more than three decades a number of child development experts and scholars have voiced concerns over increased scholastic demands on children. Widespread assumptions that the earlier children begin to master basic literacy and numeracy skills, the more likely they are to succeed at school, have been compounded by notions of educational enrichment as a mechanism for achieving such scholastic milestones. This assumption and its associated pathway to success are problematic in terms of any evidence for working with children. First of all, a focus on using environmental enrichment to improve a child's brain and mind can be traced back to studies with animals. In such studies, researchers found that rats that were raised in enriched environments had noticeable changes in some neurotransmitters in the brain along with increased synaptic density and an increase in overall size of the cerebral cortex compared with rats raised in impoverished environments (Rosenzweig, Krech, Bennett & Diamond, 1962; Renner & Rosenzweig, 1987). Human studies have shown similar results, but an important component of such findings is what the term 'enriched' actually means.

WHAT IS ENRICHMENT?

In the rat studies, enriched environments were cages with spinning wheels, tunnels, ladders and other rat-friendly toys, while impoverished environments lacked any similar apparatuses. An important caveat to such studies is that rats that grow up in natural environments and experience the types of challenges not found in enriched or impoverished environments have actually been shown to have even greater synaptic connectivity and bigger brains than either of their caged counterparts (Healy, 2004). In other words, the natural environment of rats produces better results than any contrived notions of enrichment. In an educational context, enriched environments are presented in a polemic fashion, similar to that of impoverished environments, without any consideration of what might lie between or outside the two. Current evidence suggests that environments somewhere between the two are perfectly adequate. Reiterating important points made in Chapter 3, there is little evidence, if any, to support any notion that special stimulation or enrichment activities or programs beyond normal growth-promoting experiences will lead to some measure of advanced brain development (Nagel 2012a; Shonkoff, 2010; Shonkoff & Phillips, 2000). Perhaps the greatest form of enrichment, therefore, lies in ensuring that all environments are safe and supportive and remembering that: 'in order to develop normally, a child requires progressively more complex joint activity with one or more adults who have an irrational emotional relationship with the child. Somebody's got to be crazy about that kid. That's number one. First, last and always' (Bronfenbrenner, cited in Allred, 2007, p. v).

The sentiments expressed by Bronfenbrenner are not only a reminder of the important role relationships play in learning but also that oversimplified notions of enrichment or agendas of increased stimulation can be problematic; like homework and standardised testing, they deserve much scrutiny in application and intent.

STRESS AND LEARNING DO NOT MIX

One of the most potentially deleterious influences on learning that standardised tests, homework and hyperstimulation under the guise of enrichment have in common is that of stress or anxiety arising from such practices. When discussing these practices, there is almost always some mention of the potential stress they may create but this is often overshadowed by the perceived benefits of engaging in such practices. The next time NAPLAN comes around, look in a newspaper and it is likely you will see some advice on how to beat test stress or some opinion piece suggesting that students need to endure such stress as a measure of growing up. Such views are overly simplistic and fail to consider important questions related to sound educational practice and how stress can actually diminish cognition and negatively influence learning. Once again, it is important to unpack both of these areas of concern, starting with how stress may be character building or part of growing up, particularly in any context of learning.

Stress hinders learning! This is something to be explored in more detail below but perhaps more problematic is any notion that, in order to build some measure of resilience for life in the future, stress-related activities should go unquestioned and even be tolerated. Aside from hindering learning, stress is also unhealthy and even more so in the developing brain of a student, regardless of age. There is also some concern in any belief system that suggests that children will get better at coping with stress and anxiety as adults if they are deliberately made to experience stress and anxiety during their childhood years. Arguably, one need not look at the research to see the logic in the preceding statement, but perhaps a better understanding of how stress impairs learning is enough to engender an educational philosophy that looks to alleviate stress when students are involved with any measure of schooling.

EUSTRESS AND DISTRESS

From the outset it is important to note that not all stress is harmful and life without stress is not possible. Optimum levels of stress, referred to as *eustress*, can act as powerful empathetic, motivational and creative forces while negative, chronic or traumatic stress (*distress*) is potentially very destructive for the body and mind (Nagel, 2009, 2012a; see also Lazarus, 1999; McEwen, 2002; Selye, 1974, 1975, 1978). Eustress is the type of stress we encounter when having to step out of our comfort zone and perhaps do things like public speaking, performing or engaging in team sports. Distress, however, is rather self-explanatory and is worth avoiding given what happens to the mind and body when a stress response occurs.

STRESSORS

While most people believe they can identify what stress is, they often associate it with some event or *stressor*. This is important (and discussed later) but from a neurobiological perspective, stress is an adaptive response to some environmental stimuli triggering the brain into action (Arnsten, 1998; Dickerson & Kemeny, 2004; McEwen, 2002; Selye, 1975). A stress response, once activated, facilitates a series of chemical releases and reactions. Such reactions may require great energy, oxygen, bodily fuel, muscle power, heightened pain thresholds and mental acuity, which in turn rely on the brain to stimulate various hormones, glands, the heart, lungs, immune system and blood to make everything happen (McEwen, 2002). This is the brain's way to ensure survival by focusing on fight or flight, and getting the mind and body ready for action. Significantly, while the brain is designed to ensure our survival, the goal behind the hundreds of thousands of years of evolution it took to develop this important system was for short-term use only. We now know that prolonged or continuous stress responses to the relative stressors around us may have negative effects over the long term. In a sense, the very system designed to protect us can threaten our well-being if it is activated too often.

It is likely that most people are aware that too much stress is not a good thing. They may not often consider that stress does not discriminate on the basis of age and the machinations of a stress response are no different whether you are six, sixteen or sixty years of age. Of importance here is that children are particularly vulnerable to stress compared to the adults around them because the brain of a child is still developing. Children and adults also have different stressors—and *absolute stressors* aside—*relative stressors* vary from person to person.

Absolute and relative stressors

The different nature of absolute and relative stressors is important. Absolute stressors are real threats to anyone and everyone, while relative stressors are those individual events or situations interpreted as being threatening, novel, unpredictable or out of one's control (Lupien, Maheu, Tu, Fiocco & Schramek, 2007). A natural disaster such as a cyclone or bushfire is a good example of an absolute stressor, while being late for work or having to do an exam are more characteristic of relative stressors. Perhaps it is advantageous to think of relative stress as a personal experience; as such, the origin of stress is different for each person. It worth mentioning that regardless of the specific nature of a relative stressor— injury, anxiety, fear, hunger, relational conflict, too cold, too hot, test anxiety—when individuals activate a stress response, the effects of this can be problematic, considering what happens to the mind and body (Sapolsky, 2004).

STRESS AND THE BRAIN

As noted earlier, when a stress response is triggered, the mind and body step into action, starting with the hypothalamus releasing chemicals to initiate a series of reactions. The deleterious impact of long-term exposure to stress is well documented; the very chemicals designed to ensure our survival in the short term can create numerous health and mental health concerns. For example, among the many negative effects of stress, studies with humans and other mammals have shown that chronic stress can reduce dendrite and neural growth in the brain, impair memory, damage the brain's adaptive systems, impair the immune system and diminish the body's capacity to heal wounds (Nagel, 2009; see also Avitsur et al., 2003; Cook & Wellman, 2004; McEwen, 2002; Sapolsky, 2004; Sheridan, Padgett, Avitsur & Marucha, 2004; Tanapat, Galea & Gould, 1998). Imagine then, the potential impact of stress on children. There is a substantive array of literature across many disciplinary fields noting that children who live in chronically stressful environments may be at greater risk of developing a variety of disorders and a growing body of neuroscientific research telling us that the powerful chemicals designed for our survival in stressful situations can actually affect the normal growth and development of important regions of the brain, especially during the early stages of life and through adolescence (Gunnar & Donzella, 2002; Lupien et al., 2007; McEwen, 2006; McEwen & Sapolsky, 1995; McEwen & Seeman, 1999; National Scientific Council on the Developing Child, 2007). Arguably, most children do not live in such chronically stressful environments but those who do are not likely to do well with school stressors such as homework or tests. Even children who are not chronically stressed may experience stress in school and not perform to the best of their ability, particularly if cortisol levels are elevated.

Cortisol is a powerful hormone that is activated and most potent when we are stressed. It is a safe assumption that the vast majority of people have experienced the effects of elevated cortisol levels. For example, consider a time when you were involved in some manner of conflict, perhaps a heated argument, with another person. Often such an interaction elicits anger, frustration and stress, which in turn can signal a stress response resulting in increased levels of cortisol in the bloodstream. Now think back to after that event, when some time later you appeared to regain clarity of thought, resulting in you saying to yourself, 'Why didn't I say this?' or 'How come I didn't say that?' During the argument it is almost like your brain shut down for a period of time; in a sense, that is exactly what happened. When cortisol levels are elevated, your capacity to think is diminished because you are in a fight-or-flight response and your brain is geared for survival. The brain must react and some higher order executive functions—such as analytical thought or the mediation of emotions—are literally switched off while your brain decides to fight or run away. Only after enough time has passed for cortisol to return to normal levels and the body to return to homeostasis, or a state of equilibrium, do you begin to have clarity of thought. Researchers refer to this neurological phenomenon as **downshifting**, whereby we lose a great deal of access to higher order thinking, creativity and some of our normal cognitive capacities so that we may deal with the immediacy of the stressful moment (Caine & Caine, 2001).

Downshifting
This phenomenon results in impaired cognition due to high levels of stress hormones when the brain is in a state of 'fight or flight'.

Downshifting

Downshifting is a real phenomenon that affects everyone, including children. In an educational context, there is little doubt that the anxiety and stress often felt by many students when it comes to tests and homework may actually shut down thinking. Schools are also responsible for developing emotional and social well-being: students who arrive at school stressed or encounter stress during the day will often function at very low cognitive, emotional and social levels. When stressed, they are also less likely to demonstrate curious, novelty-seeking, exploratory behaviours or take risks, which are all prerequisites for healthy emotional, social and cognitive development (Nagel, 2009; see also Jensen, 2006). It is also conceivable that too much stress, whether short or long term, markedly diminishes the opportunities for children to positively engage with others and hinders learning and higher order thinking processes Finally, for students who continually feel stress, it begs earlier questions as to the overall efficacy of continuing to engage in some of the practices that cause it. Perhaps there are better ways to consolidate or nurture learning or determine what has been learnt. It is also important to mention here that one of the most resounding findings from numerous studies is that parents and care-givers or teachers are the major players when it comes to stress management in children and students alike. With all of this in mind, it is timely to draw together some key points regarding the challenges this presents before exploring what some of the positive contributors to learning might be.

RISING TO THE CHALLENGES

We started this chapter by looking at some challenges teachers face and how such challenges can negatively affect student learning. Importantly, teachers will often encounter the types of challenges noted or different ones, depending on various social, political and cultural happenings. The key is to stay informed and to always consider how to alleviate any potential pitfalls by being proactive and finding ways to support students. For example, it is likely that standardised testing is going to be around for some time but teachers and school leaders can create an environment and learning culture that allows students to move through such events as positively as possible. How this is done depends on context. It is also incumbent upon educators to ensure that all stakeholders are aware of the issues surrounding the difficulties and challenges related to such things as standardised testing and homework rather than taking them for granted. Many parents believe homework is beneficial and, as such, dialogue between teachers and parents is important to ensure that all expectations are met and strategies put in place for the benefit of all students.

These suggestions may sound somewhat broad but the reality is that finding a single solution to overcome any educational challenge is impossible. Schools are fluid and dynamic and, while systemic or local structures or policies affect schools, no two schools are alike. Schools, and the people within them, change; it is the teachers and school leaders who are best placed to determine how to meet the types of challenges that arise. Bransford and colleagues elaborate on this point:

> the process of learning is community-centred, as it is influenced by the norms and modes of operation of the community in which it occurs. In a sense, all learning is culturally mediated; this is, it arises from cultural activity. An important implication of this perspective is that providing supportive, enriched, and flexible settings where people can learn from one another is essential.
>
> (2005, p. 33)

In summary, education systems will always present challenges and breed sacred cows, but teachers can alleviate such challenges in their day-to-day practices. One way of assisting this is to highlight some of the most recent theories and ideas that can have a positive impact on development and learning within a school. The remainder of this chapter provides insights and information into how development and learning can be positively nurtured through two avenues that are often treated as superfluous in terms of development: learning and achievement.

SOMETHING TO THINK ABOUT 10.2

HOW TEST RESULTS CAN BE USEFUL

From the information presented earlier you may think that the authors of this volume of work are anti-testing in any format. In actuality, testing is not always the problem; instead, problems arise from how the data is interpreted and presented, particularly in political or media contexts. For example, comparing the results of Year 3 classrooms denoted as 'like' classrooms on *MySchool* via NAPLAN is highly problematic, as is comparing results from one country with another, which often occurs when unpacking PISA results. Too often such comparisons fail to take in the vast social and cultural differences across Australia or between OECD countries and present the findings in a narrow fashion. NAPLAN becomes a comparative tool for erroneously promoting some notion of accountability instead of being a diagnostic measure for supporting or extending students as needed; PISA becomes an instrument for decrying the failings of the Australian education system, which is presented as falling behind other OECD nations. But, in themselves, the data derived from each instrument can be useful for teachers. One aspect of findings arising from PISA provides a good example.

One of the keys to effective learning for any student is not just prior knowledge about a particular subject but also knowledge in how learning works or what may be referred to as *metacognitive* strategies. Many studies have demonstrated this but the findings of PISA in 2009 specifically add further support to this: 'students who use appropriate strategies to understand and remember what they read, such as underlining important parts of the texts or discussing what they read with other people perform at least 73 points higher in the PISA assessment— that is, one full proficiency level or nearly two full school years—than students who use these strategies the least' (OECD, 2010, p. 12).

The points made by the OECD (2010) are valid and an important aspect of the PISA testing that can be useful for teachers. These findings have also been noted by researchers in Australia, who found that the quality of students' knowledge about how they learn influences their overall achievement (Askell-Williams, Lawson & Skrzypiec, 2012). Equally important is the fact that the quality of teachers' knowledge about how people learn influences student outcomes; worryingly, it seems that research findings supporting these important components of learning are not often evident in the day-to-day teaching and learning practices in classrooms (Askell-Williams et al., 2012). Instead, schools still tend to emphasise what students need to learn rather than training students how to go about learning in the most efficient manner, and teachers focus on ensuring that all the material in the curriculum is covered. Paradoxically, PISA and NAPLAN are then used to show what students don't know and the content focus is exacerbated.

Ask yourself...

1   There is ample evidence supporting the teaching of metacognitive strategies to students in order to assist in their learning. What metacognitive strategies are you aware of and how could you use these to teach your students how to enhance their learning?

2   What strategies might you use to enhance your learning as you work through the remainder of this chapter? One example might be to highlight important passages and paraphrase what you have read as notes in the margin or in a notebook. What other strategies could you use?

THE CREATIVE ARTS AND LEARNING

Particularly since the turn of the century, there has been much discussion about how to best prepare students for a rapidly changing world and future life and job prospects. Within such discussions many individuals have pointed to the need to develop a generation of learners who are creative, with some even contesting that creativity would be the ultimate economic resource of the future (Florida, 2005, 2010). Such assertions speak to broad questions of pedagogy and curriculum design at their nexus with the role of education in the twenty-first century given the global demand for innovation and creative endeavour in the workplace (Craft, Gardner & Claxton, 2008; Robinson, 2009, 2011; Scholes & Nagel, 2012; Treadwell, 2008). And while discussions focusing on creativity and education for the twenty-first century are informative, a tangential discussion around the role of the creative arts in learning is also worthy of exploration. In the context of this volume of work on development and learning this is especially significant due to the growing body of research suggesting that the creative arts can have a positive impact on many aspects of development and enhance many facets of learning and educational practice (Weinberger, 1998).

DEFINING CREATIVE ARTS

Before we look at the potential benefits of the creative arts to development and learning, it is important to note that 'creative arts' can mean different things to different people and organisations. In an educational context, the phrase 'creative arts' generally means visual arts, music, dance and drama. But, with the growth of technology, it is becoming common to see schools offer subjects under the broad heading of 'media arts'. Importantly, and regardless of which category, the creative arts do not usually get the same degree of importance as other subjects and are often seen as a soft subject area, or something to do when all the other hard work—such as science, mathematics or English—is completed. Indeed, if you looked at a hierarchy of subject importance, you would find that in most Western countries, including Australia, the creative arts are generally seen as the least important area of school endeavour (Robinson, 2011). The mainstream culture of schooling in Australia privileges science, maths and English above all other subjects thereby positioning the creative arts as superfluous in the eyes of many (Ewing, 2010). This is unfortunate given the growing volumes of evidence suggesting that the creative arts can significantly and positively influence many facets of development, learning and, by association, achievement.

RESEARCH FINDINGS

The positive impact of the creative arts on development and learning cannot be understated. For example, numerous international studies have demonstrated the positive contributions arising from engaging in the creative arts, including enhanced social success, motivation, learning engagement, cognitive capacities, academic achievement and improved outcomes for underachieving students (Scholes & Nagel, 2012; see also Arnold, 2001; Asbury & Rich, 2008; Colwell, 1999). Of particular note, a consortium of researchers uncovered some interesting findings in an effort to develop a deeper understanding of how to define and evaluate the possible causal relationships between creative arts training and the ability of the brain to learn in other cognitive domains (Gazzaniga, 2008). Collectively, this team of researchers noted that interest and engagement across a range of creative arts led to high states of motivation and sustained attention, improved working- and long-term memory functions, enhanced mathematical skills and improvements in literacy and reading (Gazzaniga, 2008). Other research findings have supported aspects of all the research cited above and noted that active engagement in the creative arts has a positive influence on a range of skills and attributes, including creativity, physical development and well-being, language and literacy development, mathematical and scientific aptitude, attention, memory, visual–spatial abilities, metacognition and executive functioning to name a few (Scholes & Nagel, 2012; see also Gardiner, Fox, Knowles & Jeffrey, 1996; Grafton, 2010; Hyde et al., 2009; Posner & Patoine, 2010; Rauscher et al., 1997; Richards, 2003; Richardson, Sacks & Ayers, 2003; Schellenberg, 2004, 2005, 2006; Stevens & McKechine, 2005; Wurst, Jones & Moore, 2005).

It seems clear from the studies above that the subjects found within the creative arts can influence many aspects of development and learning. It could also be that using the creative arts as a means of integrating other subject areas may also prove advantageous in an educational context, particularly in terms of enhancing retention of content. Throughout *Understanding Development and Learning* we have referred to the powerful role emotions play in learning. For example, there is substantive research to show that emotions, either positive or negative, can influence long-term memory and that, in general, information that is more emotionally arousing is better remembered than that which is emotionally neutral (Kensinger & Schacter, 2008; Rinne, Gregory, Yarmolinskaya & Hardiman, 2011). There is also evidence noting that emotional arousal can enhance attentive focus, which in turn also aids in the retention and retrieval of information (Talmi, Anderson, Riggs, Caplan & Moscovitch, 2008). It therefore seems plausible that pedagogy through artistic activities could aid recall by way of emotional arousal (Rinne et al., 2011). Consider, for example, how most people can easily recall the words or rhythm of particular pieces of music and how music or musical training could thus be used to enhance memory and the recall of information. It is interesting to note that studies have shown that musicians, compared to non-musicians, have greater volumes of grey matter in the part of the frontal cortex known to accommodate the neural networks that are involved in several significant working-memory processes (Janke, 2008; Sluming, Brooks, Howard, Downes & Roberts, 2007). In other words, musical training has enhanced working memory; if this information is coupled with the evidence noting the links between emotional arousal and memory, it seems that the creative arts might be an important avenue of study for all students across all year levels and should garner a greater degree of importance and emphasis in schools.

SUMMARY

Notwithstanding the important empirical research noted above linking the creative arts to various aspects of development and learning, research across other disciplinary areas such as cultural studies and innovation also acknowledges the importance of the creative arts, particularly in enhancing socio-emotional well-being and building creative capacities (Florida, 2005; Scholes & Nagel, 2012; Robinson, 2011). The creative arts also possess both instrumental value and are valuable in their own right; they reach beyond simplistic notions of intellect and achievement, extending the range of learning and developmental opportunities that arise in an educational context. It is also becoming increasingly evident that the creative arts play an important role in human development and enhance the growth of cognitive, socio-emotional and psychomotor pathways; they are basic to human experience and should be considered as fundamental or indeed foundational, not optional, curriculum areas (Sousa, 2001).

THE BRAIN, MOVEMENT AND LEARNING

The known physiological benefits associated with overall health and physical activity has a long history. For simplicity, this chapter will use the term 'physical activity' to denote all types of activities or exercise requiring some measure of increased aerobic function, given that such activities may vary depending on age and context. What is not without variation is the plethora of research across a number of disciplinary fields noting the health benefits associated with physical activity. For example, school-aged children and adolescents who are more physically active are generally healthier and show a trend towards continuing activity and improved health into adulthood (Ramirez, Kulinna & Cothran, 2012). Regular physical activity in such young people has also been associated with reductions in type-2 diabetes, cardiovascular risk factors, depression, sleep problems and anxiety disorders (Australian Institute of Health and Welfare, 2009; Biddle, Gorely & Stensel, 2004; Hills, King & Armstrong, 2007). The noting of anxiety disorders in the preceding sentence is important in that a great deal of research also acknowledges that regular physical activity produces psychological health benefits. For example, physical activity can lead to increased levels of serotonin, norepinephrine and dopamine, which can alleviate a variety of mental health ailments including anxiety and stress-related disorders (Ratey, 2008). It is worth remembering that, in terms of development, physical activity is an important contributor to growing and maintaining not only a healthy body but also a healthy mind. This is a noteworthy consideration for parents and teachers alike but, specifically in an educational context, it appears that physical activity can play an important role in learning and achievement.

As noted above, there has been a great deal of research identifying the positive associations between physical activity and overall physical and mental health. In the last couple of decades, a growing number of studies have suggested that regular physical activity can also positively influence cognition, brain structure and brain function during childhood, which in turn can positively influence learning (Chaddock-Heyman, Hillman, Cohen & Kramer, 2014). Brain-derived neurotrophic factor, or BDNF, as it is more commonly known, provides an important foundation for understanding why this might be.

BRAIN-DERIVED NEUROTROPHIC FACTOR

BDNF is a type of protein that activates stem cells in the brain to convert into new neurons and triggers numerous other chemicals that strengthen and protect neurons while promoting overall neural health (Cotman, Berchtold & Christie, 2007; Greenberg, Xu, Lu & Hempstead, 2009; Ratey, 2008). In addition to helping strengthen neurons, BDNF is essential for synaptic plasticity, hippocampal function and learning (Kuipers & Bramham, 2006).

In essence, BDNF could be analogous to fertilisers for plants, in that it helps to build and maintain cell circuitry, just as fertilisers strengthen the roots and structures of plants. Importantly, numerous animal studies have identified that physical activity induces BDNF to help build and strengthen neural connections in the hippocampus, a structure of the brain intimately linked with memory and learning; such findings have been supported by studies of humans, particularly in ageing populations (Berchtold, Chinn, Chou, Kesslak & Cotman, 2005; Cotman et al., 2007; Ma, 2008; Yarrow, White, McCoy & Borst, 2010). Humans have also been found to have elevated levels of BDNF in their bloodstream when engaging in physical activity and, as such, may be fertilising their brains for the better (Ratey, 2008).

OTHER EFFECTS OF PHYSICAL ACTIVITY ON THE BRAIN

Aside from the potential benefits to memory and learning from exercise and the release of BDNF, numerous studies also indicate that physical activity enhances executive functioning in people of all ages. If you recall from Chapter 3, executive functioning refers to many of the higher order functions of the prefrontal cortex. Concentrating and thinking, reasoning, exerting self-control, drawing on your working-memory systems or changing the way you think about a problem are a few examples of how you engage in measures of executive functioning (Diamond, 2012; Goldberg, 2001; Nagel, 2012a, 2014). The neural mechanisms that support such activity are available during childhood and through adolescence but are immature or less efficient than adult systems (Chaddock-Heyman et al., 2014). Significantly, numerous studies acknowledge that physical activity, both acute or moderate, appears to enhance executive functioning in children, and some studies indicate that, when physical activity is coupled with executive functioning or 'thinking while doing', executive functioning is enhanced to a greater extent (Best, 2010; Chaddock-Heyman et al., 2014; Guiney & Machado, 2013; Verburgh, Konigs, Scherder & Oosterlaan, 2014). In other words, physical activity positively affects cognition and can positively influence the very processes required for learning and achievement.

The potential cognitive benefits of physical activity are a very significant consideration for teachers, school leaders and policy-makers. There is growing evidence that integrating physical activity throughout the school day may enhance learning, given that physical activity improves attention span and concentration (Maeda & Murata, 2004; Pellegrini & Bjorkland, 1997; Shepard, 1997; Wojcicki & McAuley, 2014). This is supported by studies showing that vigorous physical activities have been associated with better school grades (Coe, Pivarnik, Womack, Reeves & Malina, 2006) and that acute bouts of aerobic physical activity reveal improved performance on academic achievement tests (Hillman, Buck & Themanson, 2009; Kohl & Cook, 2013). In terms of learning and achievement, it is also worth noting that numerous studies have shown that fitter children outperform their less fit counterparts in a variety of cognitive measures and memory tests (see Chaddock-Heyman et al., 2014 for an extensive listing of such studies). Taken in totality, the evidence is rather unequivocal; in a real-world setting such as a classroom, regular participation in physical activity has been associated with increased academic achievement (Chaddock-Heyman et al., 2014; see also Castelli, Hillman, Buck & Erwin, 2007; Coe et al., 2006; Grissom, 2005; Roberts, Freed & McCarthy, 2010). But, while the importance of physical activity to development and learning is unquestionable, there appears to be a growing pandemic of physical inactivity among today's human beings (Hillman, 2014).

PHYSICAL ACTIVITY TODAY

Concerns over physical inactivity within industrialised nations have grown markedly, given the evidence noting that physical activity has diminished significantly over the last century and is forecasted to continue to fall over the next few decades (Hillman, 2014). In Australia, the majority of children and young people are not meeting the daily recommendations for physical activity (Active Healthy Kids Australia, 2014). The reasons behind such a trend are multifarious but it is evident that across childhood and adolescence, levels of physical activity have declined and remain low (Colley et al., 2011; Salmon & Timperio, 2007; Troiano et al., 2008). Inactive lifestyles have been found to be detrimental to the health and well-being of children and adults alike, resulting in a range of disorders that accompany a sedentary lifestyle including obesity, metabolic disorders and type-2 diabetes to name a few (Booth & Lees, 2006; Wojcicki & McAuley, 2014).

The possible factors contributing to a rise in inactivity are complex. There is some evidence noting that school environments may be contributing to greater sedentary behaviours due to policies aimed at minimising or replacing physical activities in an effort to increase academic performance (Kohl & Cook, 2013). It may also be the case that schools are tacitly supporting a greater disposition towards sedentary activity through stressing the importance of technology through didactic and pedagogic endeavour as evident in curriculum and policy documents (see, for example, Ministerial Council on Education, Employment, Training and Youth Affairs—MCEETYA, 2008). This is significant given recommendations that children should not spend more than two hours a day using electronic media, particularly during daylight hours, and that children aged five to eighteen should participate in at least sixty minutes of moderate to vigorous physical activity every day of the week (Australian Government Department of Health and Ageing, 2004). Equally significant is evidence noting that approximately one-third of Australian children do not meet these physical activity guidelines (Commonwealth Scientific and Industrial Research Organisation—CSIRO, 2007). Taken in its entirety, the research supporting physical activity juxtaposed with growing levels of inactivity in children suggests that educational contexts are in a favourable position to enact positive change.

SUMMARY

It appears that students who engage in exercise and physical activity every day may be making their brains, as well as their bodies, stronger. Schools, in turn, should be promoting daily physical activity as part of a holistic curriculum across all year levels, while ensuring that they are not knowingly or tacitly making students more sedentary. The positive links between physical activity, development, brain function and learning are well established. Even moderate activity appears able to increase working memory, for example, in all children. Schools are well placed to enhance all aspects of student health, well-being, development and learning.

Refer to Chapter ❸ to review the importance of executive function.

EXERCISE IS GOOD FOR YOUR BRAIN

The benefits of physical activity and exercise appear fairly convincing to most, yet many school systems fail to embed extra opportunities for physical activity due to a belief that any time doing exercise is time lost in terms of working through the curriculum or getting better academic results. But some studies have noted unexpected tangential benefits from exercise programs that provide further support for the argument that neither the curriculum nor marks suffer from time spent exercising. One study, for example, not only found improvements in executive functioning in students but also improved maths achievement although no additional maths instruction had been provided.

From 2003 to 2006, researchers at the Medical College of Georgia, led by Dr Catherine Davis, recruited 171 overweight and inactive seven- to eleven-year-old students to participate in exercise intervention programs that lasted approximately fourteen weeks (Davis et al., 2011). The participants were divided into three groups: a control group who did no physical activity after school; a group who did 20 minutes of vigorous physical five days a week after school; and a group that did 40 minutes of such activity on those same days. The groups involved in physical activity played intermittent, high-energy running games such as capture the flag, relays, jumping rope and modified basketball. They also wore heart-rate monitors and were rewarded for maintaining a high average heart rate. All the students were also given cognitive-function tests at the beginning and end of the study. They were tested for their maths and reading achievement and executive function; the findings were quite interesting.

The children in the 40-minute activity group showed significant improvement on an executive-function test compared with the control group. They increased about 4 points on a cognitive-performance scale. Those in the 20-minute group showed about half that improvement and while there did not appear to be any signs of improvement in reading, there was an improvement in maths achievement for both exercise groups. Brain scans were also conducted on each participant and indicated that the children who were exercising appeared to have more neural activity in the frontal areas of their brains, an important area for executive function. Moreover—from the physical and cognitive benefits evident—the researchers noted that the finding of improved maths achievement was 'remarkable given that no academic instruction was provided and suggests that a longer intervention period may result in more benefit' (Davis et al., 2011, p. 96).

Other research studies, as noted earlier, have shown similar results to those found by Dr Davis and her colleagues: demonstrating positive links between exercise and cognitive capacities, and strong associations between maths performance and aerobic fitness among primary school–aged children. And while there are always limitations with any empirical study, perhaps the longer intervention alluded to in Davis's study could easily take the form of daily regularly programmed exercise for all students that goes beyond physical education classes. It could also be the case that those students who do not regularly engage in physical activity may be at an academic disadvantage compared with peers who participate in various extracurricular activities, thereby giving schools another reason for ensuring all students are physically active through ongoing school-based approaches.

Ask yourself...

1   Given the evidence provided, do you think it is important or possible to get your future students more active? Explain.

2   What might you be able to do to increase physical activity opportunities in a school setting if your school does not have such planned activities? How would you go about getting support for such programs?

CONCLUSION

Education has a number of sacred cows: that was the claim made at the start of the chapter. How and why such taken-for-granted beliefs or notions about education have arisen is a point of conjecture among most people. Perhaps such ideas exist given that anyone who has attended school likely has an opinion about how education should be conducted. In his seminal work examining the profession of teaching, Dan Lortie (1975) coined the phrase 'apprenticeship of observation', suggesting that teachers often taught the way they had been taught: their experiences as students were like an apprenticeship to the profession. It could be the case that all who have attended school believe they have sound arguments for supporting various educational practices over others and for perhaps building credibility in 'common sense' notions of how to get the best results from students. However, it could also be argued that 'common sense' ideas about 'schooling' do not always stack up well against research evidence. From standardised tests, to homework to hyperstimulation to the lack of emphasis on the arts and physical activity, it is incumbent upon future teachers to act on the best available evidence for promoting development and learning.

Schools are dynamic, as are the students who occupy them. Increasingly, the evidence requires us to question, challenge and, when necessary, change what we do to, and with, children in an educational context. As a teacher, it will be part of your role to take on such responsibilities when able—and, when you are not able to, to ensure that the support provided to your students to overcome various challenges is positive and adequate. For example, some school communities and school leaders may ardently value homework and have particular guidelines. Given that research on homework is an inexact science due to the many variables associated with it, teachers would do well to reflect on their practices and continually ask themselves if what they are doing is working. It may be the case that the students are not encumbered by homework, so nothing need be done—but if homework seems to be detrimental, then changes to its structure or approach or both are warranted. This is part and parcel of being a reflective practitioner and making changes when necessary. Remember, some of the challenges that present themselves are rooted in a long history of practice and may need similar timelines to be modified, overcome or completely abandoned. In the meantime, there are positive steps that can also be taken such as diminishing stress and promoting and engaging in daily physical activity. In the end, it is in the hands of the teacher to do what they can to nurture learning and, we hope, to continually build healthy developmental foundations while doing so.

CHAPTER SUMMARY

This chapter focused on examining a number of challenges you may face as a teacher that go beyond the curriculum, behaviour management and pedagogy. Like many professions, teaching has its share of systemic challenges that can appear contradictory or conflict with one's philosophical beliefs about how to work with children. For example, standardised testing and homework are often contentious issues that require a degree of reflection and consideration and were explored early in the chapter. The impact of stress on learning was examined, given that such things as testing and homework can certainly create a degree of anxiety or stress in students of all ages. There are positive initiatives that teachers can take to overcome such challenges; there are also some areas of endeavour that can enhance learning and academic outcomes. The creative arts and the need for physical activity are two such areas and these were explored in detail; particular attention was given to how they not only enhance numerous aspects of development but can also improve academic outcomes over time. As a future teacher you were invited to explore these challenges and opportunities with a view to always questioning what you do and why, and how any barriers and opportunities can be used to improve your practice and the learning of your students.

Implications for Teaching

The title of this chapter is 'Nurturing learning' and the chapter-opening scenario provided an example of how learning can be unknowingly hindered through a systemic process designed to determine what students know or do not know. The intent of the chapter was to draw your awareness to the fact that there can be many things that hinder learning but that, equally important, there are many things that can nurture learning in a positive manner. Given that you have, or will likely draw upon, your history as a student and experience Lortie's (1975) apprenticeship of observation, it is important that you always reflect on what you are being asked to do or plan on doing as an educator. Reflection is an important skill for any teacher and research evidence suggests that it is integral to nurturing learning.

Reflection, or what is sometimes referred to as reflective practice, has a long tradition and can be found in the work of John Dewey (1933) whose writing spoke of thinking for personal and intellectual growth. Dewey is widely considered one of education's great philosophers and thinkers, and his notions of reflective practice have been echoed by others in more contemporary times and through recent research. It has also been noted that when new teachers reflect on their own learning and educational experiences, it can help them to make their own assumptions about learning and teaching explicit, thereby improving their practice (Bransford, Derry, Berliner, Hammerness & Beckett, 2005). In a broad sense this is what this chapter has asked you, as a future teacher, to do. You have been tasked with looking into challenges you may face while also being provided with ideas about how to nurture learning. Reflection is integral to nurturing learning; we hope that this chapter has allowed you to develop your skills as a reflective practitioner by looking at how learning can be nurtured.

Ask yourself...

After working through and reflecting on the chapter, what are your current thoughts on standardised testing and homework? Are they any different from before you read the information? Why or why not? Remember that whatever views you hold are always open to scrutiny and as such it is important that you are able to support your beliefs when dealing with stakeholders and in your practice.

PRACTICAL ACTIVITIES

1   *While on practicum*, examine your school's homework policy and discuss this with your mentor teacher. Do approaches to homework conflict with your views? How do the students seem to respond to homework? Do you see any patterns of behaviour associated with homework and, if so, what do you think may be contributing to those behaviours?

2   *While on practicum*, keep a record of how much structured physical activity your students receive on a weekly basis. Note how much time they receive exploring the creative arts. Reflect on your observations by noting what you see that the research presents, and note how you might do things when you have your own class.

STUDY QUESTIONS

1   What are some of the major disadvantages with standardised testing? What are some of the benefits?

2   What are some of the problems associated with homework? How can homework hinder learning? Can it enhance learning and, if so, how?

3   Explain why any notion of hyperstimulating the brain to promote enhanced learning is erroneous and unfounded in science. What might you say to parents who have been led to believe that extra stimulation under the guise of 'enrichment' is in the best interests of their child?

4   Describe how stress can affect behaviour and learning.

5   Describe how the creative arts and physical activity can enhance learning. Provide examples from the evidence in the chapter.

FURTHER READING

Asbury, C. & Rich, B. (Eds.). (2008). *Learning, Arts and the Brain*. New York, NY: Dana Press.

Australian Government Department of Health and Ageing (2004). *Active Kids Are Healthy Kids. Australia's Physical Activity Recommendations for 5–12 Year Olds*. Canberra, Australia: Author.

Best, J. R. (2010). Effects of physical activity on children's executive function: Contributions of experimental research on aerobic exercise. *Developmental Review, 30*(4), 331–351.

Buell, J. (2004). *Closing the Book on Homework: Enhancing Public Education and Freeing Family Time*. Philadelphia, PA: Temple University Press.

Diamond, A. (2012). Activities and programs that improve children's executive functions. *Current Directions in Psychological Science, 21*(5), 335–341.

McEwen, B. S. (2002). *The End of Stress as We Know It*. Washington, DC: John Henry Press.

Nagel, M. C. (2009). Mind the mind: Understanding the links between stress, emotional well-being and learning in educational contexts. *International Journal of Learning, 16*(2), 33–42.

Posner, M. I. & Patoine, B. (2010). How arts training improves attention and cognition. In D. Gordon (Ed.), *Cerebrum: Emerging Ideas in Brain Science* (pp. 12–22). New York, NY: Dana Press.

Ratey, J. J. (2008). *Spark: The Revolutionary New Science of Exercise and the Brain*. New York, NY: Little, Brown.

Roberts, K., Freed, B. & McCarthy, W. J. (2010). Low aerobic fitness and obesity are associated with lower standardised test scores in children. *Journal of Pediatrics, 156*(5), 711–718.

Sahlberg, P. (2010). *Finnish Lessons: What Can the World Learn from Educational Change in Finland?* New York, NY: Teachers College Press.

Schellenberg, E. G. (2006). Long term positive associations between music lessons and IQ. *Journal of Educational Psychology, 98*(2), 457–468.

Wyn, J., Turnbull, M. & Grimshaw, L. (2014). *The Experience of Education: The Impacts of High Stakes Testing on School Students and Their Families*. Sydney, Australia: The Whitlam Institute, University of Western Sydney.

VIDEO LINKS

The Progessive Magazine: *Calls to Action: Noam Chomsky on the Dangers of Standardized Testing*
https://www.youtube.com/watch?v=9JVVRWBekYo

World-renowned linguist and cognitive scientist Professor Emeritus Noam Chomsky from the Massachusetts Institute of Technology provides a candid perspective on the problems associated with standardised testing.

NIBIB: *Exercise, Stress, and the Brain*
https://www.youtube.com/watch?v=xpy_rAWSWkA

Dr Paul Thompson of the National Institute of Biomedical Imaging and Bioengineering in the United States briefly describes how exercise enhances neural function while counteracting the effects of cortisol arising from stress.

WEBLINKS

Project Zero
www.pz.harvard.edu

Originally developed as a research enterprise looking at the links between learning and the arts at Harvard University, Project Zero has expanded its work into a number of areas including thinking, intelligence and creativity with a focus on learning processes in children, adults and organisations. The site offers resources, references and ideas for consideration in terms of educational practice.

GLOSSARY

Affective
Of or having to do with emotions or the feeling of emotion.

Anxiety
A negative emotional state that can impair performance and engage the body's stress-response system.

Arousal
A physiological and psychological reaction that allows for enhanced alertness, attention and, at times, performance.

Attachment
An emotional bond between an individual and attachment figure, usually the primary care-giver.

Behaviourism
A field of psychology concerned with individual behaviour.

Behaviourist
Assumes the behaviour of a human is a consequence of reinforcement and punishment.

Bio-ecological theory
A refinement of the ecological systems theory model, incorporating bi-directional influences between individuals' development and their surrounding environment.

Broca's area
Syntax centre in the brain synthesising language so we can articulate our thoughts through the regulation of facial and hand activity, allowing us to speak and write.

Cognitive ability
Brain process of acquiring knowledge and understanding.

Constructivism
A theory of learning whereby individuals construct knowledge and meaning from their experiences.

Culturally responsive teaching
A genuine interest and awareness of different cultural backgrounds of the students.

Culture
Knowledge, beliefs, values, morals, laws, customs, traditions and artefacts common to members of society.

Developmental tasks
The meeting of developmental challenges arising from maturation, context and sense of self.

Disability
Consequence of an impairment that may be physical, cognitive, mental, sensory, emotional or developmental.

Downshifting
This phenomenon results in impaired cognition due to high levels of stress hormones when the brain is in a state of 'fight or flight'.

Ecological systems theory
Posits reciprocal relationships within immediate and broader contexts.

Emotional intelligence
Capacity of individuals to recognise their own and other people's emotions.

Emotional regulation
The capacity to understand, accept and manage one's emotions.

Enquiry learning
Problem-based learning with co-enquiry by student and teacher.

Episodic memory
A type of explicit memory where we recall things said or done over time.

Executive functions
An umbrella term for the regulation and control of cognitive processes, including aspects of memory, reasoning and numerous higher order skills.

Experience-dependent stimulation
The experiences that act as adaptive processes in shaping the brain's hard-wiring and may be most commonly referred to as learning experiences.

Experience-expectant stimulation
Those ordinary day-to-day experiences the brain requires for the particular hard-wiring of important connections.

Extrinsic motivation
A type of motivation that is facilitated through the use of external rewards or punishment.

Flow
A state of intense concentration that supersedes other affective and cognitive processes.

Gender
Range of characteristics pertaining to, and differentiating between, masculinity and femininity. May be based on social and gender identity.

General mental ability
Broad mental capacity that influences performance on cognitive ability.

Gifted and talented
Broad term for those who demonstrate outstanding levels of aptitude or competence in one or more domains.

Guided participation
Builds on the concept of the zone of proximal development to include broader support such as structuring tasks and ICT.

Humanism
A philosophical and/or ethical position that emphasises and values the agency of human beings.

Hyperstimulate
Trying to enhance a child's intellect or learning by providing numerous extracurricular activities or learning programs, or through the provision of a multitude of so-called learning toys.

Inclusion
All students attend and are welcomed by schools in age-appropriate, regular classes and are supported to learn, contribute and participate in all aspects of the life of the school.

Intelligence quotient
A number representing a person's reasoning ability.

Intrinsic motivation
Motivation that is the product of an internal state or desire such as excitement, curiosity, pride or satisfaction.

Language
A body of sounds (phonemes), words, word order (syntax) and meaning (semantics)—common to people of the same cultural tradition.

Learning difficulties
Challenges associated with processing information.

Learning windows
Optimum times of neural maturation when the brain requires certain types of stimulation to create or stabilise long-lasting neural connections.

Literacy
The ability to use language, numbers, images and other means to understand and use the dominant symbol systems of a culture.

Long-term memory
As evident in the term, this type of memory stores information for a long period of time.

Long-term potentiation (LTP)
The continuous activation of synapses leading to the hard-wiring of neural connections.

Motivation
An internal state that instigates, drives, directs and maintains particular behaviours.

Multiple intelligences
Theory that proposes several independent forms of human intelligence exist.

NAPLAN
The National Assessment Program—Literacy and Numeracy is a set of standardised tests administered annually to Australian children in Years 3, 5, 7 and 9.

Nativist
Believes biological influences bring about language development.

Negative reinforcement
The removal of an undesirable stimulus or object after a desired behaviour is exhibited.

Neuromyths
The misuse or misinterpretation or both of neuroscience to perpetuate educational myths.

Neuroplasticity
The ability of the brain to reorganise neural pathways via sensory stimulation and new experiences.

Positive reinforcement
The addition of a pleasurable or desirable stimulus after a desired behaviour is exhibited.

Prefrontal cortex
The region of the frontal lobes directly connected to every distinct function of the brain and responsible for coordinating and integrating most brain functions.

Procedural memory
A type of implicit memory that is used to do things automatically and without conscious effort.

Scaffolding
Guidance received from an adult or more competent peer.

Schemata
The mental representation of an experience.

Self-efficacy
An individual's perceptions of ability of success in valued tasks.

Semantic memory
A type of explicit memory related to factual information and knowledge.

Social learning theory
A theory of learning that posits that learning is a cognitive process that occurs in a social context.

Socioculturalist
Theory that language development depends upon interactions between the child and the environment.

Special needs
Educational requirements due to learning difficulties, physical disability or emotional and behavioural needs.

Standardised testing
A systemic approach to testing students in predetermined areas of importance.

States
Temporary feelings that might drive behaviours.

Telegraphic speech
Simplified speech including most important content but combinations may not include articles, prepositions or verbs.

Temperament
A person's way of responding to novel events or experiences while regulating emotional impulses.

Traits
Stable and long-lasting predispositions that might drive behaviours.

Triarchic model
Characterises intelligence in terms of distinct components: analytic, creative, practical.

Universal grammar
Proposes the ability to learn grammar is hard-wired into the brain: that human brains have a language acquisition device (LAD), an innate mechanism allowing children to develop language skills.

Wernicke's area
Part of the brain involved in comprehension and understanding speech; processes elements of language, converting thoughts into language.

Working memory
A memory system that both stores and manipulates information and is important for reasoning, comprehension, learning and processing information into long-term storage.

Zone of proximal development
Difference between what learners can do without help and with help.

REFERENCES

Aber, J. L. & Jones, S. J. (1997). Indicators of positive development in early childhood: Improving concepts and measures. In R. M. Hauser, B. V. Brown & W. R. Prosser (Eds.), *Indicators of Children's Well-being* (pp. 395–408). New York, NY: Russell Sage Foundation.

Ackoff, R. L. & Greenberg, D. (2008). *Turning Learning Right Side Up: Putting Education Back on Track*. Upper Saddle River, NJ: Wharton School Publishing.

Active Healthy Kids Australia (2014). *Is Sport Enough? The 2014 Active Healthy Kids Australia Report Card on Physical Activity for Children and Young People*. Adelaide, Australia: Author.

Adey, P., Csapo, B., Demetriou, A., Hautamaki, J. & Shayer, M. (2007). Can we be intelligent about intelligence? Why education needs the concept of plastic general ability. *Educational Research Review, 2*, 75–97.

Adler, P. A., Kless, S. J. & Adler, P. (1992). Socialization to gender roles: Popularity among elementary school boys and girls. *Sociology of Education, 65*(3), 169–187.

Adreon, D. & Stella, J. (2001). Transition to middle and high school: Increasing the success of students with Asperger syndrome. *Intervention in School and Clinic, 32*, 266–271.

Ahola, D. & Kovacik, A. (2007). *Observing and Understanding Child Development: A Child Study Manual*. New York, NY: Thomson Delmar Learning.

Ainley, M. (2006). Connecting with learning: Motivation, affect and cognition in interest processes. *Educational Psychology Review, 18*(4), 391–405.

Allan, A. (2010). Picturing success: Young femininities and the (im)possibilities of academic achievement in selective, single-sex schooling. *International Studies in Sociology of Education, 20*(1), 39–54.

Allen, K. E. & Schwartz, I. (2000). *The Exceptional Child: Inclusion in Early Childhood Education* (4th ed.). Albany, NY: Delmar Cengage Learning.

Alloway, N., Freebody, P., Gilbert, P. & Muspratt, S. (2002). *Boys, Literacy and Schooling*. Canberra, Australia: Commonwealth Department of Education, Science and Training.

Allred, L. A. (2007). *Piggyback Rides and Slippery Slides: How to Have Fun Raising First Rate Children*. Springville, UT: Cedar Fort.

Ambridge, B. & Lieven, E. V. M. (2011). *Language Acquisition: Contrasting Theoretical Approaches*. Cambridge, UK: Cambridge University Press.

American Academy of Pediatrics (2009). *Caring for Your Baby and Young Child: Birth to Age Five* (5th ed.). New York, NY: Bantam.

Ames, D. L. & Fiske, S. T. (2010). Cultural neuroscience. *Asian Journal of Social Psychology, 13*(2), 72–82.

Amrein, A. L. & Berliner, D. C. (2002). High-stakes testing, uncertainty and student learning. *Education Policy Analysis Archives, 10*(18), 1–74.

Anderman, E. M., Cupp, P. K. & Lane, D. (2009). Impulsivity and academic cheating. *Journal of Experimental Education, 78*(1), 135–150.

Anderman, E. M. & Midgley, C. (2004). Changes in self-reported academic cheating across the transition from middle school to high school. *Contemporary Educational Psychology, 29*(4), 499–517.

Andersen, B. B., Korbo, L. & Pakkenberg, B. (1992). A quantitative study of the human cerebellum with unbiased stereological techniques. *Journal of Comparative Neurology, 326*(4), 549–560.

Anderson, N. J. (2002). The role of metacognition in second language teaching and learning. *ERIC Digest*, April, 3–4.

Annese, J., Schenker-Ahmed, N. M., Bartsch, H., Maechler, P., Sheh, C., Thomas, N., Kayano, J., Ghatan, A., Bresler, N., Frosch, M. P., Kaming, R. & Corkin, S. (2014). Postmortem examination of patient H. M.'s brain based on histological sectioning and digital 3D reconstruction. *Nature Communications, 5*(3122), 1–9.

Anning, A., Cullen, J. & Fleer, M. (Eds.) (2004). *Early Childhood Education: Society and Culture*. New York, NY: Sage Publications.

Anyon, J. (1997). *Ghetto Schooling: A Political Economy of Urban Educational Reform*. New York, NY: Teachers College Press.

Appleton, J. J., Christenson, S. L. & Furlong, M. J. (2008). Student engagement with school: Critical conceptual and methodological issues of the construct. *Psychology in the Schools, 45*(5), 369–386.

Armstrong, S. (2008). *Teaching Smarter with the Brain in Focus: Practical Ways to Apply the Latest Brain Research to Deepen Comprehension, Improve Memory, and Motivate Students to Achieve*. New York, NY: Scholastic.

Arnold, A. (2001). Towards a finer description of the connection between arts education and student achievement. *Arts Education Policy Review, 102*(5), 25–26.

Arnsten, A. (1998). The biology of being frazzled. *Science, 280*(5370), 1711–1712.

Asbury, C. & Rich, B. (Eds.) (2008). *Learning, Arts and the Brain*. New York, NY: Dana Press.

Askell-Williams, H., Lawson, M. J. & Skrzypiec, G. (2012). Scaffolding cognitive and metacognitive strategy instruction in regular class lessons. *Instructional Science, 40*(2), 413–443.

Atkinson, J. W. & Feather, N. T. (Eds.) (1966). *A Theory of Achievement Motivation*. New York, NY: John Wiley & Sons.

Atkinson, J. W. & Raynor, J. O. (1974). *Motivation and Achievement*. Washington, DC: V. H. Winston.

Au, W. (2009). *Unequal by Design: High Stakes Testing and the Standardisation of Inequality*. New York, NY: Routledge.

Aubert-Broche, B., Fonov, V., Leppert, I., Pike, G. B. & Collins, D. L. (2008). Human brain myelination from birth to 4. 5 years. In D. N. Metaxas, L. Axel, G. Fichtinger & G. Szekely (Eds.), *Medical Image Computing and Computer Assisted Intervention—MICCAI Lecture Notes in Computer Science, 5242* (pp. 180–187). Berlin, Germany: Springer.

Australian Bureau of Statistics (2015). *Migration, Australia* (cat. no. 3412. 0). Canberra, Australia: Commonwealth of Australia.

Australian Council for Educational Research (2010). *Challenges for Australian Education: Results for PISA 2009*. Melbourne, Australia: ACER Press.

Australian Government Department of Health and Ageing (2004). *Active Kids Are Healthy Kids. Australia's Physical Activity Recommendations for 5–12 Year Olds*. Canberra, Australia: Author.

Australian Institute of Family Studies (2015). *Longitudinal Study of Australian Children: Annual Statistical Report*. Melbourne, Australia: Author.

Australian Institute of Health and Welfare (2009). *A Picture of Australia's Children 2009*. Canberra, Australia: Author.

Avitsur, R., Padgettt, D. A., Dhabhar, F. S., Stark, J. L., Kramer, K. A., Engler, H. & Sheridan, J. F. (2003). Expression of glucocorticoid resistance following social stress requires a second signal. *Journal of Leukocyte Biology, 74*(4), 507–513.

Baard, P. P., Deci, E. L. & Ryan, R. M. (2004). Intrinsic need satisfaction: A motivational basis of performance and well-being in two work settings. *Journal of Applied Social Psychology, 34*(10), 2045–2068.

Baddeley, A. (2003a). Working memory and language: An overview. *Journal of Communication Disorders, 36*(3), 189–208.

Baddeley, A. (2003b). Working memory: Looking back and looking forward. *Nature Reviews Neuroscience, 4*(10), 829–839.

Baddeley, A. D. (2007). *Working Memory, Thought and Action*. Oxford, UK: Oxford University Press.

Baddeley, A. D. & Hitch, G. (1974). Working memory. In G. H. Bower (Ed.), *The Psychology of Learning and Motivation* (Vol. 8, pp. 47–90). New York, NY: Academic Press.

Bailey, R., Morley, D. & Dismore, H. (2009). Talent development in physical education: A national survey of policy and practice in England. *Physical Education and Sport Pedagogy, 14*(1), 59–72.

Baines, L. (2007). Less is more? Ideas for American schools. *Phi Delta Kappan, 89*(2), 98–100.

Baker, C. (2006). *Foundations of Bilingual Education and Bilingualism* (4th ed.). New York, NY: Multilingual Matters.

Baker, D. P. & LeTendre, G. K. (2005). *National Differences, Global Similarities: World Culture and the Future of Schooling*. Stanford, CA: Stanford University Press.

Ballet, K. & Kelchtermans, G. (2009). Struggling with workload: Primary teachers' experience of intensification. *Teaching and Teacher Education, 25*(8), 1150–1157.

Bandura, A. (1976). *Social Learning Theory*. Englewood Cliffs, NJ: Prentice Hall.

Bandura, A. (1977). Self-efficacy: Toward a unifying theory of behavioural change. *Psychological Review, 84*(2), 191–215.

Bandura, A. (1986). *Social Foundations of Thought and Action*. Englewood Cliffs, NJ: Prentice Hall.

Bandura, A. (1993). Perceived self-efficacy in cognitive development and functioning. *Educational Psychologist, 28*(2), 117–148.

Bandura, A. (1997). *Self-efficacy: The Exercise of Control*. New York, NY: W.H. Freeman.

Bandura, A. (2001). Social cognitive theory: An agentic perspective. *Annual Review of Psychology, 52*, 1–26.

Bandura, A. (2006). Toward a psychology of human agency. *Perspectives on Psychological Science, 1*(2), 164–180.

Bandura, A. & Adams, N. F. (1977). Analysis of self-efficacy theory of behavioural change. *Cognitive Therapy and Research, 1*(4), 287–310.

Bandura, A., Jeffery, R. W. & Wright, C. L. (1974). Efficacy of participant modeling as a function of response induction aids. *Journal of Abnormal Psychology, 83*(1), 56–64.

Banks, J. & Banks, C. (2013). *Multicultural Education: Issues and Perspectives* (8th ed.). New York, NY: Wiley.

Bannon, L. J. (2006). Forgetting as a feature, not a bug: The duality of memory and implications for ubiquitous computing. *Co-Design, 2*(1), 3–15.

Barber, B. (1986). Homework does not belong on the agenda for educational reform. *Educational Leadership, 43*(8), 55–57.

Barkley, R. (2006). *Attention Deficit Hyperactivity Disorder: A Handbook for Diagnosis and Treatment* (3rd ed.). New York, NY: Guilford Press.

Baron-Cohen, S. (2003). *The Essential Difference: The Truth about the Male and Female Brain*. New York, NY: Basic Books.

Baron-Cohen, S. (2009) Autism: The empathizing–systemizing (E–S) theory. *Annals of the New York Academy of Sciences, 1156*, 68–80.

Baron-Cohen, S. (2012) Autism and the technical mind. *Scientific American, 307*, 72–77.

Baron-Cohen, S., Tager-Flusberg, H. & Lombardo, M. (Eds.) (2013). *Understanding Other Minds: Perspectives from Social Cognitive Neuroscience* (3rd ed.). Oxford, UK: Oxford University Press.

Barton, D. (2007). *Literacy: An Introduction to the Ecology of Written Language* (2nd ed.). Oxford, UK: Blackwell Publishing.

Basten, U., Hilger, K. & Fiebach, C. (2015). Where smart brains are different: A quantitative meta-analysis of functional and structural brain imaging studies on intelligence. *Intelligence, 51*, 10–27.

Bauer, P. J. (2005). New developments in the study of infant memory. In D. M. Teti (Ed.), *Blackwell Handbook of Research Methods in Developmental Science* (pp. 467–488). Oxford, UK: Blackwell Publishing.

Baxter, M. G. & Murray, E. A. (2002). The amygdala and reward. *Nature Reviews Neuroscience, 3*(7), 563–573.

Bell, M. A. & Fox, N. A. (1997). Individual differences in object permanence performance at 8 months: Locomotor experience and brain electrical activity. *Developmental Psychology, 31*(4), 287–297.

Bell, M. A. & Wolfe, C. D. (2004). Emotion and cognition: An intricately bound developmental process. *Child Development, 75*(2), 366–370.

Belmonte, M. K. & Bourgeron. T. (2006). Fragile X syndrome and autism at the intersection of genetic and neural networks. *Nature Neuroscience, 9(*10), 1221–1225.

Bennett, C. I. (2003). *Comprehensive Multicultural Education: Theory and Practice* (5th ed.). Boston, MA: Allyn & Bacon.

Bennett, S. & Kalish, N. (2006). *The Case against Homework: How Homework is Hurting Children and What Parents Can Do about It*. New York, NY: Three Rivers Press.

Ben-Yehudah, G. & Fiez, J. A. (2007). Development of verbal working memory. In D. Coch, K. W. Fisher & G. Dawson (Eds.), *Human Behavior, Learning and the Developing Brain: Typical Development* (pp. 301–328). New York, NY: The Guilford Press.

Berchtold, N. C., Chinn, G., Chou, M., Kesslak, J. P. & Cotman, C. W. (2005). Exercise primes a molecular memory for brain-derived neurotrophic factor protein induction in the rat hippocampus. *Neuroscience, 133*(3), 853–861.

Berk, L. (2006). *Child Development* (7th ed.). Boston, MA: Allyn and Bacon.

Berk, L. & Spuhl, S. (1995). Maternal interaction, private speech, and task performance in preschool children. *Early Childhood Research Quarterly, 10*, 145–169.

Bermudez-Rattoni, F. (2010). Is memory consolidation a multiple-circuit system? *Proceedings of the National Academy of Sciences, 107*(18), 8051–8052.

Berninger, V. W. & Richards, T. L. (2002). *Brain Literacy for Educators and Psychologists*. San Diego, CA: Elsevier Science.

Berwick, R. C., Friederici, A. D., Chomsky, N. & Bolhuis, J. J. (2013). Evolution, brain, and the nature of language. *Trends in Cognitive Sciences, 17*(2), 89–98.

Best, J. R. (2010). Effects of physical activity on children's executive function: Contributions of experimental research on aerobic exercise. *Developmental Review, 30*(4), 331–351.

Bethea, C. L., Lu, N. Z., Gundlah, C. & Streicher, J. M. (2002). Diverse actions of ovarian steroids in the serotonin neural system. *Frontiers in Neuroendocrinology, 23*(1), 41–100.

Biddle, S. J. H., Gorely, T. & Stensel, D. J. (2004). Health-enhancing physical activity and sedentary behaviour in children and adolescents. *Journal of Sports Sciences, 22*(8), 679–701.

Binet, A. (1916). New methods for the diagnosis of the intellectual level of subnormals. In E. S. Kite (Trans.), *The Development of Intelligence in Children*. Vineland, NJ: Publications of the Training School at Vineland. (Originally published 1905 in *L'Année Psychologique, 12*, 191–244.)

Bjorklund, D. F. (2005). *Children's Thinking: Cognitive Development and Individual Differences* (4th ed.). Belmont, CA: Wadsworth/Thomson Learning.

Bjorklund, D. F. & Blasi, C. H. (2012). *Child and Adolescent Development: An Integrated Approach.* Belmont, CA: Wadsworth.

Black, J. E., Jones, T. A., Nelson, C. A. & Greenough, W. T. (1998). Neural plasticity and the developing brain. In J. D. Noshpitz, N. E. Alessi, J. T. Coyle, S. I. Harrison & S. Eth (Eds.), *Handbook of Child and Adolescent Psychiatry,* (Vol. 6: *Basic Psychiatric Science and Treatment,* pp. 31–53). New York, NY: Wiley.

Black, S. (2001). Morale matters: When teachers feel good about their work, research shows, student achievement rises. *American School Board Journal, 188*(1), 40–43.

Black, S. (2004). Whose economic wellbeing? A challenge to dominant discourses on the relationship between literacy and numeracy skills and (un)employment. *Literacy and Numeracy Studies, 13*(1), 7–18.

Blair, C. (2002). School readiness: Integrating cognition and emotion in a neurobiological conceptualization of children's functioning at school entry. *American Psychologist, 57*(2), 111–127.

Blair, C. & Razza, R. P. (2007). Relating effortful control, executive function, and false belief understanding to emerging math and literacy ability in kindergarten. *Child Development, 78*(2), 647–663.

Blakemore, S. J., den Ouden, H., Choudhury, S. & Frith, C. (2007). Adolescent development of the neural circuitry for thinking intentions. *Social, Cognitive & Affective Neuroscience, 2*(2), 130–139.

Blakemore, S. J. & Frith, U. (2005). *The Learning Brain: Lessons for Education.* Oxford, UK: Blackwell Publishing.

Blomberg, O. (2011). Concepts of cognition for cognitive engineering. *International Journal of Aviation Psychology, 21*(1), 85–104.

Bloom, F. E., Beal, M. F. & Kupfer, D. J. (Eds.) (2006). *The Dana Guide to Brain Health: A Practical Family Reference from Medical Experts.* Washington, DC: Dana Press.

Bong, M. & Skaalvik, E. M. (2003). Academic self-concept and self-efficacy: How different are they really? *Educational Psychology Review, 15*(1), 1–40.

Booth, F. W. & Lees, S. J. (2006). Physically active subjects should be the control group. *Medicine & Science in Sports & Exercise, 38*(3), 405–406.

Booth, T. (1996). Perspectives on inclusion from England. *Cambridge Journal of Education,* 26(1), 87–99.

Bornstein, M. H., Hahn, C. S. & Haynes, O. M. (2004). Specific and general language performance across early childhood: Stability and gender considerations. *First Language, 24*(3), 267–304.

Bowlby, J. (1969). *Attachment and Loss, Volume 1: Attachment.* New York, NY: Basic Books.

Bransford, J., Darling-Hammond, L. & LePage, P. (2005). Introduction. In L. Darling-Hammond & J. Bransford (Eds.), *Preparing Teachers for a Changing World: What Teachers Should Learn and Be Able to Do* (pp. 1–39). San Francisco, CA: John Wiley & Sons.

Bransford, J., Derry, S., Berliner, D., Hammerness, K. & Beckett, K. L. (2005). Theories of learning and their roles in teaching. In L. Darling-Hammond & J. Bransford (Eds.), *Preparing Teachers for a Changing World: What Teachers Should Learn and Be Able to Do* (pp. 40–87). San Francisco, CA: John Wiley & Sons.

Bransford, J. D., Brown, A. L. & Cocking, R. R. (2000). *How People Learn: Brain, Mind, Experience, and School.* Washington, DC: National Academy Press.

Breier, J., Simos, P. G. & Fletcher, J. M. (2002). Abnormal activation of tempoparietal language areas during phonetic analysis in children with dyslexia. *Neuropsychology, 17,* 610–621.

Breznitz, Z. & Share, D. L. (1992). The effect of accelerated reading rate on memory for text. *Journal of Educational Psychology, 84*(2), 193–199.

Brizendine, L. B. (2006). *The Female Brain.* New York, NY: Morgan Road Books.

Broadbent, D. E. (1975). The magic number seven after fifteen years. In A. Kennedy & A. Wilkes (Eds.), *Studies in Long-Term Memory* (pp. 3–18). Oxford, UK: John Wiley & Sons.

Bronfenbrenner, U. (1979). *The Ecology of Human Development.* Cambridge, MA: Harvard University Press.

Bronfenbrenner, U. (1989). The ecological systems theory. *Annals of Child Development, 6,* 87–250.

Bronfenbrenner, U. (1989, April). *The Developing Ecology of Human Development: Paradigm Lost or Paradigm Regained.* Paper presented at the Biennial Meeting of the Society for Research in Child Development, Kansas City, Missouri.

Bronfenbrenner, U. (2001). The bioecological theory of human development. In N. J. Smelser & P. B. Baltes (Eds.), *International Encyclopaedia of the Social and Behavorial Sciences* (Vol. 10, pp. 6963–6970). New York, NY: Elsevier Science Ltd.

Bronfenbrenner, U. (Ed.) (2005). *Making Human Beings Human: Bioecological Perspectives on Human Development.* Thousand Oaks, CA: Sage Publications.

Bronfenbrenner, U. & Ceci, S. J. (1994). Nature–nurture reconceptualized in developmental perspective:

A bioecological model. *Psychological Review, 101*(4), 568–586.

Brophy, J. (1987). Synthesis of research on strategies for motivating students to learn. *Educational Leadership, 45*(2), 40–48.

Brophy, J. (2005). Goal theorists should move on from performance goals. *Educational Psychologist, 40*(3), 167–176.

Brown, M., Keynes, R. & Lumsden, A. (2001). *The Developing Brain*. Oxford, UK: Oxford University Press.

Brown, P. C., Roediger, H. L. & McDaniel, M. A. (2014). *Make It Stick: The Science of Successful Learning*. Cambridge, MA: Belknap Press.

Brown, S. (2009). *Play: How It Shapes the Brain, Opens the Imagination, and Invigorates the Soul*. New York, NY: Penguin Books.

Bruner, J. (1978). The role of dialogue in language acquisition. In A. Sinclair, R. J. Jarvelle, and W. J. M. Levelt (Eds.), *The Child's Concept of Language*. New York, NY: Springer-Verlag.

Bruner, J. S. (1983). *Child's Talk: Learning to Use Language*. New York, NY: W.W. Norton.

Bruner, J. S. (1996). *The Culture of Education*. Cambridge, MA: Harvard University Press.

Buell, J. (2004). *Closing the Book on Homework: Enhancing Public Education and Freeing Family Time*. Philadelphia, PA: Temple University Press.

Burack, J. A., Flanagan, T., Peled, T., Sutton, H. M., Zygmuntowicz, C. & Manly, J. T. (2006). Social perspective-taking skills in maltreated children and adolescents. *Developmental Psychology, 42*(2), 207–217.

Burts, D. C., Hart, C. H., Charlesworth, R. & Kirk, L. (1990). A comparison of frequencies of stress behaviours observed in kindergarten children in classrooms with developmentally appropriate versus developmentally inappropriate practices. *Early Childhood Research Quarterly, 5*(3), 407–423.

Bush, N. R., Lengua, L. J. & Colder, C. R. (2010). Temperament as a moderator of the relation between neighbourhood and children's adjustment. *Journal of Applied Psychology, 31*(5), 351–361.

Byrnes, J. P. (2007). Some ways in which neuroscientific research can be relevant to education. In D. Coch, K. W. Fisher & G. Dawson (Eds.), *Human Behavior, Learning and the Developing Brain: Typical Development* (pp. 30–49). New York, NY: Guilford Press.

Caine, G. & Caine, R. N. (2001). *The Brain, Education and the Competitive Edge*. Lanham, MD: Scarecrow Press.

Cajochen, C., Frey, S., Anders, D., Spati, J., Bues, M., Pross, A., Mager, R., Wirz-Justice, A. & Stefani, O. (2011). Evening exposure to a light-emitting diodes (LED)—backlit computer screen affects circadian physiology and cognitive performance. *Journal of Applied Physiology, 110*(5), 1432–1438.

Campbell, S. R. (2012). Educational neuroscience: Motivations, methodology, and implications. *Educational Philosophy and Theory, 43*(1), 7–16.

Campos, J. J., Kermoian, R. & Zumbahlen, M. R. (1992). Socioemotional transformation in the family system following infant crawling onset. In N. Eisenberg & R. A. Fabes (Eds.), *New Directions For Child Development* (Vol. 55, pp. 25–40). San Francisco, CA: Jossey-Bass.

Cardinal, R. N., Parkinson, J. A., Hall, J. & Everitt, B. J. (2002). Emotion and motivation: The role of the amygdala, ventral striatum and prefrontal cortex. *Neuroscience and Biobehavioral Reviews, 26*(3), 321–352.

Carew, T. J. & Magsamen, S. H. (2010). Neuroscience and education: An ideal partnership for producing evidence-based solutions to guide 21st century learning, *Neuron, 67*(5), 685–688.

Carl, J. (2009). Industrialisation and public education: Social cohesion and social stratification. In R. Cowen & A. M. Kazamias (Eds.), *International Handbook of Comparative Education* (Vol. 22, pp. 503–518). London, UK: Springer.

Carney, R. N. & Levin, J. R. (2000). Mnemonic instruction, with a focus on transfer. *Journal of Educational Psychology, 92*(4), 783–790.

Carpenter, L. (2010). Understanding autism spectrum disorder. In M. Hyde, L. Carpenter & R. Conway, *Diversity and Inclusion in Australian Schools* (pp. 267–279). Melbourne, Australia: Oxford University Press.

Carpenter, L. & Thomson, R. (2010). Supporting behaviour change. In M. Hyde, L. Carpenter & R. Conway, *Diversity and Inclusion in Australian Schools* (pp. 37–153). Melbourne, Australia: Oxford.

Carskadon, M. A. (2002). *Adolescent Sleep Patterns: Biological, Social, and Psychological Influences*. Cambridge, UK: Cambridge University Press.

Carskadon, M. A., Acebo, C. & Jenni, O. G. (2004). Regulation of adolescent sleep: Implications for behaviour. *Annals of the New York Academy of Sciences, 1021*, 276–291.

Carter, R. (2000). *Mapping the Mind*. London, UK: Orion Books Ltd.

Carter, R. (2009). *The Human Brain Book: An Illustrated Guide to Its Structure, Function and Disorders*. New York, NY: D.K. Publishing.

Casey, B. J. & Caudle, K. (2013). The teenage brain: Self-control. *Current Directions in Psychological Science*, *22*(2), 82–87.

Casey, B. J., Getz, S. & Galvan, A. (2008). The adolescent brain. *Developmental Review*, *28*(1), 62–77.

Casey, B. J., Jones, R. M. & Somerville, L. H. (2011). Braking and accelerating of the adolescent brain. *Journal of Research on Adolescence*, *21*(1), 21–33.

Casey, B. J., Somerville, L. H., Gotlib, I. H., Ayduk, O., Franklin, N. T., Askren, M. K., Jonides, J., Berman, M. G., Wilson, N. L., Teslovich, T., Glover, G., Zayas, V., Mischel, W. & Shoda, Y. (2011). Behavioral and neural correlates of delay of gratification 40 years later. *Proceedings of the National Academy of Sciences*, *108*(36), 14998–15003.

Castelli, D. M., Hillman, C. H., Buck, S. M. & Erwin, H. E. (2007). Physical fitness and academic achievement in third and fifth grade students. *Journal of Sport & Exercise Psychology*, *29*(2), 239–252.

Cattell, R. B. (1987). *Intelligence: Its Structure, Growth, and Action*. Amsterdam: Elsevier.

Catterall, J. S., Chapleau, R. & Iwanaga, J. (1999). Involvement in the arts and human development: General involvement and intensive involvement in music and theater arts. In E. B. Fiske (Ed.), *Champions of Change: The Impact of the Arts on Learning: The Arts Education Partnership*. Retrieved from Arts Edge: The Kennedy Center: http://www.artsedge.kennedy-center.org/champions/

Catts, H. W. & Kamhi, A. G. (2005). *Language and Reading Disabilities*. Boston, MA: Allyn & Bacon.

Cervone, D. (2015). *Psychology: The Science of Person, Mind and Brain*. New York, NY: Worth Publishers.

Chabris, C. & Simons, D. (2010). *The Invisible Gorilla and Other Ways Our Intuitions Deceive Us*. New York, NY: Crown Publishers.

Chaddock-Heyman, L., Hillman, C. H., Cohen, N. J. & Kramer, A. F. (2014). The importance of physical activity and aerobic fitness for cognitive control and memory in children. In C. H. Hillman (Ed.), *The Relation of Childhood Physical Activity to Brain Health, Cognition, and Scholastic Achievement—Monographs of the Society for Research in Child Development* (pp. 25–50). Boston, MA: Wiley.

Chambers, R. A., Taylor, J. R. & Potenza, M. N. (2003). Developmental neurocircuitry of motivation in adolescence: A critical period of addiction vulnerability. *American Journal of Psychiatry*, *160*(6), 1041–1052.

Chess, S. & Thomas, A. (1977). Temperamental individuality from childhood to adolescence. *Journal of the American Academy of Child Psychiatry*, *16*(2), 218–226.

Chess, S. & Thomas, A. (2000). Interactions between offspring and parents in development. In B. Tizard & V. P. Varma (Eds.), *Vulnerability and Resilience in Human Development: A Fetschrift for Ann and Alan Clarke* (pp. 72–87). London, UK: Jessica Kingsley Publishers.

Chomsky, N. (1957). *Syntactic Structures*. The Hague, Netherlands: Mouton Publishing.

Chomsky, N. (1965). *Aspects of the Theory of Syntax*. Cambridge, MA: MIT Press.

Chomsky, N. (1971). *Chomsky: Selected Readings*. J. P. B. Allen & P. Van Buren (Eds.). New York, NY: Oxford University Press.

Chugani, D. C., Muzik, O., Behen, M., Rothermel, R., Janisse, J. J., Lee, J. & Chugani, H. T. (1999). Developmental changes in brain serotonin synthesis capacity in autistic and nonautistic children. *Annals of Neurology*, *45*(3), 287–295.

Chugani, H. T. (1994). Development of regional brain glucose metabolism in relation to behavior and plasticity. In G. Dawson & K. W. Fischer (Eds.), *Human Behavior and the Developing Brain* (pp. 153–175). New York, NY: Guilford Publications.

Chugani, H. T. (1996). Neuroimaging of developmental non-linearity and developmental pathologies. In R. W. Thatcher, G. R. Lyon & J. Rumsey (Eds), *Developmental Neuroimaging: Mapping the Development of Brain and Behavior* (pp. 187–195). San Diego, CA: Academic Press.

Chugani, H. T., Behen, M. E., Muzik, O., Juhasz, C., Nagy, F. & Chugani, D. C. (2001). Local brain functional activity following early deprivation: A study of post-institutionalised Romanian orphans. *NeuroImage*, *14*(6), 1290–1301.

Chugani, H. T., Phelps, M. E. & Mazziotta, J. C. (1987). Positron emission tomography study of human brain functional development. *Annals of Neurology*, *22*, 487–497.

Chugani, H. T., Phelps, M. E. & Mazziotta, J. C. (1989). Metabolic assessment of functional maturation and neuronal plasticity in the human brain. In C. von Euler, C. Forssberg & H. Lagercrantz (Eds.), *Neurobiology of Early Infant Behaviour*, Wenner-Gren International Symposium Series (Vol. 55, pp. 323–330). New York, NY: Stockton Press.

Cirulli, F., Berry, A. & Alleva, E. (2003). Early disruption of the mother–infant relationship: Effects on brain plasticity and implications for psychopathology. *Neuroscience and Biobehavioral Reviews, 27*(1), 73–82.

Clarke-Stewart, K. A. (1998). Historical shifts and underlying themes in ideas about rearing young children in the United States: Where have we been? Where are we going? *Early Development and Parenting, 7*(2), 101–117.

Claxton, G. (1999). *Wise Up: The Challenge of Lifelong Learning.* New York, NY: Bloomsbury Publishing.

Coe, D. P., Pivarnik, J. M., Womack, C. J., Reeves, M. J. & Malina, R. M. (2006). Effect of physical education and activity levels on academic achievement in children. *Medicine & Science in Sports & Exercise, 38*(8), 1515–1519.

Cohen, G. L. & Steele, C. M. (2002). *A barrier of mistrust: How negative stereotypes affect cross-race mentoring.* In J. Aronson (Ed.), *Improving Academic Achievement: Impact of Psychological Factors on Education* (pp. 305–331). San Diego, CA: Academic Press.

Cohen, S. & Pressman, S. D. (2006). Positive affect and health. *Current Directions in Psychological Science, 15*(3), 122–125.

Cole, M., Yarkoni, T., Repovš, G., Anticevic, A. & Braver, T. (2012). Global connectivity of prefrontal cortex predicts cognitive control and intelligence. *Journal of Neuroscience, 32*(26), 8988–8999.

Cole, P. M., Martin, S. E. & Dennis, T. A. (2004). Emotion regulation as a scientific construct: Methodological challenges and directions for child development research. *Child Development, 75*(2), 317–333.

Colley, R. C., Garriguet, D., Janssen, I., Craig, C. L., Clarke, J. & Tremblay, M. S. (2011). Physical activity of Canadian children and youth: Accelerometer results from the 2007 to 2009 Canadian Health Measures Survey. *Health Reports, 22*(1), 15–23.

Collins, C., Kenway, J. & McLeod, J. (2000). *Factors Influencing the Educational Performance of Males and Females in School and Their Initial Destinations after Leaving School.* Canberra, Australia: Department of Education, Training and Youth Affairs.

Colom, R., Haier, K., Head, J. Álvarez-Linera, M. Á., Quiroga, P. C., et al. (2009). Gray matter correlates of fluid, crystallized, and spatial intelligence: Testing the P-FIT model. *Intelligence, 37*, 124–135.

Colwell, R. (1999). The arts. In G. Calweti (Ed.), *Handbook on Research on Improving Student Achievement* (pp. 22–49). Arlington, VA: Education Service.

Commonwealth Scientific and Industrial Research Organisation (CSIRO) (2007). *Australian National Children's Nutrition and Physical Activity Survey.* Canberra, Australia: Commonwealth of Australia Departments of Health and Ageing and Agriculture Fisheries and Forestry, Australian Food and Grocery Council.

Connell, R. (2009). *Gender: In World Perspective* (2nd ed.). Cambridge, UK: Polity.

Connell, R. W. (2000). *The Men and the Boys.* Sydney, Australia: Allen & Unwin.

Connell, R. W. (2005). Change among the gatekeepers: Men, masculinities, and gender equity in the global arena. *Signs: Journal of Women in Culture and Society, 30*(3), 1801–1825.

Connolly, P. (2004). *Boys and Schooling in the Early Years.* London, UK: Routledge Falmer.

Connolly, P. (2006). The effects of social class and ethnicity on gender differences in GCSE attainment: A secondary analysis of the youth cohort study of England and Wales 1997–2001. *British Educational Research Journal, 32*(1), 3–21.

Connolly, P. (2009). *Developing Programmes to Promote Ethnic Diversity in Early Childhood: Lessons from Northern Ireland.* The Hague, Netherlands: Bernard van Leer Foundation.

Cook, S. C. & Wellman, C. L. (2004). Chronic stress alters dendritic morphology in rat medial prefrontal cortex. *Journal of Neurobiology, 60*(2), 236–248.

Cooke, S. F. & Bliss, T. V. P. (2006). Plasticity in the human central nervous system. *Brain, 129*(7), 1659–1673.

Coon, D. & Mitterer, J. O. (2010). *Introduction to Psychology* (12th ed.). Belmont, CA: Wadsworth, Cengage Learning.

Corsaro, W. (1997). *The Sociology of Childhood.* Thousand Oaks, CA: Pine Forge Press.

Cotman, C. W., Berchtold, N. C. & Christie, L. (2007). Exercise builds brain health: Key roles of growth factor cascades and inflammation. *Trends in Neurosciences, 30*(9), 464–471.

Cowan, N. (1998). Visual and auditory working memory capacity. *Trends in Cognitive Sciences, 2*(3), 77–78.

Cowan, N. (2001) The magical number 4 in short-term memory: A reconsideration of mental storage capacity. *Behavioral and Brain Sciences, 24*(1), 87–185.

Cowan, N. (2008). What are the differences between long-term, short-term and working memory? *Progress in Brain Research, 169*, 323–338.

Cowan, N. & Morey, C. C. (2006). Visual working memory depends on attentional filtering. *Trends in Cognitive Sciences, 10*(4), 139–141.

Cozolino, L. (2013). *The Social Neuroscience of Education: Optimizing Attachment and Learning in the Classroom.* New York, NY: W.W. Norton.

Craft, A., Gardner, H. & Claxton, G. (Eds.) (2008). *Creativity, Wisdom, and Trusteeship.* Thousand Oaks, CA: Corwin Press.

Csikszentmihalyi, M. (1975). *Beyond Boredom and Anxiety.* San Francisco, CA: Jossey Bass.

Csikszentmihalyi, M. (1982). Toward a psychology of optimal experience. In L. Wheeler (Ed.), *Review of Personality and Social Psychology* (pp. 13–36). Beverly Hills, CA: Sage.

Csikszentmihalyi, M. (1988). The flow experience and its significance for human psychology. In M. Csikszentmihalyi & I. Csikszentmihalyi (Eds.), *Optimal Experience: Psychological Studies of Flow in Consciousness* (pp. 15–35). Cambridge, UK: Cambridge University Press.

Csikszentmihalyi, M. (1990). *Flow: The Psychology of Optimal Experience.* New York, NY: Harper & Row.

Csikszentmihalyi, M. & LeFevre, J. (1989). Optimal experience in work and leisure. *Journal of Personality and Social Psychology, 56*(5), 815–822.

Cunningham, A. & Stanovich, K. (1997). Early reading acquisition and its relation to reading experience and ability 10 years later. *Developmental Psychology, 33,* 934–945.

Currie, D. H., Kelly, D. M. & Pomerantz, S. (2007). 'The power to squash people': understanding girls' relational aggression. *British Journal of Sociology of Education, 28*(1), 23–37.

Curtiss, S. (1977). *Genie: A Psycholinguistic Study of a Modern-Day 'Wild Child'.* New York, NY: Academic Press.

Cushner, K., McClelland, A. & Safford, P. (2000). *Human Diversity in Education: An Integrative Approach* (3rd ed.). Boston, MA: McGraw-Hill.

Dahl, R. E. (2001). Affect regulation, brain development, and behavioral/emotional health in adolescence. *CNS Spectrums, 6*(1), 60–72.

Dahl, R. E. (2003). Beyond raging hormones: The tinderbox in the teenage brain. *Cerebrum, 5*(3), 7–22.

Damasio, A. (1999). *The Feeling of What Happens: Body and Emotion in the Making of Consciousness.* San Diego, CA: Harcourt.

Damasio, A. (2004). Emotions and feelings: A neurobiological perspective. In A. S. R. Manstead, N. Frijda & A. Fischer (Eds.), *Feelings and Emotions: The Amsterdam Symposium (Studies in Emotion and Social Interaction)* (pp. 49–57). Cambridge, UK: Cambridge University Press.

Dannar, P. R. (2013). Millennials: What they offer our organizations and how leaders can make sure they deliver. *The Journal of Values-Based Leadership, 6*(1), Article 3.

Darling-Hammond, L. (2006). *Powerful Teacher Education.* San Francisco, CA: John Wiley & Sons.

Darling-Hammond, L., Banks, J., Zumwalt, K., Gomez, L., Sherin, M. G., Griesdorn, J. & Finn, L. E. (2005). Educational goals and purposes: Developing a curricular vision for teaching. In L. Darling-Hammond & J. Bransford, (Eds.), *Preparing Teachers for a Changing World: What Teachers Should Learn and Be Able to Do* (pp. 169–200). San Francisco, CA: John Wiley & Sons.

Davidson, R. J. (2004). What does the prefrontal cortex 'do' in affect? Perspectives on frontal EEG asymmetry research. *Biological Psychology, 67*(1–2), 219–233.

Davidson, R. J. (2012). *The Emotional Life of Your Brain: How Its Unique Patterns Affect the Way You Think, Feel and Live—and How You Can Change Them.* New York, NY: Plume.

Davis, C. L., Tomprowski, P. D., McDowell, J. E., Austin, B. P., Miller, P. H., Yanasak, N. E., Allison, J. D. & Naglieri, J. A. (2011). Exercise improves executive function and achievement and alters brain activation in overweight children: A randomised, controlled trial. *Health Psychology, 30*(1), 91–98.

Davis, E. L., Levine, L. J., Lench, H. C. & Quas, J. A. (2010). Metacognitive emotion regulation: Children's awareness that changing thoughts and goals can alleviate negative emotions. *Emotion, 10*(4), 498–510.

Davis, N., Gross, J. & Hayne, H. (2008). Defining the boundary of childhood amnesia. *Memory, 16*(5), 465–474.

Daw, N. C. & Shohamy, D. (2008). The cognitive neuroscience of motivation and learning. *Social Cognition, 26*(5), 593–620.

Decety, J. & Michalska, K. J. (2010). Neurodevelopmental changes in the circuits underlying empathy and sympathy from childhood to adulthood. *Developmental Science, 13*(6), 886–899.

Deci, E. L., Koestner, R. & Ryan, R. M. (1999). A meta-analytic review of experiments examining the effects of extrinsic rewards on intrinsic motivation. *Psychological Bulletin, 125*(6), 627–668.

Deci, E. L., Koestner, R. & Ryan, R. M. (2001). Extrinsic rewards and intrinsic motivation in education: Reconsidered once again. *Review of Educational Research, 71*(1), 1–27.

Deci, E. L. & Ryan, R. M. (1985). *Intrinsic Motivation and Self-determination in Human Behavior*. New York, NY: Plenum Press.

Deci, E. L. & Ryan, R. M. (1987). The support of autonomy and the control of behaviour. *Journal of Personality and Social Psychology, 53*(6), 1024–1037.

Deci, E. L. & Ryan, R. M. (2000). The 'what' and 'why' of goal pursuits: Human needs and the self-determination of behavior. *Psychological Inquiry, 11*(4), 227–268.

Deci, E. L. & Ryan, R. M. (2002). The paradox of achievement: The harder you push, the worse it gets. In J. Aronson (Ed.), *Improving Academic Achievement: Impact of Psychological Factors on Education* (pp. 62–90). San Diego, CA: Academic Press.

del Campo, N., Fryer, T., Hong, Y., Smith, R., Brichard, L., et al. (2013). A positron emission tomography study of nigro-striatal dopaminergic mechanisms underlying attention: Implications for ADHD and its treatment. *Brain, 136*(Pt 11), 3252–70

Deoni, S. C. L., Mercure, E., Blasi, A., Gasston, D., Thomson, A., Johnson, M., Williams, S. C. R. & Murphy, D. G. M. (2011). Mapping infant brain myelination with magnetic resonance imaging. *Journal of Neuroscience, 31*(2), 784–791.

Dewey, J. (1933). *How We Think*. Buffalo, NY: Prometheus Books.

Diamond, A. (2012). Activities and programs that improve children's executive functions. *Current Directions in Psychological Science, 21*(5), 335–341.

Diamond, M. & Hopson, J. (1999). *Magic Trees of the Mind: How to Nurture Your Child's Intelligence, Creativity, and Healthy Emotions from Birth through Adolescence*. New York, NY: Penguin Putnam.

Díaz-Rico, L. T. & Weed, K. Z. (2010). *The Cross-cultural, Language, and Academic Development Handbook* (4th ed.). Boston, MA: Allyn & Bacon.

Dickerson, S. S. & Kemeny, M. E. (2004). Acute stressors and cortisol responses: A theoretical integration and synthesis of laboratory research. *Psychological Bulletin, 130*(3), 355–391.

Dickinson, D. & Tabors, P. (2001). *Beginning Literacy with Language*. Baltimore, MD: Paul Brookes Publishing.

Domjan, M. P. (2014). *The Principles of Learning and Behavior*, (7th ed.). Stamford, CT: Cengage Learning.

Dondi, M., Simion, F. & Caltran, G. (1999). Can newborns discriminate between their own cry and the cry of another newborn infant? *Developmental Psychology, 35*(2), 418–426.

Donovan, J. J. & Radosevich, D. J. (1999). A meta-analytic review of the distribution of practice effect: Now you see it, now you don't. *Journal of Applied Psychology, 84*(5), 795–805.

Donovan, M. S., Bransford, J. D. & Pellegrino, J. W. (Eds.). (2000). *How People Learn: Brain, Mind, Experience and School*. Washington, DC: National Academy Press.

Doyle, T. & Zakrajsek, T. (2013). *The New Science of Learning: How to Learn in Harmony With Your Brain*. Sterling, VA: Stylus Publishing.

Driver, R., Asoko, H., Leach, J., Mortimer, E. & Scott, P. (1994). Constructing scientific knowledge in the classroom. *Educational Researcher, 23*(7), 5–12.

Duchesne, S., McMaugh, A., Bochner, S. & Krause, K. (2013). *Educational Psychology for Learning and Teaching* (4th ed.). Melbourne, Australia: Cengage Learning Australia.

Dudai, Y. & Morris, R. G. M. (2013). Memorable trends. *Neuron, 80*(3), 742–750.

Dulfer, N., Polesel, J. & Rice, S. (2012). *The Experience of Education: The Impacts of High Stakes Testing on School Students and Their Families*. Sydney, Australia: Whitlam Institute.

Dweck, C. S. (1986). Motivational processes affecting learning. *American Psychologist, 41*(10), 1040–1048.

Ebbinghaus, H. (2011). *Memory: A Contribution to Experimental Psychology*. Charleston, SC: Nabu Press. (Originally published 1885. New York, NY: Teachers College, Columbia University.)

Eccles J. S., Adler, T. F., Futterman, R., Goff, S. B., Kaczala, C. M., Meece, J. L. & Midgley, C. (1983). Expectancies, values, and academic behaviors. In J. T. Spence (Ed.), *Achievement and Achievement Motivation* (pp. 75–146). San Francisco, CA: W.H. Freeman.

Eccles, J. S. & Wigfield, A. (2002). Motivational beliefs, values and goals. *Annual Review of Psychology, 53*, 109–32.

Edwards, B. (2005). Does it take a village? An investigation of neighbourhood effects on Australian children's development. *Family Matters, 72*, 36–43.

Eisenberg, N., Eggum, N. D. & Edwards, A. (2010). Empathy-related responding and moral development. In W. F. Arsenio & E. A. Lemerise (Eds.), *Emotions, Aggression and Morality in Children: Bridging Development and Psychopathology* (pp. 115–135). Washington, DC: American Psychological Association.

Eisenberg, N. & Spinrad, T. L. (2004). Emotion-related regulation: Sharpening the definition. *Child Development, 75*(2), 334–339.

Eisenberg, N., Valiente, C. & Eggum, N. D. (2010). Self-regulation and school readiness. *Early Education and Development, 21*(5), 681–698.

Ekman, P. (1970). Universal facial expressions of emotions. *California Mental Health Research Digest*, *8*(4), 151–158.

Ekman, P. (1999). Basic emotions. In T. Dalgleish & M. Power (Eds.), *Handbook of Cognition and Emotion* (pp. 45–60). New York, NY: John Wiley & Sons.

Ekman, P. & Friesen, W. V. (1971). Constants across cultures in the face and emotion. *Journal of Personality and Social Psychology*, *17*(2), 124–129.

Eliot, L. (2000). *What's Going On in There? How the Brain and Mind Develop in the First Five Years of Life*. New York, NY: Bantam Books.

Elliot, A. J. (1997). Integrating 'classic' and 'contemporary' approaches to achievement motivation. In M. L. Maehr & P. R. Pintrich (Eds.), *Advances in Motivation and Achievement* (Vol. 10, pp. 143–179). Greenwich, CT: JAI Press.

Elliot, A. J. & McGregor, H. A. (2001). A 2 x 2 achievement goal framework. *Journal of Personality and Social Psychology*, *80*(3), 501–519.

Elkind, D. (1986). Formal education and early childhood education: An essential difference. *Phi Delta Kappan*, *67*(9), 631–636.

Epstein, D. & Johnson, R. (1994). On the straight and narrow. In D. Epstein (Ed.), *Challenging Lesbian and Gay Inequalities in Education*. Buckingham, UK: Open University Press.

Erk, S., Kiefer, M., Grothe, J., Wunderlich, A. P., Spitzer, M. & Walter, H. (2003). Emotional context modulates subsequent memory effect. *NeuroImage*, *18*(2), 439–447.

Erlauer, L. (2003). *The Brain-Compatible Classroom: Using What We Know about Learning to Improve Teaching*. Alexandria, VA: Association for Supervision and Curriculum Development.

Esch, T. & Stefano, G. B. (2006). The neurobiology of pleasure, reward processes, addiction and their health implications. *Neuroendocrinology Letters*, *25*(4), 235–251.

European Commission (2010). *Gender Differences in Educational Outcomes*. Brussels, Belgium: Author.

Evans, G. W. & Wachs, T. D. (Eds.). (2010). *Chaos and Its Influence on Children's Development: An Ecological Perspective*. Washington, DC: The American Psychological Association.

Eveleth, P. B. & Tanner, J. M. (1991). *Worldwide Variation in Human Growth* (2nd ed.). Cambridge, UK: Cambridge University Press.

Ewing, R. (2010). *The Arts and Australian Education: Realising Potential*. Australian Education Review no. 58. Melbourne, Australia: ACER Press.

Faull, J. & McLean-Oliver, J. (2010). *Amazing Minds: The Science of Nurturing Your Child's Developing Mind with Games, Activities and More*. New York, NY: Berkley Books.

Feinberg, W. (2012). I. Schooling, inequality, and commitment to the public good. *Review of Research in Education*, *36*, 1–22.

Felitti, V. J., Anda, R. F., Nordenberg, D., Williamson, D. F., Spitz, A. M., Edwards, V., Koss, M. P. & Marks, J. S. (1998). Relationship of childhood abuse and household dysfunction to many of the leading causes of death in adults: The adverse childhood experiences (ACE) study. *American Journal of Preventative Medicine*, *14*(4), 245–258.

Fernald, A., Marchman, V. A. & Weisleder, A. (2013). SES differences in language processing skill and vocabulary are evident at 18 months. *Developmental Science*, *16*(2), 234–248.

Fifer, W. P. & Moon, C. M. (1995). The effects of fetal experience with sound. In J. P. Lecanuet, W. P. Fifer, N. A. Krasnegor & W. P. Smotherman (Eds.), *Fetal Development: A Psychobiological Perspective* (pp. 351–366). Hillsdale, NJ: Lawrence Erlbaum Associates.

Findlay, L. C., Girardi, A. & Coplan, R. J. (2006). Links between empathy, social behaviour and social understanding in early childhood. *Early Childhood Research Quarterly*, *21*(3), 347–359.

Fine, J. G., Semrud-Clikeman, M., Keith, T. Z., Stapleton, L. M. & Hynd, G. W. (2007). Reading and the corpus callosum: An MRI family study of volume and area. *Neuropsychology*, *21*, 235–241.

Fiske, E. (1999). *Champions of Change: The Impact of the Arts on Learning*. Retrieved from Arts Edge: The Kennedy Center: http://www.artsedge.kennedy-center.org/champions/.

Fiske, S. T. (2004). Mind the gap: In praise of informal sources of formal theory. *Personality and Social Psychology Review*, *8*(2), 132–137.

Florida, R. (2005). *The Flight of the Creative Class*. New York, NY: Harper Collins.

Florida, R. (2010). *The Great Reset: How New Ways of Living and Working Drive Post-crash Prosperity*. New York, NY: Harper Collins.

Flynn, J. R. (2000). The hidden history of IQ and special education: Can the problem be solved? *Psychology, Public Policy and Law*, *6*(1), 191–198.

Fougine, D. (2008). The relationship between attention and working memory. In N. B. Johnson (Ed.), *New Research on Short-Term Memory* (pp. 1–45). Hauppauge, NY: Nova Science Publishers.

Fox, N. A. & Calkins, S. D. (2003). The development of self-control of emotion: Intrinsic and extrinsic influences. *Motivation and Emotion, 27*(1), 7–26.

Frackowiak, R. S. J. (1994). Functional mapping of verbal memory and language. *Trends in Neuroscience, 17*(3), 109–115.

Francis, B. (2000). *Boys, Girls and Achievement*. London, UK: Routledge Falmer.

Francis, B. (2009). The role of the boffin as abject Other in gendered performances of school achievement. *Sociological Review, 57*(4), 645–669.

Francis, B. (2010). Re/theorising gender: Female masculinity and male femininity in the classroom? *Gender and Education, 22*(5), 477–490.

Francis, B. & Skelton, C. (2005). *Reassessing Gender and Achievement: Questioning Contemporary Key Debates*. London, UK: Routledge & Kegan Paul.

Fraser, N. (2007). Feminist politics in the age of recognition: A two dimensional approach to gender justice. *Studies in Social Justice, 1*(1), 23–35.

Fredericks, J. A., Blumenfeld, P. C. & Paris, A. H. (2004). School engagement: Potential of the concept, state of the evidence. *Review of Educational Research, 74*(1), 59–109.

Fredrickson, B. L. (2001). The role of positive emotions in positive psychology: The broaden-and-build theory of positive emotions. *American Psychologist, 56*(3), 218–226.

Fredrickson, B. L. & Joiner, T. (2002). Positive emotions trigger upward spirals toward emotional well-being. *Psychological Science, 13*(2), 172–175.

Freebody, P., Ludwig, C. & Gunn, S. (1995). *Everyday Literacy Practices in and out of Schools in Low Socio-economic Urban Communities*. Brisbane, Australia: Centre for Literacy Education Research, Griffith University.

Freebody, P., Maton, K. & Martin, J. (2008). Talk, text, and knowledge in cumulative, integrated learning: A response to 'intellectual challenge'. *Australian Journal of Language and Literacy, 3*(2), 188–201.

Fries, A. B. W. & Pollack, S. D. (2007). Emotion processing and the developing brain. In D. Coch, K. W. Fisher & G. Dawson (Eds.), *Human Behavior, Learning and the Developing Brain: Typical Development* (pp. 329–361). New York, NY: Guilford Press.

Fryer-Smith, S. (2002). *Aboriginal Cultural Awareness Benchbook for Western Australian Courts* (2nd ed.). Melbourne, Australia: Australian Institute of Judicial Administration.

Furlong, M. J. & Christenson, S. L. (2008). Engaging students at school and with learning: A relevant construct for all students. *Psychology in the Schools, 45*(5), 365–368.

Fuster, J. M. (2002). Frontal lobe and cognitive development. *Journal of Neurocytology, 31*(3), 373–385.

Gaab, N. & Schlaug, G. (2003). Musicians differ from nonmusicians in brain activation despite performance matching. *Annals of the New York Academy of Sciences, 999,* 385–388.

Gable, S. L., Reis, H. T. & Elliott, A. J. (2000). Behavioral activation and inhibition in everyday life. *Journal of Personality and Social Psychology, 78*(6), 1135–1149.

Gabrieli, J. (2009). Dyslexia: A new synergy between education and cognitive neuroscience. *Science, 325*(5938), 280–283.

Gallagher, J. M. & Coche, J. (1987). Hothousing: The clinical and educational concerns over pressuring young children. *Early Childhood Research Quarterly, 2*(3), 203–210.

Galvan, A. (2010). Adolescent development of the reward system. *Frontiers in Neuroscience, 4*(6), 1–9.

Galvan, A. (2012). Risky behaviour in adolescents: The role of the developing brain. In V. F. Reyna, S. B. Chapman, M. R. Dougherty & J. Confrey (Eds.), *The Adolescent Brain: Learning, Reasoning and Decision Making* (pp. 267–289). Washington, DC: American Psychological Association.

Gardiner, M. F., Fox, A., Knowles, F. & Jeffrey, D. (1996). Learning improved by the arts. *Nature, 381*(6580), 284.

Gardner, H. (1983). *Frames of Mind: The Theory of Multiple Intelligences*. New York, NY: Basic Books.

Gardner, H. (2011). *The Unschooled Mind: How Children Think and How Schools Should Teach*. New York, NY: Basic Books.

Gardner, H. (2015). *The Components of MI*. Official Authoritative Site of Multiple Intelligences. Retrieved from http://multipleintelligencesoasis. org/about/the-components-of-mi/.

Garrett, B. (2009). *Brain and Behaviour* (2nd ed.). Thousand Oaks, CA: Sage Publications.

Gaser, G. & Schlaug, G. (2003). Gray matter differences between musicians and nonmusicians. *Annals of the New York Academy of Sciences, 999,* 514–517.

Gathercole, S. E. (1999). Cognitive approaches to the development of short-term memory. *Trends in Cognitive Sciences, 3*(11), 410–419.

Gathercole, S. E. & Baddeley, A. D. (1993). Phonological working memory: A critical building block for reading development and vocabulary acquisition? *European Journal of the Psychology of Education, 8*(3), 259–272.

Gay, G. (2000). *Culturally Responsive Teaching: Theory, Research, and Practice*. New York, NY: Teachers College Press.

Gazzaniga, M. (1998). *The Mind's Past*. Berkeley, CA: University of California Press.

Gazzaniga, M., Heatherton, T. & Halpern, D. (2010). *Psychological Science* (3rd ed.). New York, NY: W.W. Norton & Company.

Gazzaniga, M. S. (1989). Organization of the human brain. *Science, 245*(4921), 947–952.

Gazzaniga, M. S. (2008). Arts and cognition: Findings hint at relationships. In C. Ashbury & B. Rich (Eds.), *Learning, Arts and the Brain* (pp. v–viii). New York, NY: Dana Press.

Gazzaniga, M. S. & Mangun, G. R. (2014). *Cognitive Neuroscience* (4th ed.). Boston, MA: MIT Press.

Geake, J. G. (2009). *The Brain at School: Educational Neuroscience in the Classroom*. Berkshire, UK: Open University Press.

Gelbard-Sagiv, H., Mukamel, R., Harel, M., Malach, R. & Fried, I. (2008). Internally generated reactivation of single neurons in human hippocampus during free recall. *Science, 322*(5898), 96–101.

Gentile, D. A. (2014). Why don't media violence effects look the same on everyone?: Developmental approaches to understanding media effects. In D. A. Gentile (Ed.), *Media Violence and Children: A Complete Guide for Parents and Professionals* (2nd ed.), (pp. 44–69). Santa Barbara, CA: Praeger.

Gervais, J. (2009). Environmental and genetic influences on early attachment. *Child and Adolescent Psychiatry and Mental Health, 3*(25), 1–12.

Gibb, B. N. (2012). *The Rough Guide to the Brain: Get to Know Your Grey Matter* (2nd ed.). London, UK: Rough Guides Ltd.

Giedd, J. (2004). Structural magnetic resonance imaging of the adolescent brain. *Annals of the New York Academy of Sciences, 1021*, 77–85.

Giedd, J. N., Blumenthal, J., Jeffries, N. O., Castellanos, F. X., Liu, H., Zijdenbos, A., Paus, T., Evans, C. & Rapoport, J. L. (1999). Brain development during childhood and adolescence: A longitudinal MRI study. *Nature Neuroscience, 2*(10), 861–863.

Gilbert, R. & Gilbert, P. (1998). *Masculinity Goes to School*. Sydney, Australia: Allen & Unwin.

Gill, B. P. & Schlossman, S. L. (2004). Villain or saviour? The American discourse on homework, 1850–2003. *Theory into Practice, 43*(3), 174–181.

Gladwell, M. (2008). *Outliers: The Story of Success*. New York, NY: Little, Brown.

Gluckman, P. D. & Hanson, M. A. (2004). Living with the past: Evolution, development and patterns of disease. *Science, 305*(5691), 1733–1736.

Goldberg, E. (2001). *The Executive Brain: Frontal Lobes and the Civilized Mind*. Oxford, UK: Oxford University Press.

Goldman-Rakic, P. S. (1993). Working memory and the mind. *In Scientific American—Mind and Brain: Readings from Scientific American* (pp. 67–77). New York, NY: W.H. Freeman.

Goldman-Rakic, P. S. (1996). Regional and cellular fractionation of working memory. *Proceedings of the National Academy of Sciences, 93*, 13473–13480.

Goleman, D. (1995). *Emotional Intelligence: Why It Can Matter More than IQ*. New York, NY: Bantam Books.

Goleman, D. (2006). *Social Intelligence: The New Science of Human Relationships*. London, UK: Random House.

Gopnik, A., Meltzoff, A. N. & Kuhl, P. K. (1999). *The Scientist in the Crib: What Early Learning Tells Us about the Mind*. New York, NY: Harper Collins Publishers.

Goswami, U. (2004). Annual review: Neuroscience and education. *British Journal of Educational Psychology, 74*, 1–14.

Gottfredson, L. (2003). Dissecting practical intelligence theory: Its claims and its evidence. *Intelligence, 31*, 343–397.

Grafton, S. T. (2010). What can dance teach us about learning? In D. Gordon (Ed.), *Cerebrum: Emerging Ideas in Brain Science* (pp. 23–33). New York, NY: Dana Press.

Greenberg, M. E., Xu, B., Lu, B. & Hempstead, B. L. (2009). New insights in the biology of BDNF synthesis and release: Implications in CNS function. *Journal of Neuroscience, 29*(41), 12764–12767.

Greenough, W. T. & Black, J. E. (1992). Induction of brain structure by experience substrates for cognitive development. In M. R. Gunnar & C. A. Nelson (Eds.), *Developmental Behavioral Neuroscience: The Minnesota Symposia on Child Psychology* (Vol. 24, pp. 155–200). Mahwah, NJ: Lawrence Erlbaum.

Greenough, W. T., Black, J. E. & Wallace, C. S. (1987). Experience and brain development. *Child Development, 58*(3), 539–559.

Greenwood, C. R. (1991). A longitudinal analysis of time to learn, engagement and academic achievement in urban versus suburban schools. *Exceptional Children, 57*, 521–535.

Grigorenko, E. L., Geissler, P. W., Prince, R., Okatcha, F., Nokes, C., Kenny, D. A., Bundy, D. A. & Sternberg, R. J. (2001). The organization of Luo conceptions of intelligence: A study of implicit theories in a Kenyan village. *International Journal of Behavioural Development*, *25*(4), 367–378.

Grissom, J. B. (2005). Physical fitness and academic achievement. *Journal of Exercise Physiology*, *8*(1), 11–25.

Guiney, H. & Machado, L. (2013). Benefits of regular aerobic exercise for executive functioning in healthy populations. *Psychonomic Bulletin & Review*, *20*(1), 73–86.

Gunnar, M. R. & Donzella, B. (2002). Social regulation of the cortisol levels in early human development. *Psychoneuroendocrinology*, *27*(1–2), 199–220.

Hadwin J., Howlin, P. & Baron-Cohen, S. (2008). *Teaching Children with Autism to Mindread: A Practical Guide for Teachers and Parents*. New York, NY: Wiley.

Haier, R. & Jung, R. (2008). Brain imaging studies of intelligence and creativity—what is the picture for education? *Roeper Review* (special issue on giftedness and neuroscience), *30*(3), 171–180.

Haier, R., Jung, R., Yeo, R., Head, K. & Alkire, M. (2005). The neuroanatomy of general intelligence: Sex matters. *NeuroImage*, *25*(1), 320–327.

Haier, R. J. & Jung, R. E. (2007). Beautiful minds (i. e. brains) and the neural basis of intelligence. *Behavioral and Brain Sciences*, *30*, 174–178.

Halberstam, J. (1998). *Female Masculinity*. Durham, NC: Duke University Press.

Hall, G. S. (1904). *Adolescence: Its Psychology and Its Relations to Physiology, Anthropology, Sociology, Sex, Crime, Religion, and Education*. New York, NY: Appleton.

Halpern, D. F. (2009). *Sex Differences in Cognitive Abilities* (3rd ed.). Mahwah, NJ: Lawrence Erlbaum.

Hampton, A. N. & O'Doherty, J. P. (2007). Decoding the neural substrates of reward-related decision making with functional MRI. *Proceedings of the National Academy of Sciences*, *104*(4), 1377–1382.

Han, S. & Northoff, G. (2008). Culture-sensitive neural substrates of human cognition: A transcultural neuroimaging approach. *Nature Reviews Neuroscience*, *9*, 646–654.

Han, S., Northoff, G., Vogeley, K., Wexler, B. E., Kitayama, S. & Varnum, M. E. W., (2013). A cultural neuroscience approach to the biosocial nature of the human brain. *Annual Review of Psychology*, *64*, 335–359.

Hancock, P. A. & Ganey, H. C. N. (2003). From the inverted-U to the extended-U: The evolution of a law of psychology. *Journal of Human Performance in Extreme Environments*, *7*(1), 5–14.

Hanoch, Y. & Vitouch, O. (2004). Information, emotional arousal and the ecological reframing of the Yerkes–Dodson Law. *Theory and Psychology*, *14*(4), 427–452.

Hansen, M., Janssen, I., Schiff, A., Zee, P. C. & Dubocovich, M. L. (2005). The impact of school daily schedule on adolescent sleep. *Pediatrics*, *115*(6), 1555–1561.

Hanushek, E. (2005). The economics of school quality. *German Economic Review*, *6*(3), 269–286.

Harackiewicz, J. M., Barron, K. E., Pintrich, P. R., Elliot, A. J. & Thrash, T. M. (2002). Revision of achievement goal theory: Necessary and illuminating. *Journal of Educational Psychology*, *94*(3), 638–645.

Harmon-Jones, E. (2011). Neural bases of approach and avoidance. In M. D. Alicke & C. Sedikides (Eds.), *The Handbook of Self-Enhancement and Self-Protection* (pp. 23–48). New York, NY: Guilford Press.

Hart, B. & Risley, T. (1995). *Meaningful Differences in Everyday Experiences of Young American Children*. Baltimore, MD: Paul H. Brookes Publishing.

Hart, L. A. (1983). *Human Brain and Human Learning*. New York, NY: Longman.

Hattie, J. (2009). *Visible Learning: A Synthesis of Over 800 Meta-analyses Relating to Achievement*. New York, NY: Routledge.

Hayden, B. Y., Nair, A. C., McCoy, A. N. & Platt, M. L. (2008). Posterior cingulate cortex mediates outcome-contingent allocation of behaviour. *Neuron*, *60*(1), 19–25.

Healy, J. (2004). *Your Child's Growing Mind: Brain Development and Learning from Birth to Adolescence*. New York, NY: Broadway Books.

Hebb, D. (1949). *The Organization of Behaviour*. New York, NY: John Wiley & Sons.

Herschkowitz, N. & Herschkowitz, E. C. (2004). *A Good Start to Life: Understanding Your Child's Brain and Behaviour from Birth to Age 6*. New York, NY: Dana Press.

Hidi, S. (2006). Interest: A unique motivational variable. *Educational Research Review*, *1*(2), 69–82.

Hillman, C. H. (2014). An introduction to the relation of physical activity to cognition and brain health and scholastic achievement. In C. H. Hillman (Ed.), *The Relation of Childhood Physical Activity to Brain Health, Cognition, and Scholastic Achievement*, Monographs of the Society for Research in Child Development (pp. 1–6). Boston, MA: Wiley.

Hillman, C. H., Buck, S. M. & Themanson, J. T. (2009). Physical activity and neurocognitive function across the lifespan. In W. Chodzko-Zajko, A. F. Kramer & L. Poon (Eds.), *Enhancing Cognitive Functioning and Brain Plasticity*, Aging, Exercise and Cognition Series (Vol. 3, pp. 85–110). Champaign, IL: Human Kinetics.

Hills, A. P., King, N. A. & Armstrong, T. P. (2007). The contribution of physical activity and sedentary behaviours to the growth and development of children and adolescents. *Sports Medicine*, *37*(6), 533–545.

Hirsh-Pasek, K. & Golinkoff, R. M. (2004). *Einstein Never Used Flashcards: How Our Children Really Learn—and Why They Need to Play More and Memorize Less*. New York, NY: Rodale.

Hockett, C. F. (1960). Logical considerations in the study of animal communication. In W. E. Lanyon & W. N. Tavolga, *Animals Sounds and Animal Communication* (pp. 392–430). Washington, DC: American Institute of Biological Sciences.

Hofstetter, S., Tavor, I., Moryosef, S. T. & Assaf, Y. (2013). Short-term learning induces white matter plasticity in the fornix. *Journal of Neuroscience*, *33*(31), 12844–12850.

Hogg, M. A., Abrams, D. & Martin, G. N. (2010). Social cognition and attitudes. In G. N. Martin, N. R. Carlson & W. Buskist (Eds.), *Psychology* (4th ed., pp. 646–677). Harlow: Pearson Education.

Holowka, S. & Petitto, L. A. (2002). Left hemisphere cerebral specialization for babies while babbling. *Science*, *297*(5586), 1515.

Hongwanishkul, D., Happaney, K. R., Lee, W. S. C. & Zelazo, P. D. (2005). Assessment of hot and cool executive function in young children: Age-related changes and individual differences. *Developmental Neuropsychology*, *28*(2), 617–644.

Hooper, J. & Teresi, D. (1986). *The 3 Pound Universe: Revolutionary Discoveries about the Brain—From Chemistry of the Mind to the New Frontiers of the Soul*. New York, NY: G. P. Putnam's Sons.

House of Representatives Standing Committee on Education and Training, Parliament of Australia (2002). *Boys: Getting It Right*. Report on the Inquiry into the Education of Boys. Canberra, Australia: Author.

Howard, A., Robinson, M., Smith, G., Ambrosini, G., Piek, J. & Oddy, W. (2011). ADHD is associated with a 'Western' dietary pattern in adolescents. *Journal of Attention Disorders*, *15*(5), 403–11.

Howard, P. J. (2006). *The Owner's Manual for the Brain: Everyday Applications from Mind–Brain Research* (3rd ed.). Austin, TX: Bard Press.

Howard-Jones, P. (2010). *Introducing Neuroeducational Research: Neuroscience, Education and the Brain from Contexts to Practice*. New York, NY: Routledge.

Howe, M. L. & Courage, M. L. (2004). Demystifying the beginnings of memory. *Developmental Review*, *24*(1), 1–5.

Hrdy, S. B. (1999). *Mother Nature: A History of Mothers, Infants and Natural Selection*. New York, NY: Pantheon Books.

Hubel, D. H. & Wiesel, T. N. (1970). The period of susceptibility to the physiological effects of unilateral eye closure in kittens. *Journal of Physiology*, *206*, 419–436.

Hullemon, C. S., Schrager, S. M., Bodmann, S. M. & Harackiewicz, J. M. (2010). A meta-analytic review of achievement goal measures: Different labels for the same constructs or different constructs with similar labels? *Psychological Bulletin*, *136*(3), 422–449.

Hupp, S. & Jewell, J. (2015). *Great Myths of Child Development*. Chichester, UK: John Wiley & Sons.

Huttenlocher, P. (2002). *Neural Plasticity: The Effects of Environment on the Development of the Cerebral Cortex*. Cambridge, MA: Harvard University Press.

Hyde, K. L., Lerch, J., Norton, A., Forgeard, N., Winner, E., Evans, C. & Schlaug, G. (2009). Musical training shapes structural brain development, *Journal of Neuroscience*, *29*(10), 3019–3025.

Hyde, M. (2014a). Creating inclusive schools. In M. Hyde, L. Carpenter & R. Conway, *Diversity, Inclusion and Engagement* (2nd ed., pp. 354–364). Melbourne, Australia: Oxford University Press.

Hyde, M. (2014b). Understanding diversity, inclusion and engagement. In M. Hyde, L. Carpenter & R. Conway, *Diversity, Inclusion and Engagement* (2nd ed., pp. 3–9). Melbourne, Australia: Oxford University Press.

Hyde, M., Carpenter, L. & Conway, R. (2014). Inclusive education: The way to the future. In M. Hyde, L. Carpenter & R. Conway, *Diversity, Inclusion and Engagement* (2nd ed., pp. 385–393). Melbourne, Australia: Oxford University Press.

Immordino-Yang, M. H. & Faeth, M. (2010). The role of emotion and skilled intuition in learning. In D. A. Sousa (Ed.), *Mind, Brain and Education* (pp. 69–83). Bloomington, IN: Solution Tree Press.

Inhelder, B. & Piaget, J. (1958). *The Growth of Logical Thinking from Childhood to Adolescence*. London, UK: Routledge & Kegan Paul.

Isenberg, J. (1987). Societal influences on children. *Childhood Education*, *63*(5), 341–342.

Izard, C. E. (2007). Basic emotions, natural kinds, emotion schemas, and a new paradigm. *Perspectives on Psychological Science*, *2*(3), 260–280.

Jackson, C. (2006). *'Lads' and 'Laddettes' in School: Gender and a Fear of Failure*. Maidenhead, UK: Open University Press.

Jakab, A., Schwartz, E., Kasprian, G., Gruber, G. M., Prayer, D., Schopf, V. & Langs, G. (2014). Fetal functional imaging portrays heterogeneous development of emerging human brain networks. *Frontiers in Human Neuroscience*, *8*(852), 1–17.

Janke, L. (2008). Music, memory and emotion. *Journal of Biology*, *7*(21), 1–5.

Jeffries, S. & Everatt, J. (2004). Dyslexia and other specific learning difficulties. *Dyslexia*, *10*(3), 196–214.

Jensen, E. (2000). *Different Brains, Different Learners: How to Reach the Hard to Reach*. Thousand Oaks, CA: Corwin Press.

Jensen, E. (2001) *Arts with the Brain in Mind*. Alexandria, VA: Association for Supervision and Curriculum Development.

Jensen, E. (2006). *Enriching the Brain: How to Maximize Every Learner's Potential*. San Francisco, CA: Jossey-Bass.

Jensen, E. (2013). *Engaging with Students with Poverty in Mind*. Alexandria, VA: Association for Supervision and Curriculum Development.

Johnson, M. H. (2005). Sensitive periods in functional brain development: Problems and prospects. *Developmental Psychobiology*, *46*(3), 287–292.

Johnson, S., Cooper, C., Cartwright, S., Donald, I., Taylor, P. & Millett, C. (2005). The experience of work-related stress across occupations. *Journal of Managerial Psychology*, *20*(1/2), 178–187.

Jordan, E. (1995). Fighting boys and fantasy play: The construction of masculinity in the early years of school. *Gender and Education*, *7*(1), 69-86.

Jordan, R. (1999). *Autistic Spectrum Disorder: An Introductory Handbook for Practitioners*. London, UK: David Fulton.

Jorg, T., Davis, B. & Nickmans, G. (2007). Towards a new, complexity science of learning and education. *Educational Researcher Review*, *2*(2), 145–156.

Juffer, F., Bakermans-Kranenburg, M. J. & Van Ijzendoorn, M. H. (Eds.) (2012). *Promoting Positive Parenting: An Attachment-Based Intervention*. London, UK: Routledge.

Jung R. & Haier, R. (2007). The parieto–frontal integration theory (P-FIT) of intelligence: Converging neuroimaging evidence. *Behavioral and Brain Sciences* (target article), *30*, 135–187.

Kagan, J. (1970). The determinants of attention in the infant: The factors determining attention change during the first two years of life and throw light on later differences in cognitive development. *American Scientist*, *58*(3), 298–306.

Kagan, J. (1971). *Change and Continuity in Infancy*. New York, NY: John Wiley & Sons.

Kagan, J. & Herschkowitz, N. (2005). *A Young Mind in a Growing Brain*. Mahwah, NJ: Lawrence Erlbaum.

Kagan, J. K. & Fox, N. A. (2006). Biology, culture and temperamental biases. In W. Damon, R. M. Lerner, N. Eisenberg (Eds.), *Handbook of Child Psychology*, Volume 3: *Social, Emotional and Personality Development* (6th ed., pp. 167–225). Hoboken, NJ: Wiley.

Kalantzis, M. & Cope, B. (2008). *New Learning: Elements of a Science of Education*. New York, NY: Cambridge University Press.

Kandel, E. R. (2006). *In Search of Memory: The Emergence of a New Science of Mind*. New York, NY: W.W. Norton.

Kandel, E. R., Kupfermann, I. & Iversen, S. (2000). Learning and memory. In E. R. Kandel, J. H. Schwartz & T. M. Jessell (Eds.), *Principles of Neural Science* (4th ed., pp. 1227–1247). New York, NY: McGraw-Hill.

Kearney, P. (2007). Cognitive assessment of game-based learning. *British Journal of Educational Technology*, *38*(3), 529–531.

Keddie, A. (2006). Pedagogies and critical reflection: Key understandings for transformative gender justice. *Gender and Education*, *18*(1), 99–114.

Keddie, A. & Mills, M. (2007). *Teaching Boys: Developing Classroom Practices That Work*. Sydney, Australia: Allen & Unwin.

Kensinger, E. & Schacter, D. (2008). Memory and emotion. In M. Lewis, J. M. Haviland-Jones & L. Feldman Barrett (Eds.), *Handbook of Emotions* (3rd ed., pp. 601–617). New York, NY: Guilford Press.

Keown, C. L., Shih, P., Nair, A., Peterson, N. & Müller, R.-A. (2013). Local functional overconnectivity in posterior brain regions is associated with symptom severity in autism spectrum disorders. *Cell Reports*, *5*(3), 567–572.

Keuroghlian, A. S. & Knudsen, E. I. (2007). Adaptive auditory plasticity in developing and adult animals. *Progress in Neurobiology*, *82*(3), 109–121.

Kimura, D. (1999). *Sex and Cognition*. Cambridge, MA: MIT Press.

Kintsch, W. & Kintsch, E. (2005). Comprehension. In S. G. Paris & S. A. Stahl (Eds.), *Current Issues in Reading Comprehension and Assessment* (pp. 71–92). New York, NY: Routledge.

Knudsen, E. I. (2004). Sensitive periods in the development of the brain and behavior. *Journal of Cognitive Neuroscience*, *16*(8), 1412–1425.

Kohl, H. W. & Cook, H. D. (Eds.). (2013). *Educating the Student Body: Taking Physical Activity and Physical Education to School*. Washington, DC: Institute of Medicine of the National Academies.

Kohn, A. (1999). *Punished By Rewards: The Trouble With Gold Stars, Incentive Plans, A's, Praise and Other Bribes.* New York, NY: Houghton Mifflin.

Kohn, A. (2000). *The Case against Standardised Testing: Raising the Scores, Ruining the Schools.* Portsmouth, NH: Heinemann.

Kohn, A. (2006). *The Homework Myth: Why Our Kids Get Too Much of a Bad Thing.* Philadelphia, PA: De Capo Press.

Kolb, B. (2009). Brain and behavioural plasticity in the developing brain: Neuroscience and public policy. *Paediatrics & Child Health, 14*(10), 651–652.

Kolb, D. A. (1984). *Experiential Learning: Experience as the Source of Learning and Development.* Upper Saddle River, NJ: Prentice-Hall.

Kotulak, R. (1997). *Inside the Brain: Revolutionary Discoveries of How the Mind Works.* Kansas City, MO: Andrews McNeel Publishing.

Kouvelas, E. (2007) Language and the brain. In A. F. Christidis (Ed.), *A History of Ancient Greek* (pp. 75–81). New York, NY: Cambridge University Press.

Kouzma, N. M. & Kennedy, G. A. (2002). Homework, stress and mood disturbance in senior high school students. *Psychological Reports, 91*(1), 193–198.

Krapp, A., Hidi, S. & Renninger, K. A. (1992). Interest, learning and development. In K. A. Renninger, S. Hidi & A. Krapp (Eds.), *The Role of Interest in Learning and Development* (pp. 3–26). New York, NY: Lawrence Erlbaum Associates.

Krause, K., Bochner, S., Duchesne, S. & McMaugh, A. (2010). *Educational Psychology for Learning and Teaching* (3rd ed.). Melbourne, Australia: Thomson.

Kravolec, E. & Buell, J. (2000). *The End of Homework: How Homework Disrupts Families, Overburdens Children and Limits Learning.* Boston, MA: Beacon Press.

Kuhl, P. (2004). Early language acquisition: Cracking the speech code. *Nature Reviews Neuroscience, 5*(11), 831–843.

Kuhl, P. K. (2010). Brain mechanisms in early language acquisition. *Neuron, 67*(5), 713–727.

Kuhl, P. K., Tsao, F.-M. & Liu, H.-M. (2003). Foreign-language experience in infancy: Effects of short-term exposure and social interaction on phonetic learning. *Proceedings of the National Academy of Sciences, USA, 100*(15), 9096–9101.

Kuhn, D. (2006). Do cognitive changes accompany developments in the adolescent brain? *Perspectives on Psychological Science, 1*(1), 59–67.

Kuipers, S. D. & Bramham, C. R. (2006). Brain-derived neurotrophic factor mechanisms and function in adult synaptic plasticity: New insights and implications for therapy. *Current Opinion in Drug Discovery & Development, 9*(5), 580–586.

Kumanyika, S. & Grier, S. (2006). Targeting interventions for ethnic minority and low-income populations. *Childhood Obesity, 16*(1), 187–207.

Lamm, C., Batson, C. D. & Decety, J. (2007). The neural substrate of human empathy: Effects of perspective-taking and cognitive appraisal. *Journal of Cognitive Neuroscience, 19*(1), 42–58.

Lazarus, R. S. (1991). *Emotion and Adaptation.* New York, NY: Oxford University Press.

Lazarus, R. S. (1999). *Stress and Emotion.* New York, NY: Springer Publishing.

LeDoux, J. (1998). *The Emotional Brain: The Mysterious Underpinnings of Emotional Life.* New York, NY: Simon & Schuster.

LeDoux, J. (2000). Emotion circuits in the brain. *Annual Review of Neuroscience, 23*, 155–184.

LeDoux, J. (2002). *The Synaptic Self: How Our Brains Become Who We Are.* New York, NY: Penguin Books.

Lee, H. S. & Anderson, J. R. (2013). Student learning: What has instruction got to do with it? *Annual Review of Psychology, 64*, 445–469.

Lee, W., Reeve, J., Xue, Y. & Xiong, J. (2012). Neural differences between intrinsic reasons for doing versus extrinsic reasons for doing: An fMRI study. *Neuroscience Research, 73*(1), 68–72.

Lengua, L. J., Honorado, E. & Bush, N. R. (2007). Contextual risk and parenting as predictors of effortful control and social competence in preschool children. *Journal of Applied Developmental Psychology, 28*(1), 40–55.

Lenroot, R. K. & Giedd, J. N. (2007). The structural development of the human brain as measured longitudinally with magnetic resonance imaging. In D. Coch, K. W. Fisher & G. Dawson (Eds.), *Human Behaviour, Learning and the Developing Brain: Typical Development* (pp. 50–73). New York, NY: The Guilford Press.

LePine, J. A., LePine, M. A. & Jackson, C. L. (2005). Challenge and hindrance stress: Relationships with exhaustion, motivation to learn and learning performance. *Journal of Applied Psychology, 89*(5), 883–891.

Lepper, M. R., Greene, D. & Nisbett, R. E. (1973). Undermining children's intrinsic interest with extrinsic reward: A test of the 'overjustification' hypothesis. *Journal of Personality and Social Psychology, 28*(1), 129–137.

Lewin, K. (1951). *Field Theory in Social Science: Selected Theoretical Papers.* New York, NY: Harper & Row.

Lewis, M. (2008). The emergence of human emotions. In M. Lewis & J. M. Haviland (Eds.), *Handbook of Emotions* (3rd ed., pp. 304–319). New York, NY: Guilford Press.

Lexmond, J. & Reeves, R. (2009). *Building Character*. London, UK: Demos.

Li, D., Christ, S. E. & Cowan, N. (2014). Domain-general and domain-specific functional networks in working memory. *NeuroImage, 102*(Part 2), 646–656.

Li, P., Legault, J. & Litcofsky, K. (2014). Neuroplasticity as a function of second language learning: Anatomical changes in the human brain. *Cortex, 58,* 301–324.

Lingard, B., Martino, W. & Mills, M. (2009). *Boys and Schooling: Beyond Structural Reform*. New York, NY: Palgrave McMillan.

Lortie, D. (1975) *Schoolteacher: A Sociological Study*. Chicago, IL: University of Chicago Press.

Lott, B. (2001). Low-income parents and the public schools. *Journal of Social Issues, 57*(2), 247–259.

Lupien, S. J., Maheu, F., Tu, M., Fiocco, A. & Schramek, T. E. (2007). The effects of stress and stress hormones on human cognition: Implications for the field of brain and cognition. *Brain and Cognition, 65*(3), 209–237.

Lyon, G., Shaywitz, S. & Shaywitz, B. (2003). A definition of dyslexia, *Annals of Dyslexia, 53*(1), 1–14.

Lyubomirsky, S., King, L. & Diener, E. (2005). The benefits of frequent positive affect: Does happiness lead to success? *Psychological Bulletin, 131*(6), 803–855.

Ma, Q. (2008). Beneficial effects of moderate voluntary physical exercise and its biological mechanisms on brain health. *Neuroscience Bulletin, 24*(4), 265–270.

Mac an Ghaill, M. (1994). *The Making of Men: Masculinities, Sexualities, and Schooling*. Buckingham, UK: Open University Press.

Mac an Ghaill, M. (1996). What about the boys? Schooling, class and crisis masculinity. *Sociological Review, 44,* 381–397.

Macklem, G. L. (2010). *Practitioner's Guide to Emotional Regulation in School-Aged Children*. New York, NY: Springer Science + Business Media.

Macnamara, B. N., Hambrick, D. Z. & Oswald, F. L. (2014). Deliberate practice and performance in music, games, sports, education and professions: A meta-analysis. *Psychological Science, 25*(8), 1608–1618.

Maeda, J. K. & Murata, N. M. (2004). Collaborating with classroom teachers to increase daily physical activity: The GEAR program. *Journal of Physical Education, Recreation and Dance, 75*(5), 42–46.

Maguire, E. A., Gadian, D. G., Johnsrude, I. S., Good, C. D., Ashburner, J., Frackowiak, R. S. J. & Frith, C. D. (2000). Navigation-related structural change in the hippocampi of taxi drivers. *Proceedings of the National Academy of Sciences, 97*(8), 4398–4403.

Maguire, E. A., Woollett, K. & Spiers, H. J. (2006). London taxi drivers and bus drivers: A structural MRI and neuropsychological analysis. *Hippocampus, 16*(12), 1901–1101.

Maisog, J. M., Einbinder, E. R., Flowers, D. L., Turkeltaub, P. E. & Eden, G. F. (2008). A meta-analysis of functional neuroimaging studies of dyslexia. *Annals of the New York Academy of Sciences, 1145*(1), 237–259.

Mandler, J. M. & McDonough, L. (1996). Drinking and driving don't mix: Inductive generalisation in infancy. *Cognition, 59*(3), 307–335.

Markham, J. A., Black, J. E. & Greenough, W. T. (2007). Developmental approaches to the memory process. In R. P. Kesner & J. L. Martinez (Eds.), *Neurobiology of Learning and Memory* (2nd ed., pp. 57–102). Burlington, MA: Academic Press.

Marsh, C., Clarke, M. & Pittaway, S. (2014). *Marsh's Becoming a Teacher* (6th ed.). Sydney, Australia: Pearson.

Marshall, P. J., Fox, N. A. & BEIP Core Group (2004). A comparison of the electroencephalogram between institutionalised and community children in Romania. *Journal of Cognitive Neuroscience, 16*(8), 1327–1338.

Martinelli, D. (2010). *A Critical Companion to Zoosemiotics: People, Paths, Ideas* (Vol. 5). Netherlands: Springer Science & Business Media.

Martinez, M. E. (2010). *Learning and Cognition: The Design of the Mind*. Boston, MA: Allyn & Bacon.

Martino, W. (1997). A bunch of arseholes: Exploring the politics of masculinity for adolescent boys in schools. *Social Alternatives, 16*(3), 39–43.

Martino, W. (1999). 'Cool boys', 'party animals', 'squids' and 'poofters': Interrogating the dynamics and politics of adolescent masculinities in school. *British Journal of Social Education, 20*(3), 239–265.

Martino, W. (2003). Boys, masculinities and literacy: Addressing the issues. *Australian Journal of Language and Literacy, 26*(3), 9–27.

Martino, W. & Pallotta-Chiarolli, M. (2003). *So What's a Boy? Addressing Issues of Masculinity and Schooling*. Philadelphia, PA: Open University Press.

Martino, W. & Pallotta-Chiarolli, M. (2005). *Being Normal Is the Only Way to Be*. Sydney, Australia: University of New South Wales Press.

Marton, F. & Saljo, R. (1976). On qualitative differences in learning: Outcome and process. *British Journal of Educational Psychology*, *46*(1), 4–11.

Masten, A. S. & Braswell, L. (1991). Developmental psychopathology: An integrative framework. In P. R. Martin (Ed.), *Handbook of Behaviour Therapy and Psychological Science: An Integrative Approach* (pp. 35–56). New York, NY: Pergamon Press.

Maton, K. (2009). Cumulative and segmented learning: Exploring the role of curriculum structures in knowledge-building and transfer. *British Journal of Sociology of Education*, *30*(1), 43–57.

Matthews, M. R. (2002) Constructivism and science education. A further appraisal. *Journal of Scene Education and Technology*, *11*(2), 121–134.

Maughan, A. & Cicchetti, D. (2002). Impact of child maltreatment and interadult violence on children's emotion regulation abilities and socioemotional adjustment. *Child Development*, *73*(5), 1525–1542.

Mayer, J., Barsade, S. & Roberts, R. (2008). Human abilities: Emotional intelligence. *Annual Review of Psychology*, *59*, 507–536.

Mayer, R. E. (2008). *Learning and Instruction*. Upper Saddle River, NJ: Pearson Education.

McCain, M., Mustard, F. & Shanker, S. (2007). *Early Years Study 2: Putting Science into Action*. Toronto, Canada: Council for Early Child Development.

McClure, S. M., York, M. K. & Montague, P. R. (2004). The neural substrates of reward processing in humans: The modern role of fMRI. *The Neuroscientist*, *10*(3), 260–268.

McDevitt, T. M. & Ormrod, J. E. (2013). *Child Development and Education* (5th ed.). Upper Saddle River, NJ: Pearson Education.

McDonough, L. & Mandler, J. M. (1998). Inductive generalisation in 9 and 11 month olds. *Developmental Science*, *1*(2), 227–232.

McEwen, B. & Seeman, T. (1999). Protective and damaging effects of mediators of stress: Elaborating and testing the concepts of allostasis and allostatic load. In N. E. Adler, M. Marmot, B. S. McEwen & J. Stewart (Eds.), Socioeconomic status and health in industrial nations: Social, psychological, and biological pathways. *Annals of the New York Academy of Sciences, 896*, 30–47.

McEwen, B. S. (2002). *The End of Stress as We Know It*. Washington, DC: John Henry Press.

McEwen, B. S. (2006). Protective and damaging effects of stress mediators: Central role of the brain. *Dialogues in Clinical Neuroscience*, *8*(4), 283–297.

McEwen, B. S. & Sapolsky, R. M. (1995). Stress and cognitive function. *Current Opinion in Neurobiology*, *5*(2), 205–216.

McGaugh, J. L. (2004). The amygdala modulates the consolidation of memories of emotionally arousing experiences. *Annual Review of Neuroscience*, *27*, 1–28.

McGaugh, J. L., Cahill, L. & Roozendaal, B. (1996). Involvement of the amygdala in memory storage: Interaction with other brain systems. *Proceedings of the National Academy of Sciences*, *93*(24), 13508–13514.

McGregor, H. A. & Elliot, A. J. (2002). Achievement goals as predictors of achievement-relevant processes prior to task engagement. *Journal of Educational Psychology*, *94*(2), 381–395.

McInerney, D. M. (2014). *Educational Psychology: Constructing Learning* (6th ed.). Sydney, Australia: Pearson Education.

McKenna, M. C., Kear, D. J. & Ellsworth, R. A. (1995). Children's attitudes toward reading: A national survey. *Reading Research Quarterly*, *30*(4), 934–956.

McNaughton, S. (1995). *Patterns of Emergent Literacy: Processes of Development and Transition*. Melbourne, Australia: Oxford University Press.

Medina, J. (2010). *Brain Rules for Baby: How to Raise a Smart and Happy Child from Zero to Five*. Seattle, WA: Pear Press.

Mehler, J., Jusczyk, P., Lambertz, G., Halsted, N., Bertoncini, J. & Amiel-Tison, C. (1988). A precursor of language acquisition in young infants. *Cognition*, *29*(2), 143–178.

Menon, U. (2000). Analysing emotions as culturally constructed scripts. *Culture and Psychology*, *6*(1), 40–50.

Merriam, S. B., Caffarella, R. S. & Baumgartner, L. M. (2007). *Learning in Adulthood. A Comprehensive Guide* (3rd ed.). San Francisco, CA: John Wiley & Sons.

Merten, D. E. (1997). The meaning of meanness: Popularity, competition, and conflict among junior high school girls. *Sociology of Education*, *70*(3),175–191.

Meyer, D. K. & Turner, J. C. (2002). Discovering emotion in classroom motivation research. *Educational Psychologist*, *37*(2), 107–114.

Miller, D. F. (2007). *Positive Child Guidance* (5th ed.). New York, NY: Thomson Delmar Learning.

Miller, G. A. (1956). The magical number seven, plus or minus two: Some limits on our capacity for processing information. *Psychological Review*, *63*(2), 81–97.

Miller, G. R. (1967). *An Evaluation of the Effectiveness of Mnemonic Devices as Aids to Study*. El Paso, TX: University of Texas at El Paso.

Milne, H. (2010). Special learning needs: Gifted and learning disabled. In M. Hyde., L. Carpenter & R. Conway (Eds.). *Diversity and Inclusion in Australian Schools* (pp. 291–308). Melbourne, Australia: Oxford University Press.

Ministerial Council on Education, Employment, Training and Youth Affairs (2008). *Melbourne Declaration on the Educational Goals for Young Australians*. Canberra, Australia: Author.

Mischel, W. (2014). *The Marshmallow Test: Understanding Self-Control and How to Master It*. London, UK: Bantam Press.

Mischel, W. & Ebbesen, E. B. (1970). Attention in delay of gratification. *Journal of Personality and Social Psychology*, *16*(2), 329–337.

Mischel, W., Ebbesen. E. B. & Zeiss, A. R. (1972). Cognitive and attentional mechanisms in delay of gratification. *Journal of Personality and Social Psychology*, *21*(2), 204–218.

Mitchell, A. (2009). *Brainstorm: Brains—The Secret to Better Schools*. The 2008 Atkinson Fellowship in Public Policy. Retrieved from http://www.atkinsonfoundation.ca/wp-content/uploads/2013/07/brainstorm-the-secret-to-better-schools.pdf.

Montgomery, C. & Rupp, A. A. (2005). A meta-analysis for exploring the diverse causes and effects of stress in teachers. *Canadian Journal of Education*, *28*(3), 458–486.

Morris, R. G. M. (2006). Elements of a neurobiological theory of hippocampal function: The role of synaptic plasticity, synaptic tagging and schemas. *European Journal of Neuroscience*, *23*(11), 2829–2846.

Munkata, Y. (2004). Computational cognitive neuroscience of early memory development. *Developmental Review*, *24*(1), 133–153.

Murdock, T. B., Hale, N. M. & Weber, M. J. (2001). Predictors of cheating among early adolescents: Academic and social motivations. *Contemporary Educational Psychology*, *26*(1), 96–115.

Mustafa, S. M. S., Elias, H., Roslan, S. & Noah, S. M. (2011). Can mastery and performance goals predict learning flow among secondary students? *International Journal of Humanities and Social Science*, *1*(11), 93–98.

Nagel, M. C. (2008). *It's a Girl Thing*. Melbourne, Australia: Hawker-Brownlow Education.

Nagel, M. C. (2009). Mind the mind: Understanding the links between stress, emotional well-being and learning in educational contexts. *International Journal of Learning*, *16*(2), 33–42.

Nagel, M. C. (2012a). *In the Beginning: The Brain, Early Development and Learning*. Melbourne, Australia: ACER Press.

Nagel, M. C. (2012b). *Nurturing a Healthy Mind: Doing What Matters Most for Your Child's Developing Brain*. Wollombi, New South Wales: Exisle Publishing.

Nagel, M. C. (2013a). Student learning. In R. Churchill, P. Ferguson, S. Godinho, N. Johnson, A. Keddie, W. Letts, M. McGill, J. MacKay, J. Moss, M. Nagel, P. Nicholson & M. Vick, *Teaching: Making a Difference* (2nd ed., pp. 74–111). Brisbane, Queensland: John Wiley & Sons.

Nagel, M. C. (2013b). Understanding and motivating students. In R. Churchill, P. Ferguson, S. Godinho, N. Johnson, A. Keddie, W. Letts, M. McGill, J. MacKay, J. Moss, M. Nagel, P. Nicholson & M. Vick, *Teaching: Making a Difference* (2nd ed., pp. 112–143). Brisbane, Queensland: John Wiley & Sons.

Nagel, M. C. (2014), *In the Middle: The Adolescent Brain, Behaviour and Learning*. Melbourne, Australia: ACER Press.

Nagel, M. C. & Scholes, L. (2013). Gender, diversity and engagement in the classroom. In M. Hyde, L. Carpenter & R. Conway (Eds.), *Inclusivity, Diversity and Engagement in Australian Schools* (2nd ed., pp. 91–101). Melbourne: Oxford University Press.

Nash, J. B. (1930). What price home study? *School Parent*, *9*, 6–12.

National Institute of Mental Health (2006). *Attention Deficit Hyperactivity Disorder (ADHD)*. Retrieved from https://www.nimh.nih.gov/health/publications/adhd-listing.shtml.

National Research Council (2004). *Engaging Schools: Fostering High School Students' Motivation to Learn*. Washington, DC: The National Academies Press.

National Scientific Council on the Developing Child (2004). *Young Children Develop in an Environment of Relationships*. Working Paper no. 1. Retrieved from http://developingchild.harvard.edu/index.php/resources/reports_and_working_papers/working_papers/wp1/.

National Scientific Council on the Developing Child (2005). *Excessive Stress Disrupts the Architecture of the Developing Brain*. Working Paper no. 3. Retrieved from http://developingchild.harvard.edu/index.php/library/reports_and_working_papers/working_papers/wp3/.

National Scientific Council on the Developing Child (2007). *The Science of Early Childhood Development: Closing the Gap between What We Know and What We Do*. Retrieved from http://developingchild.harvard.edu/library/reports_and_working_papers/science_of_early_childhood_development/.

Neisser, U. (2004). Memory development: New questions and old. *Developmental Review, 24*(1), 154–158.

Nelson, C. A. (2000). Neural plasticity and human development: The role of early experience in sculpting memory systems. *Developmental Science, 3*(2), 115–136.

Nelson, C. A., de Haan, M. & Thomas, K. M. (2006). *Neuroscience of Cognitive Development: The Role of Experience on the Developing Brain*. Hoboken, NJ: John Wiley & Sons.

Newton, M. (2004). *Savage Girls and Wild boys: A History of Feral Children*. New York, NY: Picador.

Nichols, S. L. & Berliner, D. C. (2007). *Collateral Damage: How High-stakes Testing Corrupts America's Schools*. Cambridge, MA: Harvard Education Press.

Nicholls, J. G. (1984). Achievement motivation: Conceptions of ability, subjective experience, task choice and performance. *Psychological Review, 91*(3), 328–346.

Nigmatullina, Y., Hellyer, P. J., Nachev, P., Sharp, D. J. & Seemungel, B. M. (2015). The neuroanatomical correlates of training-related perceptuo-reflex uncoupling in dancers. *Cerebral Cortex, 25*(2), 554–562.

Nisbett, R., Aronson, J. Blair, C., Dickens. W., Flynn, J., Halpern, D. & Turkheimer, E. (2012). Intelligence: New findings and theoretical developments. *American Psychologist, 67*(2), 130–159.

Noble, K. G., Houston, S. M., Brito, N. H. et al. (2015). Family income, parental education and brain structure in children and adolescents. *Nature Neuroscience, 18*(5), 773–778.

Obach, M. S. (2003). A longitudinal-sequential study of perceived academic competence and motivational beliefs of learning among children in middle school. *Educational Psychology, 23*(3), 323–338.

Ochsner, K. N. & Lieberman, M. D. (2001). The emergence of social cognitive neuroscience. *American Psychologist, 56*, 717–734.

O'Doherty, J. P. (2004). Reward representations and reward-related learning in the human brain: Insights from neuroimaging. *Current Opinion in Neurobiology, 14*(6), 769–776.

O'Donnell, A. M., Dobozy, E., Bartlett, B., Bryer, F., Reeve, J. M & Smith, J. K. (2012). *Educational Psychology* (1st Australian ed.). Brisbane, Queensland: John Wiley & Sons.

O'Donnell, A. M., Reeve, J. & Smith, J. K. (2009). *Educational Psychology: Reflection for Action* (2nd ed.). Hoboken, NJ: John Wiley & Sons.

Organisation for Economic Co-operation and Development—OECD (2010). *PISA 2009 Results: Executive Summary*. Paris, France: Author.

Organisation for Economic Co-operation and Development—OECD (2014). *PISA 2012 Results: What Students Know and Can Do—Student Performance in Mathematics, Reading and Science* (Vol. I, rev. ed., February 2014). Paris, France: OECD Publishing.

Ormrod, J. E. (2008). *Human Learning* (5th ed.). Hoboken, NJ: Pearson Education.

Osborne, B. (2003). Around in circles or expanding spirals? A retrospective look at education in Torres Strait 1964–2003. *Australian Journal of Indigenous Education, 32*(1), 76.

Osterman, K. F. (2000). Students' need for belonging in the school community. *Review of Educational Research, 70*(3), 323–367.

Otto, H. J. (1941). Elementary education. In W. S. Monroe (Ed.), *Encyclopedia of Education Research* (pp. 444–445). New York, NY: Macmillan.

Pagel, J. F. & Kwiatkowski, C. F. (2010). Sleep complaints affecting school performance at different educational levels. *Frontiers in Neurology, 1*(125), 1–6.

Panksepp, J. (2004). *Affective Neuroscience: The Foundations of Human and Animal Emotions*. New York, NY: Oxford University Press.

Papanicolaou, A. C. (2003). *Brain Imaging in Normal and Impaired Reading: A Developmental-educational Perspective*. Paper presented at the International Dyslexia Association conference in San Diego.

Pashler, H., McDaniel, M., Rohrer, D. & Bjork, R. (2008). Learning styles: Concepts and evidence. *Psychological Science in the Public Interest, 9*(3), 105–119.

Pashler, H. E. (1998). *The Psychology of Attention*. Cambridge, MA: MIT Press.

Paul, L. K. (2011). Developmental malformation of the corpus callosum: A review of typical callosal development and examples of developmental disorders with callosal involvement. *Journal of Neurodevelopmental Disorders, 3*, 3–27.

Paus, T., Zijdenbos, A., Worsley, K., Collins, D. L., Blumenthal, J., Giedd, J. N., Rapoport, J. L. & Evans, A. C. (1999). Structural maturation of neural pathways in children and adolescents: In vivo study. *Science, 283*(5409), 1908–1911.

Pedersen, N., Plomin, R., Nesselroade, J. & McClearn, G. (1992). A quantitative genetic analysis of cognitive abilities during the second half of the life span. *Psychological Science, 3*, 346–353.

Pekrun, R., Elliot, A. J. & Maier, M. A. (2009). Achievement goals and achievement emotions: Testing a model of their joint relations with academic performance. *Journal of Educational Psychology, 101*(1), 115–135.

Pellegrini, A. D. & Bjorkland, D. F. (1997). The role of recess in children's cognitive performance. *Educational Psychologist*, *32*(1), 35–40.

Perry, B. (2002). Childhood experience and the expression of genetic potential: What childhood neglect tells us about nature and nurture. *Brain and Mind*, *3*(1), 79–100.

Peterson, E., Rayner, S. & Armstrong, S. (2009). Researching the psychology of cognitive styles and learning style. Is there really a future? *Learning and Individual Differences*, *19*, 518–523.

Piaget, J. (1952). *The Origins of Intelligence in Children*. New York, NY: International Universities Press.

Piaget, J. (1954). *The Construction of Reality in the Child*. New York, NY: Basic Books.

Piaget, J. & Inhelder, B. (1969). *The Psychology of the Child*. New York, NY: Basic Books.

Pinker, S. (1994). *The Language Instinct. How the Mind Creates Language*. New York, NY: Marrow.

Pinker, S. (1995). Language acquisition. In L. R. Gleitman & M. Liberman (Eds.), *An Invitation to Cognitive Science* (2nd ed., pp. 135–182). Cambridge, MA: MIT Press.

Pinker, S. (2009). *How the Mind Works*. New York, NY: W.W. Norton.

Pinker, S. & Jackendoff, R. (2005). The faculty of language: What's special about it? *Cognition*, *95*(2), 201–236.

Pintrich, P. R. (2000a). An achievement goal theory perspective on issues in motivation terminology, theory and research. *Contemporary Educational Psychology*, *25*(1), 92–104.

Pintrich, P. R. (2000b). Multiple goals, multiple pathways: The role of goal orientation in learning and achievement. *Journal of Educational Psychology*, *92*(3), 544–555.

Pintrich, P. R. (2003). A motivational science perspective on the role of student motivation in learning and teaching contexts. *Journal of Educational Psychology*, *95*(4), 667–686.

Pintrich, P. R. & Schunk, D. H. (2002). *Motivation in Education: Theory, Research, and Applications* (2nd ed.). Upper Saddle River, NJ: Prentice Hall.

Pliszka, S., Glahn, D., Semrud-Clikeman, M., Franklin, C., Perez III, R. et al. (2006). Neuroimaging of inhibitory control in treatment naïve and chronically treated children with ADHD. *American Journal of Psychiatry*, *163*, 1052–1060.

Plotnik, R. & Kouyoumdjian, H. (2010). *Introduction to Psychology* (9th ed.). Belmont, CA: Wadsworth Publishing Company.

Plutchik, R. (2001). The nature of emotions. *American Scientist*, *89*, 344.

Popham, J. (2007). The no-win accountability game. In C. Glickman (Ed.), *Letters to the Next President: What We Can Do about the Real Crisis in Public Education* (pp. 166–173). New York, NY: Teachers College Press.

Posner, M. I. & Patoine, B. (2010). How arts training improves attention and cognition. In D. Gordon (Ed.), *Cerebrum: Emerging Ideas in Brain Science* (pp. 12–22). New York, NY: Dana Press.

Posner, M. I. & Rothbart, M. K. (2007). *Educating the Human Brain*. Washington, DC: American Psychological Association.

Pratt, S. & George, R. (2005). Transferring friendship: Girls' and boys' friendships in the transition from primary to secondary school. *Children and Society*, *19*, 16–26.

Prensky, M. (2001). Digital natives, digital immigrants. *On the Horizon*, *9*(5), 1–2.

Pressley, M. & El-Dinary, P. B. (1992). Memory strategy instruction that promotes good information processing. In D. J. Herrmann, H. Weingartner, A. Searleman & C. McEvoy (Eds.), *Memory Improvement: Implications for Memory Theory* (pp. 79–100). New York, NY: Springer-Verlag.

Prout, A. & James, A. (1997). A new paradigm for the sociology of childhood? Provenance, promise and problems. In A. James & A. Prout (Eds.), *Constructing and Reconstructing Childhood* (2nd ed., pp. 1–7). London, UK: Falmer Press.

Purdie, N. & Hattie, J. (2002). Assessing students' conceptions of learning. *Australian Journal of Educational & Developmental Psychology*, *2*, 17–32.

Quach, D., Mano, K. E. & Alexander, K. (2015). A randomised controlled trial examining the effect of mindfulness meditation on working memory capacity in adolescents. *Journal of Adolescent Health*, *58*(5), 489–96.

Ramachandran, V. S. (2004). *A Brief Tour of Human Consciousness: From Impostor Poodles to Purple Numbers*. New York, NY: Pi Press.

Ramirez, E., Kulinna, P. H. & Cothran, D. (2012). Constructs of physical activity behaviour in children: The usefulness of social cognitive theory. *Psychology of Sport and Exercise*, *13*(3), 303–310.

Ratey, J. J. (2001). *A User's Guide to the Brain: Perception, Attention and the Four Theatres of the Brain*. New York, NY: Vintage Books.

Ratey, J. J. (2008). *Spark: The Revolutionary New Science of Exercise and the Brain*. New York, NY: Little, Brown.

Rauscher, F. H., Shaw, G. L., Levine, L. J., Wright, E. L., Dennis, W. R. & Newcomb, R. L. (1997). Music training causes long-term enhancement of preschool children's spatial–temporal reasoning. *Neurological Research, 19*(1), 2–8.

Rayner, K., Foorman, B. R., Perfetti, C. A., Pesetsky, D. & Seidenberg, M. S. (2001). How psychological science informs the teaching of reading. *Psychological Science in the Public Interest, 2*(2), 31–74.

Read, B. (2006). Gendered constructions of cooperation and competition by pupils. In A. Ross, M. Fulop & M. Pergar Kuscer (Eds.). *Teachers' and Pupils' Constructions of Competition and Cooperation: A Three Country Study of Slovenia, Hungary and England* (pp. 174–85). Ljubljana, Slovenia: University of Ljubljana Press.

Read, B., Francis, B. & Skelton. C. (2011). Gender, popularity and notions of in/authenticity amongst 12-year-old to 13-year-old school girls. *British Journal of Sociology of Education, 32*(2), 169–183.

Reber, P. J. (2013). The neural basis of implicit learning and memory: A review of neuropsychological and neuroimaging research. *Neuropsychologia, 51*(10), 2026–2042.

Reeve, J. (2015). *Understanding Motivation and Emotion* (6th ed.). New York, NY: John Wiley & Sons.

Reeve, J., Deci, E. L. & Ryan, R. M. (2004). Self-determination theory: A dialectical framework for understanding the sociocultural influences on student motivation. In D. M. McInerney & S. Van Etten (Eds.), *Big Theories Revisited* (pp. 31–60). Greenwich, CT: Information Age Publishing.

Renner, M. J. & Rosenzweig, M. R. (1987). *Enriched and Impoverished Environments: Effects on Brain and Behavior.* New York, NY: Springer.

Renninger, K. A. (1998). Developmental psychology and instruction: Issues from and for practice. In W. Damon (Gen. Ed.) & I. E. Sigel & K. A. Renninger (Vol. Eds.), *Handbook of Child Psychology*, Vol. 4: *Child Psychology in Practice* (5th ed., pp. 211–274). New York, NY: John Wiley & Sons.

Renzulli, J. S. (2005). *Equity, Excellence, and Economy in a System for Identifying Students in Gifted Education: A Guidebook.* Storrs, CT: National Research Center on the Gifted and Talented, University of Connecticut.

Reschly, A. L., Huebner, E. S., Appleton, J. J. & Antaramian, S. (2008). Engagement as flourishing: The contribution of positive emotions and coping to adolescents' engagement at school and with learning. *Psychology in the Schools, 45*(5), 419–431.

Resnick, L. B. (2010). Nested learning systems for the thinking curriculum. *Educational Researcher, 39*(3), 183–197.

Reyna, V. F. & Farley, F. (2006). Risk and rationality in adolescent decision making: Implications for theory, practice, and public policy. *Psychological Science in the Public Interest, 7*(1), 1–44.

Richards, A. (2003). Arts and academic achievement in reading: Functions and implications. *Art Education, 56*(6), 19–23.

Richardson, J. T. E. (2005). Students' approaches to learning and teachers' approaches to learning in higher education. *Educational Psychology, 25*(6), 673–680.

Richardson, M., Sacks, M. K. & Ayers, M. (2003). Paths to reading and writing through the visual arts. *Reading Improvement, 40*(3), 80–96.

Rinne, L., Gregory, E., Yarmolinskaya, J. & Hardiman, M. (2011). Why arts integration improves long-term retention of content. *Mind, Brain and Education, 5*(2), 89–96.

Ritchey, M., LaBar, K. S. & Cabeza, R. (2011). Level of processing modulates the neural correlates of emotional memory formation. *Journal of Cognitive Neurosciences, 23*(4), 757–771.

Roberts, K., Freed, B. & McCarthy, W. J. (2010). Low aerobic fitness and obesity are associated with lower standardised test scores in children. *Journal of Pediatrics, 156*(5), 711–718.

Robinson, K. (2009). *The Element: How Finding Your Passion Changes Everything.* New York, NY: Viking.

Robinson, K. (2011). *Out of Our Minds: Learning to Be Creative* (2nd edn). Chichester, UK: Capstone Publishing.

Roediger, H. L. (2013). Applying cognitive psychology to education: Translational educational science. *Psychological Science in the Public Interest, 14*(1), 1–3.

Rogers, C. R. (1969). *Freedom to Learn: A View of What Education Might Become.* Columbus, OH: Charles E Merrill Company.

Rogers, K. B. (2007). Lessons learned about educating the gifted and talented: A synthesis of the research on educational practice. *Gifted Child Quarterly, 51*(4), 382–396.

Rogoff, B. (1990). *Apprenticeship in Thinking: Cognitive Development in a Social Context.* Oxford, UK: Oxford University Press.

Rolland, R. G. (2012). Synthesizing the evidence on classroom goal structures in middle and secondary schools: A meta-analysis and narrative review. *Review of Educational Research, 82*(4), 396–345.

Ropper, A. & Samuels, M. (2009). *Adam's and Victor's Principles of Neurology* (9th ed.). New York, NY: McGraw Hill.

Rosenzweig, M. R., Krech, D., Bennett, E. L. & Diamond, M. C. (1962). Effects of environmental complexity and training on brain chemistry and anatomy: A replication and extension. *Journal of Comparative and Physiological Psychology*, *55*(4), 429–437.

Rosier, J. P. & Sahakian, B. J. (2013). Hot and cold cognition in depression. *CNS Spectrums*, *18*(3), 139–149.

Rothbart, M. K. (2004). Temperament and the pursuit of an integrated developmental psychology. *Merrill-Palmer Quarterly*, *50*(4), 492–205.

Rothbart, M. K. (2007). Temperament, development and personality. *Current Directions in Psychological Science*, *16*(4), 207–212.

Rothbart, M. K. & Bates, J. E. (2006). Temperament. In W. Damon, R. M. Lerner & N. Eisenberg (Eds.), *Handbook of Child Psychology*, Vol. 3: *Social, Emotional, and Personality Development* (6th ed., pp. 99–166). Hoboken, NJ: John Wiley & Sons.

Rothbart, M. K., Sheese, B. E. & Conradt, E. D. (2009). Childhood temperament. In P. J. Corr & G. Matthews (Eds.), *The Cambridge Handbook of Personality Psychology*, (pp. 170–190). New York, NY: Cambridge University Press.

Rowe, K. J. & Rowe, K. S. (2002). *What Matters Most: Evidence-based Research in Teacher and School Effectiveness: The Educational Performance of Males and Females in School and Tertiary Education.* Paper presented at Educational Attainment and Labour Market Outcomes: Factors Affecting Boys and their Status in Relation to Girls, Melbourne, Australia.

Royal Society (2011). *Brain Waves Module 2: Neuroscience: Implications for Education and Lifelong Learning.* London, UK: Author.

Rudd, K. & Gillard, J. (2008). *Quality Education: The Case for an Education Revolution in Our Schools.* Canberra, Australia: Commonwealth of Australia.

Ruston, H. & Schwanenflugel, P. (2010). Effects of a conversation intervention on the expressive vocabulary development of prekindergarten. *Children. Language Speech and Hearing Services in Schools*, *41*, 303–313.

Ryan, A. M., Gheen, M. H. & Midgley, C. (1998). Why do some students avoid asking for help? An examination of the interplay among students' academic efficacy, teachers' social-emotional role, and the classroom goal structure. *Journal of Educational Psychology*, *90*(3), 528–535.

Ryan, A. M. & Pintrich, P. R. (1997). 'Should I ask for help?' The role of motivation and attitudes in adolescents' help seeking in math class. *Journal of Educational Psychology*, *89*(2), 329–341.

Ryan, E. L. (2012). 'They are kind of like magic': Why U.S. mothers use baby videos with 12 to 24 month olds. *Journalism and Mass Communication*, *2*(7), 771–785.

Ryan, R. M. & Deci, E. L. (2000). Self-determination theory and the facilitation of intrinsic motivation, social development, and well-being. *American Psychologist*, *55*(1), 68–78.

Saarni, C., Campos, J. J., Camras, L. A. & Witherington, D. (2006). Emotional development, action, communication and understanding. In W. Damon, R. M. Lerner & N. Eisenberg (Eds.), *Handbook of Child Psychology*, Vol. 3: *Social, Emotional, and Personality Development* (6th ed., pp. 226–299). Hoboken, NJ: John Wiley & Sons.

Sabatinelli, D., Bradley, M. M., Lang, P. J., Costa, V. D & Versace, F. (2007). Pleasure rather than salience activates human nucleus accumbens and medial prefrontal cortex. *Journal of Neurophysiology*, *98*(3), 1374–1379.

Sahlberg, P. (2010). *Finnish Lessons: What Can the World Learn from Educational Change in Finland?* New York, NY: Teachers College Press.

Sainsbury, M. & Schagen, I. (2004). Attitudes to reading at ages nine and eleven. *Journal of Research in Reading*, *27*(4), 373–386.

Saljo, R. (1979). *Learning in the Learner's Perspective. 1: Some Common Sense Conceptions.* Report no. 76. Goteborg, Sweden: Institute of Education, University of Goteborg.

Salkind, N. J. (2004). *An Introduction to Theories of Human Development.* Thousand Oaks, CA: Sage Publications.

Salmon, J. & Timperio, A. (2007). Prevalence, trends and environmental influences on child and youth physical activity. In G. R. Tomkinson & T. S. Olds (Eds.), *Pediatric Fitness: Secular Trends and Geographic Variability* (pp. 183–199). Basel, Switzerland: Karger Medical and Scientific Publishers.

Santrock, J. W. (2011). *Educational Psychology* (5th ed.). New York, NY: McGraw-Hill.

Sapolsky, R. (2005) Sick of poverty. *Scientific American*, *293*(6), 92–99.

Sapolsky, R. A. (2004). *Why Zebras Don't Get Ulcers: The Acclaimed Guide to Stress-Related Diseases and Coping* (3rd ed.). New York, NY: Henry Holt.

Schellenberg, E. G. (2004). Music lessons enhance IQ. *Psychological Science*, *15*(8), 511–514.

Schellenberg, E. G. (2005). Music and cognitive abilities. *Current Directions in Psychological Science, 14*(6), 317–320.

Schellenberg, E. G. (2006). Long term positive associations between music lessons and IQ. *Journal of Educational Psychology, 98*(2), 457–468.

Schlaggar, B. L., Brown, T. T., Lugar, H. M., Visscher, K. M., Miezin, F. M. & Petersen, S. E. (2002). Functional neuroanatomical differences between adults and school-age children in the processing of single words. *Science, 296*(5572), 1476–1479.

Scholes, L. (2010). Boys, masculinity and reading: Deconstructing the homogenizing of boys in literacy classrooms. *International Journal of Learning, 17*(6), 437–450.

Scholes, L. (2011). *Boys, masculinity and reading: Exploring difference amongst male readers.* (Doctoral thesis: University of Queensland, Brisbane, Australia.)

Scholes, L. (2013). Clandestine readers: Boys' and girls' descriptions of going 'undercover'. *British Journal of Sociology of Education, 36*(3), 359–374.

Scholes, L. & Nagel, M. C. (2012). Engaging the creative arts to meet the needs of twenty-first-century boys. *International Journal of Inclusive Education, 16*(10), 969–984.

Scholl, R. (2014). 'Inside-out pedagogy': Theorising pedagogical transformation through teaching philosophy. *Australian Journal of Teacher Education, 39*(6), 89–106. Retrieved from http://ro.ecu.edu.au/ajte/vol39/iss6/7.

Schools Commission (1975). *Girls, Schools and Society: Report by a Study Group to the Schools Commission.* Canberra, Australia: Author.

Schopf, V., Schlegl, A., Jakab, A., Kasprain, G., Woitek, R., Prayer, D. & Langs, G. (2014). The relationship between eye movement and vision develops before birth. *Frontiers in Human Neuroscience, 8*(775), 1–6.

Scott, C. (2010). The enduring appeal of 'learning styles'. *Australian Journal of Education, 54*(1), 5–17.

Scoville, W. B. & Milner, B. (1957). Loss of recent memory after bilateral hippocampal lesions. *Journal of Neurology, Neurosurgery & Psychiatry, 20*(1), 11–21.

Selfe, L. (1985). Anomalous drawing development: Some clinical studies. In N. H. Freeman & M. V. Cox (Eds.). *Visual Order: The Nature and Development of Pictorial Representation* (pp. 135–154). Cambridge, UK: Cambridge University Press.

Selfe, L. (2011). *Nadia Revisited: A Longitudinal Study of an Autistic Savant.* Hove, UK: Psychology Press.

Seligman, M. E. P. (1972). Learned helplessness. *Annual Review of Medicine, 23*, 407–412.

Seligman, M. E. P. & Maier, S. F. (1967). Failure to escape traumatic shock. *Journal of Experimental Psychology, 74*(1), 1–9.

Seligman, M. E. P., Maier, S. F. & Geer, J. (1968). The alleviation of learned helplessness in the dog. *Journal of Abnormal Psychology, 73*(3), 256–262.

Selye, H. (1974). *Stress without Distress.* Philadelphia, PA: Lippincott Williams & Wilkins.

Selye, H. (1975). Stress and distress. *Comprehensive Therapy, 1*(8), 9–13.

Selye, H. (1978). *The Stress of Life* (2nd ed.). New York, NY: McGraw-Hill.

Semrud-Clikeman, M. (2006). Neuropsychological aspects for evaluating LD. *Journal of Learning Disabilities, 38*, 563–568.

Semrud-Clikeman, M. & Ellison, P. A. T. (2009). *Child Neuropsychology.* New York, NY: Springer.

Shapiro, M. (2001). Plasticity, hippocampal place cells and cognitive maps. *Archives of Neurology, 58*(6), 874–881.

Shaywitz, B. A., Shaywltz, S. E., Pugh, K. R., Constable, R. T., Skudlarski, P., Fulbright, R. K., Bronen, R. A., Fletcher, J. M., Shankweiler, D. P., Katz, L. & Gore, J. C. (1995). Sex differences in the functional organization of the brain for language. *Nature, 373*(6515), 607–609.

Shepard, R. J. (1997). Curricular physical activity and academic performance. *Pediatric Exercise Science, 9*(2), 113–126.

Sheridan, J. F., Padgett, D. A., Avitsur, R. & Marucha, P. T. (2004). Experimental models of stress and wound healing. *World Journal of Surgery, 28*(3), 327–330.

Sherman, S. M. (2005). Thalamic relays and cortical functioning. *Progress in Brain Research, 149*, 107–126.

Shiraev, E. & Levy, D. (2010). *Cross-cultural psychology* (4th ed.), Boston, MA: Allyn & Bacon.

Shonkoff, J. P. (2010). Building a new biodevelopmental framework to guide the future of early childhood policy. *Child Development, 81*(1), 357–367.

Shonkoff, J. P. & Levitt P. (2010). Neuroscience and the future of early childhood policy: Moving from why to what and how. *Neuron, 67*(5), 689–691.

Shonkoff, J. P. & Phillips, D. A. (Eds.) (2000). *From Neurons to Neighborhoods: The Science of Early Childhood Development.* Washington, DC: National Academy Press.

Shor, I. (1992). *Empowering Education: Critical Teaching for Social Change.* Chicago, IL: University of Chicago Press.

Shore, R. (1997). *Rethinking the Brain: New Insights into Early Development.* New York, NY: Families and Work Institute.

Siegal, M. & Varley, R. (2002). Neural systems involved in theory of mind. *Nature Reviews Neuroscience, 3*, 462–471.

Siegel, D. J., (2012). *Pocket Guide to Interpersonal Neurobiology: An Integrative handbook of the Mind.* New York, NY: W.W. Norton & Company.

Siegel, J. Z. & Crockett, M. J. (2013). How serotonin shapes moral judgment and behaviour. *Annals of the New York Academy of Sciences, 1299*, 42–51.

Siraj-Blatchford, I. & Woodhead, M. (2009). *Effective Early Childhood Programmes.* Milton Keynes, UK: Open University Press.

Skelton, C. (2001). *Schooling the Boys: Masculinities and Primary Education.* Milton Keynes, UK: Open University Press.

Skelton, C., Francis, B. & Read, B. (2010). Brains before 'beauty'? High achieving girls, school and gender identities. *Educational Studies, 36*(2), 185–94.

Skinner, B. F. (1953). *Science and Human Behavior.* New York, NY: Macmillan.

Skinner, B. F. (1957). *Verbal Behavior.* Acton, MA: Copley Publishing Group.

Skinner, B. F. (1963). Operant behavior. *American Psychologist, 18*(8), 503–515.

Sluming, V., Brooks, J., Howard, M., Downes, J. J. & Roberts, N. (2007). Broca's area supports enhanced visuospatial cognition in orchestral musicians. *Journal of Neuroscience 27*(4), 3799–3806.

Small, G. & Vorgan, G. (2008*). iBrain: Surviving the Technological Alteration of the Modern Mind.* New York, NY: Harper Collins Publishers.

Small, G. W., Moody, T. D., Siddarth, P. & Bookheimer, S. Y. (2009). Your brain on Google: Patterns of cerebral activation during internet searching. *American Journal of Geriatric Psychiatry, 17*(2), 116–126.

Smillie, L. D., Pickering, A. D. & Jackson, C. J. (2006). The new reinforcement sensitivity theory: Implications for personality management. *Personality and Social Psychology Review, 10*(4), 320–335.

Smith, B. O. (1963). Toward a theory of teaching. In A. A. Bellack (Ed.), *Theory and Research in Teaching* (pp. 1–10). New York, NY: Teachers College, Columbia University.

Snowman, J., Dobozy, E., Scevak, J., Bryer, F., Bartlett, B. & Biehler, R. F. (2009). *Psychology Applied to Teaching* (1st Australian ed.). Brisbane, Australia: John Wiley & Sons.

Sousa, D. (2001). *How the Brain Learns* (2nd ed.). Thousand Oaks, CA: Corwin Press.

Sousa, D. (2005). *How the Brain Learns to Read.* Thousand Oaks, CA: Corwin Press.

Sowell, E. R., Thompson, P. M., Holmes, C. J., Jernigan, T. I. & Toga, A. W. (1999). In vivo evidence for post-adolescent brain maturation in frontal and striatal regions. *Nature Neuroscience, 2*(10), 859–861.

Sowell, E. R., Thompson, P. M., Tessner, K. D. & Toga, A. W. (2001). Mapping continued brain growth and gray matter density reduction in dorsal frontal cortex: Inverse relationships during postadolescent brain maturation. *Journal of Neuroscience, 21*(22), 8819–8829.

Spear, L. P. (2000a). The adolescent brain and age-related behavioral manifestations. *Neuroscience and Behavioral Reviews, 24*(4), 417–463.

Spear, L. P. (2000b). Neurobehavioral changes in adolescence. *Current Directions in Psychological Science, 9*(4), 111–114.

Spear, L. P. (2007). Brain development and adolescent behaviour. In D. Coch, K. W. Fisher & G. Dawson (Eds.), *Human Behavior, Learning and the Developing Brain: Typical Development* (pp. 362–396). New York, NY: Guilford Press.

Spear, L. P. (2010). *The Behavioural Neuroscience of Adolescence.* New York, NY: W.W. Norton & Company.

Spear, L. P. (2013). Adolescent neurodevelopment. *Journal of Adolescent Health, 52*(2), S7–S13.

Spearman, C. (1904). General intelligence, objectively determined and measured. *American Journal of Psychology*, 15(2), 201–292.

Spearman, C. (1925). Some issues in the theory of 'g' (including the Law of Diminishing Returns). *Nature, 116*, (2916), 436.

Spearman, C. (1987). The proof and measurement of association between two things. By C. Spearman, 1904. *American Journal of Psychology, 100*(3–4), 441–471.

Sroufe, L. A. (1979). The coherence of individual development: Early care, attachment and subsequent developmental issues. *American Psychologist, 34*(10), 834–841.

Sroufe, L. A. (1995). *Emotional Development: The Organisation of Emotional Life in the Early Years.* New York, NY: Cambridge Press.

Sroufe, L. A., Cooper, R. G. & DeHart. (1996). *Child Development: Its Nature and Course* (3rd ed.). New York, NY: McGraw Hill.

Sroufe, L. A., Egeland, B. & Carlson, E. A. (1999). One social world: The integrated development of parent–child and peer relationships. In W. A. Collins & B. Laursen (Eds.), *Relationships as Developmental Context.* The Minnesota Symposia on Child Psychology (Vol. 30, pp. 238–259). Mahwah, NJ: Lawrence Erlbaum.

Stainback, W. & Stainback, W. C. (1989). Classroom organization for diversity among students. In: D. Biklen,

D. Ferguson & A. Ford, *Schooling and Disability*. Chicago, IL: University of Chicago Press.

Stanovich, K. (1986). Matthew effects in reading: Some consequences of individual differences in the acquisition of literacy. *Reading Research Quarterly, 21*, 360–406.

Stanovich, K. E. (2000). *Progress in Understanding Reading: Scientific Foundations and New Frontiers*. New York, NY: Guilford Press.

Steffe, L. P. & Gale, J. (Eds.). (1995). *Constructivism in Education*. Mahwah, NJ: Lawrence Erlbaum.

Stenberg, G. (2009). Selectivity in infant social referencing. *Infancy, 14*, 457–473.

Sternberg, R. (2011). Intelligence in its cultural context. In M. Gelfand, C.-Y. Chiu & Y.-Y. Hong (Eds.), *Advances in Cultures and Psychology* (Vol. 2, pp. 205–248). New York, NY: Oxford University Press.

Sternberg, R. J. (1985). *Beyond IQ: A Triarchic Theory of Intelligence*. Cambridge, UK: Cambridge University Press.

Sternberg, R. J. (1991). Death, taxes, and bad intelligence tests. *Intelligence, 15*(3), 257–270.

Sternberg, R. J. (1997). The concept of intelligence and its role in lifelong learning and success. *American Psychologist, 52*, 1030–1037.

Sternberg, R. J. (2010). Intelligence. In B. McGaw, P. Peterson & E. Baker (Eds.), *The International Encyclopedia of Education* (3rd ed., Vol. 5). New York, NY: Elsevier.

Sternberg, R. J. (2012). *Cognitive Psychology* (6th ed.). Belmont, CA: Wadsworth, Cengage Learning.

Sternberg, R. J. & Grigorenko, E. L. (2000). *Teaching for Successful Intelligence*. Arlington Heights, IL: Skylight.

Stevens, C. & McKechnie, S. (2005). Thinking in action: Thought made visible in contemporary dance. *Cognitive Processing, 6*(4), 243–252.

Stromswold, K. (1998). The genetics of spoken language disorders. *Human Biology, 70*, 297–324.

Supekar, K., Swigart, A. G., Tenison, C., Jolles, D. D., Rosenberg-Lee, M., Fuchs, L. & Menon, V. (2013). Neural predictors of individual differences in response to math tutoring in primary-grade school children. *Proceedings of the National Academy of Sciences, 110*(20), 8230–8235.

Sweeney, M. S. (2009). *Brain, The Complete Guide: How It Develops, How It Works and How to Keep It Sharp*. Washington, DC: National Geographic Society.

Sylwester, R. (2005). *How to Explain a Brain: An Educator's Handbook of Brain Terms and Cognitive Processes*. Thousand Oaks, CA: Corwin Press.

Talmi, D., Anderson, A. K., Riggs, L., Caplan, J. B. & Moscovitch, M. (2008). Immediate memory consequences of the effect of emotion on attention to pictures. *Learning & Memory, 15*(3), 172–182.

Tanapat, P., Galea, L. & Gould, E. (1998). Stress inhibits the proliferation of granule cell precursors in the development of the dentate gyrus. *International Journal of Developmental Neuroscience, 16*(3–4), 235–239.

Taumoepeau, M. & Ruffman, T. (2008). Stepping stones to others' minds: Maternal talk relates to child mental state, language and emotion understanding at 15, 24, and 33 months. *Child Development, 79*(2), 284–302.

Teicher, M. H., Andersen, S. L., Polcarib, A., Anderson, C. M., Navalta, C. P. & Kim, D. M. (2003). The neurobiological consequences of early stress and childhood maltreatment. *Neuroscience and Biobehavioral Reviews, 27*(1), 33–44.

Thomas, A. & Chess, S. (1991). Temperament in adolescence and its functional significance. In R. M. Lerner, A. C. Petersen & J. Brooks-Gunn (Eds.), *Encyclopedia of Adolescence* (Vol. 2, pp. 1131–1140). New York, NY: Garland Publishing.

Thomas, M. S. C. & Johnson, M. H. (2008). New advances in understanding sensitive periods in brain development. *Current Directions in Psychological Science, 17*(1), 1–5.

Thompson, G. (2013). NAPLAN, MySchool and accountability: Teacher perceptions of the effects of testing. *International Education Journal: Comparative Perspectives, 12*(2), 62–84.

Thompson, G. & Cook, I. (2014). Manipulating the data: Teaching and NAPLAN in a control society. *Discourse, 35*(1), 129–142.

Thompson, G. & Harbaugh, A. G. (2013). A preliminary analysis of teacher perceptions of the effects of NAPLAN on pedagogy and curriculum. *Australian Educational Researcher, 40*(3), 299–314.

Thompson, P. M., Giedd, J. N, Woods, R. P., MacDonald, D., Evans, A. C. & Toga, A. W. (2000). Growth patterns in the developing brain detected by using continuum mechanical tensor maps. *Nature, 404*(6774), 190–193.

Thompson, R. & Carpenter, L. (2014). Supporting classroom management for challenging behaviour. In M. Hyde, L. Carpenter & R. Conway. *Diversity and Inclusion in Australian Schools* (pp. 148–172). Melbourne, Australia: Oxford.

Thompson, R. A. (2006). The development of the person: Social understanding, relationships, conscience, self. In W. Damon, R. M. Lerner & N. Eisenberg (Eds.), *Handbook of Child Psychology*, Volume 3: *Social, Emotional and Personality Development* (6th ed., pp. 24–98). Hoboken, NJ: Wiley.

Thompson, R. A. & Lagatutta, K. (2008). Feeling and understanding: Early emotional development. In K. McCartney & D. Phillips (Eds.), *The Blackwell Handbook of Early Childhood Development* (pp. 317–337). Oxford, UK: Blackwell Publishing.

Tokuhama-Espinosa, T. (2011). *Mind, Brain, and Education Science: A Comprehensive Guide to the New Brain-Based Learning.* New York, NY: W.W. Norton.

Tomasello, M. (1992), The social basis of language acquisition. *Social Development, 1*(1), 67–87.

Tomlinson, C. A. (2000). Reconcilable differences: Standards-based teaching and differentiation. *Educational Leadership, 58*(1), 6–13.

Trainor, L. J., Shahin, A. & Roberts, L. E. (2003). Effects of musical training on the auditory cortex in children. *Annals of the New York Academy of Sciences, 999*, 506–513.

Trautwein, U. & Koller, O. (2003). The relationship between homework and achievement – still much of a mystery. *Educational Psychology Review, 15*(2), 115–145.

Treadwell, M. (2008) The conceptual era and the revolution: School V2. 0 a new paradigm and a new renaissance in learning. *Australian Educational Leader, 30*(3), 8–10.

Troiano, R. P., Berrigan, D., Dodd, K. W., Masse, L. C., Tilert, T. & McDowell, M. (2008). Physical activity in the United States measured by accelerometer. *Medicine and Science in Sports and Exercise, 40*(1), 181–188.

Troullioud, D., Sarrazin, P., Bressoux, P. & Bois, J. (2006). Relation between teachers' early expectations and students' later perceived competence in physical education classes: Autonomy-supportive climate as moderator. *Journal of Education Psychology, 98*(1), 75–86.

Troullioud, D. O., Sarrazin, P. G., Martinek, T. J. & Guillet, E. (2002). The influence of teacher expectations on student achievement in physical education classes: Pygmalion revisited. *European Journal of Social Psychology, 32*(5), 591–607.

Tulving, E. (2000). Concepts of memory. In E. Tulving & F. I. M. Craik F. (Eds.), *The Oxford Handbook of Memory* (pp. 33–44). New York, NY: Oxford University Press.

United Nations Educational, Scientific and Cultural Organization (1994, June). *The Salamanca Statement and Framework for Action on Special Needs Education. World Conference on Special Education Needs for Education: Access and Quality.* Salamanca, Spain.

United Nations Educational, Scientific and Cultural Organization (2009). *Policy Guidelines on Inclusion in Education.* Paris, France: Author.

Upitis, R. (2011). *Arts Education for the Whole Child.* Toronto, Canada: Elementary Teachers' Federation of Ontario.

Urdan, T. (2004). Predictors of academic self-handicapping and achievement: Examining achievement goals, classroom goal structures and culture. *Journal of Educational Psychology, 96*(2), 251–264.

Urdan, T. & Midgley, C. (2001). Academic self-handicapping: What we know, what more there is to learn. *Educational Psychology Review, 13*(2), 115–138.

Valiente, C., Lemery-Chalfant, K., Swanson, J. & Reiser, M. (2008). Prediction of children's academic competence from their effortful control, relationships and classroom participation, *Journal of Educational Psychology, 100*(1), 67–77.

van den Heuvel, M., Stam, C., Kahn, R. & Hulshoff Pol, H. (2009). Efficiency of functional brain networks and intellectual performance. *Journal of Neuroscience, 29*, 7619–7624.

Verburgh, L., Konigs, M., Scherder, E. J. A. & Oosterlaan, J. (2014). Physical exercise and executive functions in preadolescent children, adolescents and young adults: A meta-analysis. *British Journal of Sports Medicine, 48*(12), 973–979.

Vergauwe, E. & Cowan, N. (2014). Attending to items in working memory: Evidence that refreshing and memory search are closely related. *Psychonomic Bulletin and Review, 22*, 1001–1006.

Vialle, W., Lysaght, P. & Verenikina, I. (2005). *Psychology for Educators.* Melbourne, Australia: Thomson Social Science Press.

Vick, M. (2013). Historical insights into teaching. In R. Churchill, P. Ferguson, S. Godinho, N. Johnson, A. Keddie, W. Letts, M. McGill, J. MacKay, J. Moss, M. Nagel, P. Nicholson & M. Vick, *Teaching: Making a Difference* (2nd ed., pp. 34–71). Brisbane, Queensland: John Wiley & Sons.

von Glaserfeld, E. (1997). Amplification of a constructivist perspective. *Issues in Education: Contributions from Educational Psychology, 3*(2), 203–209.

Vouloumanos, A. & Werker, J. F. (2004). Tuned to the signal: The privileged status of speech for young infants. *Developmental Science, 7*(3), 270–276.

Vygotsky, L. S. (1962). *The Development of Scientific Concepts in Childhood.* Cambridge, MA: MIT Press.

Vygotsky, L. S. (1978). *Mind in Society: The Development of Higher Psychological Processes.* Cambridge, MA: Harvard University Press.

Vygotsky, L. S. (1987). Thinking and speech. In R. W. Rieber & A. S. Carton (Eds.), *The Collected Works of*

L. S. Vygotsky, Vol. 1: *Problems of General Psychology* (pp. 39–285). New York, NY: Plenum Press. (Original work published 1934.)

Walkerdine, V. (1990). *Counting Girls Out*. London, UK: Virago.

Walker-Tileston, D. (2004). *What Every Teacher Should Know about Student Motivation*. Thousand Oaks, CA: Corwin Press.

Warton, P. M. (2001). The forgotten voices in homework: Views of students. *Educational Psychologist*, *36*(3), 155–165.

Waterhouse, L. (2006). Inadequate evidence for multiple intelligences, Mozart effect, and emotional intelligence theories. *Educational Psychologist*, *41*(4), 247–255.

Watson, J. B. (1913). Psychology as the behaviorist views it. *Psychological Review*, *20*, 158–177.

Watson, J. B. (1914). *Behaviorism: An Introduction to Comparative Psychology*. New York, NY: Holt, Rinehart & Winston.

Watson, J. B. (1925). *Behaviorism*. New York, NY: W.W. Norton.

Watson, J. B. & Rayner, R. (1920). Conditioned emotional reactions. *Journal of Experimental Psychology*, *3*(1), 1–14.

Weber, R., Tamborini, R., Westcott-Baker, A. & Kantor, B. (2009). Theorizing flow and media enjoyment as cognitive synchronization of attentional and reward networks. *Communication Theory*, *19*(4), 397–422.

Weinberger, N. M. (1998). Brain, behaviour, biology and music: Some research findings and their implications for educational policy. *Arts Education Policy Review*, *99*(3), 28–36.

Weiner, B. (1979). A theory of motivation for some classroom experiences. *Journal of Educational Psychology*, *71*(1), 3–25.

Weiner, B. (2000). Intrapersonal and interpersonal theories of motivation from an attributional perspective. *Educational Psychology Review*, *12*(1), 1–14.

Weiner, B. (2010). The development of an attribution-based theory of motivation: A history of ideas. *Educational Psychologist*, *45*(1), 28–36.

Wentzel, K. R. (2002). Are effective teachers like good parents? Teaching styles and student adjustment in early adolescence. *Child Development*, *73*(1), 287–301.

Wells, G. (1986). *The Meaning Makers: Children Learning Language and Using Language to Learn*. Portsmouth, NH: Heinemann.

Wertsch, J. (1991). *Voices of the Mind: A Sociocultural Approach to Mediated Action*. Cambridge, MA: Harvard University Press.

Wiesel, T. (1982). Postnatal development of the visual cortex and the influence of environment. *Nature*, *299*, 583–592.

Wiesel, T. N. & Hubel, D. H. (1963). Single cell response in striate cortex of kittens deprived of vision in one eye. *Journal of Neurophysiology*, *26*, 1003–1017.

Wigfield, A. (1994). Expectancy-value theory of achievement motivation: A developmental perspective. *Educational Psychology Review*, *6*(1), 49–78.

Wigfield, A. & Eccles, J. S. (2000). *Contemporary Educational Psychology*, *25*(1), 68–81.

Wigfield, A. & Eccles, J. S. (2002). Students' motivation during the middle school years. In J. Aronson (Ed.), *Improving Academic Development: Impact of Physiological Factors in Education* (pp. 106–185). New York, NY: Academic Press.

Wigfield, A., Eccles, J. S. & Rodriguez, D. (1998). The development of children's motivation in school contexts. *Review of Research in Education*, *23*, 73–118.

Wigfield, A., Tonks, S. & Eccles, J. S. (2004). Expectancy value theory in cross-cultural perspective. In D. McInerney & S. Van Etten (Eds.), *Big Theories Revisited—Volume 4: Research on Sociocultural Influences on Motivation and Learning* (pp. 165–198). Greenwich, CT: Information Age Publishing.

Wigfield, A., Tonks, S. & Klauda, S. L. (2009). Expectancy-value theory. In K. R. Wentzel & A. Wigfield (Eds.), *Handbook of Motivation at School* (pp. 55–76). New York, NY: Routledge.

Wilkinson, R. & Pickett, K. (2009). *The Spirit Level: Why Equality is Better for Everyone*. London, UK: Penguin Books.

Willingham, D. T. (2009). *Why Don't Students Like School: A Cognitive Scientist Answers Questions about How the Mind Works and What It Means for the Classroom*. San Francisco, CA: Jossey-Bass.

Willis, J. (2010). The current impact of neuroscience on teaching and learning. In D. A. Sousa (Ed.), *Mind, Brain & Education: Neuroscience Implications for the Classroom* (pp. 45–66). Bloomington, IN: Solution Tree Press.

Willis, J. A. (2009). *Inspiring Middle School Minds: Gifted, Creative and Challenging*. Scottsdale, AZ: Great Potential Press.

Willms, J. D. (2003). *Student Engagement at School—A Sense of Belonging and Participation: Results from PISA 2000*. Paris, France: Organisation for Economic Co-operation and Development (OECD).

Wilson S. M., Galantucci. S., Tartaglia, M. C., Rising, K., Patterson, D. K., Henry, M. L. & Gorno-Tempini, M. L. (2011). Syntactic processing depends on dorsal language tracts. *Neuron*, *72*, 397–403.

Windschitl, M. (2002). Framing constructivism in practice as the negotiation of dilemmas: An analysis of the conceptual, pedagogical, cultural and political challenges facing teachers. *Review of Educational Research*, *72*(2), 131–175.

Winsler, A., Abar, B., Feder, M. A., Schunn, C. D. & Rubio, D. A. (2007). Private speech and executive functioning among high-functioning children with autistic spectrum disorders. *Journal of Autism and Developmental Disorders*, *37*, 1617–1635.

Winter, P. & Luddy, S. (2010). *Engaging Families in the Early Childhood Development Story: Research Findings from a Survey of Parents of Children from Birth to Age 8*. Melbourne, Australia: Ministerial Council for Education, Early Childhood Development and Youth Affairs.

Wise, R. A. (2002). Brain reward circuitry: Insights from unsensed incentives. *Neuron*, 36(2), 229–240.

Wismer-Fries, A. B. & Pollack, S. D. (2007). Emotion processing and the developing brain. In D. Coch, K. W. Fisher & G. Dawson (Eds.). *Human Behavior, Learning and the Developing Brain: Typical Development* (pp. 329–362). New York, NY: Guilford Press.

Wober, M. (1974). Towards an understanding of the Kiganda concept of intelligence. In J. W. Berry & P. R. Dasen (Eds.), *Culture and Cognition: Readings in Cross-cultural Psychology* (pp. 261–280). London, UK: Methuen.

Wojcicki, T. R. & McAuley, E. (2014). Physical activity: Measurement and behavioural patterns in children and youth. In C. H. Hillman (Ed.), *The Relation of Childhood Physical Activity to Brain Health, Cognition, and Scholastic Achievement—Monographs of the Society for Research in Child Development* (pp. 7–24). Boston, MA: Wiley.

Wolfe, P. & Nevills, P. (2004). *Building the Reading Brain: PreK–3*. Thousand Oaks, CA: Corwin Press.

Wolters, C. A. (2004). Advancing achievement goal theory: Using goal structures and goal orientations to predict students' motivation, cognition and achievement. *Journal of Educational Psychology*, *96*(2), 236–250.

Wood, D., Bruner, J. & Ross, G. (1976). The role of tutoring in problem-solving. *Journal of Child Psychology and Psychiatry*, *17*(2), 89–100.

Woolfolk, A. & Margetts, K. (2013). *Educational Psychology* (3rd ed.). Sydney, Australia: Pearson Australia.

Woolfolk-Hoy, A. (2005). *Educational Psychology, Active Learning Edition*. Boston, MA: Allyn & Bacon.

World Conference on Education for All: Meeting Basic Learning Needs (1990). *World Declaration on Education for All and Framework for Action to Meet Basic Learning Needs*. Paris, France: Unesco.

Wurst, D., Jones, D. & Moore, J. (2005). Art supports reading comprehension. *School Arts*, *104*(5), 44–45.

Wyn, J., Turnbull, M. & Grimshaw, L. (2014). *The Experience of Education: The Impacts of High Stakes Testing on School Students and Their Families*. Sydney, Australia: Whitlam Institute, University of Western Sydney.

Yang, J., Gates, K., Molenaar, P. & Li, P. (2014). Neural changes underlying successful second language word learning: An fMRI study. *Journal of Neurolinguistics*, *33*, 29–49.

Yarrow, J. F., White, L. J., McCoy, S. C. & Borst, S. E. (2010). Training augments resistance exercise induced elevation of circulating brain-derived neurotrophic factor (BDNF). *Neuroscience Letters*, *479*(2), 161–165.

Yerkes, R. M. & Dodson, J. D. (1908). The relation of strength of stimulus to rapidity of habit-formation. *Journal of Comparative Neurology and Psychology*, *18*(5), 459–482.

Yeung, M. S. Y., Zdunek, S., Bergmann, O., Bernard, S., Salehpour, M., Alkass, K., Perl, S., Tisdale, J., Possnert, G., Brundin, L., Druid, H. & Frisen, J. (2014). Dynamics of oligodendrocyte generation and myelination in the human brain. *Cell*, *159*(4), 766–774.

Yont, K. M., Snow, C. E. & Vernon-Feagans, L. (2003). The role of context in mother-child interactions: An analysis of communicative intents expressed during toy play and book reading with 12 month-olds. *Journal of Pragmatics*, *35*, 435–454.

Younger, M., Warrington, M., Gray, J., Rudduck, J., McLellan, R., Bearne, E., Kershner, R. & Bricheno, P. (2005). *Raising Boys' Achievement* (Research Report No. 636). Norwich, UK: Faculty of Education, University of Cambridge.

Zeanah, C. H., Nelson, C. A., Fox, N. A., Smyke, A. T., Marshall, P., Parker, S. W. & Koga, S. (2003). Designing research to study the effects of institutionalisation on brain and behavioural development: The Bucharest Early Intervention Project. *Development and Psychopathology*, *15*(4), 885–907.

Zhou, Q., Eisenberg, N., Losoya, S. H., Fabes, R. A., Reiser, M., Guthrie, I. K., Murphy, B. C., Cumberland, A. J. & Shepard, S. A. (2002). The relations of parental warmth and positive experiences to children's empathy-related responding and social functioning: A longitudinal study. *Child Development*, *73*(3), 893–915.

Zimmerman, F. J., Christakis, D. A. & Meltzoff, A. N. (2007). Television and DVD/video viewing in children younger than 2 years. *Archives of Pediatrics & Adolescent Medicine*, *161*(5), 473–479.

Zimmerman, M. E., Pan, J. W., Hetherington, H. P., Katz, M. J., Verghese, J., Buschke, H., Derby, C. A. & Lipton, R. B. (2008). Hippocampal neurochemistry, neuromorphometry, and verbal memory in nondemented older adults. *Neurology*, *70*(18), 1594–1600.

Zull, J. E. (2011). *From Brain to Mind: Using Neuroscience to Guide Change in Education*. Sterling, VA: Stylus, Publishing.

INDEX